I0833622

WILLARD GLAZIER.

HEADWATERS

OF THE

MISSISSIPPI;

Comprising

BIOGRAPHICAL SKETCHES OF EARLY AND RECENT EXPLORERS OF THE GREAT RIVER, AND A FULL ACCOUNT OF THE DISCOVERY AND LOCATION OF ITS TRUE SOURCE IN A LAKE BEYOND ITASCA.

BY

CAPTAIN WILLARD GLAZIER,

Author of "Three Years in the Federal Cavalry," "Capture, Prison-Pen, and Escape," "Battles for the Union," "Heroes of Three Wars," "Peculiarities of American Cities," "Ocean to Ocean on Horseback," "Down the Great River," Etc.

Illustrated.

CHICAGO AND NEW-YORK:

RAND, McNALLY & COMPANY.

1894.

TO

My Dear Daughter

ALICE,

WHO SHARED THE FATIGUES AND PRIVATIONS OF MY SECOND EXPEDITION TO THE HEADWATERS OF THE MISSISSIPPI; STOOD WITH ME AT THE SOURCE; AND DRANK FROM ITS REMOTEST SPRINGS,

This Volume

IS LOVINGLY INSCRIBED

BY

THE AUTHOR.

PREFACE.

FROM the authenticated discovery of the Mississippi by Hernando de Soto in 1541, to the location of its True Source in 1881, comparatively little is known of the early pioneers or of the series of explorations which finally led to a solution of the mystery that surrounded its Headwaters for a period of over three hundred years. The Great River and its tributaries have been revealed to the world through a multitude of daring enterprises, the motives and incidents of which are familiar to but few of the present generation. Both the early and more modern explorers wrote much, but published little, and for the latter reason, the records of their travels have seldom found their way to the eye of the general reader.

It is the purpose of this volume to present as far as possible, from all available sources, some idea of the circumstances which led to certain important discoveries in North America, together with such sketches of the old and recent explorers of the Mississippi as the plan of the work will permit. Few or no attempts were made up to 1805 to penetrate the secret of the origin of the river, in which year Lieutenant Pike, commissioned by the Government, signally failed of his object. The efforts of General Cass in 1820, and of Beltrami three years later, though well directed and zealously executed, also fell short of the attainment of the desired end—the Fountain-head of the Mississippi was unseen and unknown to them. Schoolcraft, in 1832, approached more nearly the solution of the problem than any of his predecessors, and, in the discovery of Lake Itasca, believed he had reached the extreme head of the river. He published his discovery to the world, and it was generally accepted on his authority. For fifty years Lake Itasca was laid down in the maps as the Source of the Father of Waters, still not a few expressed their doubts of the genuineness of the discovery, and the Indians of Northern Minnesota denied it altogether Nicollet, a French savant, who followed in the footsteps of Schoolcraft in 1836, strangely confirmed the latter in what has since been proved to be a geographical error.

Rumors having reached the author of the present volume, from various sources, of the doubtful correctness of Schoolcraft in assuming Itasca to be the Primal Reservoir of the river, he determined to investigate the matter in the interest of geography, and, having time at his disposal in the summer of 1881, organized an expedition to proceed to the Headwaters. The result was the discovery of a body of water lying immediately to the south of Lake Itasca, and emptying into the latter through a perennial stream, the mouth of which was entirely concealed from view by a dense growth of lake vegetation and fallen trees. This lake, having an area of 255 acres, a circumference of between five and six miles, and an average depth of forty-five feet, being *above* Itasca, necessarily invalidated the claim of Schoolcraft, and the author's location of the True Head of the Mississippi is now recognized by nearly all of the geographers and educational publishers of this country and Europe.

Between 1541 and 1881, every part of the Great River had been visited by intrepid explorers, with the exception of its almost inaccessible Source—of the final discovery of which full particulars will be found in Part Third of this volume.

During the ten years that elapsed between 1881 and 1891, spasmodic efforts, partaking for the most part of a disingenuous and personal character, were made by a few cavilers to discredit the author's discovery, and it was thought by his friends and those who believed in his claim that a further investigation at the Head of the river might have the effect of throwing more light upon the question, and possibly of convincing the opposition. Accordingly, a Second Expedition was projected, and undertaken in August, 1891, composed of geographers, scientists, practical surveyors, and men of culture, a detailed account of which appears in the following chapters, for which the author respectfully bespeaks the reader's fair and candid consideration.

An itinerary of the journey to the Headwaters of the Great River will be found in the early chapters of Part Third, in which occasional but brief reference is made to men and places, which may be of some practical utility to the tourist contemplating a pilgrimage through Northern Minnesota to the Source of the Mighty River.

The writer makes no pretension to have exhausted the topics he has treated, or to placing his work in comparison with more elaborate productions; but presents it to the reader simply as an epitome of the history of our magnificent river—a river in many respects without a peer.

* * * The illustrations accompanying this volume are from drawings by True Williams, of Chicago, and the camera of Fred J. Trost, of the firm of Van Loo & Trost, Toledo, Ohio—the latter a member of the Expedition of 1891, and the first to photograph scenery at the Headwaters of the Mississippi.

Willard Glazier

CHICAGO, January 14, 1893.

CONTENTS.

—o—

Part First.

—o—

CHAPTER III.

DE SOTO WITH PIZARRO.

CHAPTER IV.

DISCOVERY OF THE MISSISSIPPI.

CHAPTER V.

MARQUETTE AND JOLIET.

CHAPTER VI.

ROBERT CAVELIER DE LA SALLE.

CHAPTER VII.

LA SALLE EXPLORES THE LOWER MISSISSIPPI.

CHAPTER VIII.

LAST VOYAGE AND DEATH OF LA SALLE.

CHAPTER IX.

FATHER LOUIS HENNEPIN

CHAPTER X.

LA HONTAN—CHARLEVOIX—CARVER.

Part Second.

—o—

CHAPTER III.

WINONA TO MINNEAPOLIS.

CHAPTER IV

EARLY HISTORY OF MINNESOTA.

CHAPTER V

THE "TWIN CITIES."

CHAPTER VI.

PREPARATION FOR SECOND EXPEDITION.

CHAPTER VII.

MINNEAPOLIS TO PARK RAPIDS.

CHAPTER VIII.

THROUGH THE WILDERNESS.

CHAPTER IX.

HEADWATERS OF THE MISSISSIPPI.

CHAPTER X.

JOURNAL OF THE EXPEDITION.

CHAPTER XI.

RETURN TO MINNEAPOLIS.

CHAPTER XII.

INDORSEMENT AND CONCLUSION.

——o——

Appendix.

——o——

ILLUSTRATIONS.

APPENDIX

EARLY EXPLORERS OF THE MISSISSIPPI.

CHAPTER I.

ALVAR NUÑEZ CABEÇA DE VACA.

THE position which this early explorer holds among his contemporaries is very important, so far as the narrative of his travels in the New World is concerned, but historians differ widely in their estimation of what is due him as a discoverer, and will probably never be able to settle satisfactorily the question as to whether or not he was the first European to see the Mississippi.

In the confusing mazes of opinion, which are really all that are to be consulted in regard to the earliest discoveries of the Great River, there have been some suggestions of an expedition as early as 1519, under Don Alonzo Alvarez Pineda, an officer in the service of the Governor of Jamaica; justified by the Spanish historian Navarrete, who writes that Pineda discovered the Mississippi at that time, and named it "Rio del Espirito Santo," being influenced to undertake this exploration by the universal enthusiasm excited by the conquest of Mexico by Cortez.

The aim and object of those who, like De Vaca, penetrated the wildernesses of North America was ostensibly to search out the reputed mines of gold and silver, rather than to explore the unknown regions for the enlightenment of their countrymen and the advancement of science; so that the recitals of their journeyings were more the detailed accounts of the obstacles which confronted them, and the hardships which they passed through in pursuit of the coveted treasure, than careful reports of geographical research.

It is this vagueness of description in De Vaca's narrative which has caused so much speculation among those interested in the history of our Great Central River, and which has baffled those who wish to do justice to its discoverer. If he crossed the Rio Grande of the later Spaniards, he has given no evidence that would distinguish it from the other rivers of the South, and which would place him unquestionably among the great explorers. On the other hand, those who follow De Soto in his march through the wilderness can not doubt that he and his companions saw the Mississippi, or that the disappointed cavalier met death upon its shores. It is therefore to him that historians generally give the contested honor The purpose of these pages is not, however, to advance any personal theories, or to assume the championship of those who have long since passed away, and whose claims could only be considered through uncertain and intricate hypotheses, but only to give a brief account of their lives, as bearing more or less directly upon the history of the Great River

De Vaca first comes into prominence as the lieutenant of Panfilo de Narvaez in the expedition organized for the conquest and colonization of "the whole northern coast of the Gulf"; an enterprise suggested strangely enough by the personal pique of the commander, who, having failed in his raid upon Cortez, in Mexico, as the lieutenant of the jealous Velasquez, wished to redeem his somewhat tarnished record by glorious action in a new field. Appealing to the Emperor Charles V., he obtained a commission to invade the country and to assume the title of Adelantado of those lands which he should discover within the limits of what was then known as Florida—a large area embracing the present division and extending for an almost indefinite distance toward the northwest.

Thus encouraged by the crown, he sailed from San Lucar on the seventeenth of June, 1527, with a company of six hundred, and a fleet of five vessels. At Hispaniola, where a six-weeks' halt was made to further prepare for the journey, more than a hundred of the volunteers abandoned the expedition; while at Trinidad, whither two vessels had been sent, in charge of De Vaca and Captain Pantoja, to obtain provisions, both crews perished in a violent storm, those only escaping who had gone ashore. Without having sighted the coast of Florida, Narvaez had thus lost a sixth of his men.

Soon overtaking the shipwrecked party, he established winter quarters at Xagua, twelves leagues beyond, where in February he joined the expedition with reinforcements, and arranged for the final voyage.

The Land of Flowers, through which Ponce de Leon had traveled in search of fabled treasures and the magical Fountain of Youth, was still hidden beyond the blue waters of the Gulf, and the shadow of coming misfortunes, which superstition hinted at, found no place among the eager adventurers.

On the eleventh of April Florida was reached, and a landing made just north of Tampa Bay, where the colors of Spain were unfurled and the soil solemnly appropriated in the name of Charles V. It had been the intention to enter the larger bay to the south, but through a miscalculation of the pilot, Miruelo, the ships had passed it, and the destiny of the expedition became thus entirely changed.

Narvaez and his officers now anticipated a triumphal march through a country which they had peopled with a race far superior to the Mexicans or Peruvians; whose towns were to be rich in the wealth of precious metals, and whose inhabitants, milder than the South Americans, would offer them no resistance; a country whose limits they believed inclosed an empire greater than Montezuma's, and within whose confines were to be found splendors yet undreamed of.

Their illusions were soon dispelled. Advancing upon an Indian village, whose cabins could be seen at the head of the little bay in which the ships were anchored, they were fearlessly met by the natives, whose temerity somewhat surprised them. After a friendly reception they were requested by unmistakable signs to leave, and the firmness of the Indians so impressed Narvaez—who, although a man of unquestioned courage, was lacking in decision—that he called a consultation of his principal officers to determine upon the wisest course. They concluded to follow the coast by land in search of the bay which they had attempted to reach—the Espirito Santo of De Soto's later expedition—the ships to take a similar course and meet them at that point. De Vaca was strongly opposed to this plan, but his companions were thoroughly weary of the sea, and were eager to seek their fortunes on *terra firma*. Had they been more familiar with the country, the enterprise would not have terminated so disastrously; for exploring parties, sent out at the beginning of the march, found the bay they were in search of, and, failing to recognize it, believed they had been unsuccessful, while another party, meeting Indians who wore golden ornaments, were told by them of a place to the north, which they called "Abalachie," where the metal could be found. By following this direction they would have undoubtedly reached the mines of Upper Georgia, which would have amply satisfied them; but instead they entered Appalachee toward the south, where they found nothing but poor villages and no sign of the coveted treasure.

From the old narratives, full as they are of exaggerations, we catch a glimpse of a magnificent type of the Indian here, living in wretched huts in the most primitive way, and totally lacking in those graces with which the imaginative Spaniards had clothed them, yet none the less admirable, and possessed of courage, intelligence, and a certain physical elegance.

After spending more than three weeks with these Appalachians, who were described as men of gigantic proportions, the company made preparations to move on toward Hauté, where they were told they would find an abundance of food, and a very rich region.

If Narvaez had been enterprising enough at this point to verify the statements of the Indians, which were made chiefly to induce him and his men to leave their village, he would have found a broad expanse of fertile and populous country all about him; but, lacking in those active and daring qualities which have ever characterized the successful explorer, he was easily led by the cunning natives and persuaded that the "good lands" lay beyond.

At Hauté, as at Appalachee, the Spaniards met only disappointment, for the inhabitants, learning of their approach, had abandoned and burned their homes and made away with their provisions. It was as though some enchantment preceded them to destroy the villages and to lay waste the fields. They were harassed on every side by hostile natives, who watched for them whenever they ventured beyond camp, and who sent showers of arrows into their ranks on the march; until at last, worn out with hunger, sickness, and fatigue, and thoroughly discouraged, their only desire was to escape. The ships had not been heard from, and were supposed to have returned to Havana, but De Vaca, with Captains Castillo and Dorantes and an escort of fifty foot soldiers, went to the Gulf, which was about a day's journey away, to see if there might be a sail in sight. The broad expanse betrayed no sign, and they were obliged to return with the disheartening news. A council was then called and a plan discussed which only hopeless men could have determined upon. Immediately the forest was converted into a ship-yard, where two hundred and forty men worked with the energy of despair. Within six weeks they had completed a fleet of five boats out of whatever materials were available, and by the twenty-second of September, 1528, were ready to embark. "Narvaez commanded the first boat; the second was in charge of Enriquez, the controller, and Juan Suarez, the commissary; in the third went Captains Castillo and Dorantes; in the fourth, Captains Tellez and Penalosa, and in the fifth, Cabeça de Vaca—each boat carrying about forty-eight men."

As it would have been disastrous to remain longer

on shore, where provisions were becoming more scarce, where their lives were continually exposed to the attacks of the Indians, and where the miasma of the swamps began to breed a deadly fever, these two hundred and forty half-starved and disappointed men immediately put to sea, which was dangerous for loosely constructed craft at any season, but doubly so during the autumn months. They took a westerly course along the coast, with the idea of reaching the River of Palms and the Spanish settlements in Mexico—which on the maps of the time had been inaccurately placed—believing they would be less exposed than by striking out across the Gulf, but notwithstanding this caution the company was destined to destruction, and misfortune met it on every hand.

Narvaez, separated from his crew, which had gone ashore, was swept out to sea in a violent storm and never seen again. De Vaca's party, and those of Castillo and Dorantes, were shipwrecked upon the Island of Santa Rosa, where nearly all perished; while those who were with Enriquez and Juan Suarez suffered the most terrible privations and at last they too miserably perished. The ninety six men in the boats commanded by Captains Tellez and Penalosa, going ashore near Pass Christian for water and provisions, were killed by the natives, who could easily overcome them, so weak had they become bodily and in numbers.

There were now only four survivors of that great expedition which a short time before had left the Bay of the True Cross believing their arms irresistible and their success assured; these were De Vaca, Castillo, Dorantes, and the Moor Estevanico. Through the inevitable changes of a life among a strange and half-savage people, this little company soon became separated and its members subjected to a kind of servitude. For six years De Vaca stayed among the coast tribes, carrying on a system of trade with the Indians of the interior, and becoming familiar with their language and customs, until at last he was able to communicate with his companions with whom he hoped to reach the Spanish settlements in Mexico. This plan was, strangely enough, promoted by the Indians, who began to hold the white men in superstitious awe, calling them "medicine men," and believing them endowed with supernatural powers.

De Vaca, with amusing frankness, describes his *modus operandi*, which was to say a paternoster and an ave maria over the patient; and he mentions the generosity of the Indians, who, after "treatment," often gave the great "medicines" all they possessed, and accompanied them in a kind of triumphal procession from place to place. In this way they penetrated the Western Wilderness, "traversing the bison plains and the adobe towns of the half-civilized natives of New Mexico, perched on their rocky heights," and crossing the rugged and magnificent passes of the Rockies.

Mr. John O'Shea, who has made a careful study of the subject, in his "Discovery and Explorations of the Mississippi," says: "In this long wandering he (De Vaca) must have reached and crossed the Mississippi, but we in vain examine his narrative for something to distinguish it from any other large river that he met." In fact, it is entirely through conjecture that De Vaca is given the benefit of a doubt. By some unexplained circumstance, he and his companions may have entirely failed to cross the stream, and

DE VACA CROSSING THE CONTINENT

again, he may have been, as Mr O'Shea adds, "the first European who 'launched his boat upon its waters.'"

Upon coming to a large stream, to the westward, the last in that lonely journey across the country, De Vaca and his companions met a party of Indians, from whom they learned that white men had recently been seen near there, both on the water and on horseback, and traces of their late passage were soon discovered. In a short time they were overtaken, and found to be a band of Spaniards from a Mexican colony. The meeting was a strange one, and the four wanderers were greeted as those returned from the dead.

Clothed in the rough dress of the natives, which long association had thrust upon them, changed by contact with their peculiar life, and bronzed by exposure to wind and sun, their appearance produced a singular effect upon their countrymen, none the less heightened by a mysterious air, which had been capriciously assumed. They had explored the wonders of a new land, and had visited unknown peoples—what wonder, then, that they should entertain their unquestioning friends with tales of adventure, the more fascinating because the more highly colored? The Spaniards, with their natural love of the marvelous, listened spellbound while De Vaca related the experiences which he and his fellow-travelers had passed through, regarding them with mingled curiosity and admiration. They were received "with the greatest sympathy by the Spanish authorities in Mexico," and, having all their wants supplied, were soon enabled to return to their native land, where their recitals awakened even deeper interest and enthusiasm.

Estevanico, the Moor, preferred to remain in Mexico, where he became the guide of Francisco Narco de Nizza, and ultimately perished at the hands of the Indians, who suspected him of treachery, because he announced himself as the emissary of the white people.

De Vaca reached Havana on the fourth of May, remaining there a month to await the arrival of the two other vessels, on which Castillo and Dorantes had taken passage; then, eager to return to Spain, and to confer with his Sovereign upon the things which he had seen, he sailed for Lisbon, which was reached on the fifteenth of August, 1537.

It was De Vaca's policy, upon his return, to be noncommittal, as he was anxious to privately inform the King of the resources of what he called "the richest country in the world," and to beg the privilege of returning to Florida in the service of his country; but Charles, with royal partiality, was listening to the requests of his more influential subjects, and De Vaca was obliged to content himself with the title of Adelantado of the province of Rio de la Plata, a commission requiring active duty and some danger.

While discharging the functions of this office, he became involved in a quarrel with one of his countrymen, whose jealousy he had excited, which ultimately resulted in his arrest and dismissal. Eight years of exile in Africa followed, which, to one long accustomed to the privations of a strange country and possessed of a strong love of adventure, must have had its compensations.

Upon his recall in 1552 he was given a judgeship in Seville, where he died in 1564.

The story of his life, from beginning to end, is a romance, in which the scenes and people of primitive America are invested with the charm of history's "distant twilight," into whose shadows many a student has ventured in the cause of truth. Among these, several have become convinced, from their own researches, that the honor of the discovery of the Mississippi rightfully belongs to the brave lieutenant of Panfilo Narvaez; and George Fairbanks, in his "History of Florida," even pays him the tribute of saying that "upon some high bluff of that wondrous stream should be placed a monument" to this European who first visited its shores.

Whether or not future investigation will uncrown the old hero De Soto for one who may have unjustly remained unrecognized is a question which only time can answer; but whoever the claimant, we are ready to say: "Honor to whom honor is due."

SHIPWRECK OF DE VACA

CHAPTER II.

HERNANDO DE SOTO.

THE discovery of the Mississippi is very generally ascribed to Hernando De Soto, who, in his adventurous march in pursuit of gold and glory, reached the Great River in April, 1541, near the site of the present city of Natchez.

In the opinion of most historians no white man's eye had ever before beheld that flood whose banks are now inhabited by busy millions, and in following the achievements of its discoverer, we find it filled with new interest. From the cold springs that rise in the northern wilderness, to the great torrent that mingles with the tropical Gulf three thousand miles below, the Spaniard who lies buried beneath its waters still claims an undying tribute. His ambitious march westward, through treacherous swamps and over flower-dotted prairies, in pursuit of the fabled El Dorado, the desperate encounters with Indians, who at every turn tried to resist the advance of his steel-clad band; the delays and disappointments, and the ultimate shattering of their "castles in Spain," all form a narrative romantic and fascinating as one of the enchantments of the Arabian Nights. Indeed, were it not that the contemporaneous accounts tally so nearly, we of a later day would be inclined to accept the adventures of these helmeted cavaliers with much less allowance.

So closely is the life of De Soto identified with the history of exploration in the Valley of the Mississippi, and so brilliant a touch has his presence added to its early annals, that any sketch of the Great River without mention of him would lose its most attractive feature. He was born in the little walled town of Xerés, in the province of Estramadura, Southern Spain, in the year 1500, just at the threshold of the new century, destined to be one of the brightest in the annals of the Old World, and one of the most significant in the history of the New. The ancestral castle in which he first saw light, once the scene of wealth and magnificence, had become, through repeated misfortunes to his family, only the dilapidated abode of a haughty race, and Hernando found himself, like many another young Spaniard of his time, the heir of poverty and pride. His early surroundings, and the enforced idleness which peculiar circumstances pressed upon him, no doubt greatly influenced his after career. His father was unable to give him the advantages which were accessible to the sons of richer noblemen, and custom forbade that the family fortunes should be retrieved by work; so the bright boy passed his childhood in comparative idleness, indulging at his will in the out-of-door sports, for which he had a great .fondness, and visiting occasionally the neighboring monasteries, where he probably received the religious bent that afterward proved such a strong force in his character.

While a mere lad, De Soto came under the notice of Don Pedro de Avila, Count of Puño en Rostro, and this wealthy nobleman, impressed by the manly bearing of the boy, and his personal attractiveness, became his patron, and offered him all the privileges of an own son. He was sent to one of the leading Spanish universities—probably that of Saragossa—where his skill in fencing and horsemanship was perfected, and where he received the further training that fitted him for subsequent events. He was prominent at the tournaments, and always excited the envy of competitive cavaliers in these exhibitions of martial prowess.

In the intervals between the university terms, Don Pedro's protégé found a welcome in his foster-father's home, where he became a great favorite; and so sure was the confidence which his friend reposed in him, that when the former was appointed Governor of Darien, he asked De Soto to remain with his family in the castle near Badajoz. Here, during Don Pedro's absence, De Soto formed a strong attachment for the Governor's second daughter, Isabella, a beautiful girl of sixteen, who, in accordance with the custom of her country and station, had already been presented at court and received many flattering attentions. Yet, notwithstanding the attractions of her more eligible suitors, Donna Isabella showed a partial preference for her poor cavalier, and in time the mutual sentiment was sealed by a betrothal. The two were constantly thrown together, and being congenial in tastes passed many happy days in their common home. At this time young De Soto possessed all the charms of mind and person that would win for him the admiration of his associates. He was tall and erect, with the perfect grace that is acquired by familiarity with athletic exercise; his features were handsome, and suited his well-poised head; his bearing was

HERNANDO DE SOTO.

dignified, and his character without reproach. It can not be wondered at, therefore, that two such attractive beings should have been drawn together, or that they should have become an example of love and devotion for centuries afterward.

Upon the return of Don Pedro from Darien five years later, to arrange his private affairs preparatory to a more prolonged sojourn in the New World, his daughter's betrothal was made known to him. At first he was disposed to ridicule the affair; but upon being persuaded by Isabella's governess that the girl returned the affection, and that she had declared, if her wish were opposed, she would enter a convent, the matter became more serious, and finally took such an offensive aspect that the count was beside himself with vexation. He was the more disturbed from the fact that a short time before Isabella had been sought in marriage by one of the nobility—a young man near of kin to royalty itself; and that his daughter should be indifferent to the bright prospects of such an alliance, and prefer a dependent upon her father's bounty, was more than the haughty noble could endure. He began to treat his former favorite with dislike and even contempt, and, while feigning indifference to the situation, formed a scheme for the separation of the objects of his displeasure, and tried to prevent their further intercourse.

Being possessed of an extremely sensitive nature, De Soto felt keenly the rebuke of his benefactor. He could boast of an ancestry as ancient and honorable as that of Don Pedro, and by the rules of Spanish heraldry "was entitled to admission into the noble order of Santiago." He therefore resented the marked discourtesy shown him, and determined to break down the mock barrier which had been raised against him, by becoming rich. Accordingly, when Don Pedro, with every pretension of friendship, invited Hernando to accompany him upon his second voyage to the New World, with the promise of a captaincy, and suggestions of the fabled wealth of America, the offer was gladly accepted. The young man's parents were dead, and even had they not been, their circumstances would hardly have been such as to allow them to lend their son any assistance; besides, he was without wealthy friends, and this opportunity seemed to promise the fulfillment of his hopes.

Although every precaution had been taken to prevent a final meeting of the lovers, the watchers were evaded, and Hernando and Isabella met again to renew their pledge and to say farewell. They talked long and earnestly of the future, and parted with Isabella's memorable words, "Hernando, remember that one treacherous friend is more dangerous than a thousand avowed enemies." Soon after this interview Don Pedro and his followers embarked at San Lucar, and sailed toward the yet unexplored and attractive continent which had burst upon the vision of Columbus but a short time before, and which had already begun to dazzle the eye of Europe with its magnificent possibilities.

In the course of this voyage the wily Governor doubtless perfected his plans for the ruin of his unsuspecting protégé, whom he had determined to subject to such trying circumstances that he would be powerless to oppose them. With the cleverness of the arch fiend himself, he arranged perilous expeditions, in which De Soto's life would be more or less exposed, and, presupposing that the young captain would be gratified by the confidence thus placed in him, congratulated himself upon the outcome.

Upon their arrival at Darien, De Soto was given command of a troop of horse, and with these steel-clad followers began the brilliant career which has filled many a page of early history with valiant deeds, and touched them with the fascinating color of romance. The field for daring adventure was most prolific, and wherever the cavalry led, there could be seen the white plume of De Soto. His contemporaries, however, have not charged him with any of the disgusting crimes of which his brother officers were guilty, and which were often done in obedience to Don Pedro's command. Upon one occasion he refused to obey a distasteful order and sent the Governor his decided disapproval. This involved him in a duel with one of his most desperate companions, who was sent to him with the message, and whom De Soto took occasion to visit with his scorn; but his old-time training and unerring arm gave him the advantage in the encounter, and he escaped unhurt. A similar instance of his moral courage occurred during Pizarro's raid upon the territories of the Indian Uracca in 1521.

That outraged monarch, having suffered beyond endurance from the unprovoked attacks of the Spaniards, at last made preparation to resist them. He gathered about him a force of some twenty thousand warriors, armed with their deadly arrows and wooden swords, and these, under his leadership, started toward the camp of the enemy Don Pedro, learning of the intended attack, made plans to circumvent the Indians, who were much stronger in numbers, and sending a party under Espinosa by sea, along the western coast of Uracca's dominions, and another by land under Pizarro, attempted to rout the opposing forces by a surprise. De Soto and his troop joined Pizarro's division. Uracca, with a thousand men, perceiving the approach of Espinosa from the coast, went bravely to the attack, and succeeded in completely demoralizing the Spanish soldiery; but De Soto, having heard the noise of battle from a distance, left his position and hurried with all dispatch to the aid of his distressed countrymen, thus turning the fortunes of the day.

The approach to the scene of conflict was through an almost impassable part of the country, cut up by huge rocks and seamed with chasms, and over this difficult way the dauntless captain led his hesitating followers by his own example and by the electrifying war-cry, "Sant Iago to the rescue!"

The charge of this unexpected force, and above all the sight of the unfamiliar horses, whose riders were proof against the showers of arrows sent into their midst, struck terror into their hearts and caused them to retreat to the hills in consternation; but having regained their courage there, they began such a vigorous onslaught upon the Spaniards in the valley below, that those warriors quickly retreated to their ships to avoid the hail of poisoned darts. Seeing this action on the part of their recent conquerors, the Indians ran down from their shelter and renewed the attack. In a moment the quick eye of De Soto saw their movement, and, knowing their fear of horses, ordered his men to face about. This frightened the pursuers, who were now willing to watch the Spaniards from a safe distance. At this point Pizarro and Espinosa met to discuss the situation, and decided upon retreat. De Soto could not endure such cowardice. He knew that although the numbers of the Spaniards were considerably less than those of the enemy, the latter could never cope with the trained soldiers arrayed against them, and he felt besides, a certain responsibility for his country's glory. He therefore looked upon the cowardly action of his superior officers with ill-concealed disgust, and availed himself of the first opportunity to display his sentiment. This occurred but a short time afterward when, having abandoned the field, the Spanish forces fell upon a small village farther up the coast and began their murderous work.

The men of the village were away, and the pillagers, taking advantage of their absence, undertook to make prisoners of the women and children. This again excited the indignation of De Soto, who informed Espinosa that if his severe measures were not suspended, and the captives released, he would withdraw his men and leave him to his fate. Espinosa understood the strength of this threat, and considering the consequences, sullenly consented.

After this affair, De Soto went to Darien with messages to the Governor, and upon his return found the force at Borrica hemmed in by Uracca's men. By a few masterly sallies he succeeded in dispersing the besiegers, and while engaged in this way was able to save the life of one Micer Codro, who afterward returned the kindness by risking his life for him. Codro was an Italian scientist and astrologer, who had been exiled from his native country under the conviction of being a magician, and had come to America when Don Pedro's predecessor, Vasco Nuñez de Balboa, was Governor. Under this mild administration the student had pursued his favorite studies unmolested, and had won the friendship of the natives, but in the excitement of the encounter with their new foes they mistook him for an enemy, and would have killed him had not De Soto interposed. Although he showed very little gratitude at the time, being, as he afterward expressed it, too much his debtor to make a sufficient acknowledgment, he later performed a kindness which few men would have dared to undertake.

When De Avila wished to send messages to Spain, and was deliberating as to whom he might intrust with the valuable papers, knowing too well that none of his favorites was reliable, he fixed upon the simple-minded Italian.

Upon leaving Spain, Don Pedro had taken every precaution to prevent any correspondence between De Soto and his daughter. All letters were intercepted, and a violation of his commands was punishable by death; but Codro was willing to risk the penalty that he might in a small way return the obligation to his friend. For five years no communication had passed between the lovers, and now that an opportunity offered, De Soto feared to involve the bearer of his message. However, he was persuaded to accept the favor, and intrusted Micer Codro with a letter to his lady-love, for whom he still entertained feelings of the tenderest affection. The Italian gladly delivered the message to Donna Isabella, receiving her warmest gratitude in return, and offered to carry her answering letter; but unfortunately for those concerned, the incautious man stated, upon his arrival at Badajoz, that he had a packet for Don Pedro's daughter, which aroused the suspicion of the vigilant inmates of the castle.

The same ship that carried Codro back to Darien, bore communications to Don Pedro convicting the bearer of his letters, and virtually sealing his fate. Within a few days after his return he was sent upon a supposed mineralogical survey to the gulf of San Miguel and was never seen again. His fate was even unknown until after the disgraceful expedition to Nicaragua, when De Soto came by chance upon the captain and his crew whom Don Pedro had commissioned to murder Codro. These wretches were boasting of the way in which they had tortured their victim, and were laughing at his death agonies, when De Soto, overhearing the remarks, and burning with revenge, rushed upon the leader and dispatched him with his sword. Then, turning to the crew, who were long accustomed to such violent sights, and who were more than half inclined to sympathize with the avenger, he made such a bitter charge against them that they were glad to escape without punishment. When Codro was expiring, he had declared that his tormentor would soon follow him, and it was when the murderer was laughing at the possibility, that De Soto came forward and fulfilled the prophecy.

Some time before this De Soto had been sent by the Governor to Nicaragua in search of a passage, which was supposed to exist, connecting the two oceans. After having explored seven hundred miles of sea coast in a fruitless search for the imaginary strait, the expedition returned; but not without some recompense, for the rich country through which they had passed had yielded them a magnificent bounty. De Soto was beginning to realize his ambition. He had always maintained an independent attitude toward the Governor, but now that he had acquired a small fortune he could better afford to show his indifference. He was first to acquaint Don Pedro with the fact that his successor, whom the King of Spain had sent, was already on the way to Darien. This induced the guilty official to seek refuge in Nicaragua, for he hardly expected to be treated with more clemency than he himself had shown toward his predecessor, and, once in the neighboring territory, he could put an end to Cordova, for whom he entertained the strongest hatred and envy. He therefore went to Leon, and, under pretense of good will, sent messengers to acquaint that official of his coming. He was welcomed in the public square, where he drew up his soldiers in such order as to presage treachery to his kindly host; but this honest-hearted ruler had no fear of the man from whom he had received his authority. Now that his superior had arrived, he proceeded to extend the courtesies of hospitality, and to give an account of his own administration. He had not gone far in his recital when Don Pedro, according to a pre-arranged plan, ordered his headsman, who was standing in readiness, to put an end to the unsuspecting Cordova, whose head an instant later was rolling in the dust.

De Soto, who, with his men, had taken a position on the side of the square opposite to Don Pedro and his guards, now spurred to desperation at sight of his friend's murder, dashed with drawn sword upon Don Pedro and would have dispatched him, had he not, by a sudden self-mastery, forborne for the sake of Isabella, and, without a sign of resistance from the soldiers, returned to his place. An instant later, Don Pedro, having recovered from his momentary consternation, called out· "Hernando De Soto you are ordered to dismount and submit yourself to the punishment you have just seen inflicted upon your traitorous comrade. Soldiers, drag him from his horse if he refuses to obey "

For a time the men held back, but one of them at last stepped forward in obedience to the order With a powerful sweep of his sabre De Soto cleaved his helmet in twain, and Don Pedro, seeing that to insist would be dangerous, since he was not supported, allowed the matter to pass.

By a complication of circumstances the King's emissary never landed at Darien, and reassured, Don Pedro again assumed the authority which he had not really given up. Pizarro was now projecting an unprovoked raid upon Peru in quest of gold and glory, and was calling upon the Governor for reinforcements. He desired especially the coöperation of De Soto, who, he knew, would be a strong ally. The proposition was submitted to De Soto, who unaccountably accepted it, greatly to the satisfaction of Don Pedro and Pizarro, but unfortunately for his own good name. It might be said in defense of this course, however, that continued disappointments had driven the Spaniard almost to desperation, and, uncertain of the future, he recklessly joined his fortunes with the murderous adventurer in the hope that he might be able to acquire the wealth and renown which was his ultimate and absorbing aim.

CHAPTER III.

DE SOTO WITH PIZARRO.

LEAVING Darien, we turn to a new chapter in the career of De Soto—his connection with Francisco Pizarro in the conquest of Peru, which forms the most romantic, if not the most noteworthy, period of his stirring and adventurous life.

It is possible that reference to the expedition of Pizarro may not seem entirely consistent with one of the chief purposes of this volume, which is to present De Soto as the discoverer of the Mississippi River; still, the narrative of his heroic deeds would be incomplete without alluding briefly, at least, to that dark page in his history, which, were it possible, I would gladly strike from his soldier escutcheon.

It is not strange that the invasion and conquest of one of the richest countries of South America should have presented some attractions to this lover of adventure, nor that when Pizarro found himself confronted by overwhelming numbers in the mountain fastnesses of Peru, he should have remembered the gallant and chivalrous De Soto, who had given ample proof of his soldierly qualities. When, therefore, he urged the Governor to send his captain forward, holding out to that officer, meanwhile, the promise of second in command in the coming expedition, he knew that the inducement would hardly fail. In confirmation of his prediction, De Soto started southward, soon afterward, with two ships and a small but strong force, in the direction of the Island of Puna, a strip of land separated from the mainland by a narrow channel, where Pizarro had been in possession for a short time. Upon his arrival there, De Soto found to his surprise that the promise of the lieutenancy was only a ruse which had been resorted to in order to secure his services, as that position was already filled by Pizarro's elder brother, Hernando. The honor only rested nominally upon the latter, however, for from the moment that De Soto entered camp he was accorded the honors due to his deserved rank, and the general sentiment was never opposed by Pizarro, who, in his abject nature, did not dare to show any resentment toward a man so vastly his superior, and upon whose coöperation he must completely rely.

During his short stay within the territory of the Peruvian monarch, ostensibly to convert its people to Christianity, all manner of outrages had been committed by Pizarro and his confederates, and reports of his crimes had reached the mainland before the coming of De Soto. It was therefore the policy of the commander-in-chief to remain in the background, while his lieutenant, with a small following, went to reconnoitre the country and to see what manner of people they would have to encounter. As the rafts bearing the steel-clad warriors were slowly pushed ashore, the natives, naturally alarmed at the unusual sight, and determined to put an end to the invaders who were bringing destruction to their homes, attempted to make some resistance; but the invincible

Spaniards soon gained the advantage and began their march toward Tumbez. Some time previously Pizarro had visited this town, and while craftily holding in check his desire for plunder, in order that he might form some idea of its wealth, had inspired the hospitable citizens with confidence, and had been given the freedom of a trusted friend; but the later news of his cruelties on the neighboring island had given them an idea of his intentions, so that upon his second visit he found only abandoned and dismantled houses.

This was a disappointment to the "conquerors," but they were not limited in their new field. With an escort of sixty horsemen and twenty foot soldiers, De Soto was soon sent to explore the towns lying farther in the interior. The natural fearlessness of the man who, free from the guilty motives that actuated his commander, could penetrate the lonely and unknown passes of this South American country without forebodings, won for him the confidence and good-will of the peaceful Peruvians. It is not probable that he believed he was violating any moral law in pursuing this course, nor that he need expect any resistance from the natives. The expedition was approved by his Catholic Majesty, the King of Spain, and any gold of which he or his companions might come into possession was to be obtained by legitimate means, for he especially enjoined his men not to commit any violence. In fact, everything tended to give his advance into the territories of the Inca the appearance of a peaceful embassy. The gleam of shield and sword, the grace of richly caparisoned steeds, the proud bearing of the helmeted cavaliers, and the waving of silken banners contributed to make the passing of the glittering cavalcade a novel and awe-inspiring spectacle; while the lovely scenery of Peru, although lately marked by the demolition of civil war, in turn won the admiration of the Spaniards.

In slowly pursuing their course through the narrow defiles and along the fertile valleys, De Soto and his followers came upon the great highway leading to the capital of the empire, which extended for fifteen hundred miles across the varied passes of the Andes. This stupendous evidence of engineering skill, accomplished by a comparatively obscure people, intimated to the Spaniards the possible strength of a nation which they had come to molest, and which, had their ultimate aims been known, could have crushed them at a single blow. Like the native houses, this road had been constructed of great blocks of stone, so dexterously fitted together as to make it appear one solid mass of masonry. Continuing their way upon this magnificent thoroughfare, the adventurers found themselves nearing the headquarters of the Peruvian camp, which was located about three miles from the town of Caxamarca. At Guoncabama they were met by the Inca's envoy, bearing gifts and friendly greetings to Pizarro, and were asked to return with him to their chief. With some hesitation, De Soto consented, retracing his course to San Miguel, the town which Pizarro was founding, some ninety miles south of Tumbez.

It is said that the superstitious Pizarro, while engaged in a close battle with the Indians a short time before, had seen spirits hovering in the air above the contesting ranks; those on his side apparently led by one resembling Saint Michael, while those of the enemy represented the forces of the Dark Angel.

In the heat of the encounter, Saint Michael and his host were seen to meet and overcome the opposing ranks, which Pizarro took as a sign of his own triumph. With renewed vigor the battle was continued, the Spaniard vowing, if his men conquered, he would do something in honor of the friendly saint. The result was the building of a town which was to become the center of a large colony, and whose patron was to be San Miguel.

Having entered its walls, the Inca's envoy, with all the ceremony of an ostentatious court, delivered the greetings and gifts of his Sovereign to the Spanish general; but Pizarro, notwithstanding these tokens of amity, suspected Attahuallapa of treachery, and feared to be drawn into some snare.

De Soto's report of the magnificence of the larger towns through which he had passed, and the friendliness of the people, in a measure reassured him, and more effectually aroused his craving for plunder, for during De Soto's absence he had conceived a design to seize the Inca in his own stronghold, and to assume control of the rich dominions which would thus fall into his victorious hand. These designs had not been made known to De Soto, who, he knew, would have rejected them. It was therefore innocently that his lieutenant conducted him to the presence of the Peruvian ruler, and in the name of the King of Spain besought an interview.

The first meeting of the Inca and De Soto was a noble sight, and one which the historian has delighted to describe. On the wide plain beyond Caxamarca stretched the tents of the Indian army—a force

THE INCA RECEIVING DE SOTO.

numbered by thousands—with the gorgeous pavilion of the Inca in their midst; and here, sheltered by his protecting legions, the Indian ruler awaited the approach of the Spaniard. When within a few paces of the Inca, partly out of respect to the dignity of his presence, and partly to lessen the fears of the attendants, who were unable to emulate the proud indifference of their King at sight of the spirited white horse which the stranger rode, that gallant cavalier dismounted, and advanced to offer his salutations.

In reply to his request that Pizarro be granted an audience, the Inca appointed the next day, and, as De Soto noticed during their conversation that Attahuallapa betrayed some interest in the restless movements of the horse, which had been left in charge of an attendant, he mounted and performed several equestrian feats, greatly to the astonishment and terror of the awed retainers. This over, De Soto retired, bearing the royal message to Pizarro.

It was not until late in the afternoon of November sixteenth, 1532, that the Inca, with his splendid cortege, approached the public square of Caxamarca, the place which had been agreed upon for the meeting. Already the body of armed warriors, drawn up in imposing array, awaited his coming. Attahuallapa, dressed in the gorgeous robes of his office, his handsome head bound in the variegated turban from which hung the scarlet tassel, the insignia of his rank, his pensive features standing out in striking contrast against the glittering palanquins presented an impressive and suggestive spectacle to the Spaniards.

Friar Vincent, Pizarro's spiritual adviser, and the

chief among the missionary band, so-called, now advanced toward the King with upheld crucifix, and in the language of his priestly office exhorted him to embrace the Catholic faith, presenting some of its doctrines, and saying that it was for this that his countrymen had entered the Peruvian territories.

The abruptness and strangeness of the address somewhat surprised Attahuallapa, who, with becoming firmness, refused to relinquish the religion of his fathers, and awaited the further pleasure of his inexplicable guests. Friar Vincent immediately reported his non-success to Pizarro, and, incensed at the proud bearing of the Peruvian, encouraged his master to set upon the obstinate unbelievers. The time for action had come. If the opportunity were lost, the Spaniards might be surrounded and annihilated, for their leader well knew that his outrages would, sooner or later, raise rebellion. In a moment the square was a battle-ground, the Peruvian retainers, filled with consternation, and defenseless, were being hewn down, or attempting to escape the massacre; the bearers of the royal palanquin were giving way before the deadly swords of their assailants, and the Inca was at the mercy of Pizarro and his men. A body of desperate Indians had burst through the stone inclosure of the square and were fleeing toward the distant tents, hotly pursued by a body of horsemen; but their object gained, the troops were recalled and the carnage stopped.

What part De Soto took in this perfidious affair has not been recorded. With the friendly feeling he entertained for Attahuallapa, it is not probable that he would enter into any conspiracy against him, or that he would countenance such a breach of military honor.

If he was a witness of the scene, and made no attempt to prevent it, this is the darkest accusation that can be brought against him, but his subsequent kindness to the outraged monarch would seem to deny even this.

During the dark days that followed, De Soto made frequent visits to the captive, and Attahuallapa, recognizing his superior qualities and sense of honor, soon gave him his cofidence. Through De Soto the agreement was drawn up by which the Inca was to be released upon the payment of the fabulous sum which, in his desperation, he had offered. This ransom, consisting of two rooms closely filled with gold and silver ornaments, taken from temple and home, was gladly given by the faithful Peruvians for the return of their Sovereign, whom they reverenced almost to idolatry, but even this did not satisfy Pizarro. He feared to release Attahuallapa, as he might, when returned to his people, excite their sense of injustice. He therefore notified his officers of his intentions upon the Inca's life, which he had long determined to take, giving as his reason the involved position of the Spanish troops, and hinting that the Peruvians were already preparing for an attack.

De Soto, who felt that his honor, as well as that of Pizarro, was at stake, had been continually urging Attahuallapa's release, and refused to believe the report of an uprising; but Pizarro with his usual cunning, suggested that his incredulous lieutenant take a body of horse and reconnoitre that part of the country supposed to be the gathering place of the enemy's forces. This De Soto undertook without delay, hoping the sooner to set the prisoner at liberty; while Pizarro, relieved of his presence, prepared to carry out his terrible purpose.

The Inca once out of the way, the Peruvians would be thrown into a state of confusion, thus making the seizure of the capital easy. and safety assured for the "Christian missionaries."

When Attahuallapa was informed of his fate, he seemed overcome by its cruelty, and called excitedly for his friend De Soto, who he hoped might mitigate the sentence, but Pizarro mockingly informed him that De Soto was far away and powerless to lend him any assistance. Although he had received very little encouragement, he confidently believed that Pizarro would keep his promise and treat him honorably The sudden crushing of his hopes was therefore doubly cruel.

The execution was arranged to take place at nightfall, and the soldiers, bearing torches, were called together at a given signal from their leader. The Inca, his wretched captivity about to end, was once more led out under the open sky, shackled hand and foot, and bound to the stake. Friar Vincent approached and again exhorted him to embrace the faith of Rome, with the promise that the manner of his death would be mitigated by the act; but to this hypocritical appeal Attahuallapa refused to listen, accepting his fate with courageous firmness.

De Soto, soon returning from his fruitless expedition, found the Inca dead and the Spaniards planning to take possession of his dominions. His grief and anger knew no bounds. Going to Pizarro's tent, he bitterly accused him of the murder and threatened to report the crime to the King of Spain; then throwing down his glove in the presence of those who had heard his accusation, he challenged them to deny the guilt of their chief. Receiving no response, he turned and left the tent, with mingled feelings of hatred and remorse. The fact that he should have joined them afterward in their march toward Cuzco seems strangely inconsistent; but to abandon his countrymen in their hour of peril would have appeared cowardly, and Hernando De Soto was not the one to retreat.

The advance upon the capital brought ruin and desolation to the villages along the route, for while De Soto, with his stout-hearted band, was hurrying forward, sparing always private property, while occasionally plundering the temples and shrines, Pizarro, with his freebooters, was pillaging and plundering in every direction. In this way the road was cleared, and the attacks of the natives repulsed by the swords of De Soto's men, while Pizarro reaped the benefits. In the meantime, Tapaxpa, the grief-stricken son of Attahuallapa, had been seized and declared his father's successor, that Pizarro might still hold the Inca in his power. Another captive was one of the most influential of the nobility, a man trusted and loved by the Peruvians, whom Pizarro guarded and declared to be held as a hostage, threatening to put him to death at the first sign of rebellion from the people. This unfortunate victim, upon a slight outbreak during the march toward Cuzco, was notified that his end was near, and was tendered the consolations of the church; but this offer presented no attractions to one who had suffered such injustice at the hands of its fanatical devotees, and he told them that he did not understand their religion, and all he had seen of it had not impressed him favorably.

When within a short distance of the capital, De Soto's troop was assailed by a desperate band of

Peruvians, who had taken a position on high ground above the pass through which the Spaniards were moving, and who determined to make a last effort to destroy their enemies. Stones were hurled from the overhanging cliffs, and showers of arrows sent clashing down upon the steel armor of horse and rider, but De Soto quickly dashed up the steep defile, and, once on the level plain, routed the enemy The news of defeat was soon spread, and, having lost all hope, the Peruvians hurried to the city and applied the torch to every wall. As the conquering army approached, they saw its palaces and temples in flames and its inhabitants vanished. Hurrying hither and thither, they attempted to rescue part of the gold and silver which had not been carried away, but the conflagration was too great, and the splendid treasures of the Inca were lost in the ruins.

The conquest of Peru accomplished, and his desire for gold thoroughly satisfied, De Soto now turned with renewed craving to the peaceful confines of Spain, and to the long-delayed meeting with Donna Isabella. He, therefore, prepared to return, that he might claim the hand of his lady-love, and share with her his splendid fortune. A good share of Attahuallapa's ransom had fallen to him, and he had accepted it rather than allow it to go into the hands of Pizarro. While following the fortunes of his associates in Peru, he seems to have attempted in a degree the moderation of their terrible deeds, and the upholding of his country's honor. That he did not do so more effectually is the one great reproach which humanity raises against him; the one great blemish upon an otherwise admirable and chivalrous career.

CHAPTER IV.

DISCOVERY OF THE MISSISSIPPI.

TWO years of luxury and inactivity in Spain after the hardships of the Peruvian expedition, had satisfied the restless spirit of De Soto, and quite exhausted the wealth which he had accumulated.

Unsparingly the golden treasure of the Inca had been given in exchange for the extravagances which attracted the wealthier grandees, and the envied cavalier again found it necessary to seek his fortune beyond the sea. While he was still in South America with Pizarro, Don Pedro had died, leaving the greater share of his wealth for the erection of a convent, over which his elder daughter was appointed abbess, and disinheriting his former favorite on account of her faithful attachment to Don Hernando, for whom, to the last, he entertained the strongest dislike. Isabella was therefore unable to follow her generous impulses and avoid another separation.

At this time all Europe was stirred by the tales of Cabeça de Vaca, one of the adventurers who had escaped the fate of his companions under Narvaez in Florida, and who suggested to his credulous countrymen untold regions of gold in the chimerical El Dorado. His words had magical effect. Immediately the rich fields of North America were the engrossing topic, the cynosure of ambitious fortune-seekers. Very naturally, De Soto came into prominence, and was soon known to be contemplating an expedition thither. He believed that he would find an easier road to fortune in the land which De Vaca had described than in the mountains of Peru, and he accordingly appealed to King Charles V., offering to meet all expenses and to reserve a fifth of the treasure for the crown if His Majesty would sanction the undertaking.

With admirable generosity, Charles gave his consent, offering his zealous subject the governorship of Cuba, with other high-sounding dignities, and granting him an estate, with the title of Adelantado, in Florida. Enthusiastic knights from every direction now hastened to place themselves under the leadership of De Soto, and to make preparations for their voyage. The magnificence of the equipments was in accordance with their inflated ideas, representing vast sums of money, and appearing more suitable for a triumphal march through the reputed land of gold, than for the toilsome and dangerous campaigns which were actually to be endured.

The passage of De Soto and his followers through her streets, en route to the ships, formed probably the most brilliant pageant which the citizens of San Lucar had ever witnessed.

With waving pennants, and decks glittering with the armor of nine hundred knights, the fleet moved slowly out of port, taking a southerly course in the direction of the Canary Isles. Within two weeks they cast anchor at Gomera, sailing from thence to San Iago de Cuba, which was reached toward the latter part of May. As the distance lessened between them and their El Dorado, the adventurers, impatient of delay, urged the termination of the voyage, and De Soto, equally eager, hastened forward to Havana, where final arrangements were to be made. Two brigantines were sent out from here to discover the most practicable route for the expedition, and upon their return knight and lady bade adieu, the great band of explorers, now ten hundred strong, were animated with the hope of their future achievements, while Isabella having been appointed regent during the Governor's absence, assumed the responsibilities of the office with many sad forebodings.

Seven days later, on Whitsunday, 1539, the fleet reached the quiet waters of Tampa Bay, which they named Espirito Santo, in honor of the day. Here they met the first opposition. On the high hills along the shore the beacons of the unknown natives were sending out a menacing signal, and De Soto, wishing to avoid any unnecessary encounter, prudently made a landing two leagues beyond. A march of a few miles through the enchanted wilderness, gorgeous in its luxuriant tangles of tropical vegetation, brought the Spaniards to an abandoned village, the home of the Indian chief Ucita, where the first encampment was made. Here, instead of the rude dwellings of the northern tribes, they found houses of wood, some of them adorned with hangings of finely cured and handsomely colored skins, with floor mats of the same soft texture; while the dwelling of the cacique, standing apart upon a little eminence, bore traces of being more fancifully arranged than the rest.

As soon as he had taken possession of this convenient camp, De Soto sent messengers to Ucita stating the peaceful object of his journey, and asking for his friendship; but the chief ignored these advances, and kept his whereabouts a secret.

Unfortunately for those who were to follow him, Narvaez had thoroughly antagonized the natives through whose territories he had passed, and had aroused in them a stubborn and bitter hatred. Wherever he had gone he had given fresh cause for revenge, and to the chief whose good-will De Soto was now seeking, he had offered the most shocking atrocities. It was therefore useless to remain longer at this point, with the hope of receiving any information or of obtaining guides. Troops were sent out in every direction to reconnoitre. One of these parties, upon leaving camp, came upon a body of Indians, who, frightened at the appearance of the strangers, ran into the woods. One of their number, however, remained in sight, and, advancing, made the sign of the cross, greatly to the astonishment of the Spaniards. When the mysterious figure reached them, they learned that he was Juan Ortiz, a survivor of the Narvaez expedition, who had been captured by the Indians, and, after suffering many persecutions at the hands of his captors, had finally escaped and received the protection of a friendly chief.

After hearing the story of their countryman's adventures, and rejoicing in his recovery, the men anxiously questioned him concerning the reputed gold fields. But Ortiz, having been confined to the limits of a single tribe, was neither able to give them any information nor to act as their guide. Upon finding no sign of the coveted treasure, and discouraged by the hardships which had already been met with, De Soto sent the ships back to Cuba, and planned a march toward the north. Hunger had already begun to threaten the band, but, finding occasional fields of maize, and here and there a fertile stretch of country, the men bravely advanced under the leadership of their dauntless captain, baffling native treachery, and encountering the difficulties of swamp and forest, where their lives were continually in jeopardy.

Still led on by rumors of gold, De Soto and his followers reached the domain of Vitachuco, the cacique whose stratagem brought about one of the most picturesque episodes in the history of the expedition. This Indian, harboring a deadly revenge against the Spaniards, notwithstanding the passive tolerance of his brother chiefs, determined to annihilate the invaders when he should have them in his power. Under the guise of friendship he invited them to his village, and while showing them every attention formed a plot for their destruction as ingenious as it was deadly.

On an appointed day the Spaniards were to be invited to witness some maneuvers of Vitachuco's warriors, the Indian weapons to be concealed in the long grass, and at a given signal from the chief, the conspirators were to seize the hidden arms and rush upon their defenseless guests—Vitachuco, with twelve chosen braves, to single out the leader. De Soto, having been warned by the faithful Ortiz, was prepared to meet the forces of the enemy on their own ground, and when the fatal day arrived accepted the invitation of the chief with evident pleasure. The scene of conflict, as the old historians describe it, was a magnificent one. Out on the sunny plain stretched the long line of warriors drawn up in martial array, their treacherous weapons hidden in the long grass, while opposite, De Soto, with his followers, was watching with intent gaze the dexterous movements of the Indians, and waiting for the cacique's signal. In an instant the warning came. With the swiftness of eagles the traitorous band closed upon the Spaniards; but finding, to their astonishment, that they must deal with a force as carefully armed and as fully prepared as themselves, their onset was soon repulsed.

Leaving Vitachuco, the expedition moved on toward the north until the Great Morass was reached; thence to the southwest toward Appalachee Bay, where the boats from Cuba were met and sent westward in search of a favorable port. The march was then directed toward the northeast, where there was a region abounding in pearls and gold, whose Sovereign was the gentle and amiable Queen called by the old chroniclers "the Ladie of the Countree." The Spaniards seem to have received every kindness at her hands, and to have found a fabulous amount of pearls of high value, and yet they kept the "ladie" as a hostage, it is said, to insure the non-resistance of her people. Under some pretext, however, she effected her escape, a gallant Spaniard disappearing at the same time, and upon this episode a Southern writer has woven his romantic tale of "Andres Vasconselos."

Still deceived by the misrepresentations of their guides, and by the finding of the pearls, the travelers pursued their *ignis-fatuus* through the fields of South Carolina, Georgia, and Alabama, whither it led them many a weary march. Then turning southward they reached Mauvilla, from which the present town of Mobile probably derived its name. Here their slaves were captured and the pearls lost with them, but De Soto, determined to avenge the robbery, made a violent attack upon the place, setting fire to the houses in which his valuable treasures were consumed. Here also the ships sent from Appalachee were heard from, but for various reasons De Soto did not wish to have their arrival known. He had hoped to send back to Cuba glowing accounts of the country and to make presents of pearls and gold, but both these plans had become impossible. He feared, too, if those who were with him once saw the means of abandoning the enterprise, they would leave him powerless to advance, for with the disheartening opposition which he had met during eighteen months, the courageous spirit of De Soto was still unwilling to acknowledge failure. Having, therefore, planned the course he would pursue, he held no communication with Maldonado, the captain of the ships, but turned resolutely away, "determined to send no news of himself until he had found some rich country."

After waiting many weeks for some sign of the expedition, Maldonado returned to Cuba, where the Governor and those who were with him were lamented as dead.

In the meanwhile, De Soto was taking a northwesterly course through the fields and forests of what is now the flourishing State of Mississippi, and slowly approaching that Great Stream with which his destiny became so closely linked. As he advanced, the Indians became more hostile, contesting the way with arrow and tomahawk and harassing the encampment at night. His men, too, were discontented, having seen hundreds of their companions perish from exposure and violence, and having found no recompense for their wearisome marches. Yet under these embarrassments the intrepid cavalier led them on, apparently stimulated by defeat and strengthened by difficulty.

At last the shores of the Mississippi were reached, it is conjectured, between the thirty-fifth and thirty-sixth parallels of latitude, a few miles below Memphis. What impression the river made upon De Soto and his companions as they came suddenly upon it can only be imagined. It was then, as it is now, a turbulent flood, whirling along on its muddy surface a mass of logs and driftwood from the forest banks above, where the white man was unknown and the Indian was still monarch. They had found nothing in all their wanderings that would compare with it, no valley enriched by so dignified a stream, so they named it Rio Grande.

Finding it thus unexpectedly, the Great River no doubt had its effect upon the minds of the explorers, who, notwithstanding repeated disappointments, could yet find something in the hidden regions of an unknown country to stimulate their energies. Instead therefore of turning back when this new barrier crossed their way, rafts were built and the entire company carried to the other side. Parties were then sent hither and thither to explore the country and to inquire after the "yellow metal," but the interpreters gave them the old response—gold could be found farther on in the mountains to the west. Still deceived and suspected by the Indians, who only wished to be rid of them, the Spaniards passed over miles of that great Western country which remained a wilderness long after their feet had penetrated its solitudes; occasionally finding a friendly chief, or a rich section, where the confident De Soto would lay plans for the establishment of a powerful and wealthy colony So amid repeated discouragements and fruitless wanderings the expedition reached again the "Father of Waters," whence a few months before they had started forth reanimated.

De Soto, the ever buoyant leader, teeming with new schemes and always ready to face difficulties, now began to give way to an irresistible despondency. All of his hopes were vanished, his health was undermined by continued hardship, and those about him were impatient to return to Cuba.

Seeing his further efforts unavailing, he decided upon returning to the coast, and accordingly sent a party down the stream to make investigations; but they could get no information, and the canebrakes and other obstructions met with in the tortuous descent delayed their progress.

A low fever began to waste his strength and he had no power to resist it. So lay the Chevalier De Soto upon his death-bed, broken in body and spirit, and unconscious of the great part he was to play in the history of the river, within sight of whose shores he expired.

On the twenty-first of May, 1542, he called those who remained of his brave band about him, to give them his last messages and to appoint his successor.

There has been much conjecture regarding the death of De Soto, some historians expressing a conviction of foul play, and bringing together circumstantial evidence to confirm it; but whether or not their surmises were correct must ever remain a mystery.

After dark on the day of his death, the burial rites

BURIAL OF DE SOTO AT MIDNIGHT

were performed upon the shore of the river, but, finding that Indians visited the spot the next day, making strange signs, they feared to leave the remains, lest they should be disinterred and subjected to dishonor. The cacique who had accompanied them on their journey also asked where the white chief was, and they, thinking, if his death were known, some assault would be made, replied that he had gone to Heaven to confer with the Great Spirit, and would soon return to lead them to the land of gold. At midnight, under pretense of going to fish, they exhumed the body, and, cutting a place for it in the trunk of a live-oak, carried it out into the middle of the stream, and there in silence lowered it to its last resting place.

With no one of Don Hernando's force to stimulate and encourage, the band was soon disorganized and scattered in different directions, the greater number starting toward the Southwest in search of a Spanish colony said to have been founded upon the shores of the Gulf. With the energy of desperate men they launched their small fleet of rudely constructed boats once more upon the open sea, sometimes overtaken by storms and driven ashore, sometimes injured by rocks, until at last they reached the flourishing little Mexican town of Panuco. Here they were received as those returned from the dead, and were soon given an opportunity to reach their home and friends. Others tried to return to Cuba by another route, and either miserably perished on the way or were never heard from; so that of all the brilliant company which sailed from Havana three years before, only a remnant was left to tell the tale of suffering and disappointment.

De Soto, whose enterprise had been looked upon as a magnificent venture, destined, perhaps, to change the financial condition of Spain, and to establish her jurisdiction in a new and rich country, was now considered as a man who had perished in a worthless cause; whose early triumphs were shadowed by failure.

The planting of the cross upon the banks of the great North American River had not attained the significance which later chroniclers ascribed to it, and investigation had not yet been sufficiently thorough to attach importance to the event. Time, however, has, in a measure, thrown light upon the page of history, and has done justice to the Early Explorers, not least among whom is the brave knight and Christian gentleman, Don Hernando De Soto. To him falls the honor of the discovery of the Mississippi—the noble "Father of Waters."

JUAN ORTIZ THE INDIAN CAPTIVE.

CHAPTER V

MARQUETTE AND JOLIET.

BEFORE Columbus opened a new field for exploration on the Western Continent, Europe had been speculating upon a possible route to Asia and the East through untried channels. What lay beyond the great ocean, and whither would it lead the venturesome mariner, were questions already being asked by those progressive spirits, whose queries in all ages have inspired the scientist and the explorer.

When, in the attempt to solve the important problem, the shores of a new country were accidentally discovered, the excitement which this created for a time banished the original motive; but, as exploration began in turn to be directed toward the unknown regions of America, zealous adventurers hoped to find the fancied channel within its boundaries.

From the Canadian settlements along the Saint Lawrence those daring expeditions were first projected which began the spread of the Gospel among the savage tribes of the West; and which, placing within the knowledge of men untraveled territories, added new glory to the name of France. This, too, in the face of continual encounters with the treacherous natives, whose tomahawks had already dyed woodland and valley with the white man's blood.

As early as 1658, two fur traders had reached the

western end of Lake Superior, where they were told by the Sioux of a great river, whose valley their Indian fancy had enveloped in mystery and romance. Up and down its windings many a war and hunting party had passed in the centuries before the European came, investing it with traditions which even now cling to it, and which leave some faint trace of a prehistoric era. Of this the traders told upon their return to Canada, exciting the greatest interest in the western river, and reviving the old theory of an international waterway. "The Indians had described it; the Jesuits were eager to discover it," and to be the first to plant the cross upon its shores. They were very nearly deprived of the honor of first reaching it, however, by the ambitious Sieur de La Salle, who believed its course lay toward the Red Sea—by which name the Gulf of California was then known—and who was willing to put his entire fortune into an expedition for its discovery; but by a complication of events, his plans failed, and he returned without having accomplished his purpose. By the time he prepared for a second expedition, the Jesuits had explored more than a thousand miles of the river, had sown the first seeds of their religion along its shores, and had become convinced that its course lay in the direction of the Gulf of Mexico, and not, as was supposed, in the direction of the Pacific.

The two men who had been chosen by the Canadian officials to conduct this enterprise were singularly fitted for the service, and in their different rôles of explorer and missionary are admirable examples of the courage and loyalty which characterized the early pioneer

Father James Marquette, the elder of the two,

was born in 1637, in the picturesque old cathedral town of Laon, about ninety miles northeast of the French capital. Here, under the gentle guidance of his mother and the Church, he received that early training which influenced him, at the age of seventeen, to renounce the world and attach himself to the order of the Jesuits.

Twelve years were spent in the quiet pursuits of teaching and study, and then, eager to follow the example of his patron saint, Francis Xavier, whose life and death among the half-civilized nations of the Orient had deeply impressed him, he was given an opportunity to follow his bent by being transferred from the province of Champagne, which contained no foreign mission, to that of France. In 1666, he sailed for Canada, full of enthusiasm for the noble cause which he had espoused, and buoyant with life and health. His inclination toward an active career was doubtless inherited from his soldier and statesmen ancestors, who were ever ready to defend their country and their King, and whose loyal services were among the proudest records of Laon. In this country the name is also deserving of honor, not only for the sake of the priest-explorer, but because of the enlistment of three Marquettes in the cause of American independence.

At the time of Marquette's arrival at Quebec, the mission fields of the New World were greatly in need of reinforcements, and the sight of this earnest young Jesuit must have been encouraging to the good Vicar Apostolic, Francis de Laval, who, since his appointment as bishop of Petrea, had labored unceasingly to establish order in his outlying stations, and who wished to extend the influence of the Church to the more distant tribes. Filled with the zeal which has ever characterized the members of the Society of Jesus, he longed to penetrate the Great West himself, and to plant the cross in its wildest haunts. This wish he could not realize, but he was none the less ambitious in appointing others to the work. He soon sent Marquette with Father Druilletes to study the Montagnais language, which was a key to the others, that the young man might be prepared for the mission of Tadoussac, which was first planned for him; but his field was changed, and he was ordered in 1668 to the Ottawa mission on Lake Superior

Starting from Quebec, on the twenty-first of April, with three companions, Marquette was joined by a party of Nezpercés, with whom he began the journey up the Saint Lawrence and through the lakes, invoking the protection of the Virgin Mary, whom he worshiped with the simple devotion of a child, and, under her guidance, reaching his distant station of Ste. Marie du Sault.

It is impossible to mistake the sincerity of Marquette's character. Possessed of an imaginative and gentle nature, he gave all of his energies to his holy calling, and combined in his own person the sturdy qualities of the explorer with the ideal virtues of the saint. In his lonely home on Lake Superior he labored unceasingly, instructing first the Algonquins at Ste. Marie's, and later, at Lapointe, the Hurons and Ottawas, who had been driven westward by the vengeful Iroquois, writing to his superior at Quebec of the progress he was making, and the difficulties which confronted him, and, with all his Christian labors, learning the languages of the tribes who frequented the region of the northern lakes.

Through the intercourse which frequent contact with the visiting tribes thus brought about, Marquette first began to entertain the hope of some day leaving his mission in other hands, and of carrying out his favorite wish—to see the Mississippi, and to convert the tribes upon its shores. While at Ste. Marie's he had heard from the Sioux of the Great River, and again at Saint Ignace—by which name the mission at Michilimackinac was known—the Illinois brought him word of the stream into which their river found its way

For a time it seemed that his wish could not be realized. The Hurons and Ottawas became involved in a quarrel with the Sioux, and were again obliged to flee from their angry neighbors. Each tribe sought a different retreat—the Ottawas going to the Island of Manataulin followed by Father Louis André, while the Hurons took up their abode at Michilimackinac, whither Father Marquette accompanied them. To one less strong of purpose, this new field would have been discouraging, but with unfailing patience he erected a chapel and established a mission upon the bleak coast, which later became an important point for the Indians returning from their hunting excursions. Meanwhile, events were culminating at Quebec in such a way as to bring Marquette to a speedy realization of his hopes.

It was the policy of the French to explore and occupy the interior of the country as rapidly as possible, and to this end the Governor was seeking competent men to carry on the enterprise. The influence of the Jesuits was strong at that time, and therefore the choice of emissaries under their patronage would naturally follow. Probably for this reason the intendant, Talon, before leaving the colony, recommended Louis Joliet for the discovery of the Mississippi, although Joliet had proven himself worthy of the project, and was a man of wide experience. The choice of the one who was to accompany him fell to Marquette, on account of his familiarity with the Indians and their language, and of his knowledge of the country, and also, it may be supposed, in acknowledgment of his zealous labors in the remote missions of the West. To him the appointment meant the crowning of his life work; the golden opportunity for which he had waited; and if ambition for his Order entered somewhat into his thoughts, it was a pardonable ambition, in which self-glory bore a very small, and the salvation of a heathen race a very large, part.

As to Joliet, very little has been found concerning his early career beyond a few distinct facts, and the detailed record of his life only begins with the expedition to the Mississippi in company with Marquette. This omission in the old manuscripts has been a source of regret to American historians, who would have taken some pride in writing the biography of an explorer born in their own country To the efforts of Mr. Shea we are indebted for nearly all of the information that has been gained concerning him.

Born in 1645 in Quebec, then a great stronghold of the Jesuits, he was early placed under their instruction, and determined to become a priest. At seventeen he received the minor orders, and at twenty-one excited the admiration of his superiors by his intelligent reasoning in the philosophical discussions inaugurated by the sages of the colony. His real province, though, was soon found to be widely different from that of his brother priests, and, becoming convinced that his inclinations were antagonistic to his office, he soon renounced his vows and took up the practical occupation of a fur trader, remaining, however, partial to the order which he had left. His keen intelligence and natural hardihood rendered him great assistance in his roving tours over the country, and he became valuable to the authorities in Quebec as an explorer. Talon sent him, in 1669, with Péré, to search for and report upon the copper mines of Lake Superior, and although the expedition was a failure, he had made careful maps of the route passed over, and by them was able to offer suggestions to Pollier and his companions, whom, with La Salle, he met at the head of Lake Ontario, bent upon "exploring the mystery of the great unknown River of the West."

La Salle and the priests soon separated; the latter taking the route which Joliet had indicated, in order to visit those tribes which he had described as being sadly in need of their assistance, while the former, prevented from carrying out his plans for reaching the Mississippi, was obliged to postpone his undertaking and return to Canada.

As late as 1673 no important move had been made toward the interesting interior, so that the appointment in that year of Marquette and Joliet to search out the unknown river meant a new era in the history of American exploration.

Having accepted the responsibility of the expedition, Joliet started in the autumn to meet his fellow voyager, reaching the mission of Saint Ignace on the festival of the Immaculate Conception, a time singularly happy to Marquette, who wrote in his journal: "The day of the Immaculate Conception of the

Blessed Virgin Mary whom I have always invoked, since I have been in this country, to obtain of God the grace to be able to visit the nations on the River Mississippi, was identically that on which M. Joliet arrived with orders of the Comte de Frontenac, our Governor, and M. Talon, our intendant, to make this discovery with me. I was the more enraptured at this good news, as I saw my designs on the point of being accomplished, and myself in the happy necessity of exposing my life for the salvation of all these nations, and particularly the Illinois, who had, when I was at Lapointe du Saint Esprit, very earnestly entreated me to carry the word of God to their country " This entry, as indeed his entire journal, shows the enthusiasm that burned in the soul of Marquette for the uplifting of the heathen nations among whom he had chosen to pursue his life work.

As for Joliet, he had become greatly interested in the River Mississippi while on his western hunting excursions, during which he received glowing accounts of it from the Indians. It was his ambition to reach it, and, as he had promised Frontenac, "to see its mouth", yet notwithstanding the eagerness of both men, it was deemed prudent to devote the winter months to investigation, that "if the enterprise were hazardous," as Marquette says, "it should not be foolhardy " They accordingly questioned all Indians who had any knowledge of the region, and with information gathered from personal observation mapped out the route, and the tribes they were likely to encounter. In the spring their plans were matured, and, devoutly placing themselves under the protection of the "Blessed Virgin Immaculate," they began their journey on the seventeenth of May, letting their paddles "play joyously over a part of Lake Huron and that of the Illinois—Lake Michigan—into the Bay of the Fetid," according to Marquette's sprightly account.

Following the northern shore of Lake Michigan until it turns southward, they coasted on down to the inlet now known as Green Bay; then into a small tributary stream, reaching the village of the Menomonees, or "Wild Rice," Indians, where they were seriously cautioned against going farther. In vain these superstitious children of the forest sought to dissuade their white brothers. Marquette paid no heed to their stories, assuring them that he and the Sieur Joliet could protect themselves, and that he must not turn back when there were souls to save.

At the head of Green Bay the travelers were welcomed by Fathers Allouez and Dablon, who had been laboring among the savage tribes of that region for three years, in an attempt to convert them to Christianity.

Father Allouez had bravely entered the field in 1669 to found the mission of Saint Francis Xavier, where he was joined the next year by his brother missionary Together they had visited the villages of the Pottawattamies, Winnebagoes, Sacs, Mascoutins, Miamis, Kickapoos, and Foxes, who lived in what Dablon enthusiastically called "an earthly paradise," and from them they also heard of the Great River. which rose far in the north, and which they had hoped some day to see. With the natural sympathy of men of broad purpose and brave deeds, they now rejoiced with their more fortunate brothers. who were about to realize a kindred wish; and with every encouragement saw them again on their way.

The voyagers now paddled into Fox River, finding it easy of access near its mouth, but farther up, where they were obliged to get into the water and carry the boats, its stones and pebbly bottom made their passage difficult. Reading the narrative at this point, one fancies that Father Marquette and his sturdy companion must have enjoyed their journey with the relish of a modern canoeist; forgetting for the moment the perils of travel in the midst of savage tribes, and only realizing the beauties about them. For two hundred and sixty miles they followed this stream, noticing as they passed along the changes of scene, and stopping near the village of the Mascoutins "to drink the mineral waters." At Mascoutins itself, we have, through Marquette's journal, a picturesque view of an Indian village, built on an eminence overlooking the river; with a great cross in the midst of its lodges, hung with colored skins and bows and arrows as a thank offering to the great Manitou, who had given them an abundance of game during the winter, when a famine had been expected.

Soon after disembarking here, Marquette and Joliet called the chiefs about them to explain the reason of their journey, and to ask for guides, as they would soon reach unfamiliar streams. Their request was quickly granted, for the Miamis, who belonged to the head tribe of the town, were very friendly with the French.

The route beyond was through the unknown country, for exploration had ceased at Mascoutins, and the only information that had been gained concerning it was from Indian descriptions, with which considerable superstition had been mingled.

At the head of the Upper Fox River the Frenchmen

left the waters on which they had come from Quebec, and making a portage, with the assistance of their Miami guides, were soon launched upon the broad stream of the Wisconsin. Their anxiety to reach the Great River now filled their thoughts and hurried their paddles, as they glided down the sandy channel, past bar and island and forest-covered bank.

With feelings of mingled pride and gratitude the brave men approached the goal of their hopes, and, again quoting the simple but forcible words of the missionary, they "safely entered the Mississippi on the seventeenth of June, with a joy that he could not express." Evidently, from Marquette's preliminary description of the river, the Indians from whom he received his information had a very good idea of its features, for he speaks of the lakes from which it had its source in the North.

It is a characteristic of the Indian that he has very accurate ideas of location; often exerting his faculty in this direction to a remarkable degree; and if given materials, will map out familiar localities with an exactness which has often been of the greatest service to his white brothers. In changing his abode to meet the exigencies of summer and winter, this trait becomes almost an instinct.

After having gone more than three hundred miles without meeting anything more startling than the timid denizens of forest and prairie, the travelers were filled with apprehension. At every turn, they expected to come upon hostile natives or to be overwhelmed by them in ambush; and the greatest care was taken to prevent surprise. In the evening a small fire was made on the shore, where their food was prepared; but this was left as darkness came on,

MARQUETTE AND JOLIET DESCENDING THE MISSISSIPPI.

and a safer shelter found in the boats moored far out in the stream, from whose silent retreat a sentinel always kept guard. In this way they pursued their course for some time; but on the twenty-fifth of June, while passing closely to the shore, footprints were discovered on the sand, from which a path was seen to extend over the prairie. This the explorers determined to follow, leaving the boats in charge of their men and warning them to be on the lookout.

Realizing the danger to which they were exposed. Marquette and Joliet advanced in silence until within sight of the Indian village whither the path led; then, recommending themselves to the protection of Heaven, made their presence known by crying out with all their strength. At this the Indians rushed from their cabins in consternation, but perceiving the peaceful intent of the strangers, they made no attempt to prevent their approach. Four old men were sent out to greet them, bearing aloft the calumet—their universal emblem of good-will—and when they had come within a few paces of the Frenchmen, Marquette began the parley by asking the Indians who they were. To the surprise and pleasure of their visitors they replied that they were Illinois, and in token of peace offered their pipes, at the same time inviting the strangers to their village.

The reception which Marquette and his companion received at the hands of this friendly tribe is strongly characteristic of Indian customs, and of their fondness for a certain savage formality Seeing the black gown of the priest, which even then had become a truce through the faithful exertions of the earlier evangelists, the two explorers were welcomed to the village and escorted to the tent of one of the chiefs.

At his door that august personage appeared entirely naked, that he might, according to his heathen notions, show the greater respect for his guests; and lifting his hands as if to shield his face, cried out, "How bright is the sun, O Frenchmen, when you come to visit us!" then, standing aside, he bade them enter his tent. Within, a curious and silent assemblage confronted them, from whose midst, now and then, came the reassuring ejaculation, uttered in their low guttural, "Well done, brothers, to visit us!"

After observing the ceremony of smoking the calumet, a universal token of peace among the Indians, the Frenchmen were invited to visit the great sachem, whose town lay a short distance beyond. A crowd of curious Indians followed them, resorting to the most ludicrous methods in order to get a good look at their white brothers, and the scene described by Marquette is extremely amusing. "They threw themselves on the grass by the wayside, they ran ahead, they turned and walked back to see us again," he writes, and "all this was done without noise and with marks of a great respect entertained for us."

Thus escorted, they made their way to the chief, and were in turn welcomed by him with the usual demonstrativeness of the race. He had, besides, a reason for being on good terms with the French, as the Illinois nation were then the direct objects of Iroquois wrath—owing to a complicated rivalry in connection with the fur trade—and were in need of an alliance with Canada. To be skeptical, therefore, the extent of the chief's personal regard might be questioned. He tried to dissuade his guests, in the name of all the Illinois, from going farther on their perilous mission, recounting the dangers to which they would be exposed, and putting forth all his Indian eloquence in their interest; but Marquette answered that he feared nothing, and that he would gladly risk his life in the service of the Great Spirit; an assertion which he believed beyond the comprehension of his hearers, although he must have had abundant proof of their own capacity for self-sacrifice and loyalty.

On the next day, at three o'clock in the afternoon, Marquette and Joliet, having rejoined their men, embarked in the presence of six hundred Illinois, who had assembled to give them farewell.

Passing slowly down the river, the explorers stopped occasionally to notice the rare plants and fruits which grew upon the banks, and to enjoy the beauties of a scene which even now enchants the beholder.

A surprise met them in their peaceful descent, and turned their contemplation of nature to the arts of man. On the high rocks which overhung the stream, some original Indian had skillfully painted two figures, which, from Marquette's account, must have been the artist's conception of Matcha Manitou, or the Evil One. The terrible aspect of these monsters made a deep impression upon the good priest, who says they were so well painted that he could not believe the work done by an Indian, and for whose awe-inspiring effect he vouched by saying that "the boldest Indian" dared not gaze too long upon them.

While still talking of the strange impression the Manitous had exerted over them, the little party of men were suddenly aware of another surprise in their way. They were coming within the disturbing influence of the muddy Missouri, which, pouring its full flood into the main stream, seemed almost to threaten destruction to the frail fleet. Here the Indians described the course of the great tributary of the Mississippi, and suggested a route through its channel by which the Gulf of California might be reached indirectly, a course since found to be practicable by topographical surveys. This suggestion aroused Marquette's love of adventure and missionary zeal, and he wrote if God would give him strength he would "not despair of one day making its discovery."

A few days later the mouth of the Ohio, or "beautiful river," was reached, upon whose banks dwelt the peaceable Shawnees, fugitives from the unprovoked assaults of the Iroquois.

The travelers now became exposed to the attacks of the merciless mosquito, which proved to have no more reverence for a black gown than for any other garb.

Marquette, appreciating the cleverness of the Indians, describes their methods of defense in dealing with the "little animals," as he calls them. "They raise a scaffolding," he says, "the floor of which is made of simple poles, and consequently a mere gratework to give passage to the smoke of a fire which they build beneath. The Indians sleep on the poles, having pieces of bark stretched above them to keep off the rain." By following this example as far as their limited means would allow, the Frenchmen improvised a screen out of their sails, and, thus protected, kept their way down to the warmer climates.

Below the Ohio they came to an Indian village, and, anticipating trouble, Marquette held up his safeguard, the handsome calumet presented by the great sachem of the Illinois. For an instant it seemed that their friendly sign was disregarded, and Marquette's quick ear caught what he believed to be the word of battle; but it proved to be an invitation to land, which was gladly accepted by the fatigued and famished travelers, who were later treated to buffalo-steak, bear's oil, and white plums.

Upon receiving the joyful assurance that they were now only ten days' journey from the Gulf, the party again resumed their way, no longer content to glide on at the will of the current, but with vigorous paddle-strokes pushing their canoes forward. Down they sped between the solitary banks, for nearly three hundred miles, until they reached the village of Mitchigamea, where their right of way was for the first time seriously questioned.

Seeing the men on shore running back and forth brandishing their weapons, the terrified voyageurs committed themselves to the protection of Heaven, and with abated breath held the canoes in mid-stream while Marquette exposed the peaceful talisman. Its magic effect appeared to fail with the threatening warriors, who now pushed out into the water in their canoes, or swam toward the fleet with uplifted clubs. At this moment the older warriors appeared upon the scene, and, noticing the peace-pipe, averted the danger just when the party had given up hope. They asked the strangers ashore, treated them with surprising hospitality, and invited them to stay over night, an invitation which was accepted, as Marquette says, "not without some uneasiness." Besides this, they found it difficult to make each other understood, as the Indians did not speak any of the languages with which Marquette and Joliet were familiar; but at last resorting to signs, and the aid of an Indian among them who could speak a little Illinois, they told the Frenchmen that they could obtain all the information they desired at the next village below. Early the following morning, therefore, they launched their canoes, and, with some relief, started on their way toward Akamsea —Arkansas—accompanied by ten of their late entertainers, and the Illinois interpreter.

When within a mile and a half of their destination two canoes were seen approaching, in one of which stood a chief holding the calumet, and singing an Indian song of peace. These preliminaries over, the foremost canoe was turned about to guide the visitors to the town. Here Marquette and Joliet were royally received, and as soon as ceremony allowed, and the priest had made his usual exhortation, eager inquiry was made concerning the subject nearest their thoughts. How many days' journey was it to the sea? and what did the men of Akamsea know of the river beyond?

They were told that ten days' journey would bring them to the Gulf, but that the tribes below were unknown to them, since their enemies prevented any intercourse. They also warned the Frenchmen against exposing themselves to the attacks of their warlike neighbors, from whose depredations they had so often suffered.

Soon after this friendly council the sachems came together and deliberated upon the destruction of their guests, whom they had seemed but a short time before to regard with so much solicitude, but the chief became aware of their movements and prevented violence; further proving his protection by dancing the calumet and presenting the pipe to the priest at its conclusion.

Marquette and Joliet now met to discuss their

plans. They had heard of the Mexicans through the Indians, and believed it would be foolhardy to expose themselves to capture by the former—who looked upon their expedition as an encroachment—or to massacre by the latter, by further following the river, whose course they were now convinced lay toward the Gulf of Mexico. They argued that their lives were of value to their country, and that they had attained the object of their journey—namely, the discovery of the Mississippi, and the location of its mouth. Accordingly, they resolved to turn back, beginning the ascent of the river on the seventeenth of July, 1673, and believing themselves within a short distance of the Gulf, although in reality it was some seven hundred miles below.

Retracing their course up the Illinois, they encountered near its head the friendly Kaskaskias, who begged Marquette to return to them, and instruct them in the Faith This he promised to do, and, taking leave of them, he and his companions were escorted to Lake Michigan by a chief of the tribe, where they embarked for Green Bay. By September the mission of Saint Francis Xavier was reached, whence the expedition had started four months before.

Joliet now took leave of his fellow traveler, and, with the maps and papers relating to their recent explorations, started for Quebec. Down through the lakes he hurried to bear the tidings of the successful enterprise to Frontenac and to seek his deserved reward; but the good fortune which had smiled upon him thus far now seemed suddenly to desert him. Just above Montreal his boat was capsized, his papers lost, and all that remained to him was his life, which, he wrote, he ardently desired to employ in any service which his Excellency might please to direct; a loyal offer, and worthy a more generous acknowledgment than the Government deemed fit to give.

After carefully drawing up a report from memory, Joliet again presented himself to the authorities at Quebec, but the Mississippi was not then of so much importance as Canadian affairs, and its exploration was not met with the enthusiasm that it would have received later.

Upon failing to procure a grant from the King, of the countries which he had visited, Joliet next turned his attention to the Indian trade on Hudson Bay, and in this interest left Quebec in 1679. Here he found the English in undisturbed possession, and reported the case to the Canadian officials, which resulted in the establishment of competitive trading stations for the purpose of dispossessing the foreign rivals. This service was rewarded, and later Joliet received a grant of the Island of Anticosti, in consideration of his services on the Mississippi. Again in 1694, after exploring the coast of Labrabor, in the employ of a company interested in the whale and seal fisheries there, he was made royal pilot for the St. Lawrence and hydrographer at Quebec. Thus, rich in honors, the great explorer of the Mississippi passed his latter years, and was buried on one of his own Islands of Mignan, on the coast of Labrador, probably in 1700. His fellow traveler had, meanwhile, met his death in the lonely forests of Michigan, twelve hundred miles away. In fact, when the expedition to the Mississippi returned to Green Bay, Marquette was already suffering from the malady which ultimately killed him, and which he had contracted from the exposure and hardships of the journey.

During the autumn and winter he stayed at the mission to gain strength for his return to Kaskaskia, where he hoped to found the mission of the Immaculate Conception, and by October of the following year started out with a band of Illinois and Pottawattamies and two Frenchmen, Pierre Porteret and Jacques ——, to fulfill his promise to the Illinois.

The party paddled up the Bay to the northern end, and thence by portage gained Lake Michigan, which they reached in the stormy month of November. Cautiously skirting its western shore, they pushed their canoes into the Chicago River a month later, where Marquette again became prostrated, and was obliged to postpone his visit to Kaskaskia till the following spring. The Indians went on, but Pierre and Jacques built a small hut on the river bank, where game was abundant, and there they guarded their master till the snows were gone and the stream cleared of ice.

Through all the bitterness of this winter in the wilderness Marquette suffered patiently the ravages of disease, but at last, despairing of his life, and unwilling to abandon his darling wish, he begged his companions to perform with him a novina, or nine days' devotion to the Virgin. At the end of this time he believed their prayers were answered, and by the thirtieth of March again undertook to reach Kaskaskia. The route thither was familiar to Marquette and one of his men, who had passed over it on their return to Green Bay, and, excepting the inconvenience caused by the freshets and the priest's physical condition, the journey was comparatively easy.

When the party reached Kaskaskia the greatest joy

was manifested, and Marquette was urged to stay with the people and be their father; but he knew his days were numbered, and that what he had to do must be done quickly He passed from lodge to lodge explaining the mysteries of his religion, and persuading his hearers by his own magnetic earnestness, and then, that he might more deeply influence their impressionable natures, called them to a great council in the open fields, where he made a final exhortation. Some four thousand souls listened to this appeal and received the first instruction in the Faith, which was kept alive there by Marquette's successors in the mission field of his founding.

Now, satisfied that he had accomplished his purpose, and anxious to reach again the station of Michilimackinac, Marquette bade farewell to his Illinois children and started for Lake Michigan. On its waters the canoe was once more launched, in the presence of a faithful band which had followed him thither.

Along the eastern border of the lake the solitary boat sped, urged on by the steady paddle strokes of Pierre and Jacques, who, seeing the emaciated form and failing strength of their dying master, attempted to reach Saint Ignace before it was too late.

Their exertions were in vain. On the nineteenth of May, when they were yet many days' journey from their destination, Marquette, feeling his time was come, asked to be taken ashore. His companions, grief-stricken and disappointed, begged permission to hurry on to Michilimackinac; but Marquette could not mistake the approach of death, and with gentle firmness insisted that they stop at a place which he had pointed out, that he might be buried there. It was on the sloping bank of a small stream which poured its waters into the great lake from the east.

Here the two men built a rude shelter of bark and laid the dying priest, receiving at his hands the sacrament of penitence and making their last confession. Marquette in turn asked their forgiveness for the trouble he had caused them, and told them how grateful he was to be permitted to die as he had always wished, alone in the wilderness after the manner of Saint Francis Xavier Then seeing that his friends were weary, he persuaded them to rest, telling them he would call when he needed them. Shortly after, they heard a feeble voice, and, overwhelmed with sadness, answered its summons. He asked that the crucifix which he had worn be held over him, and, placing his eyes on the sacred emblem, expired

The next year, 1676, a hunting party of Kiskakon Ottawas, whom the priest had once instructed, on passing his grave, reverently opened it, and, caring for the remains after their custom, bore them to Saint Esprit with all the ceremony observed at the funerals of their great chiefs; and so, honored by those for whom he had given his best energies, the priest-explorer found his final resting place.

What Marquette accomplished as a missionary will be variously estimated, but what he and his fellow voyager Joliet accomplished in the field of early exploration can never be overestimated. They hold a place unchallenged in the history of the Mississippi, and honored by those who appreciate the heralds of civilization.

CHAPTER VI.

ROBERT CAVELIER DE LA SALLE.

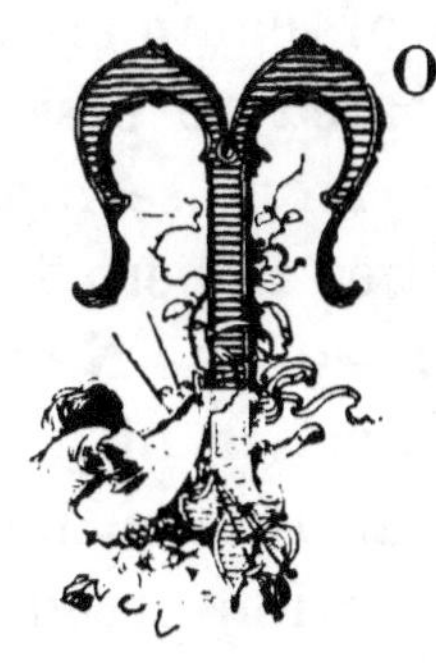

O one whose splendid ambition and unfailing patriotism won for him in his day only disappointment and the death-blow of the assassin, impartial Time has meted out his sure reward; and the La Salle of two centuries ago, now stands a giant among the great explorers. He was one of those countless heralds who proclaimed the wonders of a New World; but pre-eminently alone in the brilliant planning which sought to make the "New France" an added kingdom to the Old. Because then, he was not only the explorer but the man of thought, he has gained a loftier place among his fellows, and a truer claim to renown.

As a school-boy of Rouen, where he was born in 1643, the unusual traits of the later man began to attract the attention of his family, and he was given an education in accordance with the liberality of the Caveliers and his own capabilities; but the Order of the Jesuits, which had earlier appealed to him, became, as he reached manhood, an unbearable restraint; and throwing off the irksome bonds—together with his inheritance, which, according to a law of the Order, must be forfeited—the free-spirited La Salle obeyed his mastering impulse and sailed in 1666 for Canada.

During the quiet years in France, when all his natural love of action was confined within the chambers of his fertile brain, La Salle acquired his aptitude for great schemes; but conceiving them without the power of putting them into effect gave him also that fatal lack of attention to detail which resulted in many an ultimate defeat. His broad mind could take in with quick perception vast enterprises of commerce and colonization in America, but repeated reverses and an untimely death prevented him from seeing their successful issue. With such abilities Robert de La Salle entered the attractive boundaries of the New World. His elder brother, Abbé Jean Cavelier, of the Seminary of Saint Sulpice, belonged to an influential corporation which owned Montreal and a widespreading tract along the Saint Lawrence, and it was perhaps due to his influence that La Salle was offered gratuitously, soon after his arrival, a large property about nine miles above the city for a settlement. The object of the priests in thus dealing out their lands was to establish a line of outposts along the river in front of their island, as a defense against Iroquois incursions.

For its new proprietor the exposed position of this property had no terrors. He immediately began the building of his embryo village, hurrying up the palisades in anticipation of a surprise from the Indians, and marking out the twenty-acre farms beyond the defenses, which were offered on easy terms to those who would join his enterprise; while with the care of his new seigniory he threw himself into the study of Indian languages with a zeal which betokened design.

From time to time straggling red men were admitted within the palisade to dispose of furs or to talk with the white chief; and as La Salle had a great influence over them, he heard many a story of the unknown lands to the west, and of the river that reached to the sea. The old idea of a route to China and Japan suggested itself to him and aroused his ambition. With characteristic dispatch, he went to Quebec to confer with the Governor, obtaining authority to carry on an expedition to the Great River, but no money to aid the enterprise. This lack of co-operation in funds did not deter the young explorer, however. He soon persuaded Queylus, the Superior of Saint Sulpice, to buy back part of his lands beyond Montreal, and the rest he was able to sell to a certain Jean Milot. With this he bought the necessary equipments and secured his men.

Some time before this the Seminary had decided to send missionaries to the more western tribes, that the Jesuits might not overreach them in christianizing the heathen nations of the New World. Nor was this all. They saw that the rival Order, in penetrating the remote regions of the Northwest, would gain a foothold there which it would be difficult to supplant. For these reasons an expedition had been planned by them, and the leadership given to Dollier de Casson, a priest of Saint Sulpice.

Greatly to La Salle's annoyance, the Governor urged that Dollier join him in the exploration of the Mississippi, and as the young man was somewhat indebted to the Seminary and to Courcelles, he could offer no protest. Consequently, on the sixth of July, 1669, the two parties left the little settlement beyond Montreal, to begin the difficult ascent of the Upper Saint Lawrence. A party of Seneca Iroquois took the lead, and were to guide the expedition to the Ohio, which they had told La Salle reached to the sea; but instead of going directly to the river according to agreement, the dissimulating Indians went to their own village near the Genesee; telling the white men they would find other guides there. La Salle was not sufficiently familiar with the Iroquois language to make a personal appeal, and the expedition was delayed; but there happened to be an Indian from a neighboring tribe present at the time, who offered to take the party to his own village, promising to find some one there to act as guide. This offer was accepted, and again the march was resumed. A Shawnee prisoner was at last secured, who said he could reach the Ohio in six weeks; but just as preparations were being made to start out, news came that two Frenchmen had arrived at the next village. They proved to be Joliet and Péré, recently sent by Talon to look for the copper mines of Lake Superior.

Joliet had mapped out the route he had taken, and, giving Dollier a duplicate of this, told him of the tribes about the upper lakes who were sadly in need of spiritual guidance. The priest immediately resolved to follow these suggestions, although La Salle reminded him that the Jesuits were already in the field, but Dollier was not to be dissuaded, and he believed, moreover, that this change of plan would not interfere with the intended exploration of the Mississippi. La Salle, unwilling to follow this lead, and determined to carry out his own plans, in his own way, no doubt urged his weak physical condition as a pretext for separating from the Sulpitians. At any rate, Dollier soon started on his fruitless mission northward, while La Salle remained behind in the Indian village.

From all that has been found relating to the next two years, it is evident that La Salle was unable to reach the Mississippi; but during that time he undoubtedly made the discovery of the Ohio, and carried on extensive explorations in other quarters. Unfortunately, the only record that remains of this part of his career is an anonymous manuscript of somewhat doubtful accuracy, supposed to have been written from conversations with La Salle himself, and from which Francis Parkman, with careful explanations, has made a few extracts in his "Discovery of the Great West." These relate simply to his explorations on the Ohio and Illinois rivers, and to his voyage through the lakes. Reference is also made to the statement that La Salle, in descending the Illinois, reached a river corresponding in description to the Mississippi, which he is said to have followed as far as the thirty-sixth degree of latitude, becoming convinced that it emptied into the Gulf of Mexico; and which, the anonymous writer continues, he intended to further explore when equipped in such a way as to make it practicable. This seems to admit of question. If La Salle had made such a discovery, it is not likely that he would have remained silent in regard to it when Frontenac appointed Joliet for that service; nor that, being on the most friendly terms with the Governor, he should have made no immediate mention of it.

This doubtful period over, La Salle again emerges into the full light of authentic history, and we find him at Quebec discussing his plans with Frontenac. These plans were concerning the settlement of the Great West, and the development of commerce along the Mississippi. He saw that delay would be fatal to the interests of France, and he therefore made arrangements to confer with the King that he might obtain his approval and aid. Frontenac, fully in sympathy with his projects, was unable to give more than his hearty recommendation; but this had its value, and La Salle started for France bearing the most flattering letters from him.

Once at court, there was no difficulty in gaining attention, and Louis, recognizing the ability and zeal of his young petitioner, soon became interested in his schemes. La Salle returned to Canada with a patent of nobility in consideration of recent explorations, and with a grant of a fort at the head of Lake Ontario which he afterward named for Frontenac, and which, by its favorable position for the fur trade, would aid him in many an enterprise.

Carefully guarding every interest, La Salle now began to make improvements upon the fort, replacing Frontenac's hurriedly constructed buildings and palisades with stone, and having a few heavy boats built; for where the light Indian canoe had formerly been a convenience in making the frequent journeys up and down the river and through the lakes, when very little freight was carried, larger craft would now be indispensable. This done, La Salle again went to France to report to the minister and to receive a further sanction to his explorations. These he intended to prosecute on the Mississippi with a view to opening a direct route to France; thus to throw into her ports the monopoly of furs furnished by the great western hunting grounds of America, and to found a chain of commercial villages along its banks. He asked, besides, the privilege of holding exclusive right to the trade in buffalo skins. These petitions were favoraoly received by Colbert, and in addition large sums of money were advanced by his relatives. Men were engaged and the necessary supplies procured, and with these, La Salle again returned to Canada. On the way over he became acquainted with his new lieutenant, Henri de Tonty, who had been recommended to him during his brief stay in France, by the Prince de Conti, as a man in every respect worthy of confidence. La Salle, with keen discrimination, soon recognized this, and, himself possessed of rare personal qualities, easily made him his friend. He wrote back to the Prince extolling Tonty's "honorable character and amiable disposition," and referred to his hardihood in starting out to begin a fort at Niagara at a season when any but him would häve hesitated.

The building of this fort was a triumph for La Salle, and he had made no small effort toward its accomplishment. To this end he had encouraged La Motte to negotiate with the chief of the Senecas.

His lieutenant was, in a measure, successful; but La Salle, understanding the value of the full and friendly approval of the Iroquois, and confident of securing a personal favor, had stopped on his way up from Fort Frontenac to ratify La Motte's transactions, and had gained permission from the reluctant Indians to build a vessel above the falls for navigation on the upper lakes. An unimpeded way to success was now opened, and La Salle hastened to formulate his plans. Misfortune, however, met him at the very start. When he and Tonty reached the garrison at Niagara, they found that the boat bringing supplies, on which they had come part of the way, had been wrecked within nine or ten leagues of its destination and all the provisions lost, the crew being able to save only the anchor and cables for the new vessel.

This loss placed La Salle in an unpleasant predicament. His men, but half-hearted in their devotion to his interest, and disaffected by his enemies, were ready to desert upon the slightest provocation. At this crisis he immediately prepared to return to Fort Frontenac for provisions, leaving Tonty in command, and relying upon his Mohican hunter to supply the men with game during his absence. Nothing daunted, he began the two hundred and fifty mile journey over the midwinter snows on foot, only to find, upon reaching the fort, that the greater share of his property had been seized by over-anxious creditors, and his reputation injured by jealous enemies, but he still had friends, and these again came to his assistance. When at last he reached Niagara, after an absence of nearly six months, he found his new boat, the "Griffin," finished, and his men, under Tonty's guardianship, still committed to his service. The commander returned, affairs were quickly arranged at the fort, the "Griffin" was towed up stream, and the entire company boarded her on the seventh of August, 1679; sang the *Te Deum,* fired a salute, and set the sails for the eventful voyage across Lake Erie, whose waters had never before borne more than the fairy weight of an Indian canoe. Reaching the strait of Detroit, they passed between the forest-fringed banks and then out into the sparkling lake, which, in crossing, they called Sainte Claire; moving again through the narrowed outlet until it brought them upon the broad expanse of Lake Huron.

When the boat was well under way, promising a

speedy journey to Michilimackinac, a furious gale overtook her, and for a time caused the greatest excitement among her passengers. La Salle encouraged the men to ask the aid of Heaven, and "all fell to their prayers, but the godless pilot, who was loud in complaint against his commander for having brought him, after the honor he had won on the ocean, to drown at last ignominiously in fresh water."

With the abating of the tempest the clamor ceased, and the "Griffin" again moved forward over the becalmed lake.

Fresh trouble awaited La Salle at Saint Ignace. He found that the advance party which he had sent on to trade for him had deserted, and that the aid which he had expected from this quarter was not to be realized. He was able to secure a small cargo of furs, and this he sent back to satisfy his creditors in Canada, charging the pilot to return as soon as he had fulfilled the commission, and meet him at the mouth of the Saint Joseph. Meanwhile, La Salle, with fourteen men and four canoes, heavily laden, started down Lake Michigan toward the rendezvous, every mile of the way being contested by the stormy elements. When at last they reached the River Saint Joseph, the men, half-starved and weary, urged that the expedition move on to the village of the Illinois, where they would find shelter and provisions, but La Salle had told Tonty to meet him at this place after his journey to Saint Mary's, and therefore he would not leave. Instead, he put the men to work on a fort to divert their minds, and stolidly waited. At the end of three weeks Tonty came, bringing only half his men, the others having stopped by the way for food and rest. Soon afterward they came up with the party, and on

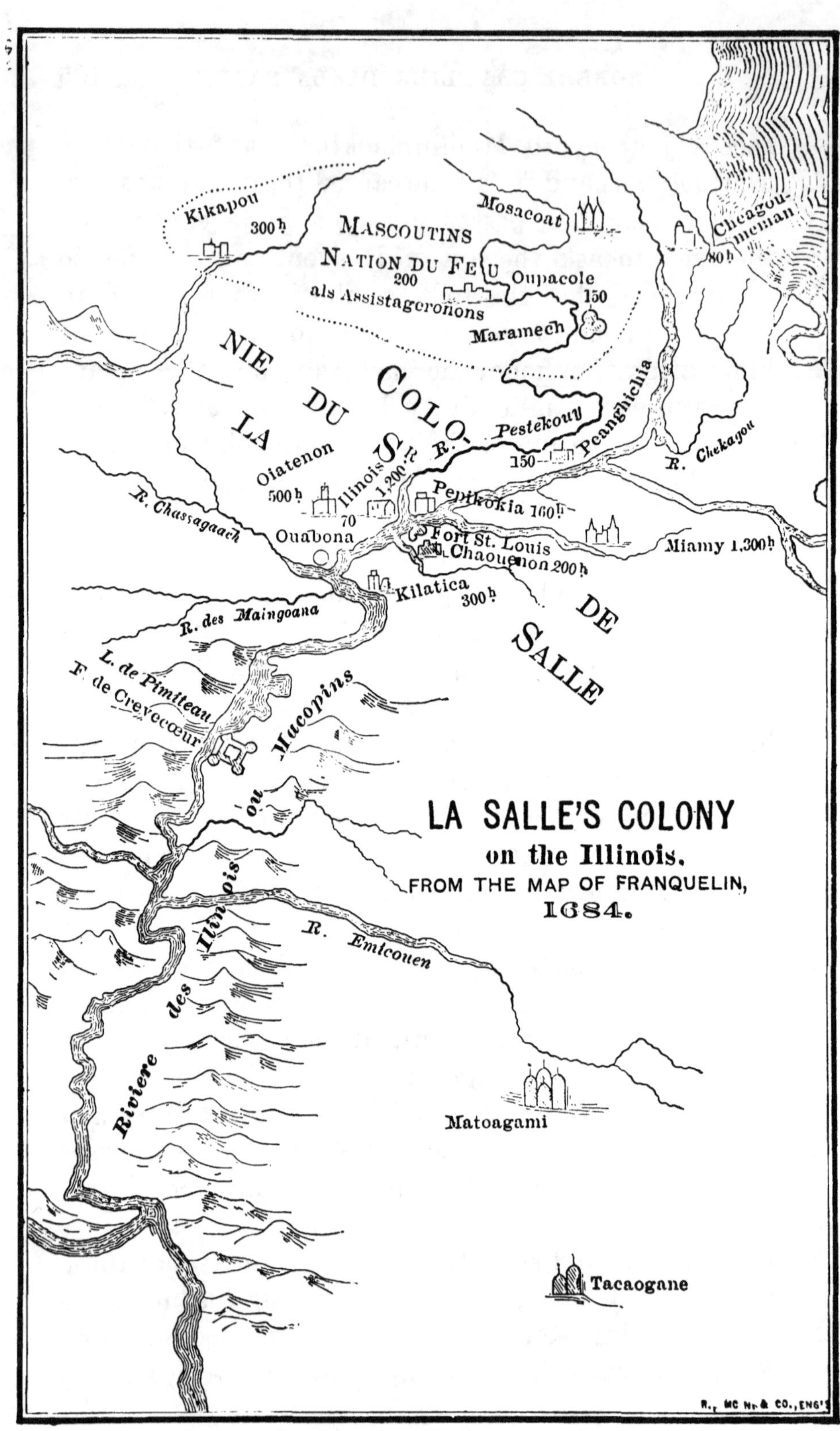

EARLY MAP OF THE ILLINOIS.

the third of December all started up the Saint Joseph.

La Salle's Mohican had remained a little behind the others, and when the expedition had reached the point where the portage was supposed to be, they were unable to discover it. La Salle went ashore to search for it, and while wandering through the forest lost his way. Night came and with it a light snow. Hurrying forward, with the hope of coming upon his party, he reached the river and fired his gun as a signal. Receiving no answer, he continued along the shore, where he saw a short distance beyond a fire in the brush. Supposing this to be the bivouac of his men he hastened toward it, but found to his surprise that the spot was deserted. Near the fire was a couch of dry grass, still warm, and bearing the impress of a recent occupant, but no answer came to his call although he used all of the Indian languages at his command. To follow Parkman's description, "La Salle then, with admirable coolness, took possession of the quarters he had found, shouting to their invisible proprietor that he was about to sleep in his bed, piled a barricade of bushes around the spot, rekindled the dying fire, warmed his benumbed hands, stretched himself on the dry grass, and slept undisturbed till morning." When he reached his party the Mohican had already found the portage, and preparations were immediately begun to transport the baggage to the Kankakee. On this stream they began the journey down to the Illinois, reaching at last the long-wished-for lodges where they were to find food and shelter.

The Indians had not yet returned from the winter's hunt, and the encampment was deserted, but La

Salle's men found the pits in which the provisions were stored, and from these a quantity of corn was taken, the intention being to meet the Indians on their return and recompense them for their intrusion. Having thus satisfied their hunger, the party pushed forward, reaching Peoria Lake on the third of January, 1680. Just below here they came in sight of the Illinois camp. La Salle had been warned by the Outagamies whom he met on Lake Michigan to beware of these, as they were angered with the French, believing they had incited the Iroquois against them. He had also to appease them for the raid upon their corn-pits. It was therefore necessary to use the utmost caution in approaching them. The canoes were put in line, the men were told to drop the oars and take up their weapons, and thus formidably the little flotilla swept down to meet friend or foe. La Salle, closely followed by his men, leaped from his boat into the midst of the astonished Indians, who, convinced of his friendliness, soon laid aside their weapons. With his usual fearlessness he then harangued them, telling them if they would permit him to build a fort in their country as a defense against the Iroquois, that he would join them in resisting those enemies in case of attack. Explanations were made and payment offered for the corn, and, while asking favors, the intrepid La Salle appeared to be conferring benefits. The Illinois received his blandishments and threats as he intended they should, and the conference ended favorably for the Frenchmen.

That same night, however, a Mascoutin chief, instigated by La Salle's enemies, came to the camp to tell the Indians in solemn council that their visitors were friends of the Iroquois, now on their way to the tribes beyond the Mississippi, whom they intended to stir up against the Illinois; and that if the Illinois wished to protect themselves they would soon be rid of them. La Salle was informed of the proceedings by a chief whose friendship he had won by generous gifts, and was thus enabled to meet the excuses which the Indians offered on the following afternoon. The chiefs resorted to a very cunning method, as they thought, to dissuade the Frenchmen from going to the Great River, telling them of terrible monsters, whirlpools, and rapids, in their way, but La Salle paid no heed to these fabrications, soon convincing the Indians of the friendliness of his visit. Some of his men fell into the snare laid for them, and, terrified by the lies invented to deceive them, deserted during the night, rather than risk the fancied dangers.

La Salle now decided to pass the remainder of the winter in the Illinois country, that he might build a fort there, and be prepared for exploration on the Mississippi in the spring. He selected a place of considerable strength, on a hill a short distance back from the river, and here palisades were thrown up and winter quarters provided. La Salle and Tonty occupied a plank cabin in the center of the inclosure, the priests were in another, and the men had their huts at the four angles. Thus sheltered from the cold, and protected from any sudden outbreak of the Indians, the isolated party waited for the snows to disappear

As an expression of his sorrow at the continued round of disappointments which had followed him, La Salle gave this fort the name of Crève-cœur Here circumstances again obliged him to undertake a journey to

Fort Frontenac, for nothing had been heard from the "Griffin" since she had left Michilimackinac, and it was now impossible to hope for her return. In her loss, the explorer once more saw his plans defeated, for she was to have brought the chains and anchor for the new vessel in which he intended to make his journey down the Mississippi, and the provisions necessary to assure the services of his men. There was no alternative, La Salle must either return to Fort Frontenac or risk the failure of his enterprise. To him the latter course was impossible, and he quickly prepared for the perilous journey, seeing half the work done on the vessel before starting, lest the men should attempt to desert during his absence or refuse to undertake its building. He also commissioned Hennepin, much against the wishes of the priest, to take two men and explore the Illinois to its mouth, and thence to the headwaters of the Mississippi—a circumstance which has a significance; for, if La Salle was not aware of the previous expedition of Marquette and Joliet, as some writers affirm, it is not probable that he would have authorized Hennepin to make this journey; for, in that case, the honor of the discovery would be lost to him. Nor is it probable that, being, as he knew, within easy distance of the Great River, he should have betrayed so little eagerness to reach it. In fact, corroborative evidence seems to show, without a doubt, that La Salle was perfectly familiar with the explorations of his predecessors, and that his aim was not to search out an unknown river, but to complete the work begun in 1673.

CHAPTER VII.

LA SALLE EXPLORES THE LOWER MISSISSIPPI.

IT was just on the verge of spring, 1681, when the streams were too full of ice to allow the passage of a canoe, and the ground too unstable for snow-shoes, that La Salle, with his Mohican and four others, began the trying journey from Fort Crève-cœur, on the Illinois, to Canada—the most arduous ever made by Frenchmen in America.

Through the dismal forests and over treacherous swamps the men made their way, braving the dangers of the wilderness and sturdily enduring the ills which exposure and hardship brought upon them. On Easter Monday they reached the Falls of Niagara, where La Salle learned that the "Griffin" was indeed lost, that a ship laden with valuable supplies coming to him from France had foundered at the mouth of the Saint Lawrence, and that twenty men sent to his assistance from Europe had in one way or another become dispersed through the machinations of his enemies. At Fort Frontenac he found only stronger evidence of disaster; but pressing on to Montreal he succeeded in making good his losses and in convincing those who attempted to thwart him that he was superior to their efforts.

In starting out with his fresh supplies for the Illinois country, the customary halt was made at the fort, and here the unhappy news from Tonty awaited him. His men, taking advantage of the temporary absence of his lieutenant, had mutinied, destroyed Fort Crève-cœur, and taking everything that was available had gone on to Fort Miami on the Saint Joseph to wage a similar destruction. At Michilimackinac they had seized a quantity of furs belonging to La Salle, and again at Niagara had continued their robberies. Word was brought that they even intended to kill their late leader, and were on their way to carry out their sinister purpose; but such reverses only tended to strengthen La Salle's determination and powers of endurance. He quickly and effectually dealt with the deserters, putting them into custody where they were to await the arrival of Frontenac, while he prepared to return to the Illinois country for the relief of Tonty and those who had remained with him. This time he took a new route, by way of the Humber, Lake Simcoe, the Severn and Georgian Bay, and thence to Michilimackinac; leaving his lieutenant La Forest at the latter place with half the men to attend to his business affairs, while he hurried southward. By chance Tonty and Father Membré were at the same time retreating from the dangerous battle-ground of the Iroquois and Illinois, and making their way to the mission at Green Bay.

Having left a small detachment on the Saint Joseph to wait for La Forest, La Salle anxiously pressed on to the Illinois, there to find the ghastly relics of war; and instead of the flourishing village which he had passed in the spring, desolated lodges and the horrid evidences of Indian vengeance. The thought of what might have befallen his friend gave him no rest, and with gloomy forebodings he continued his way down to the mouth of the river, finding all along the abandoned camp-fires of the Illinois in retreat, with those of their pursuers on the opposite bank, but no traces of those he sought. It was at this unfortunate moment that La Salle saw for the first time the Great River toward which his mind's eye had so often turned, and with whose future his thoughts had long been occupied. Even then he might have followed it to the sea, putting aside the search for his friends, and relying upon the support of the few men who had accompanied him to its shores, and who offered to make the journey with him, but he was too deeply concerned about Tonty, and too well satisfied with certain other plans to obey the temporary impulse, and therefore determined to wait. On the return to the Saint Joseph some traces were found of the recent passage of white men, which assured La Salle that Tonty had escaped the Iroquois massacre, and he was further gratified to find that during his absence the men at Fort Miami had repaired the injuries done by the deserters and had cleared a large tract of land for cultivation. Thus favored, he prepared to remain at the fort for the winter, in order to carry out his great scheme of alliance among the western tribes which the recent Iroquois invasion had made possible. It was his idea to conciliate the small tribes who had separated on account of slight grievances, and ally them, with the Illinois, to the French; nominally to resist their common enemy the Iroquois, but really to establish French interests and secure the western trade in furs. Having heard in the course of his travels of the safety of Tonty, La Salle sent La Forest on to Michilimackinac to meet him and to await his own arrival there; while he, in the meantime, continued his diplomatic mission among the red men. In these negotiations his remarkable influence with the Indians gave him the advantage, and while he intimidated, persuaded and flattered, they regarded him with mingled admiration and fear. He accomplished all that he had desired, and then hastened to Michilimackinac, where in the joy of meeting Tonty the habitual reserve of his calm nature for once broke its bonds.

Tonty, and Father Membré who had been with him, had had a very trying and dangerous experience after leaving Fort Crève-cœur. They had gone up the Illinois together to examine a hill which La Salle had suggested as a strong place in case of necessity, and during their absence the men at the fort deserted and the Iroquois war-party approached almost simultaneously The fancied presence of Frenchmen among the latter, due to the caprice of two Iroquois chiefs who had arrayed themselves in a few articles of European dress, placed Tonty and his companions in a delicate position with the Illinois, who suspected that they were being betrayed. The situation required the utmost caution. Tonty stoutly denied the charge made against his countrymen, and to prove his honesty of design, offered to negotiate with the enemy. This offer was accepted with some suspicion, but the volunteer was given a belt of wampum as a truce, and accompanied by Boisrondet and two others, started toward the band of already frenzied savages. As he came within dangerous range of their arrows and saw that hostilities were not suspended, he sent his companions back, and holding up the pacific symbol advanced alone.

Once in their midst a curious crowd of half-maddened Iroquois pressed about the mediator, and a young warrior among them, believing him to be an Illinois, thrust a knife deep into his side; but one of the chiefs, calling attention to Tonty's unpierced ears, saved him from further molestation, and wrapped a wampum belt over the wound to stop the flow of blood.

Having done all he could to awe the invaders and secure an advantage for the Illinois, Tonty returned half-fainting, with his peaceful messages; but the wary Iroquois were not thus easily to be disposed of. Under the guise of friendship they approached the Illinois village, taking in with quick comprehension the real force of their adversaries, and contemptuously provoking a quarrel.

The position of the Frenchmen soon became dangerous.

Tonty saw that the Illinois could not resist their enemies, and had done all he could to aid them; while they too began to realize the situation and were leaving the field. At this point he and his companions prudently decided to retire; and finding an old canoe, the little party embarked in it and quietly ascended the river. On the way the boat was upset, and while a halt was made to repair it Father Ribourde, who was one of the number, wandered away and was never again seen. Boisrondet also became lost in the forest, but escaped the lurking redskins and was able to find his way back. At the head of the Illinois the canoe entirely gave out, and from there on to Green Bay the three refugees were obliged to make their way on foot, finding sustenance in herbs and roots which they dug up as they went along. By the latter part of November they reached the town of a friendly Pottawattamie chief who had in several instances shown himself favorable to the French, and whose assertion that he knew but three great captains in the world, Frontenac, La Salle and himself, went far to prove his good-will.

Early the following spring they started for Michilimackinac, and there waited for La Salle.

That indefatigable traveler was now preparing to return a third time to Fort Frontenac to straighten the tangled thread of his affairs, to quiet his creditors, and to test again the unfailing friendship of Frontenac.

This time, instead of choosing a party entirely of white men, whose good faith he had found wanting in many a bitter experience, he secured eighteen Indians from the Abenaki and Mohican tribes, with the extra encumbrance of ten squaws whom the Indians insisted upon taking along to do camp work. Besides these there were twenty-three Frenchmen and three papooses, and with this strange following La Salle again undertook the exploration of the Mississippi. On the fourth of January, 1682, he reached the Chicago River, where he found Tonty, Father Membré and a small party waiting with sledges. Three weeks later they made the portage to the Illinois, passed down the river on the ice, and found the familiar village, which had been re-inhabited since the late invasion, entirely deserted, the Indians having gone down to the old site of Fort Crève-cœur on Peoria Lake for the winter. At this point the river was, as usual, open, and the canoes were put into the water, which quickly carried them down to the Mississippi. There they were delayed a week by floating ice; but at last on the thirteenth of February were able to begin the descent of the river, not as La Salle had once hoped, with spread sail and imposing ceremony, but with a modest flotilla of Indian canoes. Upon passing the Missouri Father Membré wrote that the water was "hardly drinkable," an expression which might amuse those familiar with the muddy torrent, and who know the condition of the main stream even before it is adulterated by its boisterous tributary Beyond this, on the last bank, they came upon the village of the Tamaroas, where they landed and left indications of their presence for the absent hunters; being careful to express the peaceful intent of their journey, and thus secure a friendly reception when they should return.

Notwithstanding La Salle's eagerness to push forward, the expedition was repeatedly delayed that the men might hunt and fish, for having come unencumbered with provisions excepting a quantity of Indian corn, the party relied completely upon game and an occasional donation from the Indians. During one of these halts for food near the Third Chickasaw Bluffs, one of the men, Peter Prudhomme, became separated from his companions and was not found for nine days. In the course of the search for him a report was brought to La Salle that a fresh Indian trail had been discovered. The missing man was immediately supposed to have fallen into the hands of the unknown savages; and fearing treachery to the entire party, La Salle set the men to building a fort. Prudhomme was found a few days later in an exhausted condition but unharmed, and La Salle left him with two or three others in charge of the fort which he had named in his honor, while the main party resumed the journey.

Gradually the influence of winter had passed away as the canoes sped toward the Gulf; and to La Salle who had so often felt the bitterness of the cold seasons in the northern wilderness, the gracious warmth of the South must have had its charm.

Below fort Prudhomme the voyagers were overtaken by a dense fog in which they were obliged to make their way for forty leagues, and on the third of March, while still impeded by it, they were startled by war-cries and the sound of the tocsins on the west bank. Immediately they were on the *qui vive*, while La Salle with his usual caution moved to the side of the river opposite that from which the sounds were heard, had palisades thrown up, and within an hour was ready to meet the Indians.

After an exchange of friendly signs the entire party crossed the river and entered the Indian camp, where for several days they were feasted and treated with the utmost generosity, and on the fourteenth of March they raised a cross in the village bearing the arms of France, and took possession of the country with solemn ceremony. These proceedings, while wholly incomprehensible to the Indians, were witnessed by them with apparent pleasure, and Membré had so far succeeded in explaining the sacred meaning of the cross that upon the return of the expedition it was found to be surrounded by a palisade.

This tribe, perhaps the same Akamseas which Marquette and Joliet encountered, further showed their good-will by supplying the party with provisions and giving them guides to conduct them to the villages below. The expedition embarked from here on the seventeenth of March, encountering on the downward journey several friendly tribes, and at last stopping near the village of the Taensas, which lay inland on a bayou formed by a change in the course of the river. La Salle was himself too fatigued to go to the village, but he sent Tonty and Father Membré with presents to the chief, being unwilling to miss any opportunity to gain the favor of the red men along his route.

Coming within sight of the Taensas village, Tonty and his companion were not a little surprised to find instead of the ordinary Indian lodges houses made of mud and straw, and other evidences of an approach to civilization. The people of this tribe wore garments of white cloth ingeniously woven from the bark of trees, had some furniture in their dwellings, and like the Indians whom De Soto encountered, understood the use of metals; but while the Spanish adventurer had been deceived in regard to the mines, they were now discovered to the later Frenchman, whose ambition, however, reached so far beyond the accumulation of personal wealth that he gave them hardly a passing thought.

The chief of this village paid La Salle the honor of a visit, coming to him with all the ceremony of a more civilized potentate, and returning with the pleased satisfaction of a child over the gifts which his white brother had lavishly but prudently bestowed.

From here La Salle again ordered the advance, and the expedition moved forward without encountering any Indians until the twenty-sixth of March, when a canoe was seen on the river twelve miles below. The impetuous Tonty immediately gave chase, but was ordered to return by La Salle, who saw that a band of warriors had assembled on the shore ready to greet the strange intruder with a shower of arrows. He was soon sent back with the calumet and was kindly received, learning that the Indians belonged to the Natchez tribe, and that they desired the white men to visit them at their village. It lay three leagues inland, but, says Membré, "the Sieur de La Salle did not hesitate to go there." He raised a large cross bearing the arms of France in the midst of the lodges, taking possession of the country in the name of the French King, much to the amusement of his unsuspecting entertainers.

At the village of the Koroa, who were allies of the Natchez, lying ten leagues below, the Frenchmen were again generously received, and La Salle was presented with a peace-pipe from the chief, but further down they met with a different reception, for, coming unexpectedly upon a party of Quinipissa fishermen, the frightened Indians fled, while their friends from the shore covered their retreat with drawn bows. Seeing that to further follow them was useless, the voyagers kept their way, soon reaching the last and most peaceful village on their route. Here they disembarked and advanced toward the lodges, but no one appeared to resent their intrusion, and gaining confidence as they neared the silent habitations, they cautiously peered within their gloomy recesses. There they found a sickening sight, for less friendly visitors had preceded them, and with fearful vengeance had sent their unsuspicious victims with scalping-knife and tomahawk to the "happy hunting grounds."

"At last," says Father Membré, "after a navigation of about forty leagues, we arrived on the sixth of April at a point where the river divides into three channels. The Sieur de La Salle divided his party the

LA SALLE TAKING POSSESSION OF THE VALLEY OF THE MISSISSIPPI.

next day into three bands, to go and explore them. He took the western, the Sieur Dautray the southern, the Sieur de Tonty, whom I accompanied, the middle one. These three channels are beautiful and deep. The water is brackish; after advancing two leagues it became perfectly salt, and advancing on we discovered the open sea, so that on the ninth of April, with all possible solemnity, we performed the ceremony of planting the cross and raising the arms of France." The priests then chanted the "Vexilla Regis" and the "Te Deum," the men shouted "*Vive le Roi*," and La Salle, after taking formal possession of the Great River, "of all rivers that enter into it, and of all the country watered by them," read a document certifying the fact and amply proving the credit due him. This he asked those who were with him to sign, taking in the meanwhile a careful estimate of the latitude of the mouth. By this act all of the country "from the Alleghenies to the Rocky Mountains, from the Rio Grande and the Gulf to the farthest springs of the Missouri," was appropriated by this zealous subject of the Grand Monarch, and named in his honor Louisiana.

The supply of provisions was now entirely exhausted, but when the descent of the river was commenced there were opportunities to obtain food from the Indians or by the hunt.

On the thirteenth of April the smoke of the Quinipissa village was seen, and a party was sent out to reconnoitre. Four squaws were taken, and by keeping three of them as hostages while the fourth was sent back with presents, a small quantity of corn was obtained. The gift was grudgingly given, however, and La Salle's men were obliged to act with the utmost caution in order to avoid treachery. Being invited to a feast at the village, they soon discovered that the pretended hospitality was only a ruse intended to ensnare them; for stray Indians were seen approaching, armed and evidently ready to give the white men a surprise. La Salle and his followers kept their weapons well in sight and no assault was then attempted, but the following morning before dawn the sentinel heard a rustling in the canebrakes near the camp, and giving the alarm, a band of prowling red-skins was discovered. Showers of arrows responded to the guns of the white men, and although it rained, a spirited fight ensued, but the Indians losing heavily without being able to injure their antagonists, soon fled. Thoroughly exasperated, La Salle's men were on the point of burning the village of their would-be murderers, but their leader restrained them, foreseeing a future need of their good-will. When the party reached the villages farther up the river they found that their late enemies had stirred up a feeling of distrust against them, but La Salle skillfully regained the confidence of the disaffected chiefs and was allowed to continue unmolested. He was soon delayed by something more serious than savage opposition, however, for near Fort Prudhomme he fell ill and was obliged to remain there several weeks, while Tonty in the meanwhile went on to Michilimackinac, from whence he sent a report of the recent expedition to the Governor Frontenac no longer held that office, having been replaced by La Barré, a man of altogether different character and strongly prejudiced against La Salle.

The latter, having recovered, hastened to meet Tonty and leave instructions with him regarding the fort which he intended to build on the Illinois, while he prepared to go to Quebec. His affairs were now in a lamentable condition, and it was necessary to take active steps to right them. Scores of creditors in Canada were waiting for the explorer's great schemes to materialize, while he, thoroughly confident of success, was yet able to reassure them. As before suggested, his intention was to make the new fort a large trading post and the center of a prosperous colony, while by virtue of its position it would be a stronghold against the Iroquois. Around it would gather the numerous tribes of the West seeking protection, who would pour into its storehouses the wealth of unlimited hunting grounds. It was to be the first in a chain of similar colonies which he intended to establish along the entire length of the Great River, to which the projected post at the Gulf was to be the key In this the ambitious La Salle could see the prosperous accomplishment of all his plans. France benefited, the New World committed to her interests, creditors appeased, and his own unceasing efforts crowned. But he was doomed to disappointment. Reports were brought of an impending Iroquois invasion, and instead of hastening to France as he had intended, he was obliged to remain at the new fort—Saint Louis—to prepare for attack. From here he sent men to Quebec to obtain supplies, in anticipation of a siege, but so great was La Barré's jealousy of La Salle that he detained them. It is even said that he encouraged the Iroquois in making their raid upon the western tribes, that La Salle might be involved in the general ruin, thus sacrificing his country's interests to his personal ambition; but whether or not this has any foundation, it is evident that he took extreme measures to thwart the explorer, attempting even to prejudice the King, and so far succeeding that Louis, in a letter to the Governor, expressed his belief in the uselessness of La Salle's discoveries. He then assumed the responsibility of seizing Fort Frontenac under some slight pretext, following up this piracy by sending an officer to take possession of Fort Saint Louis, with orders to La Salle to report at Quebec.

As the Iroquois had not made the expected raid, La Salle was at the time going to Canada, *en route* for France. He therefore met the Governor's emissary on the way, but maintaining his usual composure sent back word to Tonty to receive the Chevalier de Baugis well, while he, still undaunted, sought to redress his wrongs and claim an unprejudiced hearing at the Court of Versailles.

ERECTING CROSS AT AN INDIAN VILLAGE.

CHAPTER VIII.

LAST VOYAGE AND DEATH OF LA SALLE.

LOUIS, partially influenced by the opinions of his late minister, and no doubt stirred by the earnestness of the explorer himself—who, still inspired by the vast possibilities of the New World, was anxious that France should realize and profit by them—had listened favorably to La Salle's proposals, and had confirmed his approval by letters patent bearing his royal sign and seal. Colbert had previously discussed with La Salle the feasibility of "finding a port where the French might establish themselves and harass the Spaniards in those regions from whence they derive all their wealth," and this scheme, again brought to the notice of the King, prompted that enthusiasm which led him to provide more than had been asked for the success of the enterprise. Should the friendly relations maintained between France and Spain prevent any immediate encroachment upon the Mexican possessions of the latter, the policy of La Salle was to follow the original plan of establishing a colony at the mouth of the Mississippi, where he would be prepared at the slightest intimation of hostilities to make a raid upon the Mexican mines. In this case he further intimated that "if the Spaniards should delay satisfying the King at the conclusion of a peace, an expedition at this point will oblige them to hasten its conclusion, and to give His Majesty important places in Europe in exchange for those which they may lose in a country of the possession of which they are extremely jealous."

While these motives evidently excited the King's interest in the enterprise and secured his hearty coöperation, the first object of the expedition was nominally the subjection and conversion of the savage nations of America, and it was therefore in conformity to these motives that La Salle was careful to include among those who were to form his company a sufficient number of missionaries. Agents were sent to Rochefort and Rochelle to secure soldiers and artisans; several families were enlisted for the colony, and by the twenty-fourth of July, 1684, all preparations were completed, the company was aboard the boats, and together with twenty other vessels bound for Canada, the fleet sailed from Rochelle. The Canadian vessels no doubt bore the letters to La Barré expressing the King's disapproval of his late proceedings, and requiring the return of all property seized unlawfully belonging to his protégé, the Sieur de la Salle.

The naval command of La Salle's expedition had been given to Captain de Beaujeu, whom Le Clercq says was known for valor, experience, and meritorious service; who had indeed been a naval captain for thirteen years, as he himself tells Seignelay in one of his letters of complaint, but his long position of authority and natural pride made him chafe under the calm assumption of one whom he contemptuously calls a "civilian" and who was possessed of quite as much hauteur as himself. The King moreover had given La Salle almost unlimited authority, which easily gave him the advantage in matters of dispute.

Once at sea, this unfortunate feeling of antagonism soon manifested itself, and a trifling accident which occurred when the fleet was about fifty leagues out was considered by some—La Salle among them—to have been deliberately planned. This was the breaking of the bowsprit of the royal ship "Joly," which was under the personal command of Beaujeu. It was necessary to return in order to repair the injury, and in the meantime the ships bound for Canada, which were to have kept with the smaller fleet as far as Cape Finisterre, continued to that point alone. On the eighth of August La Salle's party reached the Cape, and on the twentieth sighted the Island of Madeira. Here Beaujeu wished to cast anchor for water and provisions, as there had been some misunderstanding at the start about the length of the voyage and the number of passengers, but La Salle considered this unnecessary, and feared besides that the Spaniards might hear of their coming, which would place them under suspicion.

Although La Salle's reasons for passing the island were excellent, Beaujeu and, in fact, the entire crew were out of humor with his decision, and Joutel, looking back over the disastrous period which followed, says: "These misunderstandings * * * laid the foundation of those tragical events which afterward put an unhappy end to M. de La Salle's life and undertaking, and occasioned our ruin."

Beaujeu then declared that no stop should be made but at the Island of San Domingo.

In passing the Tropic of Cancer on the way thither, the sailors prepared to carry out their usual practice of "ducking." A tub was placed on deck and everything made ready for the ludicrous and annoying ceremony, when La Salle interfered, saying that those under his command should have no part in it; thereupon Beaujeu forbade the men to put the plan into execution, and this again brought the chief into disfavor.

Together with these tempests on board the boats, the fleet was several times threatened with storms from without. The "Aimable" and the "Belle," with the heavily loaded ketch "Saint Francis," often became separated from the "Joly" and were obliged to lie to for fair weather, or follow as their heavier cargoes permitted. During one of these storms off San Domingo the vessels became dispersed, the "Joly" as usual keeping the lead. La Salle in the meantime had expressed his desire to stop at Port de Paix, which was a convenient point, and where he was to obtain supplies for the expedition according to a pre-arranged plan with M. de Cussy, Governor of the Island of Tortuga, but Beaujeu, evidently to gratify personal pique, passed the place in the night, anchoring on the twenty-seventh of September at Petit Gouave on the other side of the island. This was a great annoyance to La Salle, the more so as he was himself ill, and was every day becoming more convinced, not only of Beaujeu's indifference, but of the utter worthlessness of the men whom his agents had secured to aid him in his enterprise. He accepted the situation with characteristic fortitude, however, and on the day following the arrival at Petit Gouave, having somewhat recovered from his illness, he went ashore to send messages to De Cussy, Begon the intendant, and the Marquis de Saint Laurent, Lieutenant-governor of the islands. He then provided more comfortable quarters for the sick, who numbered more than fifty, and whose maladies in most cases had been brought on by their own excesses.

At this unfortunate time he was himself attacked by a violent fever and was delirious for several days, only regaining consciousness long enough to realize the condition of his affairs. His men being under no restraint became more dissipated than ever, and Beaujeu at this crisis held coolly aloof. Word was also brought of the loss of the "Saint Francis," one of the disastrous results of the captain's obstinacy. She had been taken by the Spaniards while attempting to come up with the other vessels after a storm. It probably afforded La Salle small satisfaction to learn from his friends on the island that this would not have occurred if Beaujeu had stopped at Port de Paix.

Having made reparation as far as possible for this loss, La Salle hastened the embarkation, as his men were fast becoming demoralized and many of them had already deserted. At a council of pilots held to decide upon the point to be reached before making the final voyage, the Island of Cuba or Cape Saint Anthony was determined upon. At night, on the fifth of December, they cast anchor in a small creek on the Isle of Pines, where they stayed for three days waiting for fair weather. Here, according to Joutel, La Salle "shot an alligator dead," which the soldiers proceeded to boil and eat; but the fastidious narrator remarks that they had "good stomachs," and that he could not relish the meat, for it had a taste of musk.

Quantities of wild swine were seen, which were probably "of the breed of those the Spaniards left in the islands when they first discovered them." One of these was killed and sent to La Salle, who divided the feast with the naval commander. Again on the eighth sails were set, with Cape Saint Anthony as the objective, which was reached four days later; but the winds being unfavorable the expedition halted only one night there, moving away on the thirteenth. The winds being again unfavorable, Beaujeu suggested that the boats return to the cape, to which La Salle agreed, being careful not to give the captain any cause to complain. On the eighteenth of the same month the fleet started forward in a fresh wind, moving generally to the northwest, and on the first of January, 1685, was driven toward the coast by the current. It was then decided that a boat be sent out to discover land, La Salle, Beaujeu, and D'Aire being among the passengers. The result was unsatisfactory, and the wind rising, forced them back to the ships. A few days later a calm tempted La Salle to go ashore again to get some idea of his position, but the pilot took exception to the number of men who were to accompany him, and he unaccountably abandoned the idea. The ships were at that time probably near one of the mouths of the Mississippi, and had an exploration been made La Salle's entire destiny might have been altered. He seemed, however, to have been entirely ignorant of the locality, believing he was yet far to the eastward—near the Bay of Appalachee. He was therefore satisfied to send out the pilot and one of the masters of the boat "La Belle," who soon returned on account of a fog. The pilot's companion reported that he believed there was a river beyond the shoals that had been sighted on the sixth, "and yet," says Joutel, "M. de La Salle took no notice of it, nor made any account of that report." Soon after this another attempt was made to reach the shore, as the supply of water had given out, Joutel being sent in charge of the boats. On nearing land a number of Indians were seen walking along the sandy beach, who signaled to the crew to come on, but the sea was very high and the boats would be in danger of going aground Joutel now determined, if possible, to get the Indians to come out, that he might take them back to the "Aimable," where La Salle could question them. He therefore signaled to them in turn, putting a handkerchief on the end of his fire-lock in token of peace. In an instant their swarthy bodies were seen battling with the waves, but they could not stand against them and were forced back to shore. With quick intelligence they devised a plan, however, and soon put it into execution. Finding a large piece of timber, they threw it into the water and arranged themselves on either side of it, each man putting one arm around it and swimming with the other. When they reached the boats they were taken in, naked and streaming, and carried back to the vessel. The trip was useless, however, for La Salle could neither understand them nor make them understand him. He gave them beads and trinkets, according to his custom, which were tied in their hair and about their necks, and thus adorned they were taken out to the place of meeting, from whence they swam ashore.

When not hindered by calms the ships now bore steadily westward, expecting to find some signs of the Mississippi, and still misguided by the advice received at San Domingo. Frequent landings were made in the meantime for fresh water and game, and having reached the sandy shores of Texas, where the western curve of the Gulf commences, without finding "the fatal river," as Joutel calls it, La Salle proposed to return and make investigations about the point which had been passed on the sixth of January; but ill success had somewhat weakened his cause, and Beaujeu, probably glad of the opportunity, now offered objections. In the first place he sent D'Aire with various grievances; among others that La Salle—who had hurried ahead in the "Aimable," eagerly seeking the Mississippi—had designedly left him. He then complained that provisions had fallen short and that there would not be enough to last for the return voyage to France; but it was not La Salle's intention to return without making another attempt to find his river, and he therefore offered to supply Beaujeu's ship, the "Joly," with two weeks' provisions from his own. Beaujeu was dissatisfied with this, and left La Salle without further discussing the matter. Meanwhile boats went ashore for water and to give the men a chance to hunt, La Salle being among the passengers. Here D'Aire again came to him to talk about the provisions, still insisting that the "Joly" be supplied for a longer period than two weeks. La Salle not only explained that this would be ample time to carry out his plans, but that a larger supply would necessitate rummaging the hold of the "Aimable." D'Aire returned with La Salle's messages, while the latter, wishing to find a river which would give a better supply of water than the one near which the vessels were then anchored, sent on a small party to explore. After following the shore line for some distance they found a "great river." Signals were raised for the boats to join them, and La Salle hoped this might be one of the mouths of the Mississippi. Soundings were made all along and stakes set to guide their passage, for La Salle desired that they come to anchor at this point. He then sent the pilot of "La Belle" to assist in bringing in the fly-boat, but Beaujeu, angry about the provisions and thwarted in his already meditated plan of desertion, refused to let him come aboard, saying he could get along very well without his help.

Another event occurring soon after seemed to presage misfortune. La Salle had set some men to hewing down a tree on the river bank, and while at work they were surprised by Indians and several of their number captured. The rest ran terrified to report to La Salle, who immediately caused the party to pursue the savages with drums beating. This had the desired effect of scaring them. He then had ten of the men lay aside their arms and with him approach the Indians, as he wished to get what information he could from them and secure the captives peaceably. This was of no avail, however, for they could not make themselves understood, and they had led away the men during the conference. La Salle was therefore obliged to follow them to their village. On the way there the Indians were attracted by the ships, which could be plainly seen, and La Salle, following their gaze, noticed with some uneasiness that the "Aimable" was under sail and moving in the wrong direction; yet he was determined to rescue the captives, and therefore did not turn back. Soon the report of a cannon broke the stillness. The Indians, terrified, fell upon their faces, while La Salle, looking over the Gulf, saw the "Aimable" with furled sails stranded upon the shoals. The signal of distress meant an inestimable loss, for on this ship were almost all the tools and ammunition for the expedition; and although the accident was due to direct opposition to La Salle's orders—perhaps even to treachery—"his intrepidity did not forsake him and he applied himself without grieving to remedy what might be." Notwithstanding the weight of anxiety pressing upon him, he waited for the release of his men, and then hurrying to the shore did all in his power to recover part of the cargo of the ruined vessel. Some gunpowder and flour were saved, but while the work was going on the sky became overcast and a storm broke upon the dismal scene.

A party of Indians taking advantage of the general confusion came down to the beach to plunder, but La Salle's effectual tactics were resorted to, and the drums soon put them to flight. Later they succeeded in stealing a roll of blankets, and volunteers were sent to recover them, but finding that the squaws had already cut them up for skirts, they indiscreetly showed their anger and further excited the savages by taking some of their canoes. The result was fatal; for, being unfamiliar with the frail craft and delayed by obstructions, they made very slow progress and were overtaken by darkness not far below the Indian village. The vengeful inhabitants had stealthily followed them, and when their victims were asleep sent a salute of arrows into their midst, killing two of the men and wounding La Salle's nephew, Moranguet. The latter, however, was not too badly hurt to discharge his gun at the unseen assailants, which for a time frightened them off.

This affair, coupled with recent disasters, tended to increase the general discontent, and Beaujeu now prepared to return, saying that as the Mississippi—or at least what was supposed to be that river—had been reached, his obligation was practically at an end. La Salle was evidently very willing to forego his assistance, merely requesting that some ammunition which belonged to him on board the "Joly" be turned over to him; but Beaujeu, perhaps with a lingering feeling of spite, gave as an excuse for not meeting this request the fact that the goods lay at the bottom of the hold, and by searching for them he would endanger the vessel. Besides this, he allowed the entire crew of the "Aimable" to follow her captain and return with him to France.

That this conduct was the result of deliberate treachery was confirmed by later events; and it has even been proved that the faithless captain after leaving La Salle went himself in search of the Mississippi, found it, and, although provisions had been alarmingly short before, remained in the vicinity of its mouth long enough to enable the engineer Minet to make two maps. He then set sail, gracefully turning his back upon the lonely shores of the Gulf, where far to the westward—within what is now known as Matagorda Bay—the abandoned and well-nigh despairing little colony under La Salle was left to accomplish the great ends which that intrepid explorer had planned.

Although the outlook was rather disheartening after the departure of the "Joly," no time was given over to idle lamenting. From the wreck of the "Aimable," Fort Saint Louis was built, the colonists and some of the men were safely domiciled within its palisades, and Joutel left in command, while La Salle went to discover if the river they had reached were indeed what he had hoped—the western mouth of the Mississippi.

Orders were left to hold no communication with Indians and to fire upon any who might approach.

La Salle hearing shots a few days afterward, and fearing they might be a signal of distress, returned to see if all was well. He had found in the meantime that the "great river" which they had haplessly come upon was not the one on which the colonists were to find a home and fortune; but their immediate wants must be supplied, and for this reason La Salle selected a more convenient place to the eastward of Fort Saint Louis, on a small river which he named La Vache.

Joutel, abandoning the old fort to join the party here some time later, found a forlorn condition of things. Owing to the scarcity of timber, the men, women, and children were living in wretched little huts and tents, the crops were a miserable failure, and in fact failure seemed to typify the whole enterprise. La Salle, however, was still hopeful and undaunted. He sent Joutel back to Fort Saint Louis with "La Belle," the only boat now left, to get the timber which had been squared and hidden in the sand. With this, new buildings were thrown up and more comfortable quarters established; yet the seeming air of prosperity still covered miserable realities, for disease and death were every day adding to the overwhelming numbers who had perished within the year.

There was now no time to be lost, and La Salle with thirty men went once more in search of the "fatal river." This time, anticipating bad faith, he left additional orders with Joutel telling him to receive no man of those who went with him except he brought a message from him in writing. It soon transpired that this order was not made without reason.

One evening a few weeks after La Salle's departure the sentinel keeping his lonely watch within the fort was startled by the sound of a voice coming from the direction of the river, calling "Dominick!" the name of the younger Duhaut. Joutel was summoned, and in an instant all the men were assembled in the open inclosure. The commander advanced to see who the intruder might be, and found Duhaut in a canoe near the shore. Joutel was in doubt as to whether or not he ought to enforce La Salle's order, but Duhaut told a very plausible story of becoming separated from the party and of being unable to overtake it, and Joutel saw no other course but to allow him to enter. "Thus it pleased God," he says, "that he who was to be one of the murderers of M. de La Salle should come off safe and surmount almost infinite dangers." Some time after this La Salle himself returned with a few ragged and weary men, after an unsuccessful tramp through forests and over prairies in quest of the river which the explorer was destined never to reach.

On the day of his arrival Joutel happened to be walking on top of one of the buildings, and seeing a body of men advancing over the prairie hurried out to meet them. They proved to be La Salle and eight of his followers, the remainder having been left on the bank of a river which was thought to be the Mississippi, while the crew of the "Belle," with the boat itself, which had kept along the coast, had disappeared and was supposed to be lost. With this the last hope of returning to France was abandoned; the Mississippi was still undiscovered; every undertaking had failed, and at last, borne down by a weight of anxiety and wearied with his fruitless wanderings, La Salle fell dangerously ill; but his sturdy frame and indomitable spirit soon overcame this weakness, and he prepared again not only to find the Mississippi, but to ascend it to the Illinois and thence tô Canada, where he intended to get vessels and provisions for the relief of his people. At the end of April his party of twenty volunteers, bearing their light packs of clothing and ammunition, issued from the gate of the little stockaded fort, quietly and resolutely, to undertake another of those journeys which had so often proved perilous and unavailing. As usual, a remnant of their number returned to tell the story of another failure; some having deserted and others perished.

These continual misfortunes were naturally disheartening, and yet the chief still planned to accomplish his purpose. Another expedition was discussed; preparations were begun; and as it was decided to wait till the end of the hot weather before undertaking it, the men were put to work making clothing out of sails, and hewing timber for future use, for work was always La Salle's antidote for discontent.

In the meantime Christmas approached, and the isolated band far away in the wilderness assembled in the rough chapel to celebrate the mass. On Twelfth Night they again came together after the usual custom, to perform the quaint old ceremony of *The King Drinks;* but when they lifted the cups their lips were moistened, not with the merry wine which their countrymen were sipping in France, but with the simple nectar of the New World's springs.

The following day, the seventh of January, those

chosen to accompany La Salle on his last journey, said farewell to the forlorn little colony left behind, once more encouraged by the words and example of their leader. Much the same direction that had been taken before was followed by this latter party—that is, toward the northeast. On the fourteenth, while crossing a prairie, herds of buffaloes were seen; some of them running as if pursued by Indians, while others, beginning to catch the infection, were moving in frightened groups toward the travelers. Soon a hunter appeared, and La Salle, having ordered one of the pack-horses to be unloaded, sent one of his men to pursue the red-skin, who, finding himself captured, concluded he was a lost man. He was somewhat surprised, however, to find himself kindly treated—which but for La Salle's wise interposition would not have been the case—and upon being released soon afterward walked cautiously away till well out of range, when he began running for dear life. Soon after this a band of Indians was seen advancing, but La Salle had his men continue the march until within hailing distance, when a halt was called. At this the natives halted also, while La Salle, laying down his gun, walked toward the chief, signaling him to come forward. A sort of peace was made, presents were distributed, and the two parties separated, La Salle and his men pushing on over the still familiar route, and occasionally meeting Indians with whom peace was established.

On the eleventh of March they came to a place near which La Salle in a previous journey had hidden some corn and beans, and as provisions were scarce Duhaut, Heins, Liotot the surgeon, Nika his Mohegan hunter, and Saget his footman were sent with a party of Indians to get the stores. They were found rotted, but when returning Nika shot two bullocks, and Saget was sent back to inform his master

Moranguet, La Salle's nephew, and De Marle were sent with horses to bring back the meat for drying; but when they reached the hunting party they found that the meat had already been smoked, although it was not ready, while Duhaut and his companions had, according to custom, laid aside the marrow-bones and a few other parts to roast. At this the quick-tempered Moranguet fell into a rage, menacing Duhaut and the others, and at the same time taking possession of all of the meat. This impassioned behavior roused like a fire-brand the smoldering hatred of the men, who already had causes of offense against the nephew of their chief.

In an instant a thousand real and imaginary grievances were recalled. In the first place, Duhaut and Liotot had invested large sums of money in an enterprise which seemed destined to fail, and in following which they had met only privations and losses; their leader, habitually cold and reserved, had unconsciously done much to help on the general disaffection, while Liotot—whose brother had been sent back alone by La Salle during one of the marches, and had been massacred by Indians on the way—had a personal sorrow to avenge. They had moreover a grudge against Moranguet and were determined to kill him.

Taking the pilot Tessier, Heins the buccaneer, and L'Archevêque into their confidence, they went aside to deliberate upon their murderous purpose; and having determined to put Nika and Saget out of the way because they were faithful to La Salle, they waited, after the manner of their kind, for the darkness.

The evening meal was eaten in silence, each man busy with his own thoughts, and when it was finished the watches were arranged. Moranguet was to keep the first, Saget the second, and Nika the third.

Taking his post, gun in hand, Moranguet guarded the apparently sleeping figures of his companions until his time was up; then calling to Saget he wrapped himself in his blanket and lay down to rest.

The end of the third watch was the signal for the assassins to begin their work. Duhaut, Heins, Tessier, and L'Archevêque stood guard while the surgeon with sure aim struck the death-blow Nika and Saget did not stir, but Moranguet made a convulsive effort to sit up, which was quickly prevented by a second stroke. "This slaughter," says Joutel, "had yet satisfied but one part of the revenge of those murderers. To finish it and secure themselves it was requisite to destroy the commander-in-chief." Their unhappy victim was already planning to meet his murderers; for becoming uneasy at the delay of Moranguet, and fearing the party might have fallen into the hands of the Indians, he determined to go in search of them. He also, it is said, had forebodings of another kind, and asked his men if Duhaut, Liotot, and Heins had not betrayed some signs of discontent. Receiving no definite answer, he started out accompanied by Father Douay, leaving Joutel in charge of the camp.

On the way he talked to the priest of God's mercy in having protected him from the countless dangers with which he had been encompassed during his twenty years of travel in America; but his manner suddenly changing, he became so overwhelmed with sadness that his companion declares he did not know him.

As they advanced toward the river, on whose farther shore the murderers had their camp, La Salle, noticing two eagles circling in the air overhead, discharged his gun at them. The shot warned the conspirators. Duhaut and L'Archevêque went up the river, crossing over without being seen. Duhaut then dropped into the long grass, while his servant remained in sight, and La Salle noticing him asked where Moranguet was. L'Archevêque replied in a broken voice that he was along the river, and at the same instant, as La Salle turned to follow the direction, Duhaut raised and fired. The bullet reached its mark and La Salle fell, pierced through the brain.

Father Douay, who was standing beside him, tremblingly expected the same fate; but Duhaut reassured him, telling him that it was despair that had driven him to the deed.

The murderers now gathered about their victim, while Liotot, remembering the death of his brother, cried out in scorn, "There thou liest, great Basha! There thou liest!" Then dragging the corpse into the bushes they left it a prey to the beasts.

Duhaut and his confederates now returned to camp, where they were soon the masters, the terror of their presence causing the most abject submission. Joutel, meanwhile, had gone off to a neighboring hill to watch some horses grazing in the bottom, and thither L'Archevêque, who had a "kindness" for him, went to warn him. The news was a great blow to this officer, and he had besides something to fear on his

ASSASSINATION OF LASALLE

own account. There was, however, no alternative, and trusting to a kind Providence he went back to camp, where he was greeted by Duhaut's menacing remark, "Every man ought to command in his turn."

Safety demanded silence, while those who would have brought the guilty ones to justice were restrained by the priest Cavelier, who reminded them that vengeance belonged to God.

With the death of the leader, whom Douay called their guardian angel, everything was thrown into confusion. The new commander took possession of all the stores and the men dared offer no resistance. There came a time, however, when their villainy was avenged; and strangely enough this was brought about by one of their number, the buccaneer Heins. While he seems to have conspired with them against Moranguet, there is no evidence to show that he took a part in the murder of La Salle, who had always been partial to him. When, therefore, Duhaut and Liotot were on their way to Canada, Heins, who refused to go with them farther, demanded his share of the goods. Duhaut and Liotot refused, giving as an excuse the fact that they were entitled to them as a recompense for their losses "So you will not give them to me?" demanded the buccaneer. "No," replied they Thereupon he drew his pistol from his belt and fired at Duhaut, saying as he did so, "You are a villain. You killed my master" A Frenchman who was then with Heins mortally wounded Liotot, and after the latter had made a confession of his crime, the same man stepped forward and discharged a blank cartridge against his head. In a moment more his hair had caught fire, then his clothing, and so, consumed by the flames, he perished.

Joutel, the two Caveliers, Father Douay, and a few others afterward made their way to Fort Saint Louis on the Illinois, where they waited for Tonty, who had gone to the Iroquois war, and from whom they later received money to return to France; concealing from him for certain reasons the fact of La Salle's death, Tonty, having previously heard that the latter was somewhere on the Gulf and in distress, had made a difficult journey to find him, with the hope of lending him succor; but, failing in the attempt, was obliged to return again to his post on the Illinois. On the way up the Mississippi he left a letter with the Quinipissa tribe—since become friendly to the French—and D'Ibberville, passing that way thirteen years later, found the message, which had been carefully preserved by one of the chiefs.

As to the little Texan colony of Saint Louis, which La Salle left when he went on his last journey in search of the "fatal river," the only record that remains of it is in the Spanish account of the expedition of Don Alonzo de Leon, where it is said that the Spaniards upon reaching Bay Saint Bernard, known by the French as Bay Saint Louis, came upon a ruined fort where the dead bodies of several foreigners were found, who had evidently been massacred by the Indians. Don Alonzo was moved to compassion at the sight, and although he afterward learned from two Frenchmen who had been with La Salle—L'Archevêque was one—the motives which had moved the explorer when he brought his people there, he still manifested the greatest concern and pity. At the same time, however, he informed his government of the affair, that its Mexican colonies might be protected from the inroads of others, which this daring though unsuccessful venture seemed to presage.

So perished the plans of one of the greatest of explorers, who "belonged not to the age of the knight-errant and the saint, but to the modern world of practical study and practical action," and to whom the enterprising spirit of a nineteenth-century civilization looks back with admiration and praise.

BUILDING OF FORT SAINT LOUIS.

CHAPTER IX.

FATHER LOUIS HENNEPIN.

THE life of this sturdy Franciscan, whose very garb has so often been the means of condemning him, possesses no small amount of attractiveness, notwithstanding the just criticisms that have been leveled against it by those who have made it a study; and even in following Hennepin's accounts, exasperating as they are by the doubts which they excite of the author's veracity, it is still impossible to resist the clever stretching of truth which made them popular above those of his fellow travelers, not only in France, but in the other countries of Europe.

With La Hontan and a few others of like reputation, he is condemned to "that amiable class who seem to tell truth by accident and fiction by inclination"; yet for want of something better we are left to the mercy of these capricious historians, who with all their fabrications have given us records of the highest value.

Moved by impulse while still a student, Hennepin entered the order of Saint Francis that he might pass the remainder of his days "in a life of austerity." This step was evidently a mistake. He soon became impatient with convent monotony, and in reading of the travels of his brother priests his craving for adventure asserted itself. He was permitted to visit the Franciscan churches and convents of Germany and Italy, which in a measure satisfied him; but returning from this tour he found his inclinations thwarted by one of his superiors who did not approve of them, and who sent him to a convent in Hainault, where he stayed a year preaching.

Anything was better than this, and at the end of that time he received permission to go to Artois, and from there was sent to Calais, where he artlessly compromised himself by confessing that he "often hid behind the tavern doors while the sailors were talking over their cruises," declaring that he could have passed whole days and nights without eating in this agreeable occupation, because by this means he was enabled to learn something new about the manners and mode of life of foreign nations.

By these stories his "old inclination" was also aroused, and starting out again he wandered about as a missionary through the towns of Holland, although the country was then shadowed by the desperate conflicts of the Prince of Orange and Louis XIV.

At Maestricht, at the time of the siege, he worked in the hospitals among the wounded for eight months, and, catching a zeal from his labors there, was next ministering to the soldiers on the bloody field of Seneff, where his unflinching charity, though in a measure vaunted by himself, was none the less admirable.

From war-scourged Holland he was recalled to Rochelle, having been elected by his superiors to make one of the quintette of missionaries to be sent to Canada at the request of Frontenac. This opportunity was gratifying to the restless priest, and he hastened back to France to prepare for the voyage.

La Salle, with his grant of Fort Frontenac and new patent of nobility, and Francis de Laval, soon to become Vicar Apostolic of New France, were two of his fellow passengers, whom he variously impressed on the way to Canada. He says that De Laval upon their arrival at Quebec commissioned him to preach the Advent and Lenten sermons to the nuns of the Hotel Dieu; but curious in the meantime to see the country about him, he traveled to the neighboring towns with his portable chapel service and snow-shoes strapped to his back, sturdily enduring hunger and fatigue, and, worse still, the frosts which "often penetrated to his very bones."

From Quebec he was sent with Father Buisset to Fort Frontenac to instruct the Indians there, and while laboring in the new field still roamed about in every direction, visiting the Five Nations, and even going as far as Albany, where the Dutch invited him to make his home.

At the end of two years La Salle had returned from France with permission to carry on his discoveries, and Hennepin, hearing of his arrival, hurried down to Quebec, where he hoped to find messages giving him permission to join in the enterprise. To his delight La Salle brought a favorable letter from Father Le Fèvre, his Provincial, and after going into retreat for a time, he went back to Fort Frontenac, where with La Motte and a crew of sixteen he was sent forward to Niagara. Then followed the building of the fort there; the negotiations with the Senecas; the triumphant sail of the "Griffin," and finally the establishment of Fort Crève-cœur.

From here La Salle sent the restless Recollet on to the Mississippi, before making his brave journey back to Canada for the relief of the men who deserted him. Hennepin was reluctant in accepting this commission, not probably for want of courage, for he more than once proved that he was not lacking in that quality, but perhaps because the journey would be a tedious one, and he was at the time suffering from an abscess in the mouth. He offered to exchange places with Father Membré, who was disgusted with the Illinois, and who came down to Fort Crève-cœur to pour his trials into the ears of his brother missionaries. "This set the Father thinking," says Hennepin, "and he preferred to remain with the Illinois, of whom he had some knowledge, rather than expose himself to go among unknown nations."

There was then no escape, for La Salle, always it seems harboring a little feeling of antagonism against the self-assertive priest, threatened to write to Hennepin's superiors in France if he refused to obey his wish; while the venerable Father Ribourde, himself one of the bravest of the band of missionaries, encouraged his younger brother with priestly consolation. On the twenty-ninth of February, 1680, La Salle and the men from the fort came down to the river to bid Hennepin and his companions farewell. By the water's edge lay moored the birch canoe which was to carry them through unknown dangers; its crannies filled with hatchets and beads, as passports to the strange tribes of the Upper Mississippi.

Hennepin embraced all the men in turn, receiving Father Ribourde's blessing and an encouraging word from La Salle, whom at the last he accuses of rashly exposing his life; then, with a stroke of the paddles the canoe was started down the stream and its occupants lost to sight.

In the evening a party of Illinois, returning to their village with the spoils of the hunt, startled the priest and his companions and almost succeeded in influencing Accault and Du Gay to abandon their journey, but the men knew if they did this the men at the fort would see them, and they decided to keep on their way. Near the mouth of the river they came to a camp of the Tamaroa and were invited to their village on the Mississippi. Hennepin, however, prevailed upon the men, who intended to do some trading, to wait until they reached the Upper River, and so prevented a delay The keen-eyed Indians had noticed in the meantime that the white men's canoe was stored with arms for their enemies, and were determined to get possession of them. They accordingly started out in pursuit, but their heavy wooden boats were no match for the canoe and they were soon far behind. Resorting to another means, they sent a party of young warriors along the shore to intercept the white men at a narrow point. The pursued saw their camp-fire at night, and, warned by it, hurried to an island on the opposite side of the river, leaving their dog in the canoe as sentinel, while they, expecting to be followed, silently waited for the signal to embark. Their fears were groundless. The Indians failing to overtake them returned, leaving them to continue their journey to the Mississippi, where they were detained by floating ice until the twelfth of March.

Here the speculations regarding Hennepin's movements begin. In his first account, published in 1683, he describes the journey northward, and his capture by the Sioux, making no reference to a descent of the river, and again in the journal published fourteen years later he declares that he descended the Mississippi to the Gulf; although he concealed the fact, he says, in order that La Salle, "who wished to keep all the glory and all the knowledge of it to himself," might not be offended! This remarkable voyage, according to a coincidence of dates in the two accounts, was made in forty-three days, but as La Salle cautiously remarks: "It is necessary to know him somewhat" to tell how much credence should be given to these declarations. It is generally believed that the earlier work is the more reliable—that it is even accurate—and therefore the experiences of the eccentric priest on the Upper Mississippi may be accepted with a good share of faith. Taking him at his word then, he and his companions passed in their upward course the rivers emptying into the main stream from the east and west, coming at last to the falls which he named in honor of Saint Anthony of Padua.

The journey was not altogether one of privations. There was an abundance of game, deer, buffalo, bear, and wild turkey, on which they had a continual feast; making amends for their Lenten indulgence by saying prayers three times a day, their chief petition at these times being that they might not be surprised by *the natives* at night, for with all their courage they valued their scalps as highly as their less venturesome brothers. This petition was granted soon after their midday devotions on the eleventh of April. A war-party of a hundred and twenty Sioux on their way to the lower tribes suddenly came upon thom. In an instant their arrows were whirring around them and their canoes had hemmed them in; but the old warriors noticing the calumet which

HENNEPIN AT THE FALLS OF SAINT ANTHONY.

Hennepin held, kept the young men from violence. The Indians then attempted to terrify the group on the shore; some of them leaping into the water and others darting up in their canoes, accompanying their maneuvers with piercing yells. All this had the desired effect. Hennepin hastened to give them the all-powerful "tabac," and they were partially appeased. Hearing them repeat the words Miamiha, Miamiha, and inferring from this that they spoke of the Miamis, whom with the Illinois they were about to attack, he took up a stick and marking with it on the sand attempted to explain that the Miamis were no longer in their villages, but had fled beyond the Mississippi, whereupon four old men placed their hands on his head and began to wail. This demonstration somewhat disturbed Hennepin, the more so as the Indians refused to smoke his peace-pipe. With quick thought, he drew forth a tattered handkerchief and made a sign as if to wipe away their tears. The stolid faces showed no evidence of pleasure. Soon, with "yells capable of striking the most resolute with terror," they crossed the river, obliging Hennepin and his companions to go with them. They then assembled in council, while the unconscious objects of their discussion, withdrawn a short distance from the camp, were making their fire for supper. In the midst of these preparations two chiefs approached to inform them by signs that the warriors had decided to tomahawk them; and Hennepin, duly impressed by the information, again hastened to appease the would-be murderers, by throwing into their midst a present of knives, hatchets, and tobacco, and at the same time resorting to diplomacy, took one of the hatchets, bowed his head before the astonished Indians and by signs gave them to understand that they might then, if they wished, carry out their purpose.

This pleased his audience, and although the peace-pipe was still refused, they invited him and his companions to share their feast of beaver with them. At night, anticipating trouble, Accault and Du Gay slept on their arms; but Hennepin affirms that he took no precaution, having determined to give himself up without resistance. He bore his part in keeping guard, however, that the Indians might not surprise them while asleep.

The night at last wore away without any disturbance, and in the morning their fears were dispelled. Narrhetoba, one of the warriors, painted from head to foot, came to them and asked for the calumet, and returning to his camp made all the Indians smoke; after which he told the white men they must return with them to his country.

Hennepin was now greatly perplexed in performing his devotions, for the Indians, watching him as he prayed, muttered, with dark faces, "Ouaĉkanché"—meaning that the book out of which he read was a spirit. Du Gay and Accault, fearing for their lives, begged the priest to go apart to pray; "but," says Hennepin, "the more I concealed myself, the more I had the Indians at my heels." Resorting to another method, he chanted his prayers aloud with the book opened on his knee, while the canoes were in motion, and the Indians, thinking the book made him sing to please them, no longer disturbed him.

Another danger threatened them in the meantime; for Aquipaguetin, a chief whose son had been killed by the Miamis, was angry with the white men because they had prevented him by their information from taking his revenge. He attempted to excite the other chiefs against them by wailing his grief every night, and Hennepin attributes the escape from this danger to the fact that the Indians wished to keep the good-will of the French, who could furnish them with "iron that has understanding," meaning guns and ammunition. The priest then complains of the harsh treatment to which he and his companions were subjected, and says that there was no opportunity to go up or down the river to explore, as the Indians kept a vigilant watch—thus denying his later assertion that he descended the river to the Gulf.

Having finally reached the end of their journey by water, the party met to decide upon what should be done with the Frenchmen, and at last they were distributed among the three families of the tribe who had lost children in battle. This done, their goods were appropriated and their canoe destroyed to prevent their return.

When within a short distance of the village the Frenchmen saw to their horror bunches of straw hanging to the posts of the cabins; and taking this as a sign that they were to perish at the stake, were filled with apprehension. Besides they noticed that the Indians, having painted Du Gay's face and fastened a tuft of white feathers in his hair, made him sing and shake a gourd filled with pebbles; but they soon found these fears to be groundless, for they were feasted and given the calumet to smoke.

Stimulated at last by hunger, Hennepin undertook to master the language of his adopted people; learning first their word "Takotchiabihen," or "What do you call that," and, with the help of the children, gradually acquiring the names of the things he saw. He also won their good-will by attempting to cure them with a little bundle of medicines which he carried in his sleeve.

In the early part of July the Sioux went southward on their annual hunting excursion, and at the same time Hennepin and Du Gay, through the influence of a friendly chief, were allowed to descend to the Wisconsin, where they expected to find traders and a supply of ammunition—Du Gay and Accault probably intending to use it to trade with the Indians for furs. On the way down they were overtaken by the hunters, and Aquipaguetin, who by an inexplicable turn of affairs had assumed the protection of Hennepin, came up to the priest and asked him if he had found the Frenchmen who were to bring the supplies. Upon receiving an unsatisfactory answer, the chief started on himself to the rendezvous, intending to seize what he could; but finding no sign of the goods or the white men he returned, thoroughly out of humor with his adopted son, and vexed that he had made the trip in vain.

Soon after this the hunting-camp was thrown into a state of excitement by a report of the old men, who as usual had been stationed on the hill-tops to keep the watch. They had seen two warriors in the distance, they said, which immediately started a pursuit.

Only two women of a neighboring band of Sioux, who had strayed from their party, were overtaken, but they said that their hunters had met five "spirits," meaning Europeans, near Lake Superior, who, knowing that there were white men with this tribe, had expressed their desire to visit them.

On the return of the party to their northern home these five "spirits" were met, and found to be Du Lhut and four companions, come to explore the Great River and to make peace with the tribes along their route.

They accompanied the Sioux back to their villages, but as the cold months were coming, and the necessity of staying longer practically at an end, Du Lhut and Hennepin came together to discuss returning to Canada. Having arranged their plans, Du Lhut then told the Indians that the Frenchmen must leave them. At first this announcement was received with some opposition, but the head chief finally consented and traced himself the route they were to take.

Everything being in readiness, the eight travelers bade adieu to their Sioux friends and started back to civilization. Descending the Mississippi as far as the Wisconsin, they followed the course which Joliet and Marquette had taken seven years before; down the Fox River, across Lake Winnebago, and thence to Lake Michigan, continuing through the chain of lakes to the settlements in Canada. From here Hennepin went to France, and was soon afterward in Amsterdam with his manuscript attempting to find a publisher. Failing there he went to Utrecht, where his second journal appeared in 1697 His later life is comparatively unknown; but from a letter dated at Rome, 1701, he is supposed to have been at the convent of Aracœli, and attempting to interest certain persons in the mission field of the Mississippi country, "where he hoped to renew his labors." As to the contradictory accounts which he published relating to his explorations and those of La Salle, there has been much comment, not only by late critics, but by the men of his time. Among the latter he made a feeble attempt to justify himself, but this effort was far from convincing his accusers then, and has even less weight now. From the doubtful pages unanswered questions still arise. What was Hennepin's real mission to the Mississippi? Why did he apparently avoid La Salle? And did he actually precede the latter in the exploration of the lower river? But with all this, the careful critic putting the journal to the test has found one certain truth, and the historian with impartial applause hails the explorer of the Upper Mississippi, Father Louis Hennepin.

FATHER HENNEPIN AT HIS DEVOTIONS.

CHAPTER X.

LA HONTAN—CHARLEVOIX—CARVER.

ITH La Salle and Hennepin, the exploration of the Mississippi was practically ended, although its farthest fountains were still undiscovered, yet, to these travelers who had followed its winding course of three thousand miles, it had not lost the old appellation of "the unknown river of the West."

One of those to follow the great explorers in the valley of the Great River was the Baron LA HONTAN, whose accounts in his own day were looked at askance generally, and loudly disclaimed by the Jesuits, but which have at last received a partial justification by Jean Nicollet and a few others.

On the twenty-fourth of September, 1688, when the tragic news of La Salle's death had reached the upper station, La Hontan left Michilimackinac on his way to the Great River, following the route of Joliet and Marquette, witnessing the calumet dance in his honor at the mouth of the Fox, and passing thence to the upper river, from which he made the portage to the Wisconsin.

When the Mississippi was reached he went northward, and, as he says, entered a river coming into Lake Pepin from the west, which he speaks of as "the Long River" At this point the critics challenge him. They find nothing that corresponds to his description, and yet the Baron, unconscious of the frowning tribunal, leads his readers up the mysterious stream, past great Indian villages and through a marvelous country in the months of November and December, when all other rivers, of that section at least, are sealed with ice before Christmas.

Nicollet, however, has an excuse for this. He finds a similarity between La Hontan's "Long River" and Cannon River, which, he says, is one of the last to freeze, and is generally a late resort of wild fowl. He finds, moreover, evidences of old Indian villages along the course of this stream, by a kind of grass that always grows where settlements have been, but he adds that he "does not pretend to justify La Hontan's gross exaggeration of the length of the river, and of the numerous population on its banks."

Nicollet's view is no doubt a just one. La Hontan knew that others were more or less familiar with that part of the Mississippi which he described, and that it would not be long before his relations would be put to the test. Perrot had been all through the region —that is, as far as any one had gone—and knew every part of it; yet the discoverer of "the Long River" did not hesitate to publish, with elaborate detail, the account of his voyage.

The geographers of Europe, quick to make additions to their incomplete maps of North America, soon gave the stream a prominent place; but the French, never over-credulous, did not accept it without question, and in 1716, a priest of Versailles wrote to De L'Isle, geographer of the Academy of Sciences, "Would it not be well to efface that great river which La Hontan says he discovered? All the

Canadians, and even the Governor-general, have told me that this river is unknown;" while Charlevoix makes the sweeping assertion that "the episode of the voyage up the Long River is as fabulous as the Barrataria of Sancho Panza."

When La Hontan re-enters the Mississippi, his account is more charitably received. In his descent of the river he made a partial exploration of the Missouri and Saint Peter, which has placed him among the men who first pushed beyond known boundaries, and which has won for him the honor of being the discoverer of those two great tributaries.

CHARLEVOIX, a man of ability and honor, was commissioned by the French government to visit New France in 1721, for the purpose of describing its condition and possibilities. Had he not accepted this commission, La Hontan would have had one critic less, and Europe, figuratively on tip-toe with curiosity, would have been deprived of one of the truest pictures of the affairs of her sister continent; but Charlevoix was a Jesuit, and an observer who had already spent four years in Canada, and he did not let pass an opportunity for wider travel.

Reaching Quebec in the spring of 1721, he began his journey westward, writing at frequent intervals to his friend the Countess Lesdigueres, who has in turn bequeathed the letters to history On his way to Three Rivers he tells her that he set out from Pointe aux Trembles "with a horse blind of an eye, which he afterward exchanged for a lame one, and then again for one that was broken-winded."

Following the route which had attracted all of the early travelers—up the Saint Lawrence and through the lakes—he modified, on the way, many of their wild exaggerations and added many details of his own. On Lake Superior he learned the strange traditions of the Indians in regard to the vast inland sea, which they believed was formed by Michabon, the god of the waters, to supply them with beaver. He found pieces of copper on its shores, and says that one of the priests of his order, belonging to the mission of Saint Mary's, had found large quantities of it in so pure a state that he was able to make ornaments of it for the mission chapel.

From Lake Michigan he entered the Saint Joseph, crossing to the Kankakee, and thence down to the Mississippi, where the light birch-bark canoes were exchanged for heavier boats, but the men, accustomed to light paddles, made awkward work of rowing, and Père Charlevoix, in his hollowed-out "walnut tree," found it perilous, as well as interesting, to descend the Mississippi. He enjoyed his experiences, however, and wrote enthusiastic descriptions of the beauties of the scenery and the pleasures of unconventional travel, which, he said, recalled the ancient Patriarchs, who lived in tents and had no fixed place of abode.

During his journey down the river, Charlevoix made frequent excursions on the tributary streams and into the adjacent country, and, traveling thus leisurely, reached in December the straggling huts of New Orleans, which, viewed from Versailles by the French Monarch and his extravagant subjects, appeared a future center of unlimited wealth. Charlevoix himself, coming upon it at a time when enthusiasm for its future was at its height, believed that this city, "the first which one of the greatest rivers of the world has seen rise upon its banks," "the wild and desert place still covered by canes and trees," would one day be an opulent city and the metropolis of a great and rich colony This, however, was his opinion when he had but entered the place. After looking about and taking a careful account of its position he wrote in quite another strain. He could not see the obstacles overcome by science after the marvelous strides of a century and a half, nor the power of steam upon the Great River, which would insure the prosperity of the "Crescent City." From here he sent the last of his witty letters to the Countess, by which his personal experiences in the New World close. Upon his return to Europe he published his "History of New France," which is valued now quite as much as when little was known of North America, while its author will always hold an important place in the scenes which he describes.

After Charlevoix, Captain JONATHAN CARVER was the next explorer of importance in the Valley of the Mississippi, and the variation from the long line of Spanish and French names which followed in succession from the early discovery of the river, tells at once of the great change which had made the English masters and dissolved the power of New France. Carver himself bore arms in his country's cause, barely escaping the massacre of Fort William Henry, and winning his captaincy by the same spirit which two generations before had given the governorship of Connecticut to an ancestor

When peace was declared, the young captain determined to explore the newly acquired British possessions, that government might be acquainted with their extent and condition. He also had in mind the discovery of a northwest passage between Hudson's Bay and the Pacific Ocean; and with these objects in view left Boston in June, 1766. At Mackinac the English governor of the fort gave him a small supply of goods for use among the Indians, promising to send him more to Saint Anthony Falls; and with this equipment he started with his men—one a French-Canadian and the other a Mohawk. As far as Prairie du Chien he had the company of two traders, but there the party separated, Carver going on up the river.

On the tenth day, at evening, the encampment was made and the boats moored near the shore. As soon as it was dark, Carver, as usual, ordered his men to take their rest, while he sat up to write his notes by the light of a candle. About ten o'clock, stepping out of his tent to see what the weather was, he saw at a little distance something that had the appearance of a herd of beasts, but, unable to distinguish them in the starlight, he stood closely watching their movements. Suddenly one of their number raised up and disclosed the figure of a man. Carver, recognizing the situation, gave the alarm, and his men, having snatched their weapons, started in the direction of the boat, toward which the savages were hurrying. "What do you want?" called out the bold Yankee, whereupon the Indians, evidently wanting only to escape alive from such an awe-inspiring white chief, fled precipitately to the woods, where Carver gave up the pursuit. The men were now badly frightened and wanted to turn back, but Carver, knowing the most effectual cure, threatened to call them "old women," and by his own example shamed them.

Below Lake Pepin the explorer discovered a strange

relic of the past, which led him—as such discoveries have led many others—to think that this continent, whose ancient history is an unsolved mystery, was once the home of civilized nations. He found the grass-grown remains of a carefully constructed intrenchment, protected in the rear by the river, and bearing the imprint of centuries.

From here he went to Saint Anthony Falls and then on as far as the Saint Francis, a distance which had been reached only by Father Hennepin and himself. Then paddling up the Saint Peter, he came to a north branch which had not been named, and in order to distinguish it he called it "Carver" River, by which name it is still known.

By the seventh of December he reached the western limit of his travels. Through the dishonesty of the men intrusted with supplies from Mackinac, it was impossible to go farther, and he was detained for the winter at the Sioux village at the head of the Saint Peter. Here he learned their language and received the honors of a great chief, for, by a service which he had rendered one of the "river bands," his fame had reached the farthest lodges. The event which had won him this distinction took place during his ascent of the river. He was stopping a day or two with the Indians at their encampment when some hunters of the band announced that a war-party of the Chippewas was approaching, large enough, they said, "to swallow them all up."

The Sioux, terrified by this news, begged their guest to lead them to battle, believing in the superior powers of the white man; but Carver, unwilling to antagonize the Chippewas, and yet wishing to retain the good-will of the Sioux, knew not what to answer.

CARVER AND THE THUNDERSTORM.

In this extremity, he offered to act as mediator, although the Indians doubted his success, as their peace-pipes had been repeatedly disregarded. Carver, however, started toward the enemy, as the brave Tonty had done before him, and so completely won over the chiefs that the war-party turned back, while the delighted Sioux quickly decamped before the enemy had time to repent of their action.

Early in the spring the Indians prepared to visit the cave below the present city of Saint Paul, which they called the dwelling of the Great Spirit, where they held their councils.

On the way down the river, the party was overtaken by a terrific storm. The Indians, terrified and imagining it to be a sign of the wrath of the Great Spirit, rushed into the woods, but Carver, who had accompanied them, afraid to be near the trees, stood out in an open space, while the savages looked on with superstitious admiration.

Having been admitted to the great council at the cave, and honored with the title of chief, Carver made use of this incident to impress the minds of his hearers. "You may remember," he said, "the day when we were encamped at *Wadepaw Minesoter*, the black clouds, the wind, the fire, the stupendous noise, the horrible cracks, and the trembling of the earth, which then alarmed you and gave you reason to think your gods were angry with you; not unlike these are the warlike implements of the English when they are fighting the battles of their great King."

At this council the gift of land was supposed to have been agreed upon which made Carver and his heirs owners of a large tract of land on the Upper Mississippi, and over which there has since been much litigation; but, as there was not sufficient proof of such a grant having been made; as Carver himself does not mention it in his writings, and as the King had made a proclamation three years before forbidding private individuals to buy or accept land from the Indians, the court having the case in hand settled it by resolving "that the prayer of the petitioners be not granted." The cave in which the meeting took place is now known as "Carver's Cave."

Disappointed in not finding his supplies at the Falls, and obliged to abandon further exploration, Carver left his Sioux friends and started down the river for Prairie du Chien. On the way he was surprised by a party of Chippewas, and, fearing it might be the same which had attempted to plunder him some time before, he was inclined to avoid them; but he knew the Indians too well to show such a disposition, and finally crossed the river to their camp. A few of the savages came down to the shore to meet him, extending their hands in welcome; but back of them stood their chief, a tall fellow, painted and tattooed, who fiercely watched the strangers. Carver, determined not to betray any signs of awe, approached this august personage and extended his hand. The chief withheld his, and, scowling down upon the white men, said in Chippewa, "English no good." Carver did not like the way the Indian grasped his tomahawk, and said he expected the laconic sentence would be followed by a blow; but drawing his pistol from his belt, he carelessly played with it as he passed the chief, and in token of his fearlessness resolved to remain with the Indians that night.

Early in the morning he continued his way to Prairie du Chien, and having attended to his affairs there, re-ascended the river with the intention of reaching Mackinac by way of Lake Superior. Entering the Chippewa River, he crossed to a branch of the Saint Croix, descended it to the fork, and thence up another branch to the source. From here the boats were launched on a little brook, which, struggling along, was gradually increased by rivulets, and at last developed into a swift stream, and on they paddled to the great lake.

From Mackinac, Carver hurried eastward, reaching Boston in October, 1768, from whence he sailed for England. There he reported to the Government, asking for reimbursements and the privilege of disposing of his manuscripts. The last petition was granted, but the explorer was afterward requested to deliver up all of his papers. This obliged him to buy back his manuscript at an advance, but no compensation was made him. He then obtained a position of clerk in a lottery office, but reverses overtook him, and finally, at the age of forty-eight, he died of want in the heart of the great metropolis.

With him ends the long line of the early explorers of the Great River. Each, looking upon the splendid stream and the valley it enriched, had prophesied; but none so well as this last, who said "There is no doubt but that, at some future period, mighty kingdoms will emerge from these wildernesses, and stately palaces and solemn temples, with gilded spires reaching to the skies, supplant the Indian huts, whose only decorations are the barbarous trophies of their vanquished enemies."

EXPLORERS OF THE UPPER MISSISSIPPI.

PART SECOND.

———:o:———

EXPLORATION

OF THE

Upper Mississippi.

———:o:———

SUBJECTS:

WINTER QUARTERS ON THE UPPER MISSISSIPPI.

CHAPTER I.

EXPEDITIONS OF LIEUTENANT PIKE.

ZEBULON MONTGOMERY PIKE was the son of a captain in the Revolutionary army, and was the first of the more recent explorers of the Mississippi and the country bordering upon it. He was born January fifth, 1779, at Lambertville, New Jersey, a village near the Delaware River, but received his education at Easton, Pennsylvania, whither the family had previously removed. At the age of twenty he became an ensign in his father's regiment, and in 1806 had attained the rank of captain.

After the purchase of Louisiana from the French in 1803, General Wilkinson was appointed by the United States Government to the military command of the Territory, with headquarters at Saint Louis. This immense acquisition embraced all the country between the Mississippi River and the Rocky Mountains, and from the Mexican dominions on the south to Canada on the north. A desire was soon felt by the Government and people to learn something of the new region, and an order was received by the general commanding to detach a competent officer for the work of exploration. Lieutenant Pike was selected for the undertaking and ordered to proceed up the Mississippi to its Headwaters, and, if practicable, trace it to its ultimate source.

Physically and mentally, Pike was well equipped for the work, and would probably have succeeded in his attempt to reach the head of the river if he had been better advised, before starting, of the difficulties he would have to encounter. He was eager for the work assigned him, and, with twenty men under his command, left Saint Louis, the capital of the newly-acquired Territory, August ninth, 1805, and commenced the ascent of the river. He labored under great disadvantages, which materially affected the results of his expedition. He was four months too late in the season to reach his destination, and was without an aide, or even a scientific observer He knew nothing of the climate of the region he was about to visit, and neither guide nor interpreter had been assigned him by the authorities. That he accomplished what he did is altogether owing to his energy, vigilance, and enterprise, his knowledge of hunting and forest life, and his habits of mental and military discipline. After great labor, many adventures, and some casualties, he reached a point one hundred and twenty miles north of Saint Anthony Falls, and here winter overtook him. The absence of all preparation against the intense cold resulted in much suffering and danger to life. To protect himself and his men, he devoted twelve days to the erection of a block-house as a temporary shelter, and after a short rest for recuperation, determined on resuming his journey up the river, which was covered with snow to a depth of several feet. Leaving a small detachment

PIKE EXPLORING ON SNOW-SHOES.

of his disabled men and his boats in charge of a non-commissioned officer at the block-house, he set forth on roughly constructed snow-shoes, with small hand-sledges, and, by great energy and perseverance, reached, at successive periods, Sandy Lake, Leech Lake, and ultimately advanced as far north as Upper Red Cedar Lake, now known as Cass Lake, an expansion of the Mississippi, in latitude 47° 42′ 30″ The whole region was covered with a mantle of snow. Here he met some straggling members of the Northwest Fur Company, of Montreal, who welcomed the explorer to their winter quarters, and extended to the party the usual hospitality to travelers.

Pike explained that the object of his visit was to discover the Source of the Mississippi, and was informed by the fur traders that the extreme Head of the river was in Turtle Lake, in confirmation of which they produced a roughly-sketched map of the section. Believing that he had now accomplished the object of his mission, he made no further effort in that direction, but prepared for a speedy return to Saint Louis. Nine months had elapsed since leaving its genial climate for the frozen North, during which interval he and his party of sturdy soldiers had undergone much suffering from the rigor of the long-continued winter—intensified by the absence of preparation in the shape of warm clothing and a proper supply of food.

The narrative of the Pike expedition was not published until 1810, in which Turtle Lake is assumed to be the Source of the Great River, which, however, has been conclusively disproved by more recent explorers.

In 1806-7, Pike was again despatched by the Government on a geographical exploration over parts of the immense Territory of Louisiana, in the course of which he reached the front range of the Rocky Mountains, and discovered what is known as Pike's Peak, 14,336 feet in height above the sea, on the summit of which there is now a United States signal station. The headwaters of the Rio Grande River were also reached. He was here taken prisoner by the Spaniards for being found on Spanish territory, and conveyed to Santa Fé, now the capital of New Mexico, where all his papers were seized; but, after trial, he was released and ordered to leave the country. He reached Nachitoches, about twenty-five miles from the Texas line, July first, 1807, and received the thanks of the Government for his enterprise and successful labors. As a reward he was promoted from the rank of major, in the following year to that of lieutenant-colonel, and in 1812, to that of assistant quartermaster-general.

In 1813, Pike was appointed to the command of an expedition against York, Upper Canada. He reached York with the fleet conveying the troops for the attack. The general, with the main body, landed, and the enemy falling back before him, he captured the main redoubt and halted his men. While General Pike and many of his soldiers were resting on their arms, preparatory to an attack on the next redoubt, the magazine of the fort exploded, and, being fatally injured, he survived but a few hours. He died April twenty-seventh, 1813, and bears the reputation of a brave and zealous officer.

CHAPTER II.

THE CASS EXPEDITION.

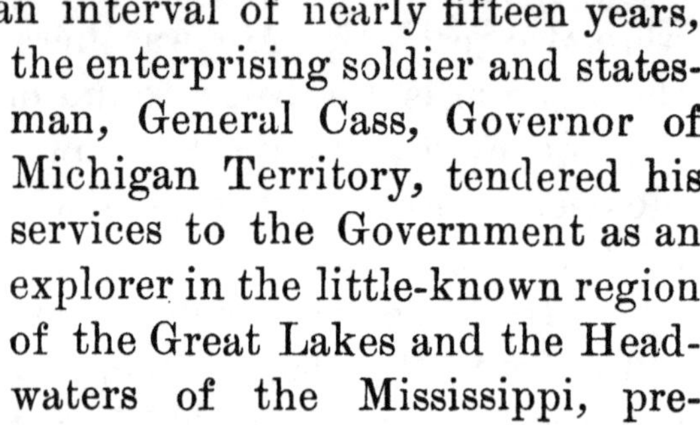

AFTER an interval of nearly fifteen years, the enterprising soldier and statesman, General Cass, Governor of Michigan Territory, tendered his services to the Government as an explorer in the little-known region of the Great Lakes and the Headwaters of the Mississippi, previously visited by Pike.

Lewis Cass was born in Exeter, New Hampshire, October ninth, 1782. He was the eldest son of Jonathan Cass, a captain in the Continental Army during the War of the Revolution. On the conclusion of peace with England, he was promoted to the rank of major and assigned to General Wayne's command, then in the territory northwest of the Ohio. Lewis remained with the family in Exeter and attended the academy. Major Cass, in 1799, removed his family to Wilmington, Delaware, in which town Lewis became a successful school-teacher.

The following year found the major and his family on their way to the West. They descended the Ohio from Pittsburg in a flat-boat, and traveled on foot for many miles. They reached Marietta, the pioneer town of Southern Ohio, in October, 1800, and near here the family settled upon a tract of land granted Major Cass by the Government in consideration of his military service. The site was on Muskingum River, near Zanesville. Lewis, however, remained at Marietta and studied law in the office of Governor Meigs. He was admitted to the bar in 1803, and began practice in Zanesville. He married Elizabeth Spencer, of Virginia, in 1806, and shortly after became a member of the Ohio Legislature.

The supposed treasonable movements of Aaron Burr were at this period a source of uneasiness to the Government, and Lewis Cass, being on the committee appointed by the local Legislature to inquire into Burr's proceedings, framed a law authorizing the authorities to arrest the men and capture the material provided for their expedition down the Ohio. He also drew up an official communication to the President, expressing the views of the Ohio Legislature on the subject of Burr's designs and movements. President Jefferson's attention was attracted to this able document, and he appointed the author marshal of the State.

On the breaking out of the second war with England, in 1812, Cass joined the forces at Dayton under the command of General Hull, with the rank of colonel of the Third Ohio Volunteers, proceeding at once to Detroit. When the army crossed the Detroit River into Canada, Colonel Cass was in command of the advance guard, and drove in the British outposts. Shortly after this, General Hull surrendered to the enemy, and Cass was included in the capitulation and paroled. He forthwith proceeded to Washington and reported the surrender to the Government. He was soon exchanged as a prisoner on parole, and was at once appointed to the Twenty-seventh Regiment of Infantry, and, shortly afterward, promoted to the rank of brigadier-general.

At the close of the campaign, General Cass was placed in command of the Territory of Michigan, with headquarters at Detroit. He also received the appointment of Civil Governor of the Territory.

In 1814, Governor Cass, associated with General Harrison, was authorized to treat with the Indians of Michigan, who had been hostile to the United States during the war. The greater part of Michigan was at this period a vast wilderness, inhabited by about fifty thousand savage Indians. No surveys had been made and no roads had been opened, the Indians being relentless in their hostility to any encroachment of the whites, who numbered only some five or six thousand, inclusive of the settlers in Detroit. Under these discouraging circumstances, Cass assumed the responsibilities of Governor and Superintendent of Indian affairs in the Territory.

The Northwestern Territory was, up to this period, imperfectly known, and, at the suggestion of Governor Cass, an expedition was organized in 1820, in which he himself bore a conspicuous part. Accompanied by Schoolcraft, the geologist and ethnologist, and six other gentlemen, with Indian guides, they embarked on the twenty-fourth of May, at Detroit, in three large canoes, for the exploration of the Great Lakes and the Headwaters of the Mississippi. The nearest approach they made to the Source of the Great River was at Upper Cedar Lake, subsequently named Cass Lake, about two hundred miles to the north of the lake now recognized as the True Head. Before returning to Detroit, the expedition had traversed five thousand miles of the Northwestern country.

General Cass was appointed Secretary of War by

CASS EXPEDITION LEAVING DETROIT

President Jackson in 1831, and during his incumbency the Black Hawk War occurred. In 1836, he submitted an elaborate report to Congress upon the military defenses of the United States, and shortly after resigned his secretaryship and was appointed United States minister to France. In January, 1845, he was elected a member of the United States Senate, and was subsequently re-elected for a second term. He was a prominent candidate for the Presidency, but was unsuccessful. In Mr Buchanan's administration he became Secretary of State. During the Civil War his sympathies were with the North, and his life was spared to witness the ultimate triumph of the Government over a rebellion that for a time threatened its existence.

General Cass was a scholar of fine attainments and a prudent and cautious legislator. He was also personally popular throughout the country. He published several works, among them, "Inquiries Concerning the History, Traditions, and Languages of the Indians Living within the United States," and "France, Its King, Court, and Government." He died at Detroit, January seventeenth, 1866, at the age of eighty-four.

CHAPTER III.

BELTRAMI AND THE "JULIAN SOURCE."

GIACOMO Constantino Beltrami, a native of Bergamo, in the Republic of Venice, son of Giambattista and Catterina Beltrami, was born in 1779, the youngest of ten children. His father held an influential position as Chief of the Customs of the Republic, and the youngest son was educated for the law At the age of twenty-eight he was appointed judge of the Court at Udine. By untiring zeal he gained the approbation of the Government, and was promoted to the office of judge of the Civil and Criminal Court. The extraordinary energy and capacity shown by him in certain important matters of state led the Minister of Justice to write and compliment him on his success, at the same time predicting his elevation to the President's chair of the Court, for which he had already been proposed to the French Emperor. This promise, however, was never realized, the Empire having met with severe reverses which crippled its exercise of authority over the foreign states annexed to France. In some way it was, moreover, strongly suspected that Beltrami had become involved in the political schemes of the Carbonari—a powerful secret society pervading Europe—whose aim was the destruction of the Empire and the deposition of all despots. In deference to the French, he was ordered into exile without trial. This was in 1821.

Beltrami had a passion for the acquisition of languages, both ancient and modern, and while still young had become familiar with Latin and Greek literature, and also with several modern languages. Frank and faithful in his intercourse with men, he was an enemy to all kinds of flattery and obsequiousness, and was, at the same time, capable of great self-denial for the sake of principle. He was well known to be a patriot, and had suffered persecution, ending in expatriation, to which latter he submitted without complaint, but loving his country none the less.

On quitting his native land, he traveled through France, England, and Germany, and made many friends among the *literati* of the continent, and, in 1822, crossed the ocean to the United States. At this period he was about forty-four years of age.

Finding himself now in the New World, with whose history he was entirely familiar, parts of which, he soon learned, were still little known to the inhabitants, his mind turned to travel and exploration. The Valley of the Mississippi was a point of great interest to him, and, desiring to know more concerning it than he could gather from books, he proceeded to Pittsburg, descended the Ohio River in company with Major Talioferra—a fellow-countryman long settled in America, an officer in the United States army, and agent for Indian affairs on the Upper Mississippi—and embarked with him for Fort Snelling, Minnesota, which they reached May twentieth, 1823. It was his wish to accompany Major Talioferra up the River Saint Peter, at that time unexplored, with the intention of proceeding farther toward the Head-waters of the Mississippi. "Major Talioferra," says Beltrami, in 'A Pilgrimage in Europe and America,' "had led me to entertain the hope that we should have proceeded together up the River Saint Peter, which has never yet been explored, the source of which is occupied by the most wild and powerful tribes of Sioux, and, as yet, only vaguely defined, while the surrounding territory abounds in buffalo. It was my intention to proceed thence to the sources of the Mississippi, which are still absolutely unknown.

"Thwarted in my project, I was on the point of changing my direction for the south, intending to traverse by land, with a Canadian interpreter and an Indian guide, the desert tracts which separate Fort Snelling from Council Bluffs. But at this period, Major Long, of the United States Topographical Engineers, arrived at the Fort, charged with an expedition to the northern boundary of the vast empire of the United States. I participated in the very great surprise manifested by the Fort at the arrival of an expedition so completely unknown to the garrison."

Beltrami's great desire of pushing his rambles farther north was mentioned to Major Long, and the former asked permission to accompany the expedition simply in the character of a foreigner who was anxious to see the country and to study the Indian character. An attempt was made to dissuade him from this. The sufferings and dangers he would have to encounter were set before him, but at these he simply laughed as childish terrors. Continuing he says: "They next attacked me on what they thought my weak side—my purse. After so long a digression from my original route, which was to lead me direct from Philadelphia to New Orleans, it might reasonably be supposed to be rather in a declining state; the more so, as the curiosities I had bought of the savages had greatly contributed to diminish its contents. But a little fund which I kept in reserve disconcerted this attack also. I even sacrificed my beautiful repeater, that I might leave this still untouched, and bought a horse, and all provisions that were said to be necessary, with the proceeds. When they saw I was determined to go, the amiable Snelling family carried their politeness so far as to offer me pecuniary assistance, with the most honorable and disinterested confidence, a thing by no means common, especially toward a person of whom they knew nothing but what they had seen."

The expedition of Major Long consisted of himself as chief, an astronomer, a mineralogist, a physician, a zoölogist, an artist, an interpreter for the Sioux, a young Canadian interpreter for the Algonquin language, twenty-eight troopers, one officer, and Mr Snelling, son of Colonel Snelling, commandant of the Fort.

"So many imaginary difficulties," says Beltrami, "were not auspicious. I foresaw all the vexations I should have to experience. * * * My intention of going in search of the real sources of the Mississippi was always before my eyes. I was therefore obliged to sacrifice my pride, and my feeling of what was due to me, to the desire of seeing places which one can hardly expect to visit twice in one's life, and of gaining information one can gain nowhere else; and I gave myself up to all I foresaw I should have to endure from littleness and jealousy."

Beltrami was possessed of a restless and adventurous spirit, and accordingly made his arrangements, despite all discouragement, to accompany Major Long's expedition through Northern Minnesota to Pembina, on the Red River of the North. They left Fort Snelling on the evening of July seventh, 1822. The expedition was divided into two bodies, one of which went by land with twenty horses, the other embarked in five Indian canoes on the River Saint Peter. "The Major traveled by canoe," says Beltrami, "and I followed him, with the intention of going sometimes by water and sometimes by land according to the curious or interesting objects either route might offer." It was arranged that the two divisions should meet every evening.

The first evening the entire party encamped on the southern bank of the Saint Peter, near the village of the chief, Black Dog, which Beltrami visited, but found vacant. "Hunger had roused these savages," he says, "from their habitual indolence, and had driven them away to hunt deer and buffalo in more distant forests and prairies. A hut, which was shut and which I opened, afforded me some shelter from the mosquitoes, which attacked me on every side. Behind the door I found, hung like a curtain, a deer-skin, which the savages doubtless looked upon as the guardian *manitou* of their dwelling. * * * We dined at the Prairie des François, so called from the first Frenchmen who pushed their discoveries from Canada to this spot, where they were all killed by the Indians." Proceeding up the Saint Peter, when sixty miles from the Fort the travelers by canoe encountered a violent rapid, and were compelled to disembark and drag their canoes through the water. It is described as a most romantic spot. "Rocks, picturesquely grouped, between which the winding stream rushes and breaks with violence; a little woody island in the middle; banks clothed with stately trees on the one side, and broken into steep and rugged rocks on the other, composed a varied and interesting picture, to which I contrived to add a touch of the grotesque. Being obliged to get on board the canoe to cross a deep gulf, my sailors were so deficient, either in strength or in skill, that they suffered it to be carried away and dashed in pieces against a rock, upon which I remained perched."

In the evening the expedition halted at an Indian encampment, and Beltrami, always observant, witnessed what he calls a most curious contrast. "A woman in the deepest affliction was tearing off her hair, which she offered as a sacrifice to the spirit of some dead relative, whose lifeless remains were stretched upon a rude scaffold, while a group of savages were eating, drinking, singing, and dancing around another dead body, exposed in the same manner to the view of passers-by."

July thirteenth they all proceeded by land. One of the interpreters pointed out the direction in which the Blue Earth River falls into the Saint Peter. "This was the highest point of the Saint Peter reached by Father Hennepin. The Blue Earth River is very celebrated among the Indians. They perform an annual pilgrimage to it to collect the blue earth off its banks, of which they make dye and paint."

Lake Traverse was reached July twenty-fourth—two hundred and eighty miles north-northwest of Fort Snelling. It is on one of the highest plateaus of North America. "It has no tributary streams,"

Beltrami asserts, "and no one knows whence it derives its waters." Its length is about eighteen miles and its width about four miles.

The party took leave of Lake Traverse with a salute of musketry The country around was all prairie, and the buffaloes appeared for the first time in large numbers, one of which was shot by Beltrami.

On July thirty-first, the expedition reached the Red River, which descends from the eastward through a lake of the same name. To quote Beltrami· "Geographers tell us that it takes its appellation from the red sand or gravel which covers its bed; but there is nothing red about it. The origin of its name is widely different. The river and the lake form the frontier line which separates the territory of the Sioux from that of the Chippewas. It may be easily imagined that the waters of a stream so situated must have often been 'red with the blood of the slain,' and that it has thus received from both the contending parties the name of the Bloody River. The lake is in like manner called the Bloody or Red Lake."

On August third the expedition arrived at the celebrated colony of Pembina, founded by the Earl of Selkirk—two hundred and sixty miles from Lake Traverse.

Altogether dissatisfied with his surroundings, Beltrami left the colony on the ninth in company with an interpreter and two Chippewas. He traveled in a southeasterly direction, and on the fourth day killed two white bears. "The white bear," he asserts, "is the only wild beast of these regions that is dangerous. He always attacks the traveler. The black bear is timid, and, on the approach of man, betakes himself to flight. He feeds entirely on fruits during summer and autumn. When the cold weather commences he hides himself in the hollow of some tree or in a hole he digs for himself in the earth. Here he remains completely motionless for the whole winter."

On the fifth day out from Pembina, still proceeding in a southeasterly direction, Beltrami and his companions arrived at Robber's River, which, he explains, was so named because a Sioux, in his flight from the vengeance which had been pronounced against him for murder, kept himself concealed, and robbed on this spot for several years, escaping the observation of his persecutors and enemies, by whom he was surrounded.

The interpreter was compelled to leave him here, and he was therefore alone with the two Indians. These also shortly left, to proceed to their destinations. This occurred on August fifteenth. After encountering many difficulties and dangers, pulling his canoe up the stream—as he was unable to handle the paddle with the dexterity required—he met, on the morning of the eighteenth, two canoes filled with Indians, including women and children, and persuaded one of the men to accompany him as far as Red Lake. On reaching the lake, another interpreter joined him—the son of a Canadian fur trader and an Indian woman. His hut was twelve miles distant, which they reached on the twenty-first.

Having rested a few days with the Canadian, Beltrami left Red Lake on the morning of the twenty-sixth, in the direction of Great Portage River. This stream, he says, is so called by the Indians because a dreadful storm that occurred on it blew down a vast

BELTRAMI SURPRISED BY INDIANS.

number of forest trees on its banks, which perfectly obstructed its channel, and so impeded its navigation by canoes as to make an extensive, or "great portage," necessary. This impediment, however, does not appear to have existed at the time of Beltrami's visit, as he embarked in his canoe and proceeded up its current. He crossed two lakes formed by the river in its course, each about five or six miles in circumference. To these lakes he gave the name of the Lakes of Wild Rice. After proceeding five or six miles farther—always in a southerly direction—he entered a large lake, or expansion of the river, with a circumference of twenty miles. This lake, he states, is situated at a very short distance from high lands, which divide the waters flowing northward from those which take a southerly direction. He at length reached the source of the Red River, which, he says, "springs out of the ground in the middle of a small prairie." * * * "A small hill overhangs the source, and I am now," he exclaims, "on the highest land of North America. Casting my eye around, I perceive the flow of waters—to the south toward the Gulf of Mexico; to the north toward the Frozen Sea; on the east to the Atlantic, and on the west toward the Pacific Ocean. A platform crowns this supreme elevation, and, what is still more astonishing, in the midst of it rises a lake. The source of the Red River is at the foot of the hill, and filtrates in a direct line from the north bank of the lake. On the other side of the hill, toward the south, and equally at the foot of the hill, other sources form a beautiful little basin about eighty feet in circumference. These waters filtrate from the lake on the top of the hill toward its southwestern extremity. These sources are the actual sources of the Mississippi. This lake, therefore, supplies the most southern source of Red or Bloody River, and the most northern source of the Mississippi—sources until now unknown. The small lake has no surface issue and no inlet. Its waters boil up in the middle. All my sounding lines have been insufficient to ascertain its depth. The lake is about three miles round. It is formed in the shape of a heart. I have given it the name of a respected lady, and have called it Lake Julia; and the sources of the two rivers, the Julian source of the Red River, and the Julian source of the Mississippi—which, in the Algonquin language, means *Father of Waters.*

"The Julian source of the Mississippi runs directly south by a narrow stream of three miles' length into Turtle Lake. If I had not been afraid of adventuring my canoe amidst the almost impassable brambles and brushwood, I should have commenced the navigation of the river from the very spot on which it springs. The famous Mississippi, whose course is said to be three thousand miles, and which bears navies on its bosom, and steamboats superior in size to frigates, is, at its source, merely a petty stream of crystalline water, concealing itself among reeds and wild rice, which seem to exult over its humble birth."

Beltrami did not visit Lake Itasca. He says it was called by the Indians "Biche Lake," from the French Lac la Biche or Elk Lake. This lake, he asserts on the authority of others, is the western source of the Mississippi.

We may here observe that the Lake Julia of Beltrami is not recognized by geographers as possessing any valid or reasonable title to be considered the Source of the Mississippi. The stream flowing from it is merely an affluent of the Great River, entering it over three hundred miles below Lake Itasca. It was shown by Schoolcraft that Lake Itasca was at least one hundred miles more distant from the mouth of the Mississippi than Lake Julia. Beltrami's enthusiasm led him into an error which is not surprising, as little or nothing was known of the region he traversed, at the period of his journey south from Pembina. In common with Pike, Cass, Schoolcraft, Nicollet, and others, he fully believed in his alleged discovery, which more modern investigation, however, has disproved.

On his return, travel-worn, from the Upper Mississippi, in the autumn of 1824, he decided to visit New Orleans, in which city he remained for a time, preparing an account of his travels and discoveries for the press. From New Orleans he embarked for Mexico, and traversed that country from east to west, after which he returned to the United States and proceeded to Philadelphia. Here arrangements were made for the publication of his book. Returning to England shortly after, his other works were given to the press in London.

The last years of the life of Beltrami were spent on his estate in Italy, surrounded by friends. His height was six feet, and it is said he was proud of bearing, high-spirited, but always the gentleman. His death occurred in February, 1855, at the age of seventy-five years.

CHAPTER IV.

SCHOOLCRAFT AND LAKE ITASCA.

HENRY ROWE SCHOOLCRAFT, who succeeded General Cass in Mississippi exploration, was born in Albany County, New York, March twenty eighth, 1793, during the second presidential term of Washington. His great-grandfather on the paternal side was James Calcraft, an Englishman, who, in the reign of George II., embarked with a detachment of troops intended to act against the French in Canada.

At the conclusion of the campaign he remained in America, settled in Albany County, and for many years conducted a school in this settlement. For some unknown reason he changed his family name from Calcraft to Schoolcraft, by which he was known for some time before his death, which took place at the great age of one hundred and two years. His son Lawrence was the father of Henry, whose youth was spent in the village of Hamilton, about thirty miles from Utica. As a boy he showed an inclination for study, and while at Middlebury College he gave much attention to the various branches of science, more especially chemistry, mineralogy, geology, and ethnology.

In 1817, at the age of twenty-four, he was led by a spirit of enterprise to the Valley of the Mississippi, traveling through Missouri and Arkansas. During this journey he collected a large number of geological and mineralogical specimens. In 1819 he published a work on the mines and mineral resources of Missouri, and proceeded to Washington, where he was favorably received by President Monroe, and by Calhoun and Crawford, members of the Cabinet.

Secretary Calhoun, who was struck by the earnestness of his views and scientific attainments, offered him the situation of geologist and mineralogist to an exploring expedition which the War Department was about to dispatch to the Headwaters of the Mississippi River under the leadership of General Cass.

The point of embarkation of this expedition was at Detroit, where the Indian canoes were secured which were to be the chosen conveyances.

At four o'clock on the afternoon of the twenty-fourth of May, 1820, the small fleet was in readiness, and in the midst of an interested assemblage the *voyageurs,* with a swift stroke of their paddles, pushed away from shore, chanting one of their animated boat songs.

From Lake Saint Clair the expedition moved along the southern shore of Lakes Huron and Superior, up the Saint Louis River, and by the Savannah to the Mississippi, which was ascended as far as Upper Red Cedar Lake, named by Schoolcraft, in honor of their leader, "Cassina," and which, he says in 1820, "may be considered the true source of the Mississippi River, although the greatest body of water is said to come down the Leech Lake Branch."

One night was spent on the shore of Cass Lake, and, as it was impracticable, at that season of the year, to go farther, preparations were made to embark before daylight the next morning, the twenty-second of July—the very day on which, sixty-one years later, my exploring party stood upon the solitary shores of the lake beyond Itasca, and knew it to be indeed the *True* Source of the Great River.

From Cass Lake the party descended the river to the Wisconsin, where Schoolcraft obtained permission from the Governor to go down to the lead mines of Dubuque. Rejoining his companions, the journey was commenced to Green Bay, where the party separated, the Governor and his escort going on to Detroit, while a detachment under Captain Douglas went around Lake Michigan to make a topographical survey. The information obtained by this expedition concerning the condition of the Indians, the natural history and mineralogy of the region along the Upper Lakes made a valuable addition to the popular knowledge of the Northwestern frontier, while, with the treaty concluded at the Sault, the safety of the country was made much more secure.

Again, in 1830, Schoolcraft was commissioned to lead an expedition into the Upper Mississippi Valley to attempt a reconciliation between the Sioux and Chippewas, who had renewed their old hostilities; but these instructions did not reach him at the Sault until August, and he reported that it was then too late to undertake such an enterprise, as the Indians would have gone to their hunting-grounds, and a return would be prevented by the frozen streams. The following year these instructions were repeated, and arrangements for it were completed at Saint Mary's. A geologist and botanist accompanied the expedition, and the small body of military were under the command of Lieutenant Robert E. Clary.

At this time Schoolcraft crossed the "lead mine"

country, carefully following trails, intercepting war parties, and enforcing the peace policy of the Government. It was evident that measures should immediately be taken to quell the discontent rising among the different tribes, and a report to this effect was sent to Washington. Mr. Calhoun, Secretary of War, approved of this suggestion, and Schoolcraft was again put in charge of an expedition which was to ascertain the condition and sentiment of the tribes of the Upper Mississippi.

A small body of infantry, commanded by Lieutenant James Allen, escorted the party, and a representative of the American Board of Commissioners for Foreign Missions joined the expedition to discover the needs of the Indians of the region.

From Saint Mary's the same course was followed as in the expedition of 1820. At Sandy Lake a council of the lower tribes was called and an appointment made to meet them again at the River Des Corbeau, and having sent a boat laden with presents and supplies down the Mississippi to await his return, Schoolcraft went on to Cass Lake, from which point he intended to prosecute his explorations about the Head of the Mississippi, which he had learned, since the expedition of 1820, was to be found beyond Cass Lake.

On one of the larger islands of this lake, called Grand Island, there was a Chippewa settlement, of which Ozawindib was chief; and, as the place was favorable for a camp, most of the men were left here in charge of an officer, while the explorers of the party, embarked in light canoes and proceeded in search of the "source" of the river. Ozawindib volunteered to guide the party.

Passing westward from Cass Lake the chief brought

the party to the junction of the East and West forks of the river, but instead of following the larger stream which leads directly to Lake Itasca he pushed his canoe into the milder current of the East Fork, and down this the voyagers paddled.

A miserable night was spent on the low shore of this stream and a day of hard paddling followed, incidents which can only be appreciated by those who have had similar experiences.

The region, rich in game, kept the men supplied, and a deer was killed beyond Lake Plantagenet; "but we were impelled forward by higher objects than hunting," writes Schoolcraft, and adds: "It was, indeed, geographical and scientific facts that we were hunting for. To trace to its source an important river, and to fix the actual point of its origin, furnished the mental stimulus which led us to care but little where we slept or what we ate."

On the thirteenth of June the source of the East Fork was reached. From here the portage was commenced over the highlands which surround the remoter lakes. The journey now became more difficult. An Indian trail was found with the usual signs of camps along its route.

Just below the highlands breakfast was prepared, as the men had not broken their fast since starting upon the trail at dawn, yet in their eagerness to move forward the journey was soon resumed and the laborious tramp through thicket and marsh begun.

With a canoe on his back, Ozawindib led the way, the voyageurs and members of the expedition following. Gradually the ground began to rise, the underbrush became less dense, and Ozawindib, throwing the canoe from his shoulders, sat down and lit his pipe in token that the first "Onwaybee," or rest, was reached. At the summit of the last hill, Schoolcraft, who had been keeping close at the chief's heels, ran ahead of him, and, as he says, "got the first glimpse of the glittering nymph we had been pursuing."

As there was no time to lose, owing to the pressing engagement made by Schoolcraft to meet Indians in council on the twenty-fourth of July, at the mouth of Crow Wing River, a small fire was at once made on the beach for the Indians to melt their pitch and repair the canoes. This done, all re-embarked and paddled for an island in the center of the lake which they had now entered. This island has since been named after Schoolcraft.

Twenty-eight years before, the fur trader, William Morrison, had built his cabin on this island, but at that time the question of the Source of the river had not assumed any especial importance, being generally understood to lie somewhere among the upper lakes. When, therefore, his successor made known the importance of this "glittering nymph," which he had named Itasca, he was given the credit of its discovery, since Morrison, either from neglect or indifference, had made no mention of it. Schoolcraft's own description of the lake as he saw it at this memorable time, is most graphic "There was not a breath of wind. We often rested to behold the scene. It is not a lake overhung by rocks. Not a precipice is in sight, or a stone, save the pebbles and boulders of the drift era which are scattered on the beach. The water-fowl, whom we disturbed in their seclusion, seemed rather loath to fly up. At one point we observed a deer standing in the water and stooping down, apparently to eat the moss."

From Photograph by F J. Trost.

SOUTHERN END OF LAKE ITASCA.

Itasca is indeed a most beautiful and tranquil sheet of water, and characteristically different from the lake beyond, which impresses the beholder, not with its tranquillity, but with a certain wild and rugged solitude, perhaps more imposing to a lover of sterner aspects.

At their island camp the travelers busied themselves with their different occupations; Schoolcraft studying the geology, the botanist examining the plants, while Lieutenant Allen made a rough map of the lake. Having faith in the descriptions of his guide, the explorer believed that an arm of the lake stretched southward, receiving a small brook at its extremity, but owing to the limitation of time, and to an apparent reliance upon Ozawindib as a topographer, no attempt was made to verify this fact or even to coast the shores. Before tents were struck in the afternoon, Schoolcraft directed a flag to be hoisted, and having made a cursory examination, the party embarked and proceeded down the West Fork of the river, en route to Cass Lake.

Here Ozawindib was dismissed, and the original party left in camp on Grand Island, joined the expedition. Having returned to Leech Lake, Flat-Mouth entertained them, and at the council which Schoolcraft called there, represented the warriors of his tribe.

In the course of his remarks this formidable Chippewa handed the "White Chief" a bundle of forty-three small sticks. "This is the number of Leech Lake Chippewas killed by the Sioux since the treaty of Prairie-du-Chien," then, lifting up a string of silver medals, smeared with vermilion, he continued, "Take notice, they are bloody. I wish you to wipe the blood off, I can not do it. I find myself in a war with this people, and I believe it has been intended by the Creator that we should be at war with them. My warriors are brave; it is to them that I owe success."

This speech evinced the feelings of the Indians at the time of Schoolcraft's visit to the Headwaters of the Mississippi. The explorer himself alludes with evident forebodings to the uprising under Black Hawk on Rock River, and found it necessary to make as imposing a display as possible of the small force with him. Several days later the rendezvous at the mouth of Crow Wing River was reached, the council held, and the usual policy observed.

In 1832 Schoolcraft was appointed Indian Agent for the tribes of the Lake Region, and established his headquarters at Mackinaw, where the following year he married the grand-daughter of a noted Ojibway chief, who had received her education in Europe. At the time of his journey to Lake Itasca he was a member of the Michigan Legislature, and was subsequently made Assistant Superintendent of Indian Affairs. In 1845, he was designated, by the New York Legislature, a commissioner to take the census of the Indians in the State, and collect information concerning the Six Nations, and having performed this task to the satisfaction of the authorities, he was authorized by Congress to obtain reports relating to all the Indian tribes of the country and to collate and edit the results of his labors. The remaining years of his life were spent in this work. He was elected a member of several scientific societies in this country and Europe; the degree of LL. D. being conferred on him by the University of Geneva. Ho is the author of thirty-one works treating of various branches of science in connection with his extended explorations through various sections of the country. He is also the author of several poems of merit, lectures, and numerous reports on Indian subjects.

In 1852 his Indian wife died, and five years later he married Miss Mary Howard of Beaufort, South Carolina; a highly educated and accomplished woman, who became his assistant and amanuensis during the preparation of his last work when he was helpless with paralysis.

The early period at which Schoolcraft entered the field of observation as a naturalist, the enterprise and interest he manifested from the outset in the geology and geography of the Great West, and his subsequent researches as an ethnologist in investigating the Indian languages and history, entitle him to the highest consideration. No explorer has done more than he to enlighten the nation on matters of the greatest importance connected especially with the Great Lakes and the Mississippi Valley. He was an example of what talent and zeal united with energy of character may accomplish in the cause of letters and science by the mere force of application, without the advantages of hereditary wealth, the impulse of patronage, or the prestige of early academical honors.

We are indebted to him for our first accounts of the mineral wealth of the great valley beyond the Alleghenies, and he approached more nearly to the True Source of the Great River of North America than any of his predecessors. His error in supposing that he had reached the Source of the Mississippi can not be placed to his discredit, as circumstances beyond his control prevented the consummation of his efforts. He pursued the stream to the points at which it had been explored in 1805 by Lieutenant Pike, and in 1820 by General Cass, and reached Lake Itasca, July twenty-first, 1832. In the following year he published the account of his discovery

In 1841, he removed from his Northwestern residence at the Sault, to the city of New York, and in the following year visited England, France, Germany, Prussia, Belgium, and Holland.

Twenty years were still left him in which to enjoy the deserved appreciation of his labors and the benefits of his wide travels. He died in Washington, December tenth, 1864, at a time when the capital was in a ferment over the Civil War; but his personality was not lost in the nation's sorrow, for as long as the great North American River has a history, the discoverer of Itasca will not be forgotten.

SCHOOLCRAFT ISLAND.

CHAPTER V.

INVESTIGATIONS OF NICOLLET.

IN his own country this scholarly explorer left some trace of his abilities; yet only such as would make him known in the circle in which he moved—the circle of the scholar and the man of science. At Chises, in Savoy, where he was born in 1786, Nicollet began life as a farmer boy, working in the fields and leading the cows to pasture; but the turning point came when, at twelve years, he commenced to read. From this time he made such rapid progress, that he soon entered the college of his native place, finishing his course there with such success that he was able at its completion to take the assistant professorship of mathematics at Chambery.

From here he went to the French capital with a recommendation to Tochon and Bouvart, two noted savants; and was soon in his favorite element studying astronomy with Laplace, and acting as secretary and librarian of the Royal Observatory.

With quick advancement, this position was soon exchanged for an appointment in the Bureau of Longitudes and a professorship of mathematics in the College of Louis le Grand; while he held at the same time the post of examiner of candidates for the Naval School. In 1825 he received the Cross of the Legion of Honor. Unfortunately, soon after this, Professor

Nicollet was seized with a desire for riches, and beginning to speculate on a small scale with satisfactory results, he finally risked all; only to find himself, after the revolution of 1830, involved in the general ruin.

All France was at this time in a ferment; Paris was the theatre of action; and the outbreak of July caused a fall in the public funds which threatened disaster to more than one fortune.

Through these events Nicollet was driven back to his accustomed labors, wiser for the bitter experience. It is only necessary to follow his life to this point to discover the spirit which led him, in December, 1831, to come to America for the purpose of contributing to the progressive increase of knowledge in its physical geography. His predecessors had, with a few exceptions, been led to make their journeys either to gratify a love of adventure or to satisfy a natural curiosity; but he dignified his explorations by making them in the name of science.

His plan was to explore the Allegheny range "in its various extensions through the Southern States," to ascend the Red and Arkansas rivers and the Missouri part way, and to explore the Mississippi River "from its mouth to its very source."

After devoting five years to the carrying out of this plan, Nicollet returned to Baltimore. His work was not unknown to Government, and he soon received a notice from the War Department to go to Washington that arrangements might be made for an expedition to the country lying about the Headwaters of the Mississippi, which would enable him to complete his map of that region, and Lieutenant Fremont, of the

Corps of Topographical Engineers had been engaged to accompany him.

The Coteau des Prairies seems to be the point from which the explorer looked out upon the region embraced within the limits of his map, and indeed it commands a view of "the green turf that forms the basin of the Red River of the North, the forest-capped summits of the Hauteur des Terres that surround the source of the Mississippi, the granite valley of the Upper Saint Peter, and the depressions in which are Lake Traverse and the Big Stone Lake."

Passing up the Saint Peter, Nicollet left the main stream at the Sioux Portage, following this trail to the mouth of the Waraju, by which he ascended to the Shetek lakes and thence to the Coteau.

In going from the Shetek lakes to the Red Pipestone Quarry, the party came upon the ruins of ancient breastworks similar to those found by Carver on the Mississippi, and recalling again the pre-historic man who fought and lived in this "old, old land which men call new."

Upon nearing the quarry where the Indians from the surrounding nations come to get the favorite material for their pipes—a place believed by them to be under the control of the Great Spirit, who salutes the visitor with thunder and lightning, Nicollet and his party were overtaken by a heavy storm and were obliged to wait until it had passed over; but the explorer humorously remarks that the Great Spirit soon showed his good favor, for the sun came out again, and the journey was resumed. Camp was made on this "consecrated ground" and the travelers had the pleasure of watching at sunset the illumined bluffs which seemed like "the ruins of some ancient city built of marble and porphyry." Nicollet mentions, in describing this remarkable place, the customs observed by the Indians when they come for the pipestone. Some one of their number is selected to work at the quarry, and before the journey is made, this one must observe a three-days' purification. At the end of this time he and his companions start out for the coveted stone, and having reached the quarry, after offering gifts to the presiding deity, the man goes to work. He cuts into the rock wherever his judgment advises; but if he fails to select the most favorable spot he is discarded and another takes his place.

In speaking of the Cannon River which Nicollet explored, and which lies within his romantic "Undine Region" toward which the Saint Peter dips in its midway curve, he gives his reason for believing this stream identical with La Hontan's "Long River" and has therefore called it after that early explorer.

With amusing incidents he describes the characteristics of each waterway which he traversed, from Devil's Lake to the smallest tributary of the Mississippi.

Returning from the former on his way to the valley of the Red River he mentions the strange behavior of his Indian "Dixon" who generally kept ahead of the party as guide. He had a habit of making the signal to rest by sitting down and lighting his pipe while he waited for the others to come up, but invariably sat facing them. On one occasion, however, Nicollet, who was closely following him, noticed that he had stopped on the crest of a hill, sat down with his back to the others and without changing his position stolidly waited. Upon reaching the inexplicable savage he found him looking off in "ecstatic contemplation" over the magnificent valley of the Red River of the North. The party had known for some time that they must be near it, but were unprepared for this strange introduction.

Upon reaching Crow Wing River on his way to the "source" of the Mississippi, Nicollet determined to follow another course than that pursued successively by Pike, Cass, and Schoolcraft; he therefore went to Leech Lake by a route lying between the Crow Wing and the Mississippi.

The first three days of his stay at Leech Lake were far from pleasant. Flat-Mouth, head-chief of the Chippewas, and father of the chief of the same name who entertained my party in 1881, was absent at the time, and the missionary of the place, Rev. Mr. Boutwell, was detained by high winds on the opposite side of the lake. Nicollet afterward discovered that the annoyance from the Indians was due to their impression that he was poor, as he had very few presents for them, and this caused them to look upon him with contempt and even to threaten his life.

When Mr. Boutwell arrived peace was in a measure restored and a mutual sympathy sprang up between the two Frenchmen.

Mr. Boutwell had come to Leech Lake some time before to work among the "pillagers," a name given the Indians there by the Schoolcraft party, whose supplies they had molested, and of which they had since proudly boasted. Boutwell was a man of zeal and devotion and no doubt exerted a strong influence.

From Leech Lake, Nicollet started for the Headwaters of the river in a canoe, accompanied by his guide Brunet, Desiré, a *voyageur,* and a Chippewa called Kegwedzissag. He followed the course of the

Kabekonaug River, whose shores were so thickly wooded that in order to make a passage it was necessary to cut away the overhanging branches. This protection, with that of the hills on either side, have given its waters a very even temperature, so that Nicollet paddling through them in August was surprised to find that they had reached only 54°.

From this stream a portage was made to La Place River which was followed to its source, and here near Schoolcraft's old camp-ground, Nicollet made some astronomical observations although he was "assailed by torrents of mosquitoes," which three times extinguished the lights of his lanterns.

Notwithstanding the party was awake by four o'clock the next morning to make the final portage to Itasca, the march was not begun until half past six; but the leader of the expedition excuses this tardiness by referring to the heat and mosquitoes which is quite enough to elicit the sympathy of those who have felt the effect of this combination. When at last the signal was given, Brunet took up the canoe, Desiré and Kegwedzissag assumed their respective burdens, while Nicollet distributed about his person his instruments, cloak, gun, powder-flask, shot-bag, and a luxury seldom known to the explorer—his umbrella. "It will be readily conceived from this description of my equipment," he says, "that although the one least loaded, I was the most inconvenienced. * * * Necessity engrossed me with the safety of my instruments. I will confess it, my mind frequently became bewildered, so that twice during the portage I lost my way; twice I got bogged in marshes from which I extricated myself by walking over slippery and decayed trunks of trees; and twice I reproached myself with the rashness that had led me upon such a journey."

The six-mile portage which has proved so trying to the travelers who have chosen to reach Itasca by this route, took Nicollet five hours to cross, bringing him to the shore of the lake before noon, where he took a barometrical observation.

Passing down the southeast arm the party halted at Schoolcraft Island and pitched tents, while Nicollet fixed his artificial horizon for observations upon the stump of Schoolcraft's flag-pole raised there four years before. He then proceeded to explore the lake, noticing the creek entering the southeast arm and others entering the southwest arm, one of which—"Nicollet Creek"—he followed to its source in a pond which at that time was connected with two lower ponds by a small rivulet; and this stream he evidently considered the source of the Great River. He says in conclusion, "*After having devoted three days to an exploration of the sources of the Mississippi, and spent portions of the nights in making astronomical observations, I took leave of Itasca Lake, to the examination of which the expedition that preceded me by four years had devoted but a short time.*"

Passing out of Lake Itasca the Indians paddled briskly enough to bring the party to Lake Bemidji for an evening encampment, and Nicollet, entering upon the unbroken sheet of water, was deeply impressed by its solitary beauty. Cass Lake was reached early the next day, and three hours were spent here to enable Nicollet to make his astronomical observations; but hearing the warning cry of the loon, which almost invariably presages a storm, all

NICOLLET AT LAKE ITASCA.

hurried toward Leech Lake, which was reached at ten o'clock at night.

Nicollet and his little following were barely under shelter when a violent storm burst upon them. During their absence, Flat-Mouth had returned from the trading posts, whither he had gone for ammunition, vowing vengeance against the Sioux and declaring that the stain of Chippewa blood had been long enough on his grounds, and that it was time he should wipe it out, but he had not succeeded in getting what he wanted and was therefore disappointed. He did not forget, however, the courtesy due Nicollet in return for the ill-treatment which he had received at the hands of his men, and accordingly called a council that he might show his white brother the esteem in which he was held. Nicollet spent three evenings with this intelligent Indian, and drank tea with him "out of fine China ware." On one of these visits he showed his host a rare snuff-box, ornamented with a picture of Napoleon at the Island of Saint Helena. Flat-Mouth examined this closely, asked many questions about the white chief, and said with eloquent conceit· "Well, it is strange, on whatever side I turn it, the figure looks at me and seems to say, 'thou art my brother warrior.'"

Having gained the required rest, Nicollet bade farewell to his friend Boutwell and to his Indian host, and began the descent of the river, deploring that ill-health and lack of time prevented him at the various points from inserting additional matter concerning them in his report, which he believed would be interesting to the general reader. This ill-health really obliged him to leave unfinished much of his work, and prevented him from revising his report, which was returned to him for that purpose while he was in Washington. He never recovered his strength, and died at the National Capital in September, 1843.

It is to be regretted that more has not been written concerning the life and works of this scientist and explorer, and that an edition of his journals has not been published for distribution beyond the Bureau of the Corps of Topographical Engineers at Washington.

His comprehensive map of the Hydrographical Basin of the Upper Mississippi, while it is not complete, in so far as it does not show the heart-shaped lake with its feeders to the south of Itasca, is, besides this, very accurate and admirable. In fact, it gives Nicollet a distinct and conspicuous place among the explorers of the Mississippi; not because he saw so much more than those who had preceded him, but because he gave the knowledge of what he saw to the world. It is this inclination, often followed at the expense of convenience and safety, which deserves appreciation.

A GLIMPSE OF THE RED RIVER

CHAPTER VI.

EXPLOITS OF CHARLES LANMAN.

THIS adventurous author and traveler published, in 1847, an interesting and somewhat sensational account of his journey to, and wanderings through the wild region surrounding the Headwaters of the Mississippi.

Leaving the city of Saint Louis in the summer of 1846, with a party of excursionists, in a small steamer that plied between that city and the head of navigation on the river, he jotted down in his diary everything he considered worthy of note. He had set out with the design of reaching, if possible, the extreme head of the Mississippi, by whatever conveyance he could secure after leaving the boat at Saint Peter—now known as the Minnesota River. The small duodecimo, in which the traveler records his experiences, is full of personal adventure of a rather romantic character; traditions picked up from loquacious and superstitious Indians, and bits of local history, are tinged by a lively imagination.

From the outset of his novel journey, the author gossips pleasantly with his readers concerning every point passed by the vessel, but his descriptions are out of date, the journey having been made over fifty years ago, when flourishing cities that now adorn the river banks, were mere villages or collections of log huts, some having no existence whatever at the time.

Passing Rock Island and Prairie du Chien, concerning both of which the traveler gives rein to an exuberant fancy, and has much to disclose in the shape of history and tradition, he discourses with enthusiasm upon Lake Pepin and its extraordinary natural beauty. Surrounded by undulating hills covered with velvety grass to their summits, and "abounding with almost every variety of game, the shores of the lake are covered with the most valuable agates and carnelians," a statement which will be received with a grain of allowance in the present day, however true it may have been a half century ago. Legends and romantic stories succeed each other, and are intensely interesting if they are not all strictly veracious. But the author gives them as he heard them from Indians and others, and himself occasionally expresses a doubt of their truth. The legend of the unfortunate "Winona" is of course related, but need not be repeated here.

The little steamer proceeded on her course up the river, passing Red Wing, "a village of about six hundred souls;" and the mouth of Saint Peter River was at length reached—the head of navigation on the Mississippi. Landing at this point the writer says: "My sojourn here has been interesting from many circumstances. I feel that I am on the extreme verge of the civilized world, and that all beyond is a mysterious wilderness." He gives an account of an encampment of Sioux and Dakota Indians near the mouth of the Saint Peter, at one of whose feasts he was permitted to be present. "It was announced throughout the village that the Indians were to have a Dog Feast, in which none but the bravest and most distinguished warriors were allowed to participate. The idea that lies at the bottom of this rite is that, by eating of a dog's liver, the heart is made strong. The feast took place on the open prairie and was attended by about one hundred braves, while there must have been a thousand spectators. The first step in the ceremony was for the Indians to seat themselves in a circle around a large pole and devote a few moments to smoking. Their only article of clothing was the clout, and their only weapon a long knife.

"Suddenly a whoop was given and the whole party rose and commenced dancing to the monotonous music of a drum. Then broke upon the ear, the howl, and in a moment more, the dying groan of a dog, from without the circle of dancers. The carcass was thrown into their midst by a woman. A chorus of deafening yells resounded through the air, the dog was immediately opened, his liver taken out, suspended on the pole by a string, and the dance resumed. The dancers then, one after another, stepped up and took a bite of the yet warm and quivering liver. Soon as this was all eaten, another dog was thrown into the ring, and the same horrible ceremony repeated, and so they continued until the carcasses of ten dogs were lying at the foot of the pole in the center of the dancing crowd."

Leaving the Saint Peter, Lanman makes his way to Saint Anthony Falls. "Their original name," he explains, "was *Owah Menah,* meaning Falling Water," adding, "they owe their reputation principally to the fact that they 'veto' the navigation of the Upper Mississippi."

Lanman journeyed from the Falls of Saint Anthony

to Crow Wing River on horseback, and, as usual, met with many adventures and some hair-breadth escapes. He was accompanied by a French-Canadian as guide. The trail lay for the most part along the eastern shore of the Great River. Their supplies consisted of a small stock of bread and pork, and a blanket, together with a gun each, and ammunition. Deer, prairie-birds, and grouse were plentiful, and at sunset the first day Lanman had fifty prairie-birds fastened to his saddle, while the Frenchman had bagged a fine deer A large wolf was also killed by a shot from the guide, and its skin taken by him. Shortly afterward they were chased by a herd of wolves, when the horses took fright, became unmanageable, and ran for their lives, leaving their enemy soon out of sight.

Crow Wing was at length reached, which the author describes as a beautiful spot, situated on the east side of the Mississippi, at the mouth of a river of the same name. Here he was fortunate in meeting William Morrison, the trader, whose "reputation as an upright, intelligent, and noble-hearted man was co-extensive with the entire wilderness of the Northwest." Lanman and Morrison became very friendly. The latter was a Scotchman by birth and at the time of meeting Lanman was somewhat advanced in life. He had resided in the Indian country about thirty-five years, and is eulogized by the author as possessing "all the virtues of the trader, and none of his vices." His wife was an Indian and had borne him a number of bright children. He was much liked by the Chippewas, to whom he was always a good friend and counselor. Lanman spent ten days with him—"the most delight-

LANMAN PURSUED BY WOLVES.

ful days I ever experienced." Morrison undertook to act as his guide for a time, and together they wandered over the region of Northern Minnesota.

Among other tales of this locality told by Lanman is the following: "A famous battle was once fought here between the Sioux and Chippewas. A party of the former had gone up Crow Wing River for the purpose of destroying a certain Chippewa village. They found it inhabited only by women and children, every one of whom they murdered in cold blood, and burned their wigwams. It so happened that the Chippewa warriors had been expecting an attack, and had consequently hidden themselves in deep holès on a high bank of the river at Crow Wing, intending to fall upon the Sioux party on their way up the river. But they were sadly disappointed. While watching for their enemy they were suddenly startled by a triumphant shout that floated down the stream. In great surprise they looked, when lo! the very party that they came after were in full view, shouting and tossing up the scalps of the women and children. The Chippewas remained in ambush for a few minutes, and when the Sioux came within reach of their arms every one of them was killed, while their canoes, plunder, and bodies were suffered to float down the stream." And the narrator adds, "the pall of night rested upon the hills, the glens, the waveless river, and the Chippewa camp."

Many legends are associated with Crow Wing, among them the following about a white panther, which was religiously believed by the Chippewas. The panther in question was the prophet or oracle of a certain Chippewa tribe and possessed the gift of speech. Lanman in all seriousness proceeds as follows: "A young Chippewa brave was anxious to avenge the death of a brother, and sought the oracle to learn the success of his projected expedition. The panther told him that he must not go, but the young man heeded him not, and, heading his party, went. Every one of his followers was killed, himself escaping by the merest accident. Thinking that the white panther had in some way caused the calamity, he recklessly stole upon the creature in the darkness of midnight and slaughtered it. The dying words of the oracle were. 'Cruel and unhappy warrior, I doom thee to walk the earth forever a starving and undying skeleton.' The Chippewas say that the specter, whenever the moon is tinged with red or the aurora borealis floods the sky with purple, may be seen flitting along the banks of Mee-see-see-pee."

Crow Wing was at the time of Lanman's visit the home of the head chief of the Chippewa nation named Hole-in-the-day Our traveler visited him in his lodge frequently, and describes him as about sixty years of age, "stern and brave, but mean, vain, treacherous, and cruel." In proof of his treachery and cruelty the following incident is related as a fact. "He and some six warriors while on a hunting tour, were hospitably entertained in a Sioux lodge, where resided a family of seventeen persons. The two nations were at peace, and for a time their intercourse had been perfectly friendly. On leaving his host, Hole-in-the-day shook him cordially by the hand, with a smile upon his countenance, and departed. At midnight, when the Sioux family were wrapped in peaceful slumber, Hole-in-the-day and his men retraced their steps, and, without any provocation, fell upon the sleeping family and cruelly murdered every member, even the lisping babe." Hole-in-the-day told this story of himself to Lanman, and boasted of it as of something creditable!

The Indian trader fifty years ago was the patriarch and counselor of the wilderness. As the agent of some fur company, his business was to trade with the Indians for their furs and pelts. He was generally of French descent, and his ancestors were traders. He was, of course, a native of the wild region he inhabited—raised in utter ignorance of civilized life. His nearest white neighbor, also a trader, would possibly be two hundred miles away. His dwelling was built of logs and contained one large room and a loft. His merchandise was composed chiefly of salt pork, flour, blankets, colored cloth, and various kinds of trinkets. His family consisted of an Indian wife and several half-breed children. Adjoining the trader's home was about one acre of ploughed ground on which he raised a few vegetables; and a solitary cow yielded him the only luxury he enjoyed.

On his way up the Mississippi, Lanman came to Lake Winnibegoshish. The river he found so winding that in some cases, by making a portage of about fifteen rods, he saved three or four miles of canoeing. The stream averaged about a quarter of a mile in breadth, and flowed rapidly over a rocky bed. Lake Winnibegoshish is fifteen miles in length and about ten miles in width. It is nearly round, has no islands, and is surrounded with a gravelly beach. The water is clear but shallow. The surrounding country is a dead level, covered with trees, interspersed with lakes and rice swamps, where immense numbers of water-fowl have lived and multiplied for centuries.

"The only inhabitants found on the shores of Winnibegoshish," says the traveler, "were three bands of Chippewas, numbering in all about three thousand souls. * * * Immediately on my arrival I heard something about a contemplated bear hunt. A number had already been killed, and there was a fording place on the Mississippi, not far away, where a good marksman might take one at almost any time. A present of tobacco soon initiated me into the good graces of the party of hunters, and I was allowed to accompany them. We started at sunset and descended the river in a canoe to the crossing, where we concealed ourselves in a recess of the forest, seated on a rock that commanded an opening between the trees. It was quite dark, as there was no moon. Here we spent an hour in perfect silence. Finally, one of the Indians tapped me on the shoulder and pointed to a large black object which I soon saw was a bear just wading into the water. Bruin took it quite leisurely, as is his wont, little dreaming that an enemy was so near. Just as his feet touched the bottom of the stream, the Indian gave me a nod, and raising our guns simultaneously, three of us fired at the animal, striking him in a vulnerable spot. We soon shipped him on board our canoe and paddled back to the village. Morrison estimated his weight to be about three hundred pounds."

Red Cedar Lake, since named Cass Lake by Schoolcraft in honor of General Cass, the Territorial Governor of Michigan, was reached in a few days. It derived its original name, in Indian, from the tree that mostly abounds upon its shores. In the center of the lake is a large island and several small islands occupy other portions of the lake. The entire region watered by the unnumbered lakes of the Upper Mississippi, was formerly inhabited by the Chippewa nation. The hospitality of the tribes was proverbial in times past, ere they came to know the whites too well and to taste of their "fire water." When a stranger entered their cabin, he was invited to a seat on their best mat, and always treated with the very best they possessed in the way of food. If a chief was visited at an untimely hour—at midnight, for example—he would arise, stir up his fire, and give the intruder a pipe with the air of a gentleman. If called upon when the caller knew the chief had reason to consider him an enemy, he would not tell the caller to leave his wigwam, but possibly in an unguarded moment, in the latter's own wigwam, he would cleave his skull with a tomahawk. They were very affectionate to their wives and children. When a party of them were in a state of starvation, and one individual happened to have a bear or deer, the latter would distribute it equally at a feast, and they would never refuse to present to a brother Chippewa, or white man whom they esteemed, any pipe, weapon, or ornament that may have been solicited. They still treat their infirm people with tender care. As the Chippewa Country was mostly covered with a dense forest, the people were unacquainted with the use of the horse. Their mode of hunting the buffalo was to drive them over bluffs, or shoot them while disguised in the skin of a wolf or buffalo. Their only vehicle for locomotion and transport was the birchen canoe. The bark of the birch tree, out of which it was made, is still found in abundance throughout the entire territory, and they used it, not only for canoes, but for their lodges, their grave-houses, their baskets, their dishes, and exquisitely worked boxes which they disposed of as curiosities.

In the month of July, 1846, Lanman entered Lake Itasca and described it as a small sheet of water about five miles long and one to two miles wide, containing only one island. Its Indian name was *Omushkos.* He followed Schoolcraft in pronouncing this lake the head of the Mississippi. This is easily understood in the light of my discovery of 1881. Neither Schoolcraft or Lanman had visited, or suspected the existence of the beautiful sheet of water to the south of Itasca, effectually screened from view by the high ridge which separates the two lakes. Schoolcraft did not see it for reasons I shall present in a future chapter, and Lanman makes no allusion to it. To the south of Itasca is the ridge or elevation of wood-crowned hills. The whole region to the north of Itasca he correctly describes as woody, low, and marshy. The trees are pine, oak, elm, maple, birch, poplar, jack-pine, and tamarack. The region around this lake was formerly famous for the number of its wild animals, and Itasca derived its name *Omushkos,* by which it is still known to the Indians, from a monstrous elk—the English of *Omushkos*—"which, according to the legend, measured the length of two canoes, and with his horns could split a pine tree."

It may be stated that Lanman is not considered a reliable authority in matters relating to the Upper Mississippi and its neighboring territory He was not in a strict sense an *explorer*, nor does he claim to have been such. His journey appears to have been undertaken chiefly for the gratification of a commendable curiosity. In 1846, the year of his romantic journey, the Valley of the Mississippi, above the Falls of Saint Anthony, was known only to Indian traders, mostly of French origin, and probably to one or two speculative and intrepid travelers prospecting for the useful and precious metals. Lanman does not pretend to have *discovered* anything. Had he given more attention to exploration, he might have made an important addition to our geographical knowledge while canoeing on the southwestern arm of Itasca, and thus have forestalled the author of the present volume. Lauman's experiences are interesting mainly from the many Indian traditions he recounts, and his descriptions of regions and scenery but little known even in the present day.

BEAR HUNTING.

PART THIRD.

———:o:———

DISCOVERY

OF THE

True Source.

———:o:———

SUBJECTS:

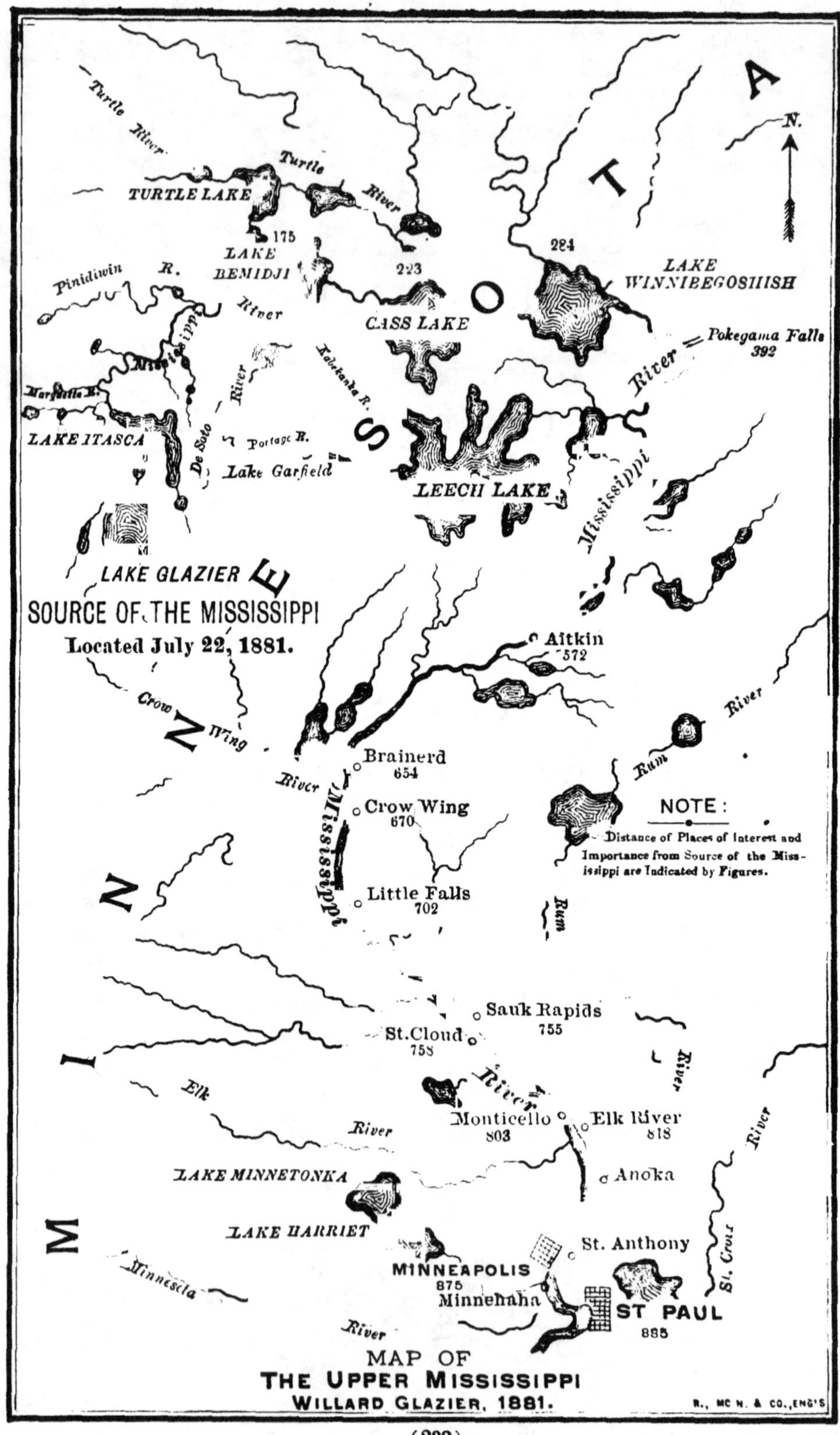

MAP OF
THE UPPER MISSISSIPPI
WILLARD GLAZIER, 1881.

CHAPTER I.

RECENT EXPLORATIONS.

FOR nearly fifty years prior to 1881, it had been generally accepted as established beyond question that the ultimate Source of the Mississippi was in Lake Itasca, Northern Minnesota. Henry Rowe Schoolcraft, geologist of the Cass expedition and leader of a subsequent exploring party, had announced to the world his discovery of this lake in the year 1832, and pronounced it the True Head of the Great River

Geographers, map-makers, educational publishers, college faculties, and teachers, invariably published and taught that the Source of the Mississippi was in the lake thus designated by Schoolcraft. A few, however, pioneers and others, who had come in contact with Indians on the Chippewa Reservation, stoutly denied the claim of Itasca to the distinction given it by its discoverer; this fact, coupled with an eager desire to ascertain the truth or error of Schoolcraft, led me to organize an expedition having for its object the possible settlement of the mooted question. That expedition resulted in locating a hitherto unrecognized lake to the south of Itasca, as the

Primal Reservoir, on the twenty-second of July, 1881.

The discovery that a lake of fair proportions above and beyond Itasca was the True Source of the Mississippi was followed by an attempt to discredit the validity of my published statements, and misrepresentations were made which rendered it expedient in the estimation of my friends, that further investigation should be undertaken in that quarter and that I should resume the pen in defense of the truth of my position.

No sooner had I announced a new source for the Mississippi than several critics jumped to their feet and declared that there was nothing beyond Itasca worthy of the slightest consideration. When, however, I had proved most conclusively that that lake was not the remotest water, some of my opponents rather reluctantly granted that there might possibly be a few ponds and puddles in that vicinity, but, if so, they were of little consequence, else the early explorers would have given them due prominence in the accounts of their explorations.

Having made it entirely clear to most geographers that there was such a lake as I had described, and that it was a direct and permanent feeder of Lake Itasca, it was now asserted by a few cavilers that it had been previously seen and that even if it were accepted as the source, I was entitled to but little credit for establishing its true relation to the Mississippi.

Again, it was the argument of certain parties who imagined that they had interests inimical to mine, that the explorations of the eminent French scientist, Nicollet, which tended largely to confirm Schoolcraft, were conducted during the "dry season," and, notwithstanding that the lake which I had fixed upon in July was between five and six miles in circumference and covered an area of two hundred and fifty-five acres, with an average depth of forty-five feet, its basin may not have exhibited water during the month of August when the region was visited by the distinguished Frenchman in 1836.

Finally, on learning that the lake in question was being almost universally adopted, one or two exceedingly zealous partisans feeling, I presume, that they had a "mission," or rather that they were called upon, to investigate my explorations, sent out what they were pleased to denominate "expeditions" to examine and report upon their findings in the locality undeı discussion. The first of the so-called expeditions visited the Head of the Mississippi in October 1886, and is alleged to have consisted of three persons although the name of but one appeared in the report. A subsequent expedition took place in the summer and autumn of 1889, and was, to say the least, conspicuous for its contradictions.

Although the leaders of both of these investigating parties were pleased to denounce me in unmeasured terms, their own reports were very conflicting; one of them even going so far as to pluck the laurel from the brow of Schoolcraft in order that he might bestow it upon his greater favorite, Nicollet, while the other was for a long time in doubt as to the propriety of deciding between a pond, a puddle, a rivulet, or spring. The investigations of this "enterprising" explorer culminated in his fixing upon two lakes having no surface connection with Lake Itasca or the Mississippi, as the Fountain-head. A very notable feature of their various "modest" reports was that they were made in the interest of their employers, and were filled with vulgar abuse of everyone connected with the expedition of 1881.

The antagonism thus developed by an honest attempt to establish a geographical truth, together with the fact that, even at this late day, some of our leading educators still believe in the error of Lake Itasca, led me to decide upon another visit to the Headwaters of the Mississippi, for the purpose of making a most thorough investigation, in an earnest effort to settle the vexed question which had occupied the attention of geographers for over ten years.

SHOOTING RAPIDS.

CHAPTER II.

JOURNEY TO MINNESOTA.

DETERMINED upon a second expedition to the Headwaters of the Mississippi, I immediately began preparations for the accomplishment of my purpose while at Milwaukee, Wisconsin, during the month of May, 1891, just ten years after starting from Cleveland, Ohio, on my first journey to that region.

Wishing to reach Northern Minnesota as early as practicable, I left Milwaukee on the fourteenth of July, accompanied by Pearce Giles of Camden, New Jersey, who assisted in the organization of my former expedition, and who has since been an earnest advocate of my position in relation to the Source of the Mississippi.

We availed ourselves of the Chicago, Milwaukee and Saint Paul Railway in our tour across Wisconsin. The season and route fixed upon for our trip were such as to present the charming scenery and rich products of its soil to the best possible advantage. Many and wonderful are the changes which have taken place in the picturesque region which lies between Lake Michigan and the Mississippi since the zealous Jesuit missionary, Father James Marquette, paddled his birch canoe down the beautiful river from which the State derives its name.

Although a slight digression, it may not be entirely foreign to our purpose, or uninteresting to the reader, if we briefly note the transformation which two hundred years have wrought in this rich and populous section of our Great Republic; for it was through the rivers of Wisconsin that not only Marquette and Joliet, but also their immediate successors, La Salle, Hennepin, La Hontan, Charlevoix, and Carver, found their way to the Father of Waters.

It is hardly probable that the old explorers, even in their most sanguine moments, ever dreamed of the brilliant future which awaited the field of their explorations. Then, all of the vast tract of country through which they passed was an unbroken wilderness. Now, its productive farms, its factories, railways, and above all the schools and churches, mark its development and tell the story of onward strides in progress and civilization.

An hour's ride from Milwaukee brought us to Waukesha, a delightful summer resort, sometimes styled the Saratoga of the West. It is the capital of Waukesha County, and is noted for the efficacy of its mineral springs. This beautiful village is situated on the Fox River, twenty-one miles southwest of Milwaukee, in one of the most fertile valleys of the State, and has many attractions aside from the health-giving properties of its famous springs.

Leaving Waukesha, our journey led us through several villages to Watertown on the Black River, forty-three miles west of Milwaukee. This quiet little city is the center of one of the richest agricultural sections of Wisconsin; it is located on both sides of the river in Dodge and Jefferson counties, in a valley from which gentle hills rise on every side.

It is reputed to have six public schools, two colleges, fifteen churches, three national banks, and four weekly papers. The river affords abundant water-power, and several mills and factories were observed as we passed through the city. The growth of Watertown has been comparatively slow, its population having increased but little over eight thousand in the course of twenty years.

Our route from Watertown was northwesterly to Portage, which is picturesquely situated at the head of navigation on the Wisconsin River, eighty-three miles from Milwaukee. This section of the State was for many years celebrated for its extensive pine forests, but they have long since yielded to the axe of the lumberman, and Portage now has graded schools, daily and weekly papers, and a flourishing trade with the surrounding country, which was not more famous in the past for its lumber than it is to-day for the rich products of the farm.

From Portage we proceeded up the Wisconsin to Kilbourn City, passing through a portion of the "Dalles," which enjoy a deservedly world-wide reputation for their scenic attractions. America has a great variety of grand and beautiful scenery, possibly excelling in this particular all other countries of the globe, and I have seen nothing anywhere so near to civilized lines that surpasses the Dalles of the Wisconsin River. Here the largest stream in the State flows through a wild gorge for a distance of nearly ten miles, so narrow in many places that there is just room for a small steamer to pass. The place is surrounded by a cluster of beautiful lakes, and the landscape resulting from such a happy combination of rural attractions is picturesque and enchanting.

DALLES OF THE WISCONSIN.

Regretting that a sojourn at the Dalles was incompatible with the chief objects of our journey, we rolled on toward our evening destination, reaching the bluffs which overlook the Mississippi at La Crosse, a few minutes after five o'clock.

Although I have often seen the Great River during the past twenty years and stood upon its banks many times since my canoe voyage of 1881, I could not, on viewing it again, readily repress emotions of affection for the mighty stream which has for so long a period occupied a large share of my time and attention. Who among reflective travelers will think it strange that long association, even with a river, may not sometimes lead to a sentiment very nearly akin to love? Who that has traced the tortuous course of any of the great streams of Earth, from source to sea, will wonder at the deep and tender regard which I always feel when looking upon this King of American rivers?

Thousands upon thousands of logs, numerous sawmills, and acres of lumber yards, betokened our proximity to La Crosse, the second city of Wisconsin and one of the most enterprising in the Valley of the Mississippi.

During my descent of the river ten years ago, I halted three days at La Crosse, at which time I learned something of its early history and development.

The name of this ambitious young city is said to be derived from the invigorating game of "La Crosse," the favorite sport of the Indians, who were wont to assemble for this purpose on the level prairie upon which the city now stands. To indulge in their athletic matches, it is recorded, that they gathered here in large numbers annually, the plain being conveniently adapted to the accommodation of the various tribes who desired to see and participate in the sport. Nathan Myrick, the first white settler, became such an enthusiastic admirer of the exciting game that he named the spot, on which his solitary cabin was built, La Crosse, and thus the name of the aboriginal sport became perpetuated in that of the city.

La Crosse claims, and with good grace, to be the second city in commercial and manufacturing importance in the State of Wisconsin. The prairie on which it is built is seven miles in length by two and a half in breadth. Its distance below Saint Paul by the river, is one hundred and ninety-seven miles; while by railway it is only one hundred and twenty-nine miles from the same city.

The Black and La Crosse rivers fall into the Mississippi at this point, the former being a most important lumbering stream.

The growth of La Crosse is in keeping with the development of the Northwest. Myrick, the first settler, landed here in November, 1841, with a boat-load of goods and notions from Prairie du Chien, which he traded with the red men for their furs. In the course of ten years the trading-post established by him, had drawn other settlers to it, and it became an incorporated town. Five years later, in 1856, it had attained sufficient size and importance to be made a city. To-day it has a population of over thirty thousand of as industrious and prosperous citizens as are to be found on the banks of the Great River.

The geographical location of La Crosse is doubtless one of the chief secrets of its rapid progress and present flourishing condition. The products of one of the leading agricultural States of the Union, together with a portion of the vast supplies which reach its shores from Minnesota and Northern Iowa, give to the city immense advantages, occupying, as it does, a commanding position on the river for attracting commercial relations with its sister cities. In addition to the facilities offered for transportation by numerous water lines, La Crosse has access to several railways which center here. The Mississippi and its tributaries embrace over sixteen thousand miles of navigable water, the former alone presenting a stretch of nearly two thousand miles of uninterrupted navigation, affording the cheapest kind of transportation, of the benefits of which La Crosse avails herself to a very large extent, and to this advantage is mainly due her growth in population and wealth.

The commerce and manufactures of a city depend, in a great measure, upon the resources of the State in which it is situated. Wisconsin is one of our richest agricultural States. It is larger than New York, Rhode Island, and Connecticut combined, and in the fertility of its soil is second to none. A considerable percentage of the wheat crop of the United States is grown in this province. Its immense cornfields, comprising several millions of acres, are another source of wealth; while the hay-producing area is double that of Iowa. Twenty-five million pounds of butter and twenty million pounds of cheese are manufactured annually in Wisconsin, most of which is shipped to Eastern and European markets. The soil and climate of this State are especially favorable to the growth of the potato. Flax raising is also a leading industry, the yield being over thirty million pounds a year. Thus in agricultural resources the "Badger" State possesses every advantage for developing great commercial and manufacturing cities, and the favorable position of La Crosse eminently fits her for reaping the full benefit of the conditions so generously provided.

After a halt of twenty minutes for connections and refreshments, we steamed out of La Crosse and were soon wending our way over the railway bridge which spans the Mississippi at this point.

Having reached the Minnesota side of the river, we rushed along toward Winona, our evening destination, where we had supper and remained for the night. The following morning a few hours were pleasantly and profitably spent in a stroll through the leading streets of the city, during which we called at the office of the *Republican* in anticipation of meeting its editor, Hon. D. Sinclair, who, we regretted to learn, was then out of town attending an editorial convention at Saint Paul. Mr. Sinclair was an early pioneer of Minnesota, and, in addition to conducting one of the first journals of the State, was at this time postmaster and prominently mentioned as a candidate for the mayoralty. He has for several years past shown much interest in the controversy relating to the True Source of the Mississippi, and the columns of his paper have ever been open to those who are disposed to discuss without prejudice the geographical question which, since 1881, has been of more than local interest.

The growth of Winona since my former visit has been gradual and substantial. Several new public buildings were noted in various parts of the city of which her intelligent citizens are justly proud.

In its location and surroundings, Winona is extremely picturesque, standing as it does on a plateau nine miles long by three broad on the west bank of the river, and environed by lofty bluffs, the surface of which, in some cases, from base to summit appears of a velvety smoothness, having more the semblance of art than of Nature.

The city is laid out with the utmost regularity, the streets wide and chiefly at right angles; the business blocks compactly built of wood and stone are generally of a very substantial character. Many of the private residences are elegantly designed and are suggestive of wealth and refinement. The whole appearance of the place betokens business activity and prosperity. In population, Winona is the fourth city in the State, and claims to be third in commercial importance. It is the river outlet of a large portion of Minnesota and several counties of Northern Wisconsin, and as a primary grain market, ranks fourth in the United States.

Besides water communication north and south, Winona has within her limits the stations of the Chicago, Milwaukee and Saint Paul; the Green Bay, Winona and Saint Paul, and several branch lines of railway.

As a lumber distributing point, this city is one of the most important of the Upper Mississippi, while its saw-mills, flour-mills, wagon factories and other manufacturing establishments give a very good idea of the extent to which its capital and industries have been developed in the course of a few years by its enterprising inhabitants.

CHAPTER III.

WINONA TO MINNEAPOLIS.

WE continued our journey up the Mississippi, at ten o'clock on the following morning, and our train making brief stops at the various stations between Winona and Minneapolis, afforded but little opportunity for obtaining glimpses of the cities and towns which dot the river banks.

Quite in contrast with my voyage down the Mississippi in a canoe, was this trip up stream by rail. Everything was reversed. Instead of leisurely disembarking at the water front, we now whirled along in rear of the numerous places which, during the descent of the river, had arrested my attention. The journey then covered a period of several days; by rail it can be completed in a corresponding number of hours.

Reflecting upon the various modes of journeying, I am led to say as the result of much experience, that he who looks at the country from the window of a railway car, can at best have only an imperfect idea of the many objects of interest which are constantly brought to his notice. During a horseback journey from ocean to ocean in 1876, I became satisfied that an equestrian tour wherein the rider mounts and dismounts at will as he jogs along over the highway, chatting with an occasional farmer, talking with the people in town and viewing rural scenes at his pleasure, presents many attractive features to the student and tourist, but notwithstanding all that may be said in favor of the horse, I can not but feel, after an equally extended experience in the canoe, that he who wishes to view the landscape, to commune with Nature, to see men and note the products of their toil, to learn something of their manners and customs from a novel standpoint, will find our rivers and the light craft, which readily thread these waterways, best adapted to his purpose.

In support of the river and canoe for a tour of observation, a contemporary says: "Other roads do some violence to Nature and bring the traveler to stare at her; but the river steals into the scenery it traverses without intrusion, silently creating and adorning it, and is free to come and go as the zephyr."

The voyager in his canoe near the surface of the water, floats along seeing hill and dale and woodland very much as they appeared to the settler in pioneer days in all their picturesque beauty Each stroke of the paddle, each bend in the river brings before the eye new scenes as the enchanted traveler glides onward in his course.

The canoe employed for such journeys need not necessarily be a birch-bark, or a "Rushton," or a "Rob Roy;" any one of these patterns and many others will meet every requirement of the voyager. In my descent of the Mississippi, I used the birch-bark at the headwaters of the river, for the reason that it is best adapted to the rough treatment which is unavoidable whenever a swift current with an uncertain bed is encountered; as this canoe is easily repaired with pitch if rendered unseaworthy by contact with obstructions. On reaching Aitkin we replaced the Indian with modern canoes in which we continued our voyage to the Gulf.

Taking it for granted that the tourist has decided upon the river as the most practicable highway for his purpose and that he has fixed upon the canoe as the most suitable conveyance at his command, he very naturally casts about for a desirable field in which to conduct his observations. If he is a resident of the Valley of the Mississippi and would like to know more of the romantic history of North America, it is not necessary that he should make an extended journey to the classic Hudson, or the Canadian lakes, or ship his canoe to the sandy shores of New Jersey, or the rugged coast of New England. Right here in the great basin of the Father of Waters, unlimited opportunities may be found for gliding through fertile regions that are as beautiful and inviting to-day as they were before the touch of civilization had wrought its mighty change. The Rock, Wisconsin, Chippewa, Saint Croix, and Minnesota are among the most interesting affluents of the Upper Mississippi, and the sights and experiences which are characteristic of this section of the Great River may reasonably be looked for upon any of the streams which are directly tributary to it.

To return to our journey, we find that we have passed Minneiska and are now at Wabasha, a small town on the west bank of the river at the foot of Lake Pepin. It is twelve miles below Lake City; is an important grain market and has a population of between three and four thousand.

Leaving Wabasha we move northward along the western shore of Pepin occupied with thoughts of the aboriginal legends which will always be associated with this beautiful sheet of water; thinking also of Father Hennepin and his adventures among the Indians, he who was the first white man to break the solitude of these northern wilds, and who suffered captivity here; for it will be remembered that having made Hennepin and his companions prisoners, the savages held a consultation near the lake for the purpose of deciding what they should do with their captives. Some were in favor of giving them their liberty, while others insisted that they should be put to death. Those who were in favor of the latter course cried and moaned throughout the night hoping by their tears to prevail upon the remainder of the tribe to consent to the murder of the whites. This experience led Hennepin to christen this magnificent sheet of water, the Lake of Tears, which title, it would seem, should have been retained when we consider the peculiar circumstances under which the adventurous Frenchman was induced to bestow it. The name which the lake now bears is evidently of French origin, but I have been unable to ascertain who applied it, or what incident led to its adoption.

Being released from captivity through the compassion and influence of Wah-zee-koo-tay, the great Nahdawessy chief, Hennepin, still undaunted, proceeded up the Mississippi to the Falls of Saint Anthony, which he named in honor of his patron saint.

Following Hennepin, Baron La Hontan journeyed through Lake Pepin, and many leagues to the northward, located his Longue Rivierre, that romance of geography, which he described as having a "due western course," but which, it was subsequently ascertained, was a creature of his imagination, or rather, a singular combination of truth and fiction.

Then came the gallant Le Sueur in 1700. Paddling up the lake, he continued the ascent of the Mississippi to the mouth of the Minnesota River, and thence up that stream to its Blue Earth tributary. This daring spirit erected a log fort on the banks of the Mankato, and was the first to break the virgin soil of Minnesota with spade and pickaxe, which was done in digging for copper ore, large quantities of which, or a green earth supposed to be ore of that metal, he had conveyed to France. Le Sueur was doubtless the first white man who supplied the Indians of the Northwest with firearms and other products of civilized labor, and to his truthful journal we are greatly indebted for much of the reliable data we possess of the Indian races of the Upper Mississippi.

After the lapse of a considerable period, Captain Jonathan Carver, a native of New England, passed through Lake Pepin during his journey up the Mississippi. He had long contemplated such an expedition, but circumstances did not favor him until 1776. With only a Frenchman and Mohawk Indian for guides, his heroic nature defied the perils of such a hazardous undertaking. Carver ascended the almost unknown river in a canoe, and exulted in the fact that he was the first of the Anglo-Saxon race to glide over these pure waters; to look upon this grand scenery and to tread the fertile soil of the Great Northwest.

Turning from the adventures of the heroic old explorers, we find our train in front of the railway station at Lake City, one of those magic towns of the West, which, under favorable circumstances, leap into existence and develop so rapidly as to far exceed the brightest anticipations of their founders. Beautifully located on the western shore of Pepin, enjoying excellent water communication with all points up and down the river, it will doubtless sustain the prominence it has already achieved.

From the beginning of our journey the scenery has been strikingly picturesque, and yet, on leaving Lake City it increases in grandeur as we move forward toward Frontenac. The broad expanse of water, charming coves and huge bluffs which, in some instances, rise abruptly to a height of from five hundred to a thousand feet above the surface of the lake, present a picture that is seldom, if ever, equaled in the Valley of the Mississippi.

As we cast our eyes to the eastward and look upon the majestic bluffs which line the Wisconsin shore our attention is arrested by Maiden Rock, and I recall the sad story of Winona and her leap from its summit, an incident that will always be of romantic interest to those who delight in the legendary lore of the Great River Her youth, beauty, and the melancholy circumstances which led to her tragic death invest her life with a peculiar charm, and will ever form a thrilling chapter in the annals of Lake Pepin.

It may be observed before proceeding further that Lake Pepin is twenty-one miles long and varies in width from one to three miles. In my descent of the Lake in 1881, I was led to conclude that the slightest breath of wind will produce a heavy swell, and from this circumstance it is the custom of voyagers on the river to pass through the lake, if possible, during the night; experience having taught them that it is gen-

VIEW OF MAIDEN ROCK—LAKE PEPIN.

erally much calmer then than during the day. Toward its outlet the valley widens considerably, owing to the entrance of the Chippewa River, which at its mouth is five hundred yards wide, and is navigable at certain seasons of the year for over one hundred miles. The general trend of the lake is from west-northwest to east-southeast. The scenery along its shores contrasts strongly with that of the river. Instead of the rapid current of the Mississippi winding around numberless islands, some of which display well-wooded surfaces, the lake when calm presents a smooth and sluggish expanse unrelieved by a single island; nothing limits the view but the towering bluffs which enclose its basin and seem like so many giant sentinels standing guard over the accumulated flood of the mighty stream as it passes quietly onward to the sea.

Arrived at Frontenac we halt for a moment only. This is a growing hamlet of perhaps three hundred souls. In appearance it is a most romantic spot, with its white sand beach in front and bluffs in the background. Frontenac has already attracted some attention as a summer resort, and will doubtless in the course of a few years attain sufficient importance in this particular to meet in a measure at least the bright anticipations of its liberal and philanthropic founder—General Israel Garrard.

Passing Frontenac we hurry on to Red Wing, situated on the west bank of the Mississippi, six miles above the head of the lake. Like many other cities of Minnesota, Red Wing has an interesting history, and is a striking illustration of what an intelligent and industrious people can accomplish in the course of a very few years when naturally zealous, and their energies are properly directed. The standard of civilization was originally planted here by two Swiss missionaries, bearing the names of Denton and Garin, who arrived, accompanied by their wives, in 1838. The savage Dakotas at this period were in possession of the territory, and these brave, self-denying Christians labored among them until the health of Denton failed in 1846, when the American Board of Missions appointed as their successors, John Aiton and J. W. Hancock, two clergymen of Vermont. Two white families and about three hundred Indians were at that time the sole occupants of what is now the flourishing little city of Red Wing.

In June, 1852, the Government entered into a treaty with the Indians which authorized the occupation of the Territory by settlers, but the close of the same year saw only about forty people on the present site of Red Wing. On the following Christmas day the entire white community dined at the residence of William Freeborn, one of the first settlers. Soon after this pleasant event in its pioneer history, the place began to grow, and although its development has been moderate it has reached a population of between twelve and thirteen thousand.

Red Wing enjoys the reputation of being one of the largest primary wheat markets in the country, having handled over three million bushels in a single year. Its manufactures also are quite extensive, while the clay deposits in its immediate vicinity are among the finest and richest in America. In addition to clay, a very superior quality of sand is found in this locality, in large quantities, and I was informed that it was the intention to establish a glass factory there at an early date. Being within a few miles of Lake

Pepin, and enjoying every advantage which has favored her sister cities, Red Wing may reasonably anticipate a steady growth and a rapid development of her great natural resources.

Less than an hour's ride from Red Wing and we are at Hastings on the west bank of the river, twenty miles below Saint Paul. In my journey between these two points I again saw in striking contrast, my canoe voyage of 1881, and my present trip up river by rail. Then a thunder-storm, which had been slumbering for a few hours, broke out afresh at ten o'clock in the morning and followed us throughout the day—drenching us to the skin and making our experience anything but agreeable. Now, we were favored with a cloudless sky, and the most delightful weather in every particular

We passed the mouth of the Saint Croix River just below Hastings. This stream enters the Mississippi from the east and forms the boundary between Wisconsin and Minnesota. For a considerable distance below the Saint Croix the water of the Mississippi, where shallow, is of a reddish tint, but very black in deep water. The red is occasioned by the sand seen at the bottom which is of that color. It may be said in explanation that the dark color is invariably common to deep water when moderately limpid.

Hastings is a pretty little city of modest pretensions, claiming a population of only about five thousand. In pioneer days it aspired to first place among the leading cities of Minnesota, and I am told was at one time considered the rival of Saint Paul and Minneapolis. While it has not been able to reach the goal of its ambition, it has made considerable progress, and will doubtless in the course of another decade show a creditable increase in population and commercial importance.

The route from Hastings to Saint Paul led us through one of the most fertile and picturesque regions of Minnesota. Some of the finest farms in the State are to be found here, while the scenery, if we except that along the shores of Lake Pepin, is not surpassed anywhere in the Northwest.

Soon after leaving Hastings, we passed what is termed, and unquestionably is, the narrowest place in the Mississippi below the Falls of Saint Anthony. The river at this point is clear of islands and not more than one hundred yards wide. Pike states that his men rowed across in forty strokes of the oar; another traveler affirms that he crossed in 1857 from a dead start in sixteen strokes. This sudden contraction of the stream gives it a greatly increased depth, and in my soundings of 1881, I discovered it to be over one hundred feet deep, while its velocity was nearly doubled.

At two o'clock in the afternoon, the church spires of Saint Paul were seen in the distance, and a few moments later we entered the hospitable gates of the capital city of Minnesota.

CHAPTER IV.

EARLY HISTORY OF MINNESOTA.

LESS than fifty years ago the present State of Minnesota was a wilderness of woodland and of prairie—the home of the red man. In the deep recesses of her forests the Sioux, Chippewas, Winnebagos, and many other savage tribes met and contended for supremacy; while vast herds of buffalo grazed and roamed at will over her fertile prairies.

Here the dark-browed Indian, in his birch canoe, floated and paddled down the rivers and over his own loved lakes; and from the rocky bluffs and hill-tops, whence to-day floats the banner of civilization, arose only the smoke of the council-fire, and was heard the war-whoop of the savage. Across these sky-tinted waters, once the battle-field of the red men, now reverberate the soft, sweet strains of the organ, the peaceful chimes of the church-going bell, and the busy hum of commerce.

The sights and scenes which were characteristic of this region in aboriginal days have passed away. The remnants of a few Indian tribes still linger at the Headwaters of May-see-see-bee—their ideal river; and an occasional straggler from these bands is now and then seen in the streets of Saint Paul, but in a very few years at most, their homes, their hunting-grounds, and even their very burial-places will be forgotten.

On this ground, the warlike Sioux and their implacable enemies, the equally fierce and uncompromising Chippewas, were for ages engaged in an exterminating conflict which spared neither age, nor sex, nor condition. This fair land has been the scene of many a sanguinary combat. Here thousands of the brave sons of the forest have sung their last wail of despair, and, suffering indescribable tortures, met death uncomplainingly.

The bitter feuds of the Indians descended to pioneer times, and among the early settlers of Minnesota there are many yet living who were reluctant witnesses of their incessant warfare. The soil upon which we tread to-day is impregnated with the blood of untutored savages, who, though denizens of the wild forest, and filled with hatred of their fellow-men, still, however, heard the voice of the Great Spirit in the morning breeze; beheld him in the dark cloud that rose in the west; recognized his presence in the setting sun, as he sank, enthroned under a glorious canopy, to his burning bed. Here they loved, fought, and delighted in the sports of the chase.

Over two centuries ago the attention of Europeans was directed to the region now known as Minnesota. Fact and fancy had already invested this portion of North America with a romantic interest rarely, if ever, equaled in the history of exploration. From the year 1658, when the Jesuit missionary and explorer, Father Menard, was lost in the wilderness, down to the present time, Minnesota has ever been a most fruitful field for research.

It has been observed in a previous chapter, that Father Louis Hennepin was the first white man to ascend the Upper Mississippi; then came La Hontan,

Le Sueur, and Carver; the last of whom acquired great influence over the Indians; made several treaties with them, was elected to the chieftainship of a tribe, and given a vast tract of land embracing millions of acres and covering the very ground on which Saint Paul now stands. Although this gift is said to have been ratified by George III. it was not sustained by our Congress, and the heroic and adventurous Carver was, for several years, suffered to feel the annoyances of poverty, and, after a fruitless effort to obtain adequate compensation for his services, died of want in the city of London, where for a long time previous to his death he endured greater privations than had fallen to his lot in the American wilderness.

Within the present century, Pike, Cass, Beltrami, Schoolcraft, Nicollet, Fremont, Long, and Keating have visited and explored Minnesota. The maps, journals, and works of these eminent explorers, and the narratives of their heroic predecessors, enable us to follow chronologically the leading events in its annals since Father Hennepin first looked upon the Falls of Saint Anthony, and to connect, with some degree of accuracy, the past with the present. These then are our sources of information, and these men the landmarks in a most romantic and interesting history

In addition to those who have visited Minnesota for the specific purpose of exploration, it is but just to mention a few of the pioneers and fur traders whose daring and enterprise have rendered their names historic. Of this class, Renville, Provençalle, Morrison, and Faribault are worthy of especial notice in the early records of the State. First in the list of these sturdy sons of the border was Joseph Renville, who was born upon the soil of Minnesota in the year 1779. His father was a French trader and his mother an Indian. At this period there were not more than a half-dozen white families within the limits of the vast territory now comprising Northern Illinois, Wisconsin, Iowa, and Minnesota.

The story of the life of this Christian pioneer forms an interesting link between the past and present history of Minnesota. At the age of ten years, young Renville was taken to Canada by his father and his education intrusted to a Roman Catholic priest. Longing for his home and friends, he left school before completing the prescribed course of study and returned to the land of his birth—the wilderness of the Northwest.

Soon after his return from Canada, Renville acted as guide to General Pike and conducted that officer and his command to the Falls of Saint Anthony. In recognition of this service, Pike subsequently secured for him the appointment of Government interpreter. For many years he was an influential citizen of Minnesota and for a long period held various local offices of importance. He was among the first, if not the very first, to plant corn and raise stock in the territory.

Although bred in the Catholic faith, missionaries, without regard to religious denomination, received a cordial welcome at his trading-post. Years before there was a church within three hundred miles of his cabin, he made a journey to Prairie du Chien in order that he might wed in accordance with the forms of the Christian service. His Indian bride, who, it may be added, was the first Dakota to unite with the church and the first to die in its faith, through the teaching of her husband had embraced

Christianity some years before she had even seen a missionary. After a long, eventful, and useful life Renville died in 1856, and his death is said to have been peaceful and happy, and a valuable legacy to the church of which he had been an exemplary member for more than a half-century.

Contemporaneous with Renville, was Louis Provençalle, one of the most daring pioneers of Minnesota, whose death occurred at Mendota in 1850. Stalwart in physique and possessed of an inflexible will, he was in every way well qualified for the rough duties of a frontier trader.

Provençalle was possessed of but little education, and his books of Indian credit were understood only by himself, as all of the entries were made in hieroglyphics, and yet his white and dusky customers never questioned their accuracy. This bold and fearless trader was ever ready for the various emergencies which often confronted him, and never shrank from danger when the odds were against him. On one occasion, a band of Indians entered his store and threatened to seize his goods, whereupon he snatched up a firebrand and holding it to a keg of gun-powder avowed his determination to blow himself and them into the air if they took a single article. The prospect of being sent so suddenly to their "Happy Hunting-Grounds" quite disconcerted the pillagers, and they rushed headlong from the cabin, leaving Provençalle in possession of his entire stock. It is sufficient to add that after this episode, the Indians were most careful not to incur the displeasure of their white brother, and never gave him further trouble.

Among the most successful fur traders of Minnesota at the beginning of the present century, William Morrison is justly given a position in the front rank. As early as 1802, he established a line of trading-posts far up the Mississippi, which in succeeding years he extended to the Headwaters of the river.

This enterprising trader was doubtless the first white man to look upon Lake Itasca, which he saw in 1804, and had he known at the time that its outlet was the Mississippi, would have been entitled to all the credit which, twenty-eight years later, was accorded to Schoolcraft. It was not the business of Morrison to give much attention to the geography and topography of the country; on the contrary he confined himself to the matter-of-fact duties of his occupation. He saw Itasca simply as one of the thousands of lakes of Minnesota, but not in its distinctive relation to the Great River. As an agent of the American Fur Company, Morrison continued his operations on the Upper Mississippi until 1826, during which period he did much to encourage immigration to this interesting section of the country.

Before Wisconsin was admitted to the sisterhood of States, all of that region lying east of the Mississippi was regarded as part of Wisconsin Territory; but after her admission as a State there was a considerable population beyond her western boundary without any state or territorial government. At this juncture of affairs, John Catlin, who had been secretary of the Territory of Wisconsin and had just been elected Governor of the new State, believing that the hitherto unclaimed portion of Minnesota was within his jurisdiction, ordered an election for delegate to the House of Representatives of the United States. This election, which was held October thirtieth, 1848, resulted in nominating as candidates, Henry H. Sibley and Henry M. Rice, the former of whom being duly elected, proceeded to Washington and took his seat early in 1849.

Sibley had scarcely had time to realize that he was a representative of the State of Wisconsin, when, at the close of the session of Congress on the third of March, Minnesota was organized as a Territory and that portion of Wisconsin which he had formerly represented was now within the limits of Minnesota. On the next day, March fourth, General Taylor was inaugurated President, and a few days later, appointed the following officers for the government of the Territory. Alexander Ramsay, Governor, Charles K. Smith, secretary; A. Goodrich, chief-justice; and B. B. Meekers and David Cooper, associate-justices of the Supreme Court; H. L. Moss, United States district attorney; and A. M. Mitchell, United States marshal. All of these officials took the oath of office soon after and entered upon their respective duties. On the first of June, 1849, Governor Ramsay issued a proclamation announcing the organization of the territorial government. The Governor also ordered an election of members to the legislative assembly, and a delegate to Congress; the latter office being given to General Sibley, who was now returned to Washington as the representative of Minnesota.

County officers were elected in November of the same year; but the regular election for all officers, including a delegate to Congress, was not held until the first Monday of September, 1850. At this election, General Sibley was returned to Congress and A. M. Mitchell became his colleague.

Minnesota was now fairly launched upon her political career, and nothing seemed wanting to assure for her a prosperous and enviable future. Her great natural resources, her splendid commercial advantages, and her confident and enterprising citizens, all tended to make her outlook most promising and insure for her a brilliant and glorious destiny.

SAINT PAUL IN 1841

CHAPTER V.

THE "TWIN CITIES."

OF the numberless cities which have sprung into existence since the discovery of the American continent, few have attracted such wide-spread attention as Saint Paul and Minneapolis, and although the growth of some of our great commercial centers has been phenomenal, none have advanced more rapidly in wealth and population than the "Twin Cities" of the Northwest. What they were and what they have become, the remarkable development of their resources, and when, how, and by whom the foundations of an unparalleled prosperity were laid, constitute one of the most interesting chapters in the history of Minnesota.

SAINT PAUL.

After the explorations of Hennepin, only an occasional missionary or adventurous traveler found his way to the Falls of Saint Anthony, and no permanent settlement was attempted in this vicinity until 1838, when the first building was erected and a trading-post located on the site of the present city of Saint Paul. In 1841, the Jesuits established a mission here and built a log chapel, which they dedicated to Saint Paul, the name subsequently given to the town which quickly sprung up around it.

Although the embryo Saint Paul was surveyed in 1845, there were but three families on the ground in 1847. In the same year it was laid out into village streets, and in 1849 became the capital of the Territory. At this time its entire population did not exceed three hundred souls. A municipal government was established in 1854, when three thousand inhabitants were claimed. At the close of 1856 the population had increased to ten thousand. Very few of the original buildings were to be seen at this period, as the greater share of these relics of pioneer days had been replaced by more commodious and imposing residences and substantial business blocks. In 1880, twenty-four years later, its population had been multiplied by five, the census returns giving fifty thousand. In 1849 the business of the place amounted to $131,000, which increased so rapidly that in 1854 it amounted to $6,000,000, with a capital of $700,000 invested. Since that date its financial development has been phenomenal, perhaps not equaled by more than two or three cities in this country.

Saint Paul is most fortunate in its location, resting as it does upon three elevations or plateaus overlooking the Mississippi, and in the rear, surrounded by a gracefully undulating and elevated ridge, which, for the most part, constitutes the residence portion of the city. The central plateau is from eighty to ninety feet above the surface of the river, with an excellent steamboat landing at each extremity.

The original town was regularly laid out, but the additions are irregular. The streets are well graded and generally paved. The upper terrace or plateau is underlaid by a stratum of limestone from twelve to

VIEW OF SAINT PAUL IN 1891

twenty feet thick, and of this material many of the buildings are constructed. Five bridges span the river; electric street-car lines connect all parts of the city, and reach also to Minneapolis, while a splendid sewerage system drains it of all impurities.

Saint Paul is nominally at the head of navigation of the Mississippi, the further progress of steamboats up the river being checked by the rapids below the Falls of Saint Anthony. The river at this point is open from two hundred to two hundred and forty days in the year, and many steamboats arrive and depart daily. It is a thorough business city, its chief thoroughfares being lined with large and well-built stores and warehouses, the movement of its citizens on the streets indicating the hurry and preoccupation of pressing business pursuits. The casual visitor is reminded of Chicago more than of any other city of the West. At its back lie the lumber and grain producing regions of Minnesota, Dakota, and Wisconsin, which are yearly filling up with an intelligent and industrious people. Much of their produce finds an outlet at this port, and here they look for a great portion of their supplies. The retail trade of Saint Paul is very large, and it is also in great part the wholesale center of a large circle of smaller towns.

Its double line of river bank affords ample wharfage; while its network of railways connect it with Minneapolis and every town of importance in Minnesota and adjoining States. These secure permanence to its prosperity, since railroads, even more than rivers, make flourishing cities at the present day.

The State Capitol occupies an entire square on an elevation overlooking the city and river. The ground upon which this building stands is sightly, and it is to be hoped that the present structure will soon be replaced by something more in keeping with the resources, enterprise, and bright anticipations of Saint Paul, and the grandest State of the great Northwest.

Among the institutions which are worthy of notice the Library Association, the Minnesota Historical Society, and Academy of Natural Sciences deserve especial mention. The Library Association and Historical Society have fine libraries, and are open to the public daily, while the Academy of Sciences has upon its shelves over a hundred and forty thousand specimens in natural history.

In its early days the Historical Society was the pride of Minnesota, and counted among its members many of the representative men of the State and country. To be named as its president or secretary was an evidence of distinguished citizenship. Dating from the organization of the territorial legislature in 1849, this society has had a most eventful and interesting career. Through the enterprise of Governor Ramsey and Rev. E. D. Neil, its first president and secretary, much valuable information has been obtained relating to aboriginal times and the early settlement of the State.

Saint Paul enjoys superior religious and educational advantages, as its numerous schools, and churches of all denominations, attest. Many of the churches are elegant structures, and the ministrations of the clergy are characterized by well-directed zeal.

The press of a city has much to do in promoting its welfare and shaping its destinies, and the importance of this powerful and influential factor in any community can hardly be overestimated. A sketch of Saint Paul and Minneapolis would therefore seem incomplete without some reference to the enterprising journalists and journals of these cities that have contributed so largely to their development. Through their unbounded faith in the resources and future of this section of our country and their unceasing labors in its behalf, they have accomplished a work whose value it would be difficult to determine, and which entitles them to rank among the benefactors of the Northwest.

The first to establish a newspaper at Saint Paul was Professor A. Randall of Cincinnati, who had been for some years identified with the Geological Survey of Minnesota, its name was the *Minnesota Register,* and the date of its birth April twenty-seventh, 1849. Although the initial number of this sheet was printed in Cincinnati, it was dated at Saint Paul, and was in every sense a Saint Paul newspaper —a Minnesota newspaper, and the first ever published in the Territory.

On the day following the issue of the *Register* another paper, bearing the significant title of *Pioneer,* made its appearance. Although the *Register* had twenty-four hours the start of its rival, it soon fell behind in circulation and popularity, and but for its timely union with the *Chronicle* would doubtless have collapsed on the very threshold of its career. In the meantime, Randall of the former and James Hughes, who had established the latter, severed their connection with their protégé, the *Chronicle and Register,* leaving it in the hands of Major McLean and D. Owens, under whom it was conducted with success for some months in the interest of the Whig party.

Having interests outside of their paper, McLean and Owens sold the establishment to David Olmstead, a democrat, and it now became the organ of that party in Minnesota. It is said by some local writers that during the period the *Chronicle and Register* was owned by Olmstead it had several editors, but "for the most part, it edited itself."

The first number of the *Minnesota Democrat* was brought out in December, 1849, by D. A. Robertson, and at about the same time, C. J. Henniss, formerly of Philadelphia, purchased the *Chronicle and Register*. A few months later this sheet succumbed—the type and presses being transferred to the *Democrat*.

The *Minnesotian* was an offshoot of the *Pioneer*, and its first number was issued September seventeenth, 1851. Its publication was undertaken by a committee, with J. P. Owens in charge of the editorial and J. S. Terry at the head of the financial department. On the sixth of January following it passed into the hands of Owens and Moore, under whose names it continued for several years.

Since 1849 over a hundred daily and weekly newspapers have been established in the "Twin Cities," many of which have proved successful ventures and justified the enthusiastic confidence of their enterprising founders. The history of these papers alone, if presented in detail, would furnish material for a large and interesting volume, but is entirely beyond the aim of the present work, which is simply to deal with the press of to-day, making slight reference only to its early beginnings.

Prominent among the existing journals of Saint Paul is the *Pioneer-Press*, an ably edited and influential daily, originally the *Pioneer*, founded in

1849 by James Goodhue. Its success as a newspaper and organ of public opinion may be inferred from the fact that since its publication it has superseded or absorbed no less than twenty-five of its contemporaries. The *Press,* the latest and most important of those acquired, was founded in 1861 by James Wheelock, and united its fortunes with the *Pioneer* in 1875, from which date to the present the paper has borne the compound title of *Pioneer-Press.* Journalism can not be said to have had any real existence in Minnesota before the establishment of this paper. The *Pioneer-Press* now extends its circulation and influence over Minnesota and the adjoining States. Its office in Saint Paul is said to be one of the finest buildings of its kind in the country

Next in point of seniority is the Saint Paul *Dispatch,* an evening paper, founded in February, 1863, by H. P. Hall, David Ramaley, and John W. Cunningham. The *Dispatch* has been a consistent exponent and advocate of Republican principles from its foundation to the present day, and an eminently successful sheet from its start, when it presented only four columns of news to its subscribers, a fifth column being devoted to the editorial exposition of its politics. It was enlarged twice during its first year owing to an increasing demand and the growth of Republican views. Its size has been considerably increased since, and to-day it presents an amplitude of surface nearly equal to that of the dailies of Chicago and New York. In 1870, Ramaley withdrew from the partnership, Cunningham having parted with his interest shortly after the founding of the paper. Thus, Hall, in 1870, became sole proprietor and retained the ownership until September, 1876, when the plant was disposed of to a company, at the head of which was H. A. Castle. In July, 1880, the proprietorship passed to W. R. Marshall and C. C. Andrews, the latter gentleman retiring in the following year, Castle again becoming the owner of the paper In 1885, George K. Shaw succeeded Castle, and a few months later, George Thompson, its present proprietor, undertook the management of the paper.

The *Dispatch*, after frequently changing hands, has, at length, found its place as a powerful representative and index of public opinion. Under its present vigorous management it has succeeded beyond all precedent, and is to-day the recognized leading Republican journal of the Northwest. It is an eminently "wide-awake" channel of news, having the franchise of the Associated Press and the exclusive day news of the United Press—the two greatest news-gathering associations in the world. It has also a corps of several hundred special correspondents in various parts of the country and in nearly every city of the Northwest. The decided views of the *Dispatch*, in politics, have gained for it a host of friends and supporters and added greatly to its influence and circulation. It is to-day *par excellence* the Republican paper of Saint Paul, and its tone in all social and political matters has secured for it a distinction second to no other newspaper in Minnesota and the adjoining States. Its prominent position to-day is doubtless an augury of still greater success in the future.

January fifteenth, 1881, the first issue of the Saint Paul *Globe* appeared as an organ of the Democracy of the Northwest. In 1885 it passed into the control of the *Globe* Publishing Company, and has since been recognized as a great and influential journal under the efficient management of Hon. Lewis Baker, formerly of the Wheeling *Register*, assisted by Henry T. Black. It has deservedly attained an immense circulation in Saint Paul and Minneapolis; in the latter of which its patrons are nearly as numerous as in the former city. It also circulates throughout Minnesota and all the adjoining States. The *Globe* publishing office in the capital city is a stately ten-story, brown stone building, while in Minneapolis, the company has erected a magnificent edifice similar to their headquarters in Saint Paul. Under its able management the *Globe* has attained the position of the leading Democratic journal of the Northwest.

The *Daily News*, founded in December, 1887, is the junior member of the Saint Paul daily press. In February, 1892, its control passed to the *News* Publishing Company, of which Clarence E. Sherin is the president and general manager. It was originally a sheet of four pages, but is now composed of eight and on Saturdays of sixteen pages. Independent in politics, it is earnest in its advocacy of measures promotive of the public good. The great increase of its circulation has rendered necessary an enlargement of its premises and an important addition to its plant. It has already attained a well-recognized standing as a purveyor of news and an index of public opinion.

The current literature of Saint Paul is not confined to the daily press. Some of its ablest periodicals are published in the form of weeklies and monthlies, and cater to the wants of the citizen under various titles. Herein the threads of history, science, and art are woven into Northwestern life. The numerous departments of industry are well and faithfully represented, while room is found to minister to the religious sentiment of the various churches.

Among the weekly publications of Saint Paul the following may be enumerated· The *Herald, Journal of Commerce, Northwestern Chronicle, Trade Reporter,* West Saint Paul *Times,* and others of equal merit. The monthlies and bi-monthlies are probably still more numerous and varied, including the *Northwestern Magazine, Book Talk, Financial News, Odd Fellow, Woman's Record,* and *Northwestern Farmer.*

There are many points of interest and places of resort in and around Saint Paul, among which Carver's Cave, Fountain Cave, White Bear and Bald Eagle lakes are the most frequently visited.

On the eastern bank of the Mississippi, near the shore, and within the city limits, is the celebrated Carver's Cave, which is reached by an opening in Dayton Bluff. It was in the interior of this cave that Captain Carver made his famous treaty with the Dakota Indians. He describes it as a "remarkable cave of amazing depth, having an entrance about ten feet wide, and an arch within about fifteen feet high and about thirty broad, the bottom consisting of clear white sand."

Concerning the lake and some other features which constitute striking peculiarities of this cave, Carver doubtless gave more or less exaggerated accounts; still, in view of the fact that he had no instruments or other means of taking measurements, it is perhaps after all not strange that he differs materially from the figures given by more recent investigation. Continuing his description of the cave, he explains that about thirty feet from its entrance he came to a lake, the water of which was transparent and extended to an indefinite distance. Being unable to acquire a correct knowledge of its dimensions, he says: "I threw a pebble toward the interior part of it with my utmost strength; I could hear that it fell into the water, and notwithstanding it was of a small size, it caused an astonishing noise that reverberated through all these gloomy regions. I found in this cave many Indian hieroglyphics, which appeared very ancient, for time had nearly covered them with moss, so that it was with difficulty I could trace them. They were cut in a rude manner upon the inside of the wall, which was composed of a stone so extremely soft that it might be easily penetrated with a knife."

It is to be regretted that while Carver found sufficient excuse for complaining that Hennepin and La Hontan were often in error as to their estimates, he was frequently wide of the mark himself in many of his calculations, and those who visit Carver's Cave to-day will hardly reconcile their own view to that portrayed by its famous discoverer.

Fountain Cave is two miles from the city, and derives its name from a small stream which flows through it, and which, doubtless, was the originating cause of the cave. It contains several chambers, some of ample dimensions, and it is said that at one thousand feet from the opening in the rock no termination has yet been discovered. The rock is of pure white, soft sandstone, and the entrance to the cave

WHITE BEAR LAKE.

about fifteen feet in width. About three hundred feet from its mouth a cascade, some twenty feet in height, falls into the stream. This cave is a favorite retreat during the summer months, and presents many features of interest to the geologist.

White Bear Lake, twelve miles from Saint Paul, and about an equal distance from Minneapolis, is already a popular pleasure resort. This lake is about four miles in length, and nearly midway between its eastern and western shores is a long forest-covered islet. The water of the lake is clear, pure, and of the color of the bright-blue sky overhead.

The largest fleet of sailing yachts to be found on any western lake is seen floating on White Bear, many of them costly and of elegant construction. Large hotels have been erected on the eastern and southern banks for the accommodation of visitors, while picturesque villas dot its western shore, owned chiefly by wealthy business men of Saint Paul and Minneapolis, who send their families here to reside during the summer, and join them each evening after the close of business.

White Bear is the oldest summer resort in the State, and "camping out" on its shores is reduced to a science. We found several encampments near the lake large enough to be called villages, many of the tents being as commodious and comfortably furnished as the parlors and bedrooms of a well-ordered city residence.

Bald Eagle Lake lies a mile beyond White Bear. It is a beautiful sheet of water, but not so large as the latter. It has high banks and is well stocked with several varieties of fish, which have made it quite famous in this particular. A few pretty cottages have been built here and occupied as summer residences. Some years since a mineral spring was discovered a short distance from the lake and a pavilion erected over it by the late Dr. Post of Saint Paul, who also built a summer home near by.

In the country adjacent to White Bear and Bald Eagle there are numerous smaller lakes, which are frequently sought by those who delight in fishing and duck hunting. The city park and race-course are located on the shores of Lake Como, two miles from the center of Saint Paul.

MINNEAPOLIS.

Having viewed Saint Paul and its surroundings, we now proceed to a brief description of its sister city. Saint Anthony, now within the corporate limits of Minneapolis, saw its beginning in December, 1849, although a single log cabin stood upon its site twelve years before this date. The first dwelling in Minneapolis proper was erected during the same winter by Colonel John H. Stevens, who had served with distinction under Scott and Taylor in Mexico. When his services were no longer required upon the tented field, this gallant soldier sought a home on the frontier, and, proceeding to Minnesota, built his rustic cottage on the west bank of the Mississippi near the Falls of Saint Anthony.

The name "Minneapolis" is compounded of Indian and Greek—*Minne* being the Sioux for water, and *polis* the Greek for city, thus signifying the Water City, or City of Waters. In a lecture before the Minneapolis Lyceum in 1855, Colonel Stevens said:

"One of our early and most perplexing difficulties was the selection of a name for our embryo city.

Colonel James M. Goodhue thought 'All Saints' to be a good name. Miss Mary Schofield wrote many letters for publication in Eastern papers and always dated from 'All Saints.' At our first claim meeting in 1851, 'Lowell' was adopted. At a public meeting in November of that year our entire population was present and we hit upon 'Albion.' This name the citizens soon got tired of, and at last as a compromise it was left to George D. Bowman, editor of the Saint Anthony *Express*. Mr. Bowman proposed, 'Minneapolis,' which met some opposition at first, but he came out every week with an article in his paper on 'Minneapolis,' and all finally swallowed it."

Whatever may be said of the various names which were suggested, discussed, and applied to this growing metropolis of the Upper Mississippi, it is now universally admitted that Minneapolis is a happy combination of the native Sioux and classic Greek, and beautifully expresses the idea which its author desired to convey.

Minneapolis is located on what was formerly known as the Military Reserve of Fort Snelling, a tract of land nine miles square, assigned to and surrounding the fort for purposes of forage. In 1855 Congress granted the right of pre-emption to the settlers, since which its growth has been most remarkable. The city proper is situated on the west side of the river, while Saint Anthony, which was united to it by mutual agreement, is on the east side, the two forming one city under the name of Minneapolis.

Minneapolis is ten miles above Saint Paul and is built on a broad esplanade overlooking the river and its falls, rapids, and picturesque bluffs. The streets are generally laid out at right angles eighty feet in width, bordered by sidewalks twenty feet wide, with double rows of trees on each side throughout the residence portion of the city. The founders of Western cities have gained wisdom from the mistakes of those of the Eastern coast. Notwithstanding the broad expanse of country, which to the early colonists seemed limitless, the cities and towns built on and near the Atlantic seaboard were modeled upon European plans, even to the narrow streets and compact rows of buildings. Not so in the West. The original plans of our Western towns are so wisely designed that no future increase of population, with its attendant demands for dwelling and business houses, can ever transform them into an aggregation of dense, stifling streets and lanes, such as are too often found in most of our Eastern cities. Health and beauty are two objects which have been kept steadily in view in their foundation. Though their rude beginnings have not always been attractive, the possibilities of beauty are always there, and time is sure to develop them.

A suspension bridge connecting Saint Anthony with Minneapolis was built in 1855. It was not only the first bridge built in Minnesota, but was also the first to span the Mississippi. A ferry-boat established here in 1851 brought its proprietor, that summer, three hundred dollars. In 1855, the receipts from this ferry had increased to twelve thousand. The population of the united towns amounted to over a hundred and fifty thousand in 1890, with the certain prospect of doubling and even trebling these figures in a very few years. The river here is about six hundred yards in width, and above Saint Anthony Falls rushes through low banks in foaming, tremulous rapids, until it reaches the precipice, whence it springs in a single leap down a distance of sixteen feet. Thence it proceeds in a series of rapids over piles of rock in its bed for several hundred yards, the great descent of eighty-two feet being made in a little less than two miles. Below the Falls the cliffs are bold and picturesque, the character of the scenery varying.

Concerning the height of the Falls and the breadth of the river at this point, much incorrect information has been published. Hennepin, who was the first white man to visit the spot, states them to be from fifty to sixty feet high. It was this explorer who gave them the name which they now bear, in honor of Saint Anthony of Padua, whom he had taken for the protection of his discovery. Carver reduces their height to about thirty feet. His strictures upon Hennepin, however, whom he charges with exaggeration, might with propriety be retorted upon himself, and we feel strongly inclined to speak of this daring adventurer as he spoke of his predecessor: "The good Father, I fear, too often had no other foundation for his accounts than report, or, at most, a slight inspection." Lieutenant Pike, who is more accurate than any traveler whom we have followed, states the perpendicular fall to be sixteen and a half feet. It was again measured in 1817, with a plumb-line, from the table rock from which the water was falling, and found to be the same. The measurement at this time was made with a rough water-level, which made it about fifteen feet. The difference of a foot is trifling and might depend upon the place where the investigation was made; but we can not account for the statement made by Schoolcraft that the river has a perpendicular pitch of forty feet, and this as late as fourteen years after Pike's measurement.

The breadth of the river near the brink of the fall is five hundred and ninety-four yards. Below the fall it contracts to about two hundred yards. There is a considerable rapid both above and below, and a portage of two hundred and sixty poles in length was usually made here in pioneer days. The difference of level between the place of disembarking and reloading was stated by Pike to be fifty-éight feet, which is undoubtedly very near the truth. The entire fall to the foot of the rapids, which extend down the river several miles, may be estimated at about one hundred feet.

The Falls of Saint Anthony are not without a legend to hallow their scenery and enhance the interest which of themselves they are well calculated to awaken. The following tragic story was current some years ago among the Indians and white settlers in the neighborhood of the Falls: A Chippewa girl, bearing the name of Ampato Sapa, which signifies "The Dark Day," was wedded to an Indian of the Dakota tribe. Ampato was not beautiful but young and proud, and the mother of two lovely children. For several years they lived together happily, and both doted on their little ones with a depth of feeling seldom equaled by more civilized races. Becoming great as a hunter, the husband of Ampato was considered a man of importance, and many of the surrounding families sought his friendship and protection, and shared the products of his chase. Some of them, anxious to strengthen their interest with the successful hunter, urged him to form a connection with their family, telling him that a second wife was indispensable to a man of his standing, who would probably soon be acknowledged as a chief. The daughter of an influential man was finally presented to him, and, animated with the desire of attaining to high honor in his nation by a union with the daughter of a man of influence, he took a second wife without mentioning the subject to the young mother of his children. Desirous of conciliating his first wife, for whom he still retained much regard, he introduced the subject to her in these words:

"You know, Ampato, that I can love no woman so fondly as I do you. With deep regret I have seen you subjected to toils which must be oppressive and from which I would gladly release you, yet I know of no other way of doing so than by associating with you in the duties of our household one who shall relieve you from the trouble of entertaining the numerous guests whom my growing importance in the nation collects around me. I have therefore resolved upon taking another wife, but she shall always be subject to your control."

With the deepest concern, his wife listened to this unexpected announcement. She remonstrated with him in the kindest terms, and tearfully entreated, by every consideration her devoted love could suggest, that he would not let another take her place in his affections. The Indian, with much duplicity, still concealed from her the secret of his marriage with another, while she put forth her strongest appeals in the effort to convince him that she was equal to the tasks imposed upon her. She pleaded all the endearments of their past life, dwelling on his former fondness for her, his regard for her happiness and that of their children, and cautioned him to beware of the consequences of uniting himself to a woman of whom he knew very little. Finding her still opposed to his wishes, he at length informed her that further opposition on her part was useless, as he had already selected another partner; and that if she could not receive his new wife as a friend, she must receive her as an encumbrance, for he had resolved she should reside with him.

Deeply distressed at this information, she stole away from the cabin with her infant and fled to her father She remained with him for a time, until some Indians with whom he lived went up the Mississippi on a winter hunt. When they returned in early spring, with their canoes loaded with skins, they encamped near the Falls. After they had left in the morning, Ampato lingered near the spot, and soon launching a light canoe, entered it with her babes. She paddled down the stream chanting her death-song. Her friends saw her only too late, and their attempts to arrest her progress were of no avail. She was heard to sing in doleful strain of the past happiness she had enjoyed while she was the sole object of her husband's affections. Finally her voice was drowned in the roar of the cataract; for a moment the canoe and its hapless freight trembled on the brow of the watery precipice, and in an instant more mother and children were lost forever in the foam below.

"Yet, that Death-Song, they say, is heard
Above the gloomy waters' roar,
When trees are by the night-wind stirred,
And darkness broods o'er wave and shore."

The Falls are divided by Cataract Island, from which a dam has been constructed to the eastern shore to furnish water-power for manufacturing purposes, and nearly the whole volume of water now rushes through the western channel. The Falls may be seen with equal advantage from either shore, but the best view is obtained from the center of the suspension bridge which crosses the river above them and from which the rapids may be seen boiling and rushing immediately beneath.

These Falls furnish abundant power for manufacturing purposes, and as early as 1856, large mills were already in operation at Saint Anthony, in which millions of feet of lumber were annually sawn. The logs which fill the Mississippi above the Falls, sometimes even to the point of obstructing navigation, all have their destination at Minneapolis. Here they are converted into lumber and laths and sent to distant sections of the country, perhaps in the form of huge rafts again set afloat upon the river. The lumber business of this city is immense, probably exceeding that of any other city in the country. It is equaled only by the flour-mills of this rapidly growing western giant.

Although originally termed the "City of Waters," Minneapolis is to-day more widely known as the "Flour City," owing to its numerous flour-mills which now line both banks of the river from the southern to the extreme northern limit of the city. There is no doubt that Minneapolis stands at the head of the flour manufacturing of the world. She certainly has no equal in this particular in this country or Europe. The wheat raised in such immense quantities on neighboring farms is ground

FALLS OF MINNEHAHA.

into flour and shipped to every corner of the habitable globe.

The tourist who visits the "Twin Cities" will discover at a glance that Minneapolis is more a manufacturing than a commercial city. Saint Paul monopolizes much of the commerce of the Upper Mississippi, as steamboats can only ascend to Fort Snelling, some miles below the Falls of Saint Anthony, hence Minneapolis depends largely upon the railroads for transportation. But while Saint Paul measures miles of streets lined with stores and warehouses, the "Flour City" exhibits an equal number of mills and factories.

Minneapolis is a city of beautiful homes, and it is perhaps no exaggeration to say that few, if any, of our American cities present greater natural attractions. The streets, as we have said, are broad and amply shaded, and the residences are, many of them, very handsomely built, and surrounded by ornamental gardens.

The University of Minnesota is located here, and there are also several other important educational institutions; while the public schools are in every respect among the best in the country. Of her libraries, the Athenæum ranks first, having an excellent and commodious reading-room, and on its shelves over twenty thousand volumes; the University possesses a library of several thousand, chiefly works of a scientific character. There are over a hundred churches of all denominations, and some of the sacred edifices are very elegant structures.

The press of Minneapolis is not among the least of the latter's claims to distinction. It is in most respects on a par with that of cities many times its size, its editors and managers being, for the most part, men of large and liberal views, and writers of experience, judgment, and tact. The dailies supply all the news up to the latest moment of going to press, and the editorials, as a rule, are tolerant yet earnest in dealing with local, state, or national issues.

Almost coeval with the city itself is the Minneapolis *Tribune,* an important journal, founded in 1866. It is a morning paper, and publishes also a noon and an evening edition. In 1877, the plant was purchased by David Blakely, whose energy and tact may be said to have laid the foundation of its ultimate success as an exponent of Republican principles and a purveyor of cosmopolitan news. Blakely was joined by General A. B. Nettleton, who took a half interest in the paper in 1884. These gentlemen sold out to A. J. Blethen of the Kansas City *Journal,* and W. E. Haskell, son of E. B. Haskell, editor and joint proprietor of the Boston *Herald.* In 1888 Haskell purchased the interest of of his partner, and, in conjunction with Charles M. Palmer of the *Northwestern Miller,* assumed entire control of the paper. In the following year Haskell became sole proprietor, C. M. Schultz being managing editor. The ownership is now vested in ex-Senator Gilbert A. Pierce and W. J. Murphy of Grand Forks, North Dakota. These gentlemen are thoroughly identified with the newspaper business, and under their able management the *Tribune* has attained a great success, its circulation embracing Minnesota and extending to the adjoining States of Wisconsin, Iowa, and the Dakotas.

In 1890 the *Tribune* met with a great disaster, its handsome building having been destroyed by fire. A commodious structure has since been erected, and at the present date, 1892, the paper is a potent factor in all that concerns the interests of the section it represents.

The *Evening Journal* was established in 1878, and has attained a comparatively wide circulation. In November, 1885, it passed under the control of its present management, Lucius Swift, J. S. McLain, W E. Brownlee, and W B. Chamberlain. In politics the *Journal* claims to be independent, with a leaning toward Republicanism, and aims to mold public opinion upon most topics of general interest. In the discussion of social and public questions it expresses its views fearlessly, and occasionally with effect. Its news columns are supplied by the Associated Press and the United Press, and furnish liberally the latest intelligence of the day upon every matter of importance to its readers. Special correspondents throughout Minnesota, Wisconsin, Michigan, Dakota, Iowa, and in the East, add interest to its columns.

The *Times* is the junior member of the Minneapolis daily press, having made its first appearance October first, 1889, in the form of a single sheet. Its growth in size has been rapid to a double sheet on week days and a sixteen-page paper on Sundays. The reports of the Associated and United Press are utilized in its news columns, while a large number of well-known correspondents in most of the principal cities enliven its pages with well-written articles on general topics of interest. The *Times* is a consistent advocate of Democratic principles, and in the discussion of politics and social questions is uniformly fair and liberal. The paper is owned by a company, of which F G Winston of Minneapolis is the president; John Blanchard, a gentleman of large experience in the conduct of a newspaper, is editor-in-chief; the management being under the able supervision of Frank L. Thresher.

Intellectually and materially, Minneapolis presents all the features of a progressive city, and, if space permitted, extended reference could be made to several of its numerous weekly and monthly publications, which are mostly of a high order, and contribute to the moral and physical advantages of its citizens. Prominent among the weeklies is the *Northwestern Presbyterian*, under the able editorship of Rev. John B. Donaldson, D.D.; the *Saturday Spectator*, an admirably conducted paper, replete with reliable information upon most subjects of interest to the reading public. The *Mississippi Valley Lumberman*, edited by J. Newton Nind, is the representative of the immense lumber interests of the Northwest. The *Northwestern Miller*, of vast practical utility to the milling interest and, indirectly, to the growers of wheat. The *Farmers' Tribune;* the *Temperance Review;* the *Canadian-American*, and others with equal claim to notice, including Sunday German, Swedish, and Norwegian weeklies.

Among the leading monthlies are the *Minnesota Farmer*, *Mechanical World*, *Midland Monthly*, and *Housekeeper*. In short, the journalism of this modern city of scarcely a half century's growth would be creditable to any Eastern city of its size and thrice its age.

A summer resort has become almost indispensable to many during the heated period of the year. Failing health, the desire for change from city life, or the demands of fashion, seeks some favorite watering-place or rustic retreat for rest, recuperation, or pleasure. These are found in the East at more or less considerable distances from the principal cities. In the Northwest the change or relief is found within easy reach of the home, and no cities in the United States are more happily situated in this respect than Saint Paul and Minneapolis. Beautiful lakes and scenery, at comparatively short distances from either city, are reached by railway or electric cars within the space of a half hour, and afford all the rest and enjoyment tired nature craves, or that is obtainable at an inland watering-place. A healthful, invigorating climate, surrounded by natural beauty and facilities for bathing in the crystal waters, or sailing in magnificently appointed yachts or steamboats, form an essential element of pleasure and relief to be found within, or a little beyond, the city limits. The summer tourist can here indulge in the delights of fishing or hunting. Points of special beauty and interest, gratifying to the senses, are numerous in the neighborhood of these lakes, and a month's residence on their banks will not exhaust their treasures and possibilities.

We have before alluded to the system of beautiful lakes easily accessible from Saint Paul, but those in the immediate vicinity of Minneapolis are equally inviting and attractive, and in the opinion of some, still more so.

Before visiting the lake resorts, however, we have a word to say about the Falls of Minnehaha, a spot invested with romance by Longfellow's poetical allusion to them in his deathless song of "Hiawatha," as the "Laughing Water" of the Indian. These Falls are about six miles in a southeasterly direction from the city, and can be reached by railway or the electric cars. The flow reaches them through a silvery stream which issues from several lakes on the western and southwestern sides of the city, and that of the large and beautiful Minnetonka, the current itself, having passed the Falls, winding its way to the Father of Waters. The height of the cataract is about fifty feet, and the "Laughing Water" plunges over a semicircular ledge of rock, while a cloud of spray ascends from the basin beneath, and together they produce an extremely pleasing picture.

Lakes Harriet and Calhoun, whose proximity to the city has rendered them, perhaps, less select than others at a somewhat greater distance, are, nevertheless, highly attractive as resorts, and multitudes of tired citizens flock to them during the summer months for relaxation and pleasure. Lake Calhoun, the nearest, is not much occupied by "campers," probably owing to its want of seclusion. Many summer guests take rooms at the Lyndale Hotel on the margin of the lake, and find health and recreation at this pleasant retreat so conveniently accessible from the city.

Lake Harriet, about a mile beyond Lake Calhoun, is also very attractive. A large number of pretty cottages surround it, and quite a number of well-appointed tents, made habitable and comfortable by their tenants for the season. Fishing in this lake is invariably productive of excellent results.

The surrounding scenery is picturesque and beautiful, the air pure and dry, and the summer heat rarely exceeds 75°. Pleasure-boats float on the surface of the clear water, affording agreeable relief from weariness to the jaded citizen whose temporary

VIEW OF LAKE MINNETONKA IN 1845.

home, with his family, is on the banks of pretty Lake Harriet.

Lake Minnetonka, in point of extent, far exceeds, and in beauty of environment is unapproached by, the smaller lakes above named. This is the favorite retreat of well-to-do citizens of the "Twin Cities" and tourists in search of the beautiful. It is only fifteen miles southwest of Minneapolis. The length of the lake is eighteen miles by five in width. The virgin forest surrounding it lends enchantment to the scene, and shade and repose are found by the weary tourist or transient visitor on the greensward beneath the foliage. Small villages have sprung up on the banks of the lake, with artistic summer cottages, villas, and handsome hotels in their near neighborhood. The woods and more sequestered portions of Minnetonka abound with pheasants, woodcock, rabbits, and squirrels. The village of Excelsior, on the south shore of the lake, eighteen miles from the city, was incorporated in 1879, and has a haven for the large and elegant steamboats that ply on its waters. Wayzata rests on the opposite shore, and is fifteen miles distant from Minneapolis. Many pretty cottages cluster around these lake villages, and several fine yachts are owned by the visitors—residents of Minneapolis and of neighboring cities. Strangers from outside the city, and from a distance, are in most cases quartered at the hotels and hostelries overlooking the beautiful lake. Outdoor life at Minnetonka can be indulged in and enjoyed with the most beneficial hygienic effects, and visitors from all parts of the country, with impaired vitality, come during the summer months to seek and find the boon of restored energies.

VIEWS OF MINNEAPOLIS IN 1891

CHAPTER VI.

PREPARATION FOR SECOND EXPEDITION.

NEARLY a month was spent in Minneapolis, occupied chiefly in correspondence with those whom I desired to form my party, and in such other preparation as was deemed necessary to place the expedition on a practical footing.

Preferring the companionship and co-operation of those who were naturally interested in the geographical problem which I had undertaken to solve, invitations were extended to many eminent geographers and scientists throughout the country, especially to those who had doubts as to the propriety of accepting the lake beyond Itasca as the True Source of the Mississippi. This correspondence led to the acceptance of several who were invited, while some others, for reasons stated in their replies, were not then in a position to leave for so long a period their business and professional duties.

It was the opinion of a few cavilers that our expedition would not include any who were not thoroughly committed to my views on the question of the Ultimate Source of the Great River. This supposition, however, was without the slightest foundation, and in order to disabuse the mind of the reader at once of the impression that I could have been in any sense partial to advocates of my claim, I herewith append the names of those who were solicited to accompany me to the Itascan Basin, many of whom are among our leading geographers, map and educational publishers, who, I felt, were likely to be more or less interested in the objects of the proposed explorations. I may here add that I especially desired to make it clear to my critics that I courted the fullest investigation, and determined that no pains or expense should be spared to insure the attainment of this purpose.

The following is a list of those who were invited to form my Second Expedition, or send representatives Pearce Giles, Camden, New Jersey, journalist; General E. W. Whitaker, Washington, late chief of staff to Generals Custer, Kilpatrick, and Sheridan; Rev. John Calvin Crane, Worcester, Massachusetts; Winfield Scott Shure, York, Pennsylvania, artist and journalist; Fred J. Trost, Toledo, Ohio, photographer; Rev. George A. Peltz, D. D., LL. D , Philadelphia; George F. Cram, Chicago, map and atlas publisher; Rand, McNally and Company, Chicago, Mathews, Northrup and Company, Buffalo, E. H. Butler and Company, Philadelphia; Dr. Jacques W. Redway, New York, editor, *Geographical Magazine;* W. H. Gamble, Philadelphia, geographer; D. S. Knowlton, editor, Boston *Times,* George Thompson, editor, Saint Paul *Dispatch;* Alfred James Murphy, secretary, Michigan State Senate; J. E. Calkins, city editor, *Democrat-Gazette,* Davenport, Iowa; N. D. H. Clark, superintendent, Station C, New York post office; Hon. D. Sinclair, postmaster; editor, Winona *Republican,* Minnesota; Captain A. N. Husted, professor of mathematics, State Normal College, Albany, New York; R. G Thwaites, secretary, Wisconsin Historical Society, Madison; Dr. A. Munsell, editor.

Trade Journal, Dubuque, Iowa; J. L. Smith, map publisher, Philadelphia; Dr. Charles E. Harrison, secretary, Academy of Natural Sciences, Davenport, Iowa; Prof. H. H. Rassweiler, geographer, Chicago; William M. Bradley, map publisher, Philadelphia; Charles H. Ames, of the firm of D. C. Heath and Company, educational publishers, Boston; George H. Adams, map publisher, New York; Charles L. Davis, editor, *Argus*, Red Wing, Minnesota; George H. Benedict, map publisher, Chicago; Charles Lubrecht, map publisher, New York; Prof. H. D. Densmore, Beloit College, Wisconsin; Prof. W. H. Pratt, Davenport Academy of Natural Sciences, Iowa; C. B. Palmer, attorney at law, Saint Paul, Minnesota; Gaylord Watson, map publisher, New York; Albert W. Whitney, botanist, Beloit College, Wisconsin; Hon. W. H. H. Johnston, Saint Paul; Dr George Crocker, Minneapolis; A. H. Hubbard, publisher, Philadelphia; Hon. Samuel Adams, member of the Minnesota Historical Society, Monticello, Minnesota; Hon. L. A. Evans, Saint Cloud, Minnesota.

In addition to the foregoing, several colleges and universities were also invited to send representatives; among these were Oberlin College, Ohio, Cornell University, Ithaca, New York, Beloit College, Wisconsin, and the University of Michigan. Of those who responded to my invitation the following, and several others who joined us at Park Rapids, were duly enrolled as members of the expedition: Pearce Giles, Rev. John C. Crane, Winfield Scott Shure, Dr. A. Munsell, Fred J. Trost, Daniel S. Knowlton, Dr Charles E. Harrison, Albert W. Whitney.

As some zealous critics have seen fit to question the qualifications of the gentlemen who composed my former party, it has been suggested that it might not be inappropriate to introduce with brief reference the companions of my second journey to the Headwaters of the Mississippi. I therefore conclude to present a short sketch of each, which is done with the full conviction that several are worthy of more extended mention than can consistently be accorded them within the limits of this volume.

The oldest in years and the first to avail himself of my invitation was Pearce Giles, formerly of London, England, now of Camden, New Jersey. Mr. Giles, who had just passed his seventy-fifth year, came to America over twenty years ago. His father was an officer in the British navy, and himself a graduate of the Royal Naval College, Greenwich, near London. He was thirty years in the Home Department of the English Government, and retired with a handsome pension in 1871. He has traveled extensively in Europe, Asia, Africa, and America, and the record of his observations in the various countries he has visited constitutes a most interesting chapter in a long and eventful life. Although not an active member of my expedition of 1881, Mr. Giles accompanied me to the Upper Mississippi, assisted in the organization of the party, and was indirectly identified with us throughout.

Rev. John Calvin Crane of Worcester, Massachusetts, is a native of Grafton in that State, and was born October sixteenth, 1837. He graduated at the Lancaster Academy at the age of sixteen, and soon after was recognized as a special correspondent of the Boston *Post*. Mr. Crane was among the pioneers of Minnesota, having been a resident of the State as early as 1858. A year or two later he returned to the "Bay State," and became a contributor to the Worcester *Gazette,* and several other New England publications. He is a member of the Worcester Antiquarian Society; a resident member of the New England Historical and Genealogical Society, and a member and correspondent of the historical societies of Cheshire and Lancashire, England. From boyhood, Mr. Crane has been deeply interested in everything relating to the Mississippi and its True Source, and joined me as a correspondent of the Boston *Herald.*

Winfield Scott Shure is a native of Maryland, but has been for several years past a resident of York, Pennsylvania. Mr. Shure is a young man of considerable promise as an artist and journalist. He joined me as the representative of the York *Daily Age* and other papers, and rendered much valuable assistance in the organization and equipment of our expedition.

Dr A. Munsell of Dubuque, Iowa, is a native of Kentucky, a man of mature years, the editor and proprietor of the Dubuque *Trade Journal,* and a gentleman of comprehensive literary attainments. Residing on the banks of the mighty river, he has been for many years greatly interested in the controversy relating to its Headwaters, and the columns of his paper have ever been open to all who were disposed to discuss the question of the Fountain-head.

Fred J. Trost of Toledo, Ohio, the photographer of the expedition, was born at Volknitz, Pomerania, Prussia, March sixteenth, 1852. He came to this country with his parents in 1854, and at the age of sixteen began the study of photography, which has since been his occupation. Mr. Trost has been connected with some of the best establishments of the country, and for many years has been a member of the American Photographers' Association. His gallery at Toledo ranks among the first establishments of its kind in Ohio.

Daniel S. Knowlton, editor and proprietor of the Boston *Times*, was born in Biddeford, Maine. Completing a preparatory course in the schools of his native State, he entered Yale College at the age of eighteen, from which he graduated four years later with the highest honors of his class. Mr. Knowlton is a young man of advanced attainments in most branches of learning, and his long journey from Boston to Minnesota sufficiently attests his interest in the geographical question which led him to set aside important business engagements in order that he might join us in our investigations.

Dr. Charles E. Harrison, formerly president and now librarian of the Davenport Academy of Natural Sciences, is a native of Kentucky, but has been for many years a citizen of Iowa. His connection with the Academy at Davenport brought him to my notice, and I found him an enthusiast upon every topic relating to the natural history of the Valley of the Mississippi.

Albert W. Whitney of Beloit, Wisconsin, is a graduate of Beloit College, in which his father, H. N. Whitney, is professor of English Literature. Although the youngest in years, Mr. Whitney possesses many excellent qualifications as an explorer, and came highly indorsed by the college faculty as a botanist and arborologist.

My daughter Alice, who had just graduated from the Saint Agnes School at Albany, New York,

MEMBERS OF SECOND EXPEDITION.

pleaded very earnestly to be allowed to accompany me. I hesitated for some time, but at length yielded, on her assurance that she was confident she could endure the rigors of such a journey. She was anxious to stand at the head of the Father of Waters, and, being a very fair artist in water colors, I felt that her talent might prove of some utility to the objects of the expedition.

Although it was the original intention to complete our organization at Minneapolis, I soon ascertained that from an economic point of view it would be to our advantage to secure surveyors, guides, and other assistants in Northern Minnesota; hence only a portion of those who accompanied me were brought together before entering upon our journey.

The route decided upon was by way of the Northern Pacific Railway to Wadena, and thence by a branch of the Great Northern to Park Rapids; the latter road having been completed but a few days before our start from Minneapolis. In my journey across Northern Minnesota, in 1881, the Leech Lake route was preferred for the reason that the region between that point and the Source of the river had not been previously traversed, and for the further reason that we could, at that time, reach our destination more readily by canoe and portage through that section of Minnesota than by any other. Then, too, the facilities now presented by rail and wagon for the transportation of necessary supplies, via Park Rapids, were an important consideration, in view of the large party I had brought together, and rendered that route by far the most practicable.

All arrangements having been completed, we assembled at my residence, on Harmon Place, Monday morning, August seventeenth, where we discussed briefly the objects of our expedition. I took occasion at this time to say that our party was the largest ever organized for purposes of investigation at the Headwaters of the Mississippi, and sought to impress upon the minds of all present that it was my earnest wish that their examination of that region should be most thorough and complete. I especially recommended that they should determine, by careful measurement, the relative length and importance of all streams falling into Itasca and the beautiful lake lying immediately to the south of it, in order that they might be prepared on their return to submit a clear and conclusive verdict as to the True Source of the Great River.

My re-appearance in Minnesota, with the intention of making further explorations, led the press of the country to comment more or less freely upon the probable outcome of my proposed expedition. These expressions of public opinion may be deemed worthy of some consideration, inasmuch as they discuss quite fully the question at issue, and set forth very clearly the results of former investigations; they show, also, something of the character of the opposition which I have had to contend with during the past ten years. In view therefore of all that has been said and written on the subject, for and against, it will perhaps be thought consistent with the purpose of this volume to invite attention to a few quotations from articles which were from time to time brought under my notice.

The *Dispatch*, a leading journal of Saint Paul, has evinced considerable interest in the location of the Source of the Mississippi, and since the date of its discovery in 1881 has, in the discussion of my claim, yielded it a fair, temperate, and disinterested support. Under date, July twenty-third, 1891, the *Dispatch* had the following editorial.

"The arrival in Saint Paul of Captain Glazier has revived interest in a subject which, three or four years ago, was a topic of world-wide discussion. His claim to have discovered, in 1881, the True Source of the Mississippi, while accepted by many, was denied by some, and doubts were thrown upon the accuracy of his conclusions. Even yet there are those who will not admit that Lake Glazier is the Source of the Father of Waters. Professor Aiton of Minneapolis has recently expressed himself on this question, disputing Captain Glazier's claim, but offering no satisfactory solution of the problem.

"From the discovery of Lake Itasca by Schoolcraft in 1832, down to the year 1881, very little was attempted in the way of exploration at the Headwaters of the Mississippi. In the latter year, Captain Glazier organized and assumed the entire expense of an expedition which had for its object a thorough investigation of the Itascan Basin. The thought had long been in his mind that if Pike, Cass, and Beltrami had been in error as to the Source, Schoolcraft also, might have been mistaken in his conclusions as to Lake Itasca.

"On the return of his first expedition, Captain Glazier announced that a lake above and beyond Itasca was the Primal Reservoir; asserted that it had not been so recognized prior to 1881; and claimed that his party was the first to correctly locate its feeders and establish its true relation to the Mississippi. From the position then taken, Glazier has never retreated, and to-day, notwithstanding the opposition of a few unreasoning critics, Lake Glazier is accepted as the True Source of the Great River by nine-tenths of the geographers, map and educational publishers of this country"

The Albany *Knickerbocker* ranks among the first journals of the country in the discussion of geographical questions, and gave much attention to the results of my First Expedition. In one of its articles, this paper observed:

"Many geographical beliefs have in course of time, and in the advancement of knowledge, been proven the veriest myths. It was for some ages contended that there was no world beyond the Pillars of Hercules. It has taken hundreds and hundreds of years to arrive at the most simple and primitive truths. Captain Glazier contends that he has exploded the myth that Itasca is the source of the Father of Waters. His claim is supported by a volume of expert and disinterested testimony, and the gentlemen composing his Second Expedition will doubtless confirm his announcement of 1881, that the origin of the Mississippi is in the lake to the south of Itasca, now generally known and accepted by geographers as Lake Glazier."

Since 1881, the *Argus* of Red Wing, Minnesota, has steadfastly maintained, in common with nearly all the leading papers of the State, that the body of water which my party located in that year should be regarded as the Head of the Mississippi. In its issue of July sixteenth, 1891, the *Argus* spoke as follows:

"The True Source of the Mississippi River does not appear to be a settled question, even though the Minnesota Legislature has decided it, so far as it was able by law to do so. Captain Glazier claimed the discovery of the real Head of the river in 1881, which was named by his companions Lake Glazier Lake Itasca had for many years been considered the source and had been so placed on the maps, but the lake discovered by Captain Glazier was beyond Itasca and flowed into it through a perennial stream. For some reason a few of the savants of our Historical Society disputed the Glazier claim, and appealed to the Legislature for an enactment to prevent its recognition. Notwithstanding this opposition, however, our leading geographers and map publishers, as well as most of the encyclopedias, recognize the fact that Glazier was the real discoverer of the lake now called after him.

"Captain Glazier is about to organize another expedition to the Headwaters of the Mississippi, which is expected to leave Saint Paul this month. His chief object in making a second visit is to obtain sketches and photographs of scenery at the source of the river, and to give some attention to the natural history of the surrounding country, as well as to secure additional information concerning the feeders of Lake Glazier An artist, photographer, surveyor, and several gentlemen of scientific attainments will be members of the expedition. These gentlemen, it is presumed, will be fully qualified to pass final judgment upon the claim of Captain Glazier to have definitely located, in 1881, the True Source of the Mississippi."

The *Trade Journal* of Dubuque, Iowa, edited by Dr. A. Munsell of that city, has been for several years an ardent participant in all discussions concerning the Head of the Great River. In its July issue of 1891 the *Journal*, in referring to the subject, said·

"Since the discovery and announcement of Lake Glazier as the Source of the Mississippi, it has been very generally recognized by the geographical world and by writers in the later encyclopedias. There are those, however, who have denied the newly asserted fact, and have even taken some pains to contradict and argue against the propriety of according it recognition. It is often difficult to sympathize with a new truth which dispels the illusion of a lifetime, and the views, customs, and complacency ingrained by education and habit. So, when called upon to surrender the honor that has for more than a half century clung to the Itasca of Schoolcraft, and bid good-by to the associations that have been pleasantly connected with the charming Indian word, it is perhaps little wonder that prejudice and conservatism are reluctant. But truth and duty have no heed save for the verities of the actual, and the modern day is a time when the white light of science and fact is allowed to fall safely and freely on that which is in the realm of reality"

Foremost among the leading newspapers of New England, the Boston *Herald* exhibited its usual enterprise in sending a special correspondent to join us in Minnesota. Commenting on my proposed visit to the Headwaters, the *Herald* said:

* * * "Captain Glazier believed that Schoolcraft was at fault in locating the source of the Mississippi in Lake Itasca, and during the summer of 1881 began a thorough personal investigation of the subject. Standing on the shore of the beautiful heart-shaped lake to the south of Itasca—the *Pokegama* of the Chippewas—he announced to the geographical world the fact that the True Head of the Father of Waters was there to be found. A geographical error had existed for nearly half a century and it was hard to change the order of things. Would-be explorers, and geographers unheard of before, sprang up in a night and sought in some way to immortalize their names in connection therewith. Some denied the truth of Captain Glazier's statements; but when it was established that the position he had taken was impregnable, they objected to having his name applied to the lake. It was in opposition to the wishes of Glazier that his name was given, but his white and Indian companions persisted and it was finally adopted. So firm is Captain Glazier in the conviction that his position is unassailable that he will lead the largest party of gentlemen to the Headwaters of the Mississippi that has ever visited that region."

The *Times* of Philadelphia has devoted much space and attention to the Mississippi and its Source, and while its columns have been open to both sides of the controversy, its editorial utterances have been clearly in support of the lake beyond Itasca as the Primal Reservoir. In its issue of July twelfth, 1891, the *Times* thus referred to the matter.

"In 1881, Captain Willard Glazier organized, equipped, and led a party through Northern Minnesota for the purpose of determining, if possible, the exact location of the Source of the Mississippi. Under the guidance of a Chippewa Indian, named Chenowagesic, he located, on the twenty-second of July of that year, a beautiful body of water to the south of Lake Itasca, having an average depth of forty-five feet, a circumference of between five and six miles, and an area of 255 acres.

"This lake was known to the Indians as *Pokegama*, meaning 'the place where the waters gather' It has for its feeders three small creeks which have their origin in springs at the foot of sand hills from two to three miles distant. After consultation, the members of the expedition unanimously voted that this body of water be named Lake Glazier, after the man who had organized the expedition and led them, at his own expense, to its shores. Since that time a few critics have seen fit to question, doubt, and finally declare that the Fountain-head of the river is in Lake Itasca; that there was no such lake as Captain Glazier described; or if there was, it was of little consequence. And again, if such a sheet of water did exist, he was not the first white man to see it. Just as if Schoolcraft was the first white man who saw Lake Itasca. It should not be a question of 'who first saw it,' but 'who first discovered its relation to the Mississippi.'

"In view of the various doubts that have been raised, and for the purpose of satisfying scientific, educational, and all other parties who take any interest in the correction of error and the advancement of truth, Captain Glazier is now fitting out a Second Expedition. This party will be composed of naturalists, surveyors, artists, photographers, correspondents of the press, and others who wish to look upon the Source of our Great Central River The country will be carefully examined, prominent views and scenes photographed, and levels and measurements taken. The botanist and geologist will report on the flora and formation of that region. It is confidently expected that the Source of the Mississippi will be established without further cavil or dispute, and that Captain Glazier will give a faithful description and photographic view of that hitherto practically unknown section of Minnesota which enjoys the distinction of embracing the Headwaters of the greatest river of North America."

The press of Minnesota, with but two or three unimportant exceptions, favored a further exploration, and said much to encourage my companions in the prosecution of their self-imposed task. The *Globe* of Saint Paul took an active interest in everything pertaining to the controversy. The subjoined article appeared in its columns under date of August sixteenth, 1891:

"On to-morrow, August seventeenth, Captain Glazier will start from Minneapolis with his Second Expedition to the Source of the Mississippi. The explorer goes with the determination of substantiating his claim of 1881, that he discovered, in a body of water beyond Itasca—since known as Lake Glazier—the True Source of the Father of Waters. Among those who will accompany him in his later visit is Rev. J C. Crane of Worcester, Massachusetts, who is now in Saint Paul. Speaking of the expedition, he said.

"'The attention of a large portion of the people of this country is at present directed to a wild and unsettled region of Minnesota. The particular locality referred to is that lying about the Source of what is, in many respects, the greatest river in the world. The complete history of this wonderful waterway, if written, would fill volumes. The chief reason for the interest now taken, arises from investigations made at the Headwaters of the river in 1881. In July of that year, Captain Willard Glazier led a party by a new and untried route to a lake which he claimed as the Ultimate Source of the Mississippi.

"'From 1832 to 1881, the statements of Schoolcraft with regard to the Fountain-head of the mighty stream were unquestioned. The announcement by Glazier that there was a beautiful lake above and beyond Itasca was a great surprise to the geographical world, and as one somewhat versed in the geography and history of the country, I became interested in his claim to have definitely located the Origin of the Great River I had been an early pioneer in Minnesota—had journeyed days and nights on the pure waters of the Upper Mississippi. As a hunter I had sailed its tributaries and camped along their shores. What more natural than that I, although no longer a resident of the State, should take an interest in the Source of her ideal river? I began anew the study of the Mississippi and its place of beginning. I investigated the claim of Captain Glazier and read its numerous indorsements. I digested also the pamphlet of General Baker, and heard and read of the progress of Mr. Brower in that locality, and in fact made a thorough study of all the reports on the question of the True Source since Glazier announced his discovery in 1881. One thing became very evident to my mind, and that was that the latter gentleman had never receded in any measure from the position first taken, which was that the Fountain-head was in a lake to the south of Itasca, known to the Indians as *Pokegama*. After a long and careful study of the question, and hearing all the pros and cons, I could not help the belief that the claim put forth by Captain Glazier was based upon careful investigation and honest conviction. I had never seen the lake of Schoolcraft, neither had I looked upon the *Pokegama* of the Chippewas, but I had seen the flowing stream as it fell in beauty over the Falls of Saint Anthony, and had noted its onward rush to the Gulf, three thousand miles away I had observed with what tenacity Glazier clung to his announcement of 1881. The thought came to me, this man is honest in his premises, and the more I studied the subject, the more I became satisfied that Lake Glazier answered all the requirements of geographers. Upon investigation, I found many who agreed with me in this belief. The written testimony of eminent educators, map publishers, and compilers of encyclopedias was examined with care.

"'Early in the present year, rumors of another expedition to be made by Captain Glazier reached my ear. Later an opportunity was presented me to become a member of the party of gentlemen who are to leave Minneapolis to-morrow to ascertain for themselves on what ground Willard Glazier bases his claim to have definitely located, in 1881, the True Source of the Mississippi River. So strong is the captain in his convictions and statements then made, that he has called about him the largest and most influential body of men that has ever been brought together for this purpose. As an humble member of that expedition, I go with the honest purpose of seeing for myself the foundation upon which I have built my belief. As a historian of some repute in the 'Old Bay State,' it would ill become me to give my sanction to a claim which upon investigation should fail to uphold opinions previously expressed.'"

Henry R. Cobb, editor of the Hubbard County *Enterprise* of Park Rapids, Minnesota, enjoys the distinction of having among his subscribers several pioneers whose claim-cabins are within a few miles of the Source of the Mississippi. In referring to my First and Second expeditions, Mr. Cobb said in his paper:

"On the twenty-second day of July, 1881—ten years ago this summer—Captain Glazier passed through Lake Itasca into a lake beyond, known to the Indians as Po-keg-a-ma. In this body of water he believed he had found the True Source of the Mississippi, which was christened Lake Glazier by his companions. Despite the criticisms of subsequent expeditions Captain Glazier still holds to his convictions, and the present party go for the purpose of adding their evidence on this much discussed question. Whatever their decision as to the Captain's claim, the latter may be credited with having gathered together, from all parts of the Union, a body of men whose testimony will be of weight."

From the time that Lake Itasca was first called in question, the religious press of Minnesota manifested much interest in the controversy. Of these publications, the *Northwestern Presbyterian* of Minneapolis, gave considerable attention to the subject. Referring to it at some length, this journal said in clear and unmistakable terms

"All who live in the valley of America's greatest river will be especially interested in knowing something of its Source, its course, and the cities that line its banks. Since De Soto first discovered the Father of Waters in 1541, many eminent explorers have been associated with its history Marquette, Joliet, La Salle, Hennepin, La Hontan, Charlevoix, Carver, Pike, Cass, and Beltrami preceded Schoolcraft. The last named discovered a lake which he supposed to be the Source, but the Indians and missionaries said there was a lake beyond. A learned few believed them. It remained for some explorer to make further investigation and publish the truth more widely to the world. This was done by Captain Glazier in 1881, who visited the lake, explored its shores, and found it to be wider and deeper than Itasca."

The following quotation from an article which appeared in the *Geographical News,* is from the pen of its publisher, George F. Cram, a leading geographical authority of Chicago, who, I should conclude from his interesting and exhaustive treatment of the subject, must have made a thorough study of everything relating to the question of the Origin of the Great River;

"In 1832, Henry Rowe Schoolcraft traced the upper courses

of the Mississippi and believed he had found its Source in Lake Itasca, and for nearly fifty years it was so shown on our maps and in our geographies, and so taught in our schools. In 1881, however, Willard Glazier made further explorations, and discovered that Itasca was connected with another lake by a permanently flowing stream which enters the southeast side of the southwest arm of the former. Captain Glazier's companions named this body of water Lake Glazier, and announced it as the Primal Reservoir of the river. Unwilling to abandon the theories of the earlier explorers, certain parties strongly antagonized the Glazier claim, and exerted so great an influence with the Historical Society of Minnesota that that body rejected his discovery altogether and refused to admit the source to be beyond Itasca. A long newspaper war followed, sufficiently acrimonious on both sides. Geographers are now divided on the question, so that scholars and students who use the geographies of one publisher will be taught that the Source of the Mississippi is Lake Itasca, while those who use the publications of another will learn that it is Lake Glazier Just who is benefited by this condition of things it is somewhat difficult to ascertain.

"The actual facts in the case are these: That all the investigations made since the Glazier discovery was first disputed, tend to show very conclusively that the True Source of the river is in the lake immediately to the south of Itasca, known to the Indians as Po-keg-a-ma; that Captain Glazier's party christened this sheet of water Lake Glazier; that Glazier was the first who discovered and proclaimed the Source to be in that lake. This being the case, it seems but just that the honor of the discovery should no longer be withheld from him. At all events, our school geographies should teach the truth as to where the Source really is."

Those who have glanced over the preceding editorial comments will probably have found some evidence of the interest taken by the general public in the question that brought me again to Minnesota. They may also have noted the trend of opinion, and if they are candid and in search of truth, I feel confident they will reach the conclusion that the press at least, throughout the country, is not only not opposed to, but favorable and strongly corroborative of my views.

From Photograph by F J. Trost.

PINE PARK, BRAINERD, MINNESOTA.

CHAPTER VII.

MINNEAPOLIS TO PARK RAPIDS.

LEAVING Minneapolis at an early hour on the morning of August seventeenth, we reached Saint Cloud at ten o'clock. Here we had dinner, and spent a few hours in strolls through the leading streets of the city. Resuming our journey, we went on to Brainerd in the evening, where we remained for two days. It was at this point that the equipment of my First Expedition was completed.

Brainerd, sometimes familiarly styled the "City of Pines," is situated in a bend of the Mississippi, on the border of an extensive pine forest, at the point where the Northern Pacific Railway makes its crossing. Although but twenty-eight miles south of Aitkin, by railway, it is ninety-five miles below that city, by the river The town was originally built among the pines, and when I saw it in 1881, it was the most picturesque village I had ever looked upon. The streets had been cut directly through the virgin forest, and only such trees removed as were absolutely necessary to make room for business houses and residences. Brainerd is the third town from the Source of the Mississippi, and, after Saint Paul and Minneapolis, one of the most advanced above the Falls of Saint Anthony. Viewed from the river, which winds around its front, a picture of rare beauty is pre-

From Photograph by F J. Trost.

LOG-BOOM ON THE UPPER MISSISSIPPI.

sented to the tourist who delights in Upper Mississippi scenery. Without a history, this town leaped into existence with a considerable population, mostly of New England origin, and at one time seemed destined to become a city of respectable proportions. Its rapid growth for several years was probably due to its large and increasing lumber interest, and the location at that point of the shops of the Northern Pacific Railway, which gave it prominence and prospective importance as a center of industry. The removal of the shops, a short time since, to Staples seriously interrupted the development of Brainerd and greatly benefited the former place; hence, although the Brainerd of to-day possesses a greater population than the Brainerd of 1881, it gives less promise for the future.

One of the attractive features of this little city, and a favorite resort during the summer months, is Pine Park, situated within the city limits. This park is thickly studded with tall gray and Norway pines from sixty to a hundred feet in height, which give the traveler an excellent idea of the appearance of this region before the axe of the settler was heard in the unbroken wilderness.

Among the objects of interest visited here were the Sanitarium and the rooms of the Young Men's Christian Association; the former of which was built by, and is entirely in the hands of, the Northern Pacific Railway—a wise and, indeed, generous provision for the sick and disabled employés of the road. The ample quarters of the Y. M. C. A. are quite up to the modern idea, having a library, gymnasium, and well-appointed reading-rooms.

A pleasant incident of our sojourn at this frontier town was a call from Miss Lotta Grandelmeyer, a

From Photograph by F. J. Trost.

THE MISSISSIPPI AT BRAINERD.

great-granddaughter of William Morrison, the pioneer fur trader, who saw Lake Itasca in 1804, the year previous to the visit of Lieutenant Pike to Cass Lake. Had the latter met Morrison then, it is hardly probable that the explorer of 1805 would have laid down the Source of the Mississippi in Turtle Lake. Since that time, the descendants of William Morrison and his brother Allan have been residents of Minnesota, and the high esteem in which the family is held was shown many years ago, in bestowing the name of Morrison upon one of the largest and most-flourishing counties in the State.

Miss Grandelmeyer is a young lady of intelligence and refinement, proud of her ancestors, and much interested in everything relating to the geography and history of Minnesota. The information which she furnished us, concerning the Morrisons and other early settlers of the northern portions of the State, was of especial value to myself and companions.

Later in the day, Dr. F. A. Seal, Government physician at the Leech Lake Indian Agency, paid his respects, and talked with us in regard to Indian affairs in that region. He has been four years among the Chippewas, and his stories of their peculiar manners and customs were eagerly listened to by those of our party who had never before been so near the dominions of their red brothers.

From Dr. Seal I learned the particulars of the death and burial of Chenowagesic, the guide of my First Expedition, to whom I made frequent reference in "Down the Great River," and other publications relating to the source of the Mississippi. I was already aware of his death, which occurred at Leech Lake in March, 1891, but knew nothing of its cause, or of his funeral and place of burial.

Dr. Seal explained that a severe cold led to pneumonia, and that he lived but a few days after his condition was considered critical. The ceremony attending his funeral was strictly in accordance with his wishes, and in conformity with usual Chippewa practices on such occasions. Since retiring from my service in 1881, he had been elevated to the chieftainship of a tribe, and later had been appointed captain of Indian police by the Government agent at Leech Lake. Having expressed a desire, during his illness, to stand once more at the head of his company, his family and friends insisted that his request should be respected. Their cabin was on the shore of the lake, about five miles from the Agency, and when the Government wagon arrived for his remains, the entire Indian police force of the Leech Lake Reservation was drawn up in line, and the body of Chenowagesic, clothed in the uniform of his office, was placed, standing, on the right of the line, where it was held in position by a relative for some moments; then, placing the corpse in a coffin, it was preceded by the police, and followed by his sorrowing family and friends to the Chippewa village near the Agency, where his remains were given a Christian burial.

While at Brainerd, I had the pleasure of again meeting Judge Holland, Dr Rosser, Captain Seelye, George S. Canfield, and several others with whom I became acquainted during my descent of the Mississippi. These gentlemen seemed greatly interested in the objects of our expedition, and furnished us much valuable information concerning the region through which we intended to pass on our way to Park Rapids. Captain Seelye and Mr. Canfield, particularly, were untiring in their efforts to place at my

BURIAL OF CHENOWAGESIC.

disposal their large experience in Northern Minnesota. The former is widely known as a veteran explorer for pine, and had, since my explorations of 1881, visited the Headwaters of the Mississippi in pursuit of his calling.

We moved from Brainerd to Wadena on the afternoon of August nineteenth, where we found quarters for the night at the Merchants' Hotel and Wadena House. On the following morning, the entire party was up at daylight, and, after an early breakfast, spent an hour in conversation with citizens, and in rambles through the place. Mr. Trost photographed a railway station, park, and two or three street scenes.

The birth of Wadena dates from the advent of the Northern Pacific Railroad, since which its growth has been consistent with the development of the surrounding country. In 1880, the population was but three hundred and seven; in 1890, it was between three and four thousand. This growing and prosperous little town is the capital of Wadena County; is forty-seven miles northwest of Brainerd, and was, until the completion of the branch road to Park Rapids, the nearest railway station to the Source of the Mississippi. Situated in the midst of one of the most productive wheat-growing sections of Minnesota, and with every facility for the receipt and shipment of this staple, the prediction of a prosperous future need hardly be questioned.

Leaving Wadena at nine o'clock, we proceeded on our journey to Park Rapids by way of the Wadena and Park Rapids branch of the Great Northern Railway. A halt of nearly an hour was made at a half-way house known as Menahga, where we had a very satisfactory dinner; the conductor favoring the land-

From Photograph by F. J. Trost.

MAIN STREET, WADENA, MINNESOTA.

lord, and ourselves at the same time, by holding his train until we could dine in detachments, the table and service not being equal to so large a party. After dinner the conductor still further delayed his train in order to give Mr. Trost an opportunity to photograph the Menahga House and its guests.

Our brief stop at this pioneer establishment was, it may perhaps be considered, an event in its history, and the worthy host seemed anxious to make the most of it. We may also explain that the new railway from Wadena to Park Rapids was, at this date, in an unfinished condition; there were no stations north of Wadena, except at its terminus at Park Rapids. The obliging conductor, therefore, consented to accommodate the passengers, of whom our party formed the majority, so far as he could do so consistently.

Continuing our journey from Menahga, we reached Park Rapids at three o'clock. Here we were most cordially received by a delegation of citizens, and escorted to the Central House by Henry R. Cobb, postmaster, and editor of the Hubbard County *Enterprise*; and E. M. Horton, clerk of the County Court, who had anticipated our arrival.

Park Rapids is a typical frontier village, the county seat of Hubbard County, and, as previously noted, the nearest inhabited point to the Source of the Mississippi. It is situated on Fish-hook River, near a beautiful lake of the same name. The region surrounding the place is familiarly known as the Shell Prairies, and the soil is said to be favorable to the growth of wheat, corn, oats, and other cereals. The first house is stated to have been erected in 1882, the year after my first journey across Northern Minnesota.

From Photograph by F. J. Trost.

WAITING FOR THE TRAIN, WADENA.

CHAPTER VIII.

THROUGH THE WILDERNESS.

THREE days were spent at Park Rapids in organization and equipment. Here we were opportunely reinforced by several gentlemen who proved a very valuable addition to the party, and having previously introduced to my readers those members of the expedition who joined us in Minneapolis, I now give the names of the Park Rapids contingent, beginning with Henry R. Cobb, to whom allusion has already been made.

Mr. Cobb is a native of Maine, and although still a young man, was a pioneer in Northern Minnesota and one of the first settlers at Park Rapids. Through his paper, the *Hubbard County Enterprise,* he has done much to invite attention to, and encourage the development of, this section of the State.

Hon. C. D. Cutting of Howard County, Iowa, was the guest of Mr. Cobb at the time of our arrival, and curtailed his visit in order to make one of our number. He began life in the "Pine Tree State," but, like thousands of others, left New England in boyhood to seek his fortune in the Great West. An ample competency, resulting from earnest toil beyond the Mississippi, and his election to the Legislature of his adopted State, are sufficient proofs of industry and good citizenship. Senator Cutting was accompa-

VIEW OF PARK RAPIDS.

nied by his son Frank, a young man of eighteen years.

E. M. Horton of Park Rapids, at present clerk of the Hubbard County Court, is a surveyor and civil engineer by profession, and was recently in the employ of the Northern Pacific Railway. Mr. Horton was introduced by Postmaster Cobb, and highly indorsed as a surveyor by many of his fellow-townsmen.

Oliver S. Keay, formerly of Maine, but now a resident of Minnesota, was accepted on the recommendation of Mr Horton and other citizens of Park Rapids for the position of guide and assistant surveyor. He has had large experience as an explorer of pine lands in the northern sections of the State, and was the only member of our party besides myself who had seen the Source of the Mississippi.

Daniel Adams and his son Grant were employed as teamsters, and, although pursuing an humble calling, are highly respected as good citizens and neighbors in Park Rapids. Louis Delezene was engaged as cook and general assistant.

In the matter of equipment for our explorations, we were provided with canoes, tents, blankets, rations, guns, ammunition, fishing tackle, surveyor's compass and chain, barometer, thermometers, pocket compasses, and a portable photographic apparatus.

Having ascertained that it was now possible to journey on wheels from Park Rapids to within a few miles of the Source of the Mississippi, three wagons were employed to carry our canoes, camp equipage, and rations to the southeastern arm of Lake Itasca; these wagons were drawn by horses, with the exception of one mule, bearing the euphonious title or nickname of "Jerry" This long-eared companion of one of the horses possessed all the peculiarities of his kind, and, as will be seen farther on, frequently converted serious into amusing and ludicrous situations.

Although we had learned from pioneers that wagon conveyance at best would be difficult, and at times even hazardous, it was a relief to know that for the greater part of the trip, at least, teams could be used for the transportation of our luggage.

Our organization and equipment completed, we started from Park Rapids at eight o'clock on Saturday morning, August twenty-second, and soon plunged into the interminable primitive forest which lies between this frontier town and the Headwaters of the Mississippi. The road, which is but little more than a trail, winds among the tall pines, over huge boulders, across marshes, and up and down sand-hills, in descending which it was necessary to chain the wagon-wheels, and in their ascent the combined strength of horses and men was required.

For the first six miles our route led us across a shell prairie to the west of Park Rapids, and then over rather indifferent sand roads, through a partly cultivated country, and past an occasional log cabin. As we moved forward, however, all traces of cultivation gradually disappeared, and by noon, after having advanced but ten miles, nothing remained to suggest the existence of humanity aside from our own party and the rugged and slightly travel-worn trail we were following. We were confronted on all sides by the apparently endless virgin forest, in which gray, Norway, and jack-pines largely predominated. From the hill-tops many of the pines rear their evergreen

STARTING FROM PARK RAPIDS.

crests to the enormous height of over a hundred feet, while in the marshes and lowlands the tamarack and underbrush are seen on every hand.

We succeeded in reaching at noon a stream known to frontiersmen of that locality as "Dinner Creek." Here, where we found excellent water, we had our first meal in the open air.

The fording of "Dinner Creek" was the first of many novel and exciting experiences in our march through the wilderness, and gave us a foretaste of what we might reasonably anticipate at intervals during the remainder of the journey, for it may be explained at once that the region about the Head of the Mississippi is a series of diluvial sand-ridges and numberless lakes, ponds, streams, marshes, and in brief everything conceivable that could impede and obstruct locomotion.

When we had reached a slight elevation overlooking the creek, it was evident that the most feasible way of crossing the stream would be to ford it in the wagons, as the depth of water was sufficient to make fording on foot impracticable without the annoyance of a severe and unnecessary wetting; we therefore mounted the wagons promptly and rode forward.

On approaching the stream, the mule divided with his mate the honor of leading our column, and no sooner had the ford begun than "Jerry," tempted by the clear sparkling water, and delighting in its cooling effects upon his overheated legs, mule-like, wanted to drink; and halt he would, doubtless oblivious of the difficulty he was sure to experience in again starting. After drinking all he could hold conveniently, he raised his head and put up his ears in a knowing manner as if in contemplation of the steep ascent beyond.

When "Jerry" received from his driver the word "go," he attempted to climb over his companion, but failing in this he next tried to push himself bodily through his collar, and, although unable to accomplish what he undertook, succeeded in landing horse, wagon, and freight on the opposite shore, where with one wheel in the road, and another against an embankment, he, with characteristic mischief, made a sudden and unexpected disposition of the passengers.

As "Dinner Creek" was the first stream encountered, and the first barrier to uninterrupted travel, a brief sketch of it may prove of some interest to those tourists who incline to follow our footsteps to the Mecca of the Upper Mississippi. Rising to the southward of the basin which incloses Itasca and Glazier lakes, it flows in a southeasterly direction through Becker and Hubbard counties, and ultimately falls into the Crow Wing River, of which it is an important tributary. Its banks, for some distance above and below the point where we effected a crossing, are high and well-defined, with an average width of about sixty, and a depth of from three to four feet, at the time we saw it on the twenty-second of August.

I may add that it was the sentiment of many of our party, that this water-course was of sufficient importance to receive a more dignified title than "Dinner Creek"; and I therefore suggest that, if entirely in accord with the views of the residents of that section of Minnesota, it be named Morrison River in honor of Allan and William Morrison, who were among the first white men to penetrate the wilds, and leave their foot-prints on the hills and in the valleys of the "North Star State."

Dinner over, and "Jerry" having been coaxed into

the "notion," we again moved forward. Obstacles to progress were found to be more numerous and difficult as we advanced; the trail being hardly discernible at many points, while the hills were steeper and more frequent. The wagons were pulled and pushed up one hill after another; then, when they were at the summit, some of our number moved in front of the teams with long sticks, as they descended, beating the animals in their faces, in order to assist the drivers in forcing them to hold back; other members of the party took position behind and on the sides of the wagons, exerting all the muscle they could command, in their efforts to keep canoes and luggage from being precipitated into the valley below.

Thoroughly exhausted by the fatigues of the day, we halted at six o'clock on the crest of a stony-capped ridge, about twenty miles northwest of Park Rapids. Here we pitched tents, and built a camp-fire, naming the encampment "Munsell," after a senior member of the expedition. Camp Munsell overlooked an apparently fine body of water, but the discovery was soon made that its appearance was misleading, and what had tempted us to go into camp early in the evening proved to be only a dead lake, the water of which was unfit for use by either man or beast.

The water near the margin of this lake was stagnant, and filled with dead and decaying vegetable matter. The horses were led down to the shore, but seemed disgusted, and would not drink. "Jerry" alone appeared satisfied, and in consideration of his approval of what seemed obnoxious to all others, we at once named it Mule Lake.

Being unable to use, in a raw state, the water refused by the horses, we boiled it, and made a kettle of rather insipid coffee, which in a measure appeased thirst, and afforded us slight refreshment.

A careful exploration of the region adjacent to Camp Munsell made it clear that living water could not be found in that immediate vicinity, and had we not already made considerable preparation for the night, we should have moved forward in the hope of finding a more desirable location.

All were astir at sunrise on the following morning, and had breakfast soon after It being Sunday, I had originally intended to remain in camp the entire day, and resume march on the morning of the twenty-fourth, but owing to the want of good water, all voted to strike tents, and move on without delay.

The event of this day's tramp was the shooting of a large black bear, early in the forenoon, by Whitney and Delezene, who, at the time of catching their first glimpse of bruin, were about a hundred yards in advance of the column. Being armed with rifles, both fired at the same instant, but their shots were not immediately fatal, and the bear made good his escape, leaving a trail of blood behind to indicate his line of retreat. Several members of the party joined Whitney and Delezene in pursuit of the wounded animal, but wishing to establish our evening encampment on Schoolcraft Island, there was no time to lose, and I therefore recalled the hunters and pushed on toward Lake Itasca.

On returning from the hunt, we were not a little amused by an incident doubtless quite in keeping with the reportorial profession. Arriving upon the ground from which the shots had been fired but a few moments before, the correspondent of the Boston *Herald* seated himself on a log, deliberately pulled

BRUIN AT BAY

his note-book and pencil from a side-pocket, and proceeded to "interview" his companions; inquired the time bruin was first seen, his size and appearance, the precise moment that fire was opened on him, and the direction he had taken after being wounded; then, putting his note-book back in his pocket, he arose with becoming dignity, and wiping the perspiration from his brow, threw his rifle over his shoulder, and, apparently "ready for action," said, "Gentlemen, my article for the *Herald* is ready; now bring on your bear!" It occurred to us that if bears could select their hunters, there would be a very large premium on reporters and correspondents of leading dailies, when fully provided with note-books, sketch-books, and all other paraphernalia known to knights of the quill; for, while the representative of the newspaper was perfecting his notes, bruin could readily betake himself to safer and more peaceful quarters beyond the reach of the enemy.

Our course was still northwesterly, and the interest in the region traversed increased as we approached the Height of Land, usually described as the watershed, and which separates the great river systems of North America.

The prevailing growth observed at this stage of our journey was thick bramble, pine, spruce, white cedar, and tamarack. The hills were found to be higher and more rugged as we advanced, while we experienced much difficulty in penetrating the dense undergrowth of the valleys. The trail often plunged into marshy and matted thickets, which required all the strength we could muster to press through; then rose to an elevation covered with cedar or jack-pines, and anon dropped into a swamp, strewn with fallen trees covered with moss, from which it again led to the summit of a sand-hill, steeper and higher than the one that preceded it; and so on, *ad infinitum,* until the goal of the expedition was reached.

Notwithstanding some of the disagreeable features enumerated, that portion of Minnesota lying at, and in the immediate vicinity of, the Headwaters is, and will always be, a region of much interest to the student and tourist who has the hardihood to climb the hills and wade through the marshes that conceal the mysterious Fount of the Great River.

It may be further observed that this particular section of Minnesota is likely to remain in a wild state for many years to come, as the soil is hardly worth tilling and the timber at present inaccessible. The surface is cut up by glacial ridges which leave many depressions, of from a few hundred feet to many miles in extent, mostly without outlet. The basins thus formed by these elevations and depressions hold the myriad lakes for which this region is celebrated.

When within a short distance of Lake Itasca, the guide drew my attention to the claim cabin of an enterprising pioneer, who had, a year or two previous, built a log house, and attempted to hold the pine land, which is allowed in case certain requirements of the State are complied with. Disappointed in his estimate of soon having neighbors, and unwilling to remain longer in his isolated position, the settler abandoned his claim and returned to the haunts of civilization, heartily glad to be rid of his enterprise in the wilderness.

Continuing our journey, the trail led us along the shore of a small lake having a length of about a half mile and a width of between two and three hundred yards. It is nearly a mile to the south of the southeast arm of Lake Itasca, into which it falls through a swift brook with a sandy and pebbly bed. This pretty little lake was seen during my former visit and christened Gamble, after W. H. Gamble, a leading geographer of Philadelphia. The stream connecting it with Itasca was named Bear Creek, from the circumstance of our adventure referred to in a previous paragraph.

A little farther on, we came to the last of the series of ridges which we had been successively climbing, since we struck tents in the morning. From the summit of this elevation we had a very good view of Lake Itasca, which was seen from the crest of the pine-covered bluff overlooking the southeastern arm of the lake. Here we bivouacked, and drank our coffee on the very spot from which I had my first glimpse of Itasca in 1881. I may further observe that Schoolcraft, also, first looked upon this lake from the same point in 1832, and Nicollet in 1836.

We had now reached the terminus of our conveyance on wheels, and, having lunched, the wagons were unloaded, and the canoes and baggage carried down to the lake. It being the intention to camp for the night on Schoolcraft Island, we embarked without delay, and an hour later were pitching our tents on the northeast side of the island, on the ground selected by my faithful guide, Chenowagesic, for the encampment of my First Expedition ten years before.

CHAPTER IX.

HEADWATERS OF THE MISSISSIPPI.

AFTER an early breakfast at Camp Shure on the morning of the twenty-fourth, tents were struck, and an hour later we were in our canoes, paddling up the southwestern arm of Lake Itasca, it being the intention to establish a permanent camp and base of operations on the south side of the elevation of land which separates that arm of Itasca from the beautiful sheet of water, now generally recognized as the True Source of the Mississippi.

As we approached the southern end of the lake, my companions seemed more than usually interested, and, resting on our paddles, we paused a few moments to scan its shores. To me the scene was quite familiar, but to them it was new and strange and full of material for future investigation; for it was this portion of Itasca, together with the fine lake beyond, and their respective feeders, which had occupied the attention of geographers for more than ten years. Entering on our right is a trickling rivulet having no well-defined course, and of little consequence. Directly in front is a small stream usually denominated Nicollet Creek—the outlet of ponds situated in marshes to the southward. This creek and the insignificant ponds in which it originates were seen and entered by Nicollet in 1836, Julius Chambers in 1872,

HEADWATERS OF THE MISSISSIPPI

WILLARD GLAZIER
1881-1891

APPROXIMATE SCALE OF MILES.
0 1 2 3 4 5 6 7 8 9 10

Route of First Expedition

EXPLANATORY

First Expedition Started from Brainerd	July 12,	1881
Canoes launched at Leech Lake	" 17,	"
Located Source of Mississippi . . .	" 22,	"
Began Voyage from Source to Sea	" "	"
Reached Gulf of Mexico.	November 15,	"

MINNESOTA

Turtle Lake
Turtle River
Lake Bemidji
Mississippi River
Lake Winnibigoshish
Mississippi
Alleroga River
River
Pinidiwin
L. Beltrami
L. Marquette
L. La Salle
Hennepin R.
River
L. Copes
L. Joliet
L. Hennepin
La Salle R.
Nicollet
Mississippi
L. Beaulieu
Marquette R.
L. Hampton
L. Wright
L. Lemon
L. Itasca
L. Gamble
L. Elvira
Lagard River
De Soto River
Paine R.
Kabekanka River
White Cloud
Portage R.
L. Garfield
L. Benedict
L. George
L. Sheridan
L. Chenowagesic
Wolf Pond
L. Alice
Leech Lake River
River
Leech Lake
Lake Agency
Canoes launched July 17, 1881

LAKE GLAZIER
Source of the Mississippi River,
3.184 Miles from the Gulf of Mexico.

Brainerd on the Mississippi
40 Miles below.

R., MC N. & CO., ENG'S

MAP OF THE HEADWATERS.

and again, by my party, in 1881; and have since been visited, christened, and re-christened so many times, by two or three enterprising parties from Saint Paul, that it is now extremely doubtful if the people of Minnesota, or elsewhere, have any definite idea of their claim to serious consideration.

It is perhaps sufficient to add, that a certain representative of the Minnesota Historical Society, who has wasted much effort in his attempt to disprove my position, has moved up the valley of this stream, and, utterly ignoring the time-honored practice of geographers, has presumed to name, successively, bogs and ponds as important feeders of the Mississippi, until he has reached the limit of running water; then, scaling sand-hills, has imagined subterranean connection with isolated dead lakes which he has exalted to the dignity of Fountain-head of the Great River. His ridiculous pretensions having finally been disposed of in this quarter, he springs a coup-de-main upon his unsuspecting followers, and announces to his "select class of scientists" at Saint Paul, that "all our rivers have their sources in the clouds." It having been the purpose of my party to confine its observations to *terra-firma*, we surrendered the department of the "clouds" to the individual above referred to, and decided to ascend Nicollet Creek with compass and chain as soon as practicable.

Resuming our observations, I may explain that we are still in our canoes, looking southward. On our right the west shore of Itasca is fringed with pine, while in our front its southern end and the eastern shore on our left are covered with tamarack, excepting an open space at the summit of a hill near the southern extremity of the lake. The Hauteur de

Terre range of hills, which constitutes the Height of Land, may be clearly seen in the distance, and between these hills and the knoll there is a peculiar light which indicates to the practiced eye of the woodsman that there is a large body of water beyond. No portion of Itasca presents so many features of striking interest as this, and were it not that imperative duties urged us forward to other fields of equal and even greater interest, we would gladly have lingered longer where there was so much to excite our admiration.

Passing from the scene which had held our attention for nearly half an hour, I carefully scanned the eastern shore for the mouth of the Infant Mississippi, the view being obstructed now, as in 1881, by a rank growth of weeds, rushes, and wild rice. Fixing my eyes upon a small pine, which marks the precise point of entrance, we turned the canoes and pushed them through the dense vegetation out into the clear waters of the inlet. I was now in my old tracks, ascending the stream which leads to the lake that has been for more than a decade the central figure in geographical discussion in this country.

We continued to move up the stream in our canoes until stopped by fallen trees, then, disembarking, we hastened forward on foot to the crest of the hill which overlooks the Source of the Mississippi and its outlet. Here we halted a few moments to survey the scene before us and to reflect upon the history of exploration in this quarter. Much has been said and written, since my earlier visit, tending to throw discredit upon my announcement of that date, and yet I honestly believe, and feel confident that I shall be able to maintain, that this beautiful body of water,

MOUTH OF "INFANT MISSISSIPPI."

the Po-keg-a-ma of the Chippewas—re-named *Lake Glazier* by the companions of my First Expedition—is the Primal Reservoir; that it was not so considered prior to my exploration of 1881, and that we were the first to correctly locate its feeders and establish its true relation to Lake Itasca and the Great River.

It has been said, by some writers, that Schoolcraft saw this lake in 1832 and Nicollet in 1836. As to the former, it may be observed that there is not a line in the narrative of his explorations to indicate that he was south of the island which bears his name. On the contrary, he plainly states that he reached the upper end of the southeastern arm of Lake Itasca about one o'clock in the afternoon of July tenth, 1832, floated down to the island, had dinner, made a few observations, and having an appointment to meet Indians at the mouth of Crow Wing River a few days later, passed out of the lake and immediately began the descent of the Mississippi, reaching a point twenty-five miles below the outlet of Itasca in season for his evening encampment. An examination of his map will convince any unprejudiced mind that he could not have coasted this lake for its feeders; nor could he even have ascended its southwestern arm. Were his map faithful to nature, it is certainly not the result of personal observation, as I venture to assert that few men could do more within the time allotted by Mr. Schoolcraft for his investigations than he himself accomplished. To resume, therefore, and taking his own account as the most reliable authority which can be cited, he was less than three hours within the limits of the Itascan Basin. Much of the knowledge which he possessed of Lake Itasca and its environs must have been obtained from his Indian guide Ozawindib.

I here introduce a few quotations from Schoolcraft, in support of my position that he omitted to explore Lake Itasca, and give in his own language his reasons for not doing so. It will readily be seen by the following extract from his "Narrative of the Expedition," page 235, "Sources of the Mississippi"—Lippincott, 1855—that his engagement to meet Indians at a date previously agreed upon, precluded the possibility of his making anything more than a very limited investigation He says

"Besides, I had agreed to meet the Indians at the mouth of the Crow Wing River on the twenty-fourth of July, and that engagement must be fulfilled."

Again, on the ensuing day, at the time of his arrival at Lake Itasca, he remarks, on page 242·

"After passing down its longest arm we landed at an island which appeared to be the only one in the lake. I immediately had my tent pitched, and, while the cook exerted his skill to prepare a meal, scrutinized its shores for crustacea, while Dr Houghton sought to identify its plants. While here, the latter recognized the *mycrostylis ophioglossoide*, *physalis lanceolata*, *silene antirrhina*, and *viola pedata*."

Further, as a proof that it was utterly impossible for Schoolcraft to have explored Itasca between the time of his arrival on its shores and his going into camp on the afternoon of the same day, on the Mississippi, twenty-five miles below the outlet of the lake, I submit the following, from the same and a succeeding chapter, which shows very conclusively that his time on the island was fully taken up with astronomical observations, the coining of a name for the newly discovered lake, geological investigations, raising the flag, and other ceremonies in connection therewith, and the composition of a commemorative poem. Referring to his observations and the naming of the lake, he tells us that.

"The latitude of this lake is 47° 13′ 35″. The highest grounds passed over by us in our transit from the Assowa Lake lie at an elevation of 1,695 feet. The view given of the scene in the first volume of my 'Ethnological Researches,' page 140, is taken from a point north of the island, looking into the vista of the south arm of the lake; I inquired of Ozawindib the Indian name of this lake; he replied, *Omushkōs*, which is the Chippewa name of the elk. Having previously got an inkling of some of their mythological and necromantic notions of the origin and mutations of the country which permitted the use of a female name for it, I denominated it Itasca."

Assuming that Schoolcraft was three hours at, and in the vicinity of, Itasca, and allowing an hour for the descent of its southeastern arm to the island, and another hour for passing out of the lake after his investigations were completed, it will be seen that not over one hour, at most, could have been spent in other employments, and that hour was fully occupied in pitching and striking tents, in a study of the botany, arborology, and mineralogy of the island and the finding of its latitude, together with the production of his expressive "Stanzas on Reaching the Source of the Mississippi," which alone would have taxed the wits and inspiration of many explorers a week instead of the fraction of an hour.

Proceeding with his examinations at the island, Mr. Schoolcraft observes, on page 246

"On scrutinizing the shores of the island on which I had encamped, innumerable *helices*, and other small univalves, were found; among these I observed a new species, which Mr. Cooper has described as *planorbis campanulatus*. There were bones of certain species of fish, as well as the bucklers of one or two kinds of tortoise, scattered around the sites of old Indian camp-fires, denoting so many points of its natural history. Amidst the forest trees before named, the *betula papyraceæ* and spruce were observed. Directing one of the latter to be cut down and prepared as a flagstaff, I caused the United States flag to be hoisted on it. This symbol was left flying at our departure. Ozawindib, who at once comprehended the meaning of this ceremony, with his companions fired a salute as it reached its elevation."

Concluding his scientific investigations, Schoolcraft devoted the remainder of his exceedingly brief visit to the island in evolving the poem to which previous allusion has been made. It is, perhaps, not too much to add that few writers have been favored with so happy a theme, or have written under more romantic circumstances, and whatever its poetic merit, I feel very confident that it will at least convince the reader that if its author did not see the True Head of the Great River, he was certainly not idle during his sojourn of an hour on Schoolcraft Island.

I present, without apology, Mr. Schoolcraft's beautiful poem as a part of the record of his visit to Lake Itasca

STANZAS ON REACHING THE SOURCE OF THE MISSISSIPPI RIVER IN 1832.

I.

Ha! truant of Western waters! Thou who hast
So long concealed thy very sources, flitting shy—
Now here, now there—through spreading mazes vast,
Thou art, at length, discovered to the eye
In crystal springs that run, like silver thread,
From out their sandy heights, and glittering lie
Within a beauteous basin, fair outspread,
Hesperian woodlands of the western sky,
As if, in Indian myths, a truth there could be read,
And these were tears, indeed, by fair Itasca shed.

II.

To bear the sword, on prancing steed arrayed;
To lift the voice admiring senates own;
To tune the lyre enraptured muses played;
Or pierce the starry heavens, the blue unknown,
These were the aims of many sons of fame,
Who shook the world with glory's golden song.
I sought a moral meed of less acclaim,
In treading lands remote, and mazes long;
And while around aerial voices ring,
I quaff the limpid cup at Mississippi's spring.

—H. R. S.

His examinations completed and his poem finished, we follow Schoolcraft to his evening encampment on the Mississippi, twenty-five miles below the outlet of Itasca. Continuing his narrative, he writes, on page 246.

"Having made the necessary examinations, I directed my tent to be struck, and the canoes put into the water, and immediately embarked. The outlet lies north of the island. Before reaching it we had lost sight of the flagstaff, owing to the curvature of the shore. Unexpectedly, the outlet proved quite a brisk brook, with a mean width of ten feet, and one foot in depth. The water is as clear as crystal, and we at once found ourselves gliding along, over a sandy and pebbly bottom, strewed with the scattered valves or shells, at a brisk rate. After descending some twenty-five miles, we encamped on a high sandy bluff on the left hand."

When it is considered that the foregoing quotations are taken from the record of a single day, and that almost the entire forenoon was occupied in making a portage between the east and west forks of the Mississippi, and that, in addition to passing through a portion of Lake Itasca, he descended the river twenty-five miles, it is as clear as the noonday sun that he could not have had more than an hour at his disposal on the island, and during his passage through the lake; and the assumption of a few critics that he must have seen the lake to the south of Itasca is not within the bounds of reason. It is, therefore, to be conclusively inferred that Schoolcraft saw Lake Itasca, accepted it as the Source of the Mississippi—probably on the authority of his Indian guide—passed out of the lake and descended the river. Hence, it was impossible that he could have coasted Itasca, or given any attention to its affluents, and, in support of this view, I find that he makes no claim to having done so in the narrative of his expedition.

Did Nicollet see the Source of the Mississippi? If

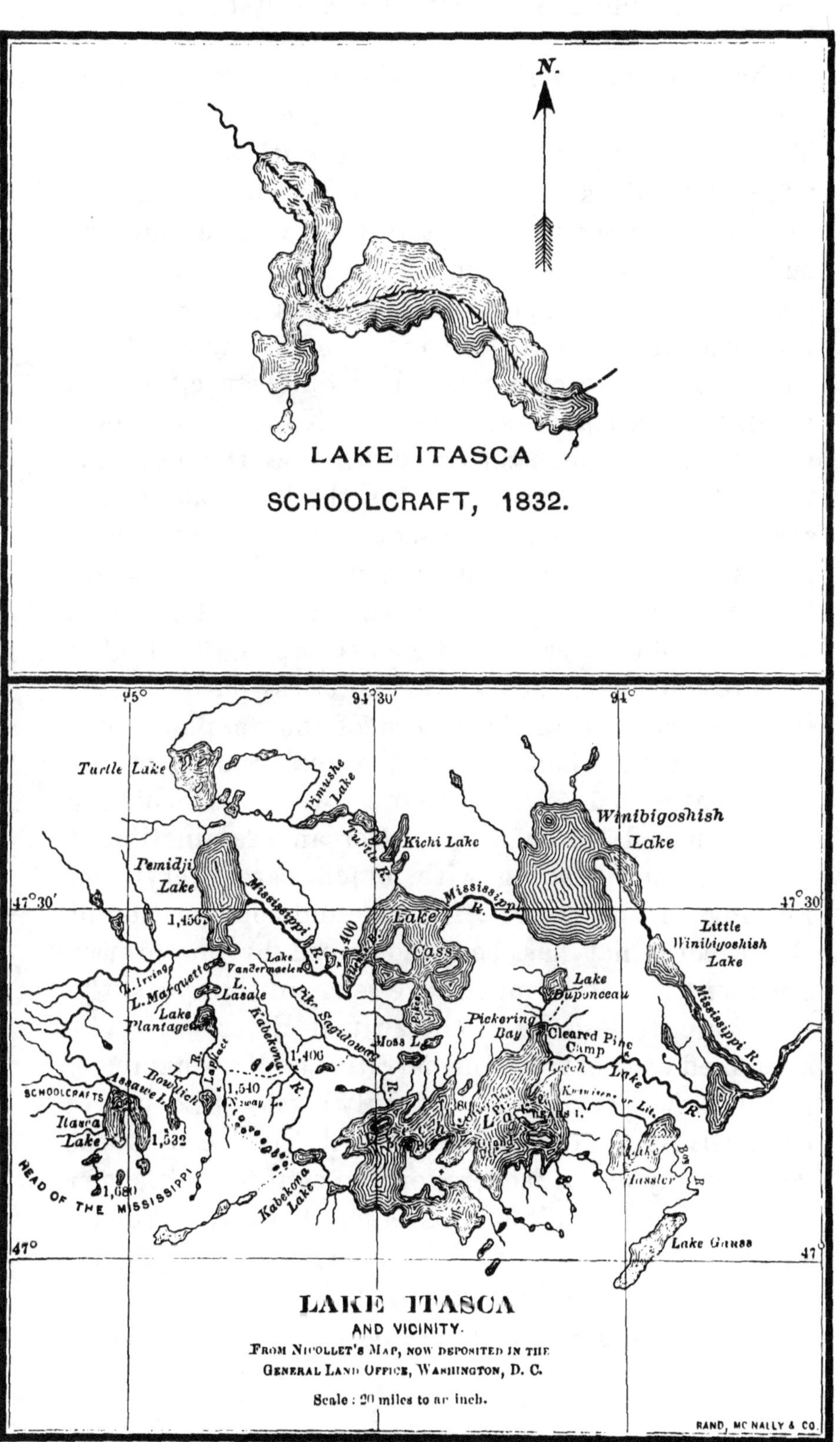

MAPS OF SCHOOLCRAFT AND NICOLLET

so, he does not describe the lake which more recent investigation has located as the Origin of the river. There is nothing on his map, to the southeast of Itasca, which resembles the delineations of later explorers, except the creek which enters the extreme southern end of the southwest arm of the lake, and the small ponds which are expansions of the stream. He doubtless coasted Itasca in his canoe, and as the mouth of this tributary is open and clear of obstructions, he readily entered and ascended it. No recent explorer will think it strange that he did not see the more important stream proceeding from the large lake to the southeastward, when we reflect that its inlet into Itasca is obstructed by reeds and rushes, and completely hidden from view. Had Schoolcraft and Nicollet ascended this stream, and looked upon this highly picturesque lake, they would doubtless have given it its true character in the record of their explorations.

Was Julius Chambers at the real Source of the Great River in 1872? No! unless we are to disbelieve his published statements. After an examination of his map, and reading with much care everything relating to the subject, I fail to find confirmation of the theory that has been advanced by one or two opponents, that he must have seen, in that year, the lake which I describe as the Primal Reservoir The subjoined extract from the narrative of Mr. Chambers, in the New York *Herald* of July sixth, 1872, proves conclusively that he did not visit the Head of the river, or any of its feeders; on the contrary, it is very evident that he paddled his canoe, "Dolly Varden," up Nicollet Creek to its first pond, which he clearly describes in the following language.

"Here, then, is the source of the longest river in the world;

in a small lake, scarcely a quarter of a mile in diameter, in the midst of a floating bog, the fountains which give birth to the Mississippi."

Before concluding with Mr. Chambers, let me ask: Is there one, among the many who are to-day familiar with the nomenclature and characteristics of this region, who will so far stultify himself, and mislead others, as to assert that the foregoing quotation refers to the True Head of the Mississippi—an expanse of water nearly two miles in diameter, having a circumference of between five and six miles, and an area of 255 acres, presenting high and wooded shores, and with no swamps or "floating bogs" in its vicinity?

What was accomplished by the Government survey of 1875 in the direction of throwing light upon the vexed question? Very little, beyond showing the area and relative proportions of the two lakes under discussion. It was not within its province to trace streams to their sources, to determine heights and levels, or meander lakes of less than forty acres in extent. Hopewell Clarke, a contemporary, and a surveyor by profession, who did me the honor to investigate and report upon my explorations of 1881, comments thus upon the survey in question:

"A singular mistake, however, on the Government plat is easily accounted for The course of the stream from lake H, until it crosses the south line of Section 22, is substantially correct as laid down on the Government map; but when they ran the line between Sections 21 and 22, this stream was not crossed again, and they naturally supposed it ran due north through the western edge of Section 22, and that the stream flowing out of Section 21 into 22 was a branch running into the main stream; whereas, this is the main stream, which, passing westward under their feet into Section 21 by an outlet which they they did not see, because it was underground, takes its course through the eastern part of Section 21, and crosses into Section 22 again at the point where the Government surveyors had indicated a feeder to the main stream. The two small lakes, C and D, on Section 22, and the two, A and

B, on Section 21, would not be crossed by a section line; hence, they were not indicated by the surveyors. At a point where the section line, between Sections 21 and 28, crosses the branch of the spring flowing out of Section 28, the course of the stream is through a boggy swamp, and it would hardly be noticed as the stream, without going a considerable distance north or south of the section line; hence, it is not shown on the Government maps, but in place of it, is shown a marsh."

It will be seen by the foregoing that Mr. Clarke had excellent reasons for excusing the inaccuracies of the survey, when, as he informs us in this connection.

"Their business was to establish sectional corners; blaze lines between the sections; note all lakes intercepted by the section lines; meander all lakes of more than forty acres in extent; note streams crossed, and indicate their apparent direction. Errors will creep into their work, but when we take into consideration the difficulties they had to contend with, it is not to be wondered at."

I quite agree with Mr. Clarke that the mistakes committed by the survey are not to be wondered at, and can readily understand their excuse for omitting to show on their map a most important feeder of the True Source. Had they traced its affluents to the springs at the foot of the sand-hills, they would have discovered, in 1875, what I learned, in 1881; that, instead of being a mere feeder of Itasca, the large lake beyond it is the Fountain-head of the Mississippi.

With the exclusively topographical survey, under Edwin S. Hall and his assistants, began and ended all investigation of an authentic character at the Headwaters of the Mississippi, up to 1881. Just what this survey really developed has been presented in preceding paragraphs. After an interval of ten years, I returned, with the largest body of explorers and surveyors that had ever stood on this ground, to examine my former work, and to submit my claim to impartial consideration.

NIGHTFALL AT OUR ENCAMPMENT

CHAPTER X.

JOURNAL OF THE EXPEDITION.

HAVING reviewed the explorations of those who preceded my earlier visit, and briefly alluded to recent investigation, I now present in detail, from our daily field notes, the observations of my Second Expedition.

Preliminary to the exploratory work of the following seven days, I may explain that our tents were pitched, and a permanent headquarters established on the south side of the ridge, or elevated land, which separates Itasca from the lake beyond, near the outlet of the latter This rendezvous we named Camp Trost, in compliment to our photographer. For convenience, the beautiful sheet of water in our front will be referred to in future pages as Lake Glazier.

Camp Trost, August 25, 1891.—Messrs. Trost and Shure were up at five o'clock, and off in a canoe with their trolling-hooks, on Lake Glazier, in quest of fish. Their efforts were rewarded with a fine mess of bass, pike, perch, and pickerel, which were caught in season for an early breakfast.

At seven o'clock, a detail was made to accompany Surveyors Horton and Keay in an examination of Nicollet Creek. It was decided that Messrs. Cobb, Crane, Cutting, Whitney, and myself should form

LAKE GLAZIER.

this committee of investigation; and that the length, width, depth, and velocity of current of this stream should be ascertained by careful measurement. Launching our canoes on Itasca, we were soon at the extremity of the southwest arm of the lake, and a moment later at the mouth of the creek This we found, by the aid of the chain, to be ten feet wide and two and a half feet deep. We then ascended this feeder to a small pond, or, more correctly, a floating bog. The area of the pond, or bog, was found to be less than three acres; and the only water exposed to view was nearly filled with lily-pads. Continuing up the creek, we came to a second pond, somewhat larger than the first, and, a few yards farther on, to the origin of the stream, in a spring at the foot of a sand hill. Our measurement enabled us to determine that the distance of the spring from Lake Itasca is 7,307 feet, or only a mile and three-eighths.

Before returning to camp, I may explain that this is the creek which Nicollet ascended in 1836, and roughly estimated to be from two to three miles in length; and which Hopewell Clarke, in 1886, reduced to two miles. A still more recent visitor, clothed with "a little brief authority," under the State Government, has such an unaccountable penchant for exaggeration, that, in his report to the Governor of Minnesota, he calls this creek a river, and elevates its insignificant ponds to the dignity of lakes. It may be observed that our careful measurement of the stream by chain shows its length to be only one mile and three-eighths.

If we pause to consider the difficulties encountered by Nicollet, while wading through a tamarack marsh, we can easily believe that this is the stream he describes

From Photograph by F. J. Trost.

EAGLE'S NEST

Western Shore of Lake Glazier.

as two or three miles in length, but there is no excuse, at the present day, for any exaggeration on the part of my successors, who allege that they "carried instruments," and whose unworthy motive for misrepresentation is clearly seen to be a predetermination to misplace me, and by so doing mislead geographers and the public.

Concluding our investigations at the head of Nicollet Creek, we returned to the encampment, and later in the day I coasted Lake Glazier. Messrs. Cobb and Cutting accompanied me, and seemed greatly surprised and pleased with the size and appearance of the lake.

Camp Trost, August 26, 1891.—All hands were astir at six o'clock. Most of the party complained of being cold during the night, although each had a covering of from two to three heavy woolen blankets.

The forenoon was devoted to the work of coasting Lake Itasca for its feeders. The committee appointed for this purpose reported on their return that they had found the outlets of six small streams—two of them with well-defined mouths, and four filtering into the lake through bogs. The stream leading to Lake Glazier, properly designated as the "Infant Mississippi," and the one leading up the Nicollet Valley, to both of which allusion has already been made, are the only affluents of Lake Itasca worthy of any consideration; the other four being insignificant rivulets, rising at very short distances from the lake, and having no definite course.

In the afternoon, I again coasted Lake Glazier, accompanied by my daughter, Trost, and Shure. Starting on the right of the outlet, we passed entirely around the lake, a distance of between five

From Photograph by F J. Trost.

MOUTH OF EXCELSIOR CREEK.

Longest and Highest Feeder of Lake Glazier.

and six miles, halting at the mouths of Eagle, Excelsior, and Deer creeks, its principal affluents. Alice made a sketch of the *Eagle's Nest*, which was plainly seen in the branches of a tall pine near the mouth of Eagle Creek. This same nest had been observed during my previous visit, ten years before, and I was then informed by Chenowagesic that he had seen it there for the past thirty years. It was the circumstance of seeing this nest, and several eagles in its vicinity, that led me to name the stream which enters this side of the lake, Eagle Creek.

On reaching the mouth of Excelsior Creek, at the southern end of the lake, we disembarked, and walked up the western bank of this tributary to the crest of a hill. On returning to our canoe, Mr. Trost photographed the Eagle's Nest from the mouth of the creek, and also produced a picture of the jutting headland, named *Harriet Promontory*, with its mantle of foliage. On this spot my party of 1881 had landed, and talked over the results of our expedition of that year. To revert to Excelsior Creek, I may observe that it was so named for the reason that it is the longest, and, in its origin, the highest stream that pays tribute to the Primal Reservoir of the Great River.

Leaving Harriet Promontory, we continued our course along the southern shore to the mouth of another tributary, where we again landed, and walked along the white sand beach, which is a peculiar and striking feature of this locality. Our attention was arrested by the great number of deer and moose tracks indenting the sandy shore. A similar incident during my previous visit led me to give to the stream falling into the lake at this point the name of Deer Creek.

On our way back to camp, the quick ear of Mr.

CAUGHT IN LAKE GLAZIER.

Shure caught the sound of falling water on the eastern shore. Upon examination, a stream was found issuing from a mammoth fountain on the side of a steep hill, about forty feet above. A current of great velocity rushed down the hillside, and, meeting broken ground in its descent, formed a cascade midway between its source and the lake. The water was largely impregnated with iron. This spring was christened *Shure*, and the cascade was named *Florence*, after his wife.

During our circuit of the lake, my daughter had her trolling-hook over the stern of the canoe, and captured a pike, a perch, a rock bass, and twelve pickerel, one of the latter weighing nearly fifteen pounds.

It may here be observed that the Primal Reservoir of the Mississippi is nearly an oval in shape, its greatest diameter being a fraction less than two miles. Its area is 255 acres, and the average depth, forty-five feet. The water is exceedingly clear, revealing, in the shallower parts, a pebbly bed. Its high and thickly wooded shores are extremely picturesque, the regularity and uniformity of the trees and their luxuriant foliage giving the scene the resemblance to an extensive park improved by art, rather than a wild product of nature. The pine, spruce, tamarack, and several varieties of hardwood, including oak, beech, birch, and maple, were observed from our canoe, gracefully bending their crests to the passing breeze.

Camp Trost, August 27, 1891.—Called the party together after breakfast, and formed committees of investigation for the day. Messrs. Crane, Trost, Keay, Shure, Munsell, Harrison, Knowlton, and myself, it was arranged, should proceed forthwith

From Photograph by F. J. Trost.

ON AN INDIAN TRAIL, AT THE HEADWATERS.

to the lake, to which a recent pretentious explorer had applied the name, "Hernando de Soto," claiming it to be the "source" of the Mississippi, while he admits, at the same time, I believe, that it has no surface connection with Lake Itasca or that river. With this admission, we hardly recognized the utility of making any investigation in this direction, but, being determined to examine everything that has occupied the attention of geographers and the public, with the utmost care, we imposed upon ourselves a duty which, in the light of former and recent investigation, was felt to be somewhat superfluous and unnecessary. I can not admit that, in a search for the source of a river, there can be any good reason for passing the limit of running water. We, however, set apart this day for the examination of "Lake Hernando de Soto." On our way up, Trost photographed the bog, pond, and spring in Nicollet Valley. We reached "Hernando" at three o'clock in the afternoon, and found, as I had anticipated, that its character and dimensions had been greatly overdrawn. That it has no visible connection with Lake Itasca or the Mississippi was the verdict of our entire party; in fact, it is an insignificant dead lake, like others in its vicinity. It has no inlet or outlet that we could discover, and if it has an underground communication with any other body of water, it is more likely to discharge itself into Lake Glazier than Lake Itasca. All returned to camp disgusted with the loss of a day, uselessly spent in tramping through bogs and over sand hills in pursuit of an imaginary source of the Great River

However it may appear to some, to me, at least, it seems an insult to the memory of the illustrious De Soto to apply his name to anything so unimportant

STRANGE MEETING IN THE WILDERNESS.

as an isolated dead lake, having no surface connection with the Great River, with which he will be eternally associated. I, therefore, respectfully suggest to the Minnesota Historical Society that the name of the renowned Spaniard be withdrawn, and that of the pseudo discoverer of this lake be conferred upon it. Let Hernando de Soto be inseparably connected with lakes and streams that pay *living* tribute to the majestic river which will be forever a monument to his fame, rather than consign it to the oblivion of a *dead lake.*

On our way out to "Hernando," a pleasing incident occurred. We had not proceeded far from camp when our ears were suddenly startled by a prolonged shout or "call-whoop," which echoed through the silent woods from some one at a distance. We, of course, answered in the language of the forest. Soon a crashing of the underbrush revealed to us an Indian, who approached me with an expression of pleasure on his bronze countenance, and I at once recognized in our sturdy visitor my old interpreter of 1881—Moses Lagard. Upon receiving a cordial greeting, he explained his presence by telling us that he had heard through the missionary at Leech Lake—his home, nearly one hundred miles away—of our expedition, and at once resolved to find us. With a small wallet of food and some matches he had started forthwith on his long tramp, which occupied him several days. When night overtook him, he had lain down in the forest and slept as only an Indian can sleep, with no roof over him but the sky, and no other covering than the clothes he wore. He said he fully believed he would find his old employer wherever he might be in that region. Need I say that I

OUTLET OF LAKE GLAZIER.

was more than glad to see him again, and gratified by his loyalty and devotion? The distance he had traveled was little less than a hundred miles, but fatigue was unknown to him. I introduced him to my companions, and engaged him to remain with us until our return to Park Rapids. He was useful to us in many ways, although we had no need of an interpreter; and, around the camp-fire at night, his tales of adventure and translations of English words into Chippewa were very entertaining to his audience. I will only add that he was faithful in all things, and always on the alert to serve us to the best of his ability.

It may be here observed that before our start in the morning, Surveyor Horton and Mr. Whitney were detached with instructions to chain and report upon the length of Excelsior Creek, also its width, depth, and velocity at three different points. They found its length to be 8,778 feet; its width at the mouth, seven feet; its depth, two and a half feet. About midway between its mouth and the spring in which it originates, the width was reported at three feet and its depth six inches. The following is the result of careful measurement.

From Lake Itasca to Lake Glazier .	1,100 feet.
Across Lake Glazier to mouth of Excelsior Creek..	4,228 feet.
Length of Excelsior Creek	.8,778 feet.

It will thus be seen that from Lake Itasca to the head of Excelsior Creek is 14,106 feet, clearly demonstrating that this stream is not only the most important feeder of Lake Glazier, but that its source is nearly twice as far from Lake Itasca as is the head of Nicollet Creek, and furnishes the most convincing evidence to the impartial investigator that the lake located by me is the Primal Reservoir—the source

From Photograph by F. J. Trost.

LAKE ALICE.
A Feeder of Lake Glazier

of Excelsior Creek being at a much greater distance from Lake Itasca than that of any stream directly tributary to it.

Camp Trost, August 28, 1891.—Breakfast at 7.30, after which Surveyor Horton and Mr. Whitney crossed to the southern shore of Lake Glazier in a canoe, and ascended Deer Creek for the purpose of taking its measurements. They reported its length to be 6,864 feet; its width at the entrance into the lake, three feet, and depth at this point, fifteen inches. This stream, which enters the extreme southern end of the lake, is about half a mile east of Excelsior Creek, and is second only in importance to the last-named tributary.

While coasting the southern shore of Lake Glazier for the mouth of Deer Creek, Horton and Whitney discovered a small stream which, on ascending, they found had its source in a lakelet about half a mile inland.

In the afternoon, Keay, Munsell, my daughter and I walked out to Lake Alice. Alice expressed her surprise and delight on viewing the beautiful little lake to which her name had been given in 1881. While we were at Lake Alice, Horton and Whitney returned to the creek they had discovered in the morning. They found upon investigation with compass and chain, that their little stream was 1,188 feet long, and that the lakelet at its head had an area of between two and three acres. With one exception, this tributary is the smallest and shortest of the five permanent affluents of Lake Glazier, but when looked upon from a geographical point of view, as a feeder of the Primal Reservoir of the Great River, it may be regarded as of considerable importance.

GLEN ALICE.

Valley of Eagle Creek.

Camp Trost, August 29, 1891.—In the morning Messrs. Horton, Keay, Shure, Trost, Harrison, Knowlton, and my daughter walked out again to Lake Alice for the purpose of surveying and sketching the lake and its surroundings; also, of measuring the length of Eagle Creek. The measurement of the creek gave it a length of 6,978 feet from its entrance into the lake to its origin in springs some distance beyond Lake Alice.

It may here be noted that Eagle Creek ranks third in importance as a feeder of Lake Glazier. It has a well-defined mouth, a sandy and pebbly bed, and an average width of about three feet.

After dinner I crossed Lake Glazier with Horton, Harrison, and Knowlton, and walked up the banks of the creek discovered by Horton on the previous day. We then proceeded to Harriet Promontory, on which our party of 1881 had assembled after the investigations which had led to the conviction and subsequent announcement that the lake to the south of, and beyond, Itasca was the True Source of the Mississippi.

Upon reaching the point of the promontory, we signaled our friends on the northern shore of the lake to join us, and on their arrival, every member of the expedition being present, we raised the Stars and Stripes to the top of a neighboring pine, the same flag, I may state, that my party had assembled under, on the same spot, in 1881.

Our investigations of the Source and alleged sources of the Great River were now ended, and so far as I could gather, there appeared to be a consensus of belief as to the Primal Reservoir. I had hitherto, however, received no direct communication of the views of any member of the party, as it had been given me to

FIRST SERMON AT THE SOURCE OF THE MISSISSIPPI.

understand that a joint consultation would be held upon the subject, and the result submitted in a formal report.

I now proceeded to offer a few remarks in terms prompted by my own feelings and the conclusions I had long since reached, and spoke substantially as follows:

"FRIENDS AND COMPANIONS OF MY SECOND EXPEDITION TO THE HEADWATERS OF THE MISSISSIPPI:

"The ground on which we are assembled to-day has a peculiar interest for me, for it was on this spot, in 1881, that I stood surrounded by the little band which had followed me through lake and portage in my long journey from the then frontier town of Brainerd, across Northern Minnesota. It was here I pronounced the beautiful lake upon which we are now looking the True Source of the Great River. It was also here that we embarked on our voyage from source to sea; and now, after a lapse of ten years, you, who represent nearly every section of our country, have come together to discuss the results of your investigations as to the truth of my announcement that this lake is the Primal Reservoir of the Mississippi.

"I had long been of the opinion that Lake Itasca occupied an erroneous position in our geography, but when I came to the Mississippi in 1881, that lake was everywhere considered and laid down as the Source of the 'Father of Running Waters,' while many Indians of Northern Minnesota affirmed that there were other lakes and streams beyond. Our geographers and educational publishers still believed in the announcement made by Schoolcraft in 1832, and confirmed by Nicollet in 1836. Several persons have visited this region since their day, but not in the capacity of explorers. These later visitors looked upon this lake and went away, still accepting the source designated by the earlier explorers. They did not see or search for its feeders. They were not aware of the proportions of these feeders. They did not measure their length or width or depth. They did not ascertain by actual investigation that this lake was the center of a large basin; that some of its affluents extended to the sand hills, and that it was what its Indian name, 'Pokegama,' implies, 'The Place where the Waters Gather,' the Primal Reservoir or True Fountain-head, from which the Mississippi starts on its long and tortuous journey to the tropical Gulf, 3,000 miles away. Careful investigation showed all this in 1881; and now, gentlemen, you, who form my Second Expedition of 1891, have been able to verify or disprove my published statements. You have seen every lake and stream which has occupied the

From a Sketch by Miss Alice Glazier.

A TALK ON THE PROMONTORY

attention of geographers during the controversy which has followed. Let me indulge the hope that you will, at an early day, report the result of your investigations, as I feel sure you will thereby enable all fair-minded persons to determine definitely that the origin of our Great River is found in the lake which meets every requirement of geographers and scientists. I feel, furthermore, that you are called upon to give an impartial account of what you have seen, as I have reason to believe the geographical world is looking forward with much interest to the outcome of your investigations."

At the conclusion of my remarks, Mr. Giles was called upon to read his record of the expedition, which he did, commencing with the day on which the party left Minneapolis, and ending on that on which our explorations were concluded. The record was in the form of a diary, and, therefore, recounted the proceedings of each day.

Then followed the surveyors' report on Lakes Itasca and Glazier and their affluents. This report, of the particulars of which I had previously no cognizance, appeared to me in every respect confirmatory of all I had advanced in 1881, and subsequently, upon the subject of the True Source. The report is here given verbatim:

LAKE GLAZIER, MINNESOTA,
August 29, 1891.

CAPTAIN WILLARD GLAZIER.

DEAR SIR: In compliance with your request, we hereby submit a statement covering our investigations as to the length of affluents flowing into the southwestern arm of Lake Itasca, and into Lake Glazier The following are the results:

"NICOLLET CREEK, from Lake Itasca to source, 7,307 feet. Equal to 1 mile and 2,027 feet.

EAGLE CREEK, from Lake Itasca to source, viz.:

Length of Infant Mississippi, or stream connecting Lakes Glazier and Itasca	1,100	feet.
Across Lake Glazier, northern end	1,980	"
From Lake Glazier to Lake Alice	4,356	"
Length of Lake Alice	924	"
Length of Inlet to Lake Alice	1,518	"
Total from Lake Itasca to source of Eagle Creek	9,878	"

Equal to 1 mile and 4,598 feet.

EXCELSIOR CREEK:

Infant Mississippi	1,100	feet.
Across Lake Glazier from its outlet to mouth of Excelsior	4,228	"
From mouth of Excelsior Creek to its source in Sandhills	8.778	"
Total distance from Lake Itasca to source of Excelsior	14,106	"

Equal to 2 miles and 3,546 feet.

DEER CREEK, from Lake Itasca to source, viz.:

Infant Mississippi	1,100	feet.
Across Lake Glazier to mouth of Creek	5 940	"
Length of Deer Creek	6,864	"
Total from Lake Itasca to source of Deer Creek	13,904	"

Equal to 2 miles and 3,344 feet.

HORTON CREEK, from Lake Glazier to source in Whitney Pond	1,188	"
Length of Whitney Pond	396	"
Total length of Horton Creek	1,584	"
Area of Lake Glazier	255	acres
Average depth of Lake Glazier	45	feet.
Area of Lake Alice	9½	acres
Area of Whitney Pond	2	"

In all cases our measurements of streams were made, as nearly as practicable, along the shore. We measured all the affluents flowing into the southwest arm of Lake Itasca, and also those emptying into Lake Glazier, and found that Excelsior Creek, a feeder of Lake Glazier, was by far the longest tributary of either lake, its source being 6,799 feet farther from Lake Itasca than the source of Nicollet Creek, erroneously supposed by some to be the most important feeder of Itasca. It is, therefore, our firm belief that the Primal Reservoir or True Source of the Mississippi is in Lake Glazier—the only well-defined body of water lying above Itasca, and having any connection therewith, or with the Great River.

Respectfully submitted,
(Signed) E. M. HORTON, OLIVER S. KEAY, } *Surveyors.*

Mr. Whitney, the botanist of the expedition, who had been diligent in the investigation of the flora of the surrounding region, being next in order, said in substance, that he was preparing, and would submit later, a detailed report, but for the present would only state in general terms, that the vegetation at the Headwaters of the Mississippi bore a strong affinity to that found in Northern Michigan and Wisconsin, and the region bordering upon the Great Lakes. He had collected many specimens of the native plants, and proposed to carefully analyze them and submit his views.

Mr. Crane then announced that he was requested by his companions of the expedition to express their appreciation for the opportunity afforded them of visiting the Head of the mighty river. Having seen and carefully surveyed the Headwaters, they felt competent to report intelligently as to its Source. But one conclusion had been reached by the entire party, and that was that Lake Glazier was the Primal Reservoir and the only body of water that could consistently be designated the Fountain-head. Mr. Crane added that a report embodying this view would shortly be formulated and submitted. He closed his remarks by proposing a vote of thanks for the arrangements I had made for their convenience and comfort during their investigations.

Dr. Harrison seconded the motion, and in a few words expressed his entire concurrence in Mr. Crane's remarks with reference to the True Head of the river. The motion was carried unanimously. Dr. Harrison complimented my daughter on her courage in accompanying her father into so wild a region, to which she briefly responded.

The party was then formed in line on the beach, and each member having brought his rifle, shotgun, or revolver, twenty-five volleys were fired as a salute to the FLAG, six rounds for the party of 1881, and nineteen for that of 1891.

We now got into our canoes and returned to camp, skirting the eastern shore of the lake, and reaching the encampment on the northern shore between five and six o'clock.

Sunday, August 30, 1891.—This day was spent quietly in camp, the morning being for the most part devoted to writing up journals and preparing letters for home, to be mailed upon our return to Park Rapids.

In the afternoon it was suggested by Mr. Crane that divine service be conducted, a suggestion immediately approved by the entire party. We accordingly assembled in front of the tents and sat in a semicircle on the dry grass, while our pastor for the occasion stood on rising ground facing us. Bible in hand, he commenced the service by reading a chapter from the New Testament. Then followed a very impressive prayer, and this by an excellent discourse on the calling of the fishermen, Simon and Andrew, to the discipleship. Mr. Crane had a most attentive audience during his sermon, following which, all united in singing "Nearer My God to Thee," Mr. Knowlton leading. The service occupied about an hour, and closed with the doxology and benediction Mr Crane may doubtless claim the credit of having delivered the first sermon ever preached at the Source of the Mississippi.

From Photograph by F. J. Trost.

LAKE CRANE.

CHAPTER XI.

RETURN TO MINNEAPOLIS.

AFTER an early breakfast at Camp Trost, on the morning of August thirty-first, I went down to the shore of Lake Glazier, accompanied by my daughter and Lagard. Getting into a canoe on the right of the outlet, we passed entirely around the lake, halting at the mouths of Eagle, Excelsior, Horton, and Deer creeks, also at Harriet Promontory, where we landed. Here Lagard erected a tablet which had been previously prepared, commemorative of my First Expedition; and another on which was engraved the names of the members of the expedition of 1891.

Before leaving the promontory we discharged our firearms three times, as a parting salute to the FLAG which was still flying from the top of the small pine to which it had been nailed during our ceremonies at that point on the twenty-ninth. Our salute was responded to by an equal number of rounds on the opposite shore. We then re-entered the canoe and returned to the encampment.

Our investigations concluded, and everything being ready, tents were struck, outfit put into the canoes, and the journey back to Minneapolis begun. Passing down the southwestern arm of Itasca to Schoolcraft Island, we bore to the right and ascended its south-eastern arm to the point where we had embarked at the time of our arrival at the lake on our way out. The teamsters awaited us by appointment, and as soon as we had eaten our noonday meal, assisted them in loading the wagons.

So much time had been consumed in the farewell circuit of Lake Glazier in the morning, and later in the forenoon in breaking camp, and our passage through Itasca, that it was nearly three o'clock in the afternoon when our little column was put in motion and the march commenced, which led over the sand-hills and through the marshes to Park Rapids.

We were favored with clear, cool weather throughout the afternoon; and it was the intention to reach a high and wooded slope, some thirteen miles south of Itasca, but owing to the steep and rugged condition of the road, or, more correctly speaking, the trail which we were following, but little progress was made, and at nightfall we had advanced only about ten miles.

The site selected for our encampment was not what we could have wished; but in a measure answered the requirements, as it was on a hill-side covered with pines, and in close proximity to a small lake which afforded good water for man and beast. Although our experience on this ground reminded me more of the bivouac than the camp, we named it Camp Horton, in honor of our surveyor, E. M. Horton, of Park Rapids, who had not only faithfully and efficiently performed the duties of his position, but had, in many ways, rendered himself agreeable to the entire party.

Before supper was over, our camp-ground was enveloped in darkness, and being too much exhausted to pitch tents, except one for my daughter, we slept under the open sky.

Although only at the end of August, the night air of this elevated region was decidedly chilly, and before curling up in our blankets, a large camp-fire was built, around which all hands gathered and spent an hour in story-telling, and a discussion of the events of our sojourn at the Headwaters. The temperature fell rapidly as we approached midnight, and we found it necessary to draw the tent canvas over our blankets, and to feed the fire at intervals in order to make ourselves sufficiently comfortable for sleep.

We were on our feet at dawn the next morning, and while the cook was preparing breakfast the hunters shouldered their fowling-pieces and went in pursuit of game. Nothing was bagged, however, worthy of notice, which doubtless was due to the noise and confusion of the camp—a condition of things always unfavorable to the art of the sportsman. A few partridges were seen in the underbrush, and deer and moose tracks noted along the shore of the lake.

A very noticeable feature of the hill on which Camp Horton was situated was the great number of red squirrels seen at every turn. Many were observed skipping about on the ground, while overhead in the trees there seemed to be hundreds of these lively little rodents engaged in a general frolic. So striking was this peculiarity of our camp-ground that, in referring to the locality afterward, most of our party spoke of it as "Squirrel Hill."

Delezene called breakfast at six o'clock, and as soon as we had drunk our coffee, the wagons were reloaded and the journey continued. The day opened with a fair sky at Camp Horton; but the clouds lowered early in the forenoon, and, although there was no

From Photograph by F J. Trost.

EXPEDITION FORDING A STREAM.

rainfall, the mosquitoes were out in full force, and made our tramp anything but agreeable when passing through the marshes and lowlands that lay along our route. The clouds lifted at ten o'clock, and brought us welcome relief from the torment of our persistent and sanguinary little enemy.

Between ten and eleven o'clock we came to a beautiful expanse of water on the left of the road, which we had also seen during our journey out. Leaving the column, Crane and Lagard walked down to the lake and carefully scrutinized its shores to discover if it had an inlet and outlet. They estimated its dimensions at a mile in length by about three-quarters of a mile in width. At its northern end there is a wooded island with an area of, perhaps, an acre. Its distance from the Source of the Mississippi is about sixteen miles. Crane discharged his fowling-piece at several ducks that were observed a few feet from the shore, but only succeeded in killing one; this Lagard secured by wading into the lake, which, at that point, was shallow, with a sandy bed. At the suggestion of a member of the party, the lake was named in honor of Mr. Crane.

The stream described in a previous chapter, and referred to as Morrison River, was reached in season for luncheon, which was eaten on the north bank, near the spot where we had taken our first refreshment in the open air after leaving Park Rapids. As soon as we had lunched and rested, all mounted the wagons except Mr. Trost, who went forward in his high rubber boots in order to find a position from which to photograph the party while fording the stream. Men, horses, wagons, and surroundings presented a picturesque appearance while crossing the

From Photograph by F J. Trost.

AN ABANDONED CLAIM.

river. Dr. Harrison rode the leader and carried over his shoulder the pole which was used to keep "Jerry" in position. The remainder of the party were piled up in the wagons like so much furniture on moving day.

Our afternoon tramp was uneventful. A half-dozen straggling settler-cabins were seen as we drew nearer Park Rapids, the same we had noted on our journey out, and at five o'clock we emerged from the wilderness and were now wending our way at a more rapid gait over the "Shell Prairies" toward the little frontier village we had left on the twenty-second of August. The feature of our march from Camp Horton to Park Rapids, and that which, perhaps, excited most comment, was the endurance displayed by my daughter, who walked by my side throughout the day, without once complaining of fatigue, a distance of at least twenty miles, although the road was so hilly and rugged in many places as to threaten to precipitate horses and wagons, with their loads, to the bottom of the declivities.

A hearty welcome met us at Park Rapids, and it was at once apparent that the inhabitants were deeply interested in the results of our expedition. We had barely re-entered our old quarters at the Central House, when several of the leading villagers, headed by Dr. Winship, called and plied us with questions concerning our journey and explorations. It may be explained that, although the Head of the Mississippi is within fifty miles of their doors, and the people feel a special interest in the question of the True Source, we found on inquiry that not more than two or three had ever ventured to traverse the wretched road that leads to it.

From Photograph by F J Trost

A FRONTIER BANK

During the whole of our journey out and back, and while making our investigations at the Head of the river, we were highly favored by the weather. On one occasion only, during the night, a little rain fell on our tents, but not enough to inconvenience us, and the clouds passed away as the morning dawned. Almost immediately on our return to Park Rapids, however, a heavy storm crept up from the northwest and rain fell in torrents.

To return to the hour of our arrival at the Central House, the first thing thought of by the entire party was rest, after the severe jolting we had endured in the wagons and the long and trying march over hill and dale. Having made our ablutions and donned clean linen, a hot supper was placed before us, although it was now late in the evening, and we gladly partook of it before retiring. The supper, I may add, consisted, in part, of bear steaks, two of these animals having been shot on the outskirts of the village the day before our return. As may be supposed, bear meat was a novelty to most of the party, but, on trial, was generally pronounced a palatable change after the canned meats, wild fowl, and fish of the previous two weeks.

Our hotel was, unfortunately for us, undergoing repair and enlargement; workmen were employed throughout the building, and the accommodation, therefore, was not of a luxurious character. The walls of the rooms were not plastered, but simply lathed, and the floors without carpet or matting. There was no furniture whatever, except a bed, and no toilet articles. To crown all, there were no doors to the rooms, so that, in order to secure a modicum of privacy, calico curtains had to be suspended on nails across the open doorways. Moreover, to add to our cheerless condition, a strong northerly wind, with torrents of rain, had considerably reduced the temperature, and, although it was early in September, the cold was piercing, which made some of our party long for a warmer latitude. The absence of the usual appliances of a hotel, and consequent discomfort, could not justly be charged against our worthy host, Ben. Inman, who could hardly have anticipated such an influx of patrons while his house was undergoing repair, and so we all resolved to make the best of it, and resume our journey homeward with the least possible delay.

Before proceeding further, I may here add a few words concerning the senior member of the expedition, Mr. Giles—who, notwithstanding his advanced age, bore the journey, both ways, bravely. While at the encampment, he kept a diary of every event that transpired, and was very enthusiastic in his admiration of the picturesque and beautiful lake embosomed in the dense forest to the south of Itasca. He passed over and around it several times, and among other piscatorial feats, was successful in landing with his trolling-hook a seventeen-pound pickerel—the finest catch made by any of the party. By common agreement he was exempted, on account of his years, from the rougher and more fatiguing duties of the survey, in which all the others participated.

Moses Lagard, my old interpreter of 1881, who, it has already been stated, came out from Leech Lake in search of me, accompanied the party on our way back to Park Rapids. He had rendered himself extremely useful in many ways, and was always willing and prompt in the performance of any service re-

From Photograph by F J. Trost.

THE MENAHGA HOUSE.

Between Wadena and Park Papids, Minnesota.

quired of him. I was very sorry to be obliged to part with him, and he seemed much affected on leaving us.

Having rested as much as possible under the circumstances, and having conversed on the following morning with most of the leading inhabitants, we took our leave of them and our friends Postmaster Cobb and Dr. Winship; and finally of Horton and Keay, of both of whom I can not speak too highly During the time they were with me they were indefatigable in the discharge of the responsible duties for which they had been engaged—Mr. Horton as a professional surveyor, and Mr. Keay as his assistant, and both repeatedly assured me of their unqualified belief in my position with reference to the True Source of the Mississippi. This testimony I value the more highly because they are both quite familiar with the region around the Headwaters of the river. On parting, they each handed me a written document expressing their decided views, and fully endorsing all my published statements on the subject.

On the afternoon of September second, we boarded the one o'clock train for Wadena, arriving in the evening of the same day, and finding very superior accommodations at the Merchants' Hotel. On our journey out, this house was too full to receive our large party, which obliged us to seek rest and shelter under other roofs. At the "Merchants'" we now had supper, bed, and breakfast. J. E. Reynolds, editor of the Wadena *Pioneer*, called upon me in the evening, and we spent an hour in conversation. Mr. Reynolds gave me much valuable information upon the early history of the city, and of that section of Minnesota.

The following morning, Mr Trost, assisted by Mr.

From Photograph by F. J. Trost.

MERCHANTS' HOTEL AND PARK, WADENA, MINNESOTA.

Shure, took an excellent photograph of the Merchants' Hotel, and the little park in front of it. While at Wadena, several members of the party sent off their dispatches to the press, having prepared them, for the most part, while in camp at the Headwaters. Mr. Knowlton sent his narrative of the expedition to the New York *Herald;* Mr. Crane to the Boston *Herald;* and others to sundry Eastern papers and the Saint Paul and Minneapolis journals. Time allowed of our taking a stroll through the principal streets of the town in the morning, and we found everything wearing an air of prosperity.

About eight o'clock, we left our agreeable quarters at the "Merchants'" and boarded a train of the Great Northern for Little Falls. The journey was attended with no event; but, in the opinion of all, the country looked beautiful under the rays of the morning sun—the fields under cultivation giving promise of an unusually fine harvest.

Little Falls was reached at eleven o'clock in the forenoon; and we at once proceeded to "The Antlers," a hotel which would do credit to a much larger city. I have seldom met a more agreeable man than mine host of The Antlers, who very kindly drove me to Mayor Richardson's office, whose acquaintance I had made on passing Little Falls on my canoe voyage ten years before. His Honor remembered the circumstance, and conversed with me on the subject of my second visit to the Headwaters and the results attending it.

In 1881, Little Falls was a straggling village of a few hundred inhabitants. In 1891, I found it an incorporated city of several thousand. On the occasion of my first visit, I received a very cordial welcome. I must not omit to state, before leaving The Antlers, that I found in John E. Sutton, the proprietor, a comrade who had served with me under Custer and Kilpatrick, in the cavalry arm of the service, during the Civil War. This unexpected meeting of old comrades revived memories of the past, but our train was nearly due, and comrade Sutton insisted on driving me to the station in his carriage.

My companions were ready and anxious to start, and myself not less so, especially as our next point was Minneapolis—the beginning and end of the expedition. We arrived at the Union Depot at five o'clock, and soon dropped back into our old quarters on Harmon Place. All were in the enjoyment of excellent health, and expressed themselves well satisfied with their rough trip to the Headwaters, and with what had been accomplished. They promised to submit to me a joint report on the following day, which they did, unanimously certifying that the True Head of the Mississippi is in the lake designated by me in 1881.

The duties which devolved upon us in our investigations at the Source of the Great River having been satisfactorily fulfilled, the gentlemen composing the party spent a few days in sight-seeing, visiting the several beautiful resorts in and around Minneapolis, and finally took leave of each other, and departed for their respective homes in different States widely separated. It affords me much pleasure to add that, throughout the trip, although all were strangers to each other, the most perfect harmony had prevailed.

CHAPTER XII.

INDORSEMENT AND CONCLUSION.

ON the following day, and several days succeeding our return to Minneapolis, the subjoined indorsements were placed in my hands, with the exception of three received at a later period from Park Rapids. This corroborative testimony is presented with a view to establishing the fact that every member of my Second Expedition fully confirmed my announcement of 1881 that the heart-shaped lake lying above, and immediately to the south of, Itasca, is the True Source of the Mississippi. It may be added that the chief reason for introducing these indorsements is found in the statements of a few cavilers, who have gratuitously asserted that my companions were divided in their conclusions as to the real origin of the Great River. In a word, the decision of the party was unanimous, as will be clearly seen in the report and unsolicited letters given in this chapter.

E. M. Horton of Park Rapids, to whom allusion has been made in previous chapters, and who accompanied the expedition in the capacity of surveyor, thus expresses his views

CENTRAL HOUSE,
PARK RAPIDS, MINNESOTA,
September 2, 1891

I was engaged by Captain Willard Glazier on August 22, 1891, to accompany his expedition to the Itascan Basin for the purpose of measuring the streams flowing into Lake Itasca and Lake Glazier; which I did with the following results:

Assisted by Oliver S. Keay, I measured all the creeks flowing into the southwest arm of Lake Itasca, and those emptying into Lake Glazier, and found that Excelsior Creek, an affluent of Lake Glazier, is by far the longest feeder, its source being 6,799 feet farther from Lake Itasca than the source of Nicollet Creek. It is my belief that the Source of the Missis-ippi is in Lake Glazier—the only well-defined body of water, beyond Itasca, having a visible connection therewith.

(Signed) E. M. HORTON,
Surveyor to Second Glazier Expedition.

From Oliver S. Keay of Park Rapids.

PARK RAPIDS,
September 4, 1891.

Being familiar with all the lakes, creeks, springs, elevations, and depressions in the Itasca and Glazier basins; having many times visited the same, and the surrounding country, I unhesitatingly affirm that the Glazier Basin is the larger of the two. Lake Glazier presents the larger volume of running, or living, water; and, from my acquaintance with the Mississippi Headwaters, and the adjoining region, I firmly believe that Lake Glazier is the Primal Reservoir of the river. All unprejudiced persons who have ever visited the two basins agree that the Glazier Lake is the Source of the Mississippi.

(Signed) OLIVER S. KEAY,
Assistant Surveyor

From Dr A. Munsell of Dubuque, Iowa.

THE WAVERLEY,
MINNEAPOLIS, MINNESOTA,
September 4, 1891.

I was one of a party of gentlemen who accompanied Captain Willard Glazier to the Headwaters of the Mississippi in August, 1891, for the purpose of making a thorough investigation of that region, in order to ascertain what was the real source of our Great River From all that I there saw—and in accordance with the rule which recognizes the source of a river in the remotest living water, and in a lake, if possible—I have no hesitation in agreeing with all the other members of our expedition that Lake Glazier is the True Source of the Mississippi River

(Signed) A. MUNSELL,
Editor, Dubuque Trade Journal.

From Pearce Giles of Camden, New Jersey.

1215 HARMON PLACE,
MINNEAPOLIS, MINNESOTA,
September 4, 1891.

On August 17, 1891, I left Minneapolis in company with Captain Willard Glazier and a party of gentlemen who had volunteered to proceed with him to the Headwaters of the Mississippi in Northern Minnesota, to ascertain, by investigation, whether his claim to have located the True Source of that river was entitled to the recognition of geographers. We arrived at the Headwaters August 23d, and left September 1st, having thus devoted ten days to the duty we had assumed of solving the question as to the exact source of the Great River We were ably assisted by Messrs. Horton and Keay of Park Rapids, Minnesota, two practical surveyors, having large acquaintance with the region; and the affluents of Lakes Itasca and Glazier were all, on different days, duly meandered, and their length, width, and depth carefully measured. The result, as shown by the joint report of the surveyors, confirmed by the gentlemen assisting in the survey, is most convincing to my mind that Lake Glazier, lying to the south of Lake Itasca, and separated from the latter by an elevated ridge of land, is unquestionably the True Head of the Mississippi, being united to Lake Itasca by a permanently flowing stream —the "Infant Mississippi." From what I have personally witnessed and carefully investigated on the spot, I believe that no honest inquirer can arrive at any other conclusion.

PEARCE GILES.

From Rev John C. Crane of West Millbury, Massachusetts:

1215 HARMON PLACE,
MINNEAPOLIS, MINNESOTA,
September 8, 1891.

I was a member of the Second Glazier Expedition to the Headwaters of the Mississippi in August and September, 1891, and made a thorough personal investigation of all lakes, creeks, and springs around Lakes Itasca and Glazier. I was accompanied by the other members of the exploring party, and together we traced the feeders of both lakes to their origin, The conclusion I have arrived at is forced upon me—after laborious efforts to discover the truth—that Lake Glazier, lying directly to the south of Itasca, is the real Head or Source of the River; and that Lake Itasca is the first expansion of the stream after leaving its source in Lake Glazier.

(Signed) JOHN C. CRANE,
Correspondent of the Boston Herald.

From D. S. Knowlton, Boston:

THE WAVERLEY,
MINNEAPOLIS, MINNESOTA,
September 4, 1891.

As a member of Captain Glazier's Second Expedition to the Headwaters of the Mississippi, in August, 1891, I desire to add my testimony to the validity of his claim—that the lake to the south of Itasca, 255 acres in extent and 45 feet deep, is the veritable Source of the Father of Waters. I made a most careful personal investigation of the region around the Itasca and Glazier lakes, and the latter has unquestionably the strongest claim to be considered the Source of the river. Geographers, scientists, and others will be entirely justified in recognizing and designating Lake Glazier as the Ultimate Source of the Mississippi.

(Signed) D. S. KNOWLTON,
Editor, Boston Times.

From Dr. Charles E. Harrison of Davenport, Iowa.

THE WAVERLEY,
MINNEAPOLIS, MINNESOTA,
September 4, 1891.

Having been a member of the company of gentlemen who, during the month of August, 1891, made a careful investigation of the several streams and bodies of water emptying into Lake Itasca from the south, I believe that the claim of Captain Glazier in locating the Source of the Mississippi River is fully justified, and that geographers and others should recognize the Glazier Lake as its True Head.

(Signed) C. E. HARRISON,
Davenport Academy of Natural Sciences.

From Henry R. Cobb of Park Rapids:

September 2, 1891.

I accompanied the Glazier expedition to the Headwaters of the Mississippi, in the month of August, 1891, and found Lake Glazier, to the south of Itasca, to be the largest well-defined body of water which has any visible connection with the Mississippi through Lake Itasca.

(Signed) HENRY R. COBB,
Postmaster, Park Rapids.

From Fred J. Trost of Toledo, Ohio.

900 HENNEPIN AVENUE,
MINNEAPOLIS, MINNESOTA,
September 3, 1891.

I had the pleasure of being one of a party to accompany Captain Glazier to the Headwaters of the Mississippi. I made photographs of all the lakes and streams flowing into Lake Glazier, and into Lake Itasca; and, from personal observation and investigation, I feel perfectly certain that Lake Glazier is the True Source of the Mississippi River.

(Signed) FRED J. TROST,
Photographer, Second Glazier Expedition.

From Albert W. Whitney of Beloit College, Wisconsin:

THE WAVERLEY,
MINNEAPOLIS, MINNESOTA,
September 4, 1891.

Of all the bodies of water at the head of the Mississippi, I consider that Lake Glazier fulfills the greatest number of conditions necessary to make it the Source of that river.

(Signed) ALBERT W WHITNEY,
Botanist to Expedition.

From Winfield Scott Shure of York, Pennsylvania.

900 HENNEPIN AVENUE,
MINNEAPOLIS, MINNESOTA,
September 8, 1891.

I have explored, in company with the other members of Captain Glazier's expedition of August and September, 1891, all the region within the limits of the Itasca and Glazier basins, and certify to the following facts:

First.—That there is no other body of water to the south of Itasca, and tributary to it, that is so large and well defined as the fine lake known as Lake Glazier

Second.—That the two ponds, called, by some, "Nicollet's First and Second lakes," emptying into Lake Itasca, are, in their origin, not of sufficient remoteness or importance to be considered the source of the Great River; and, consequently, have no claim to that distinction.

Third.—That Lake Glazier, above and beyond Itasca, fed by five permanently flowing affluents, having their sources more remote from Itasca than any other feeders falling into that lake, is the True Source of the Mississippi.

(Signed) W. S. SHURE.

CONCLUSION.

I feel very confident that all who are interested in the question discussed in Part Third of this volume will find ample evidence to sustain the author in his claim to have been the first to definitely locate the True Head of the Mississippi. As I have said in a previous publication, I am well aware that I assume grave responsibility in locating the Source of the greatest river of North America, and correcting a geographical error of half a century's standing; especially, since I follow in the footsteps of such eminent explorers as Pike, Cass, Beltrami, Schoolcraft, and Nicollet; and in view of the fact that I have presumed to pass the limit of their explorations.

The statement that the lake now generally accepted by geographers as the Primal Reservoir was so regarded prior to the organization of my First Expedition can not be substantiated; on the contrary, both press and people throughout Minnesota were ignorant of its importance, or even of its existence, so far as we were able to ascertain by diligent inquiry, from Winona to Brainerd, and, in fact, I may add, that the missionary, Indian agent, and post-trader at Leech Lake knew no other source of the Mississippi than Lake Itasca, except what they had been told by my chief guide, Chenowagesic, and a few other Chippewas in that vicinity. Barrett Channing Paine, a member of my party, fully confirms me in this assertion in his letters to the Saint Paul and Minneapolis papers of that period. These letters prove most conclusively that the people of Minnesota had no knowledge whatever of the lake beyond Itasca, until it was announced by us through the medium of the press, in 1881.

I assume that my position, with regard to locating the True Source, is precisely the same as that of Schoolcraft in connection with Lake Itasca. When William Morrison, the fur trader, pitched his tent on Schoolcraft Island, in 1804, he was probably not aware that the outlet of the lake on which he looked was the Mississippi. Schoolcraft followed, at the head of an expedition, twenty-eight years later, and claimed the lake as the Source of the Great River. It is very generally admitted that Morrison had seen Itasca before Schoolcraft, but no one questioned that the latter was entitled to the credit of discovery, since he was the first to establish the fact that the Mississippi was its outlet.

I do not desire to pass a reasonable limit in my effort to establish a geographical truth, but, having announced that the lake to the south of Itasca—the Pokegama of the Chippewas—is the Ultimate Reservoir, I do not feel disposed to be thrust aside by those who know comparatively little or nothing of that region. Assuming that the conclusions arrived at by every member of both my First and Second expeditions are incontrovertible, it naturally follows·

First.—That Lake Itasca can not longer be considered as the origin of the Mississippi, for the reason that it is the custom, agreeably to the definition of geographers, to fix upon the remotest water, and a lake, if possible, as the source of a river.

Second.—That the lake to the south of Itasca, connected therewith by a perennial stream, is the Primal Reservoir, or True Source, that it was not so known or recognized prior to the visit of my party in 1881, and that we were the first to locate its feeders correctly, and establish its true relation to the Great River.

Third.—That Schoolcraft could not have seen the lake located by me, else he would have assigned it its true character in the narrative of his expedition.

Fourth.—That Nicollet, who followed Schoolcraft, could not have been aware of its existence, as he gives it no place upon his map, or description in the account of his explorations.

Fifth.—That Julius Chambers did not see this lake,

as his published statements prove very conclusively that he ascended Nicollet Creek to the first pond on that stream, and describes a lakelet in a floating bog, instead of the large and beautiful lake which is now generally regarded as the Source of the Mississippi.

Finally.—Whatever the verdict upon the merits of my claim to have been the first to definitely locate the lake beyond Itasca as the Source of the Mississippi, and to have published it to the world, it was certainly not known to the white inhabitants of Northern Minnesota prior to 1881. Lake Itasca was still recognized as the Fountain-head, was so placed upon all maps, and taught as such in all the schools. I simply claim to have established the fact that there is a beautiful lake above and beyond Itasca, wider and deeper than that lake, with woodland shores, with five constantly flowing streams for its feeders, and in every way worthy of the position it occupies as the Primal Reservoir or True Source of the Father of Waters.

FIRST GLAZIER EXPEDITION AT THE SOURCE OF THE MISSISSIPPI, 1881

APPENDIX

———:o:———

CONCERNING

The True Source

OF THE

MISSISSIPPI

BY

PEARCE GILES,

MEMBER OF

Second Glazier Expedition,

1891

APPENDIX.

I HAVE undertaken to prepare an APPENDIX to Captain Glazier's book on the "HEADWATERS OF THE MISSISSIPPI." I am well acquainted with every detail of his claim to have located the Primal Reservoir of that river; have read all that he has written upon the subject, and much that has been written by others, in favor of, and opposed to, his views. I have known him intimately for many years; have conversed with him frequently upon the subject of his expeditions through Northern Minnesota to the True Source of the Great River; have journeyed with him over thousands of miles of this country; have looked, and floated with him, upon the beautiful sheet of water which he asserts and demonstrates is the reservoir of the remotest springs of the Mississippi, to which his companions, in 1881, gave the name of LAKE GLAZIER. I have, with great care, personally investigated the grounds upon which he bases his claim; and for these reasons I feel competent to lay before the readers of his book some material which I trust may be of interest to geographers and educators, and to those who have given any attention to the ten years of controversy which have followed his announcement of 1881, that a certain lake, immediately to the south of Lake Itasca, is the Fountain-head of the Father of Waters.

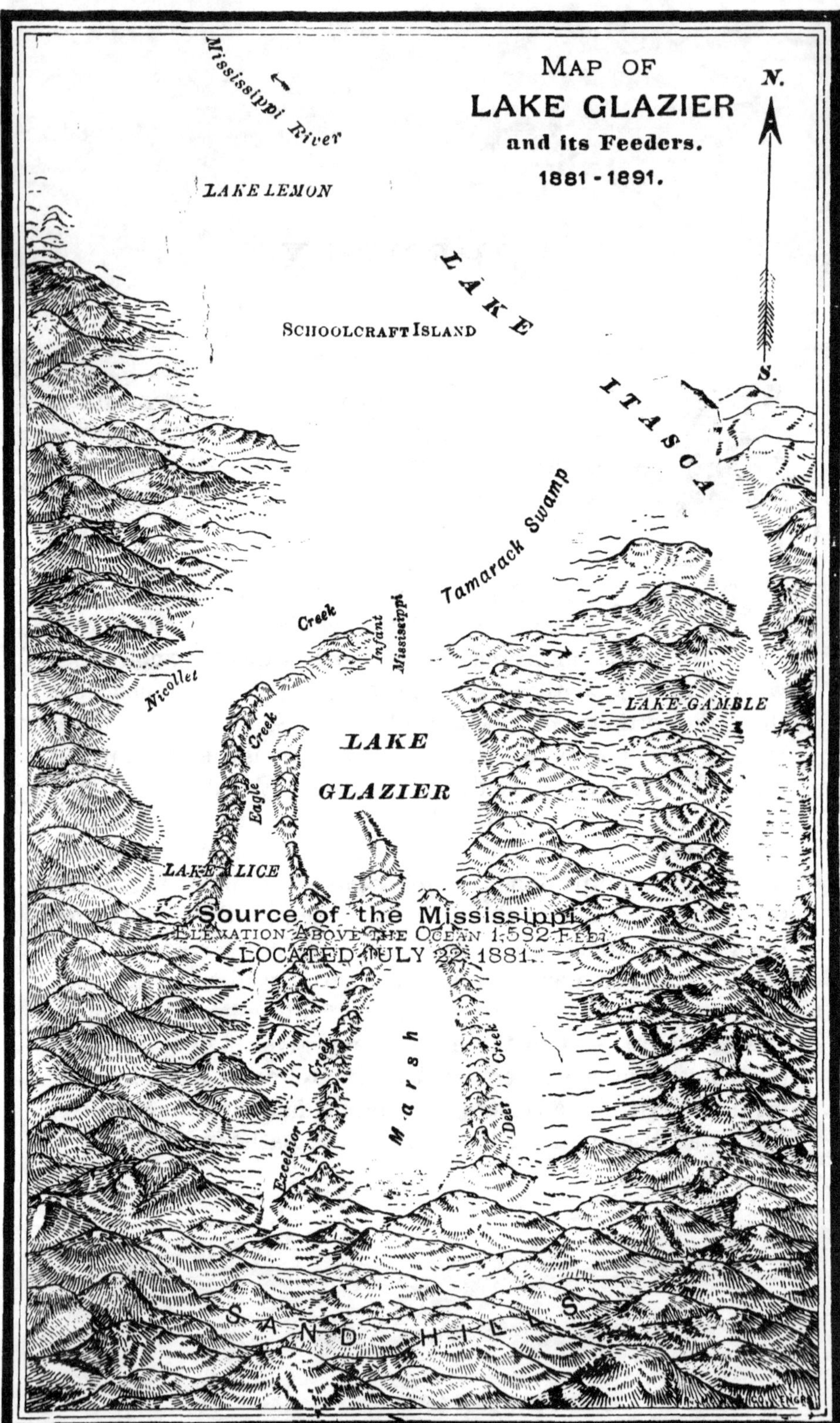
MAP OF
LAKE GLAZIER
and its Feeders.
1881 - 1891.
N.
S.
Mississippi River
LAKE LEMON
SCHOOLCRAFT ISLAND
LAKE ITASCA
Tamarack Swamp
Creek
Infant Mississippi
Nicollet
LAKE GAMBLE
Creek
Eagle
LAKE
GLAZIER
LAKE ALICE
Source of the Mississippi
ELEVATION ABOVE THE OCEAN 1,582 FEET
LOCATED JULY 22, 1881.
Marsh
Creek
Excelsior
Deer Creek
SAND HILLS

A.

FIRST GLAZIER EXPEDITION AND ITS RESULTS.

In his work, "Down the Great River," Captain Glazier clearly explains his motive for projecting his First Expedition to the Headwaters of the Mississippi. He therein states that he had heard that much uncertainty prevailed on the subject of the exact location of its Source, and decided to investigate the matter for himself, and for the satisfaction of others who, possibly, had less time at their disposal to devote to such an inquiry. He was not over-sanguine as to the issue of his venture, but little dreamed of the acrimonious and unreasoning opposition and contradiction he was fated subsequently to encounter. He believed that he was about to engage in a laudable undertaking, the result of which might possibly prove of some interest to students of geography and others. Hence, he employed his means to attain an object which appears to have eluded the efforts of all previous explorers—the Source of the Mississippi was still in doubt, although its mouth had been known over two hundred years before. This was sufficient reason, he thought, for further exploration; and possessed of a strong desire to see a part of the country but little known, he resolved to organize and equip an expedition, proceed to Lake Itasca and investigate its right to the distinction long accorded it of standing at the Head of the Mississippi.

July 4, 1881, Captain Glazier, accompanied by his brother George of Chicago, and Barrett Channing Paine of the Saint Paul *Pioneer Press*, boarded a train at Saint Paul, *en route* to the then frontier town of Brainerd, near the boundary of the Chippewa Indian Reservation. They reached Brainerd July seventh, and remained there five days to complete their commissariat supplies, and make arrangements for a journey through the wilderness and a possible detention at the Source of the river Captain Glazier also gathered much information at this point concerning the topography of the country, and finally decided to proceed via Leech Lake as a more direct course to his destination than that adopted by previous explorers, who had passed up the Mississippi through Lakes Winnebegoshish, Cass, and Bemidji, a longer and less-inviting route. He therefore secured wagon conveyance to Leech Lake, distant seventy-five miles from Brainerd, which led through an immense forest and jungle of pine and underbrush.

Leech Lake is a small settlement standing on the banks of the lake of that name, and consists of about a dozen Government buildings and log cabins, with several wigwams. It was formerly the seat of the Chippewa Indian Agency, which is now united with the White Earth and Red Lake agencies, and at the period of Captain Glazier's visit was under the superintendence of Major Ruffee, as Agent. Captain Glazier was fortunate, at this stage of his journey, in securing the valuable services of a Chippewa Indian, named Chenowagesic, who was well informed concerning the Itascan Basin and the region surrounding it. He told the Captain that the country around the Headwaters of the Great River had been his hunting-ground for many years, and being informed of the wish of the party to discover whether Itasca was the Source of the river, Chenowagesic declared emphatically that Itasca was *not* the True Head of May-see-see-bee, a fact well known to himself and many Indians who had hunted with him.

Two other Indians were also engaged at Leech Lake, one as interpreter, the other as *voyageur* The three placed their birch canoes at the disposal of the party for use on their journey through and across the numerous lakes and streams that intervened between Leech Lake and their destination. July seventeenth witnessed the departure of the party from the settlement. An hour's paddling carried them across one of the several arms of the lake, and a short portage brought them to another arm from fifteen to twenty miles long, crossing which they came to the mouth of the Kabekanka River. Guided by Chenowagesic, they ascended this stream until a small lake or expansion of the river was reached, and ultimately a large and picturesque lake, nearly seven miles in length. On its banks they pitched tents for the night, and at break of day July eighteenth again launched and pushed on to the upper end of the lake. Chenowagesic, on being asked, informed the Captain that the Indians had no name for this lake, whereupon he conferred upon it the name of "Garfield," in honor of the President.

Arrived at the head of Lake Garfield, a long portage of nearly three miles confronted them. This was accomplished by the Indians without the slightest sign of fatigue or discomfort, notwithstanding the heavy packs they bore upon their heads and shoulders, including the canoes; but the white men suffered much from the intense heat, the roughness of the trail, and the mosquitoes, which hovered like a cloud over the lowlands.

Rested and recovered from the tiresome portage of the forenoon, they resumed their line of march. Late in the afternoon the party reached a series of five lakes—a not unwelcome sight after their tramp in the broiling sun. Again on the water, they passed through three of the lakes, with, necessarily, intermediate portages, and reaching the fourth, concluded to encamp for the night.

At sunrise the following morning they breakfasted, and at seven o'clock re-embarked. By ten o'clock the fifth lake was entered. Here the guides informed Captain Glazier that these lakes had never before been seen by white men. He therefore, after consulting with his brother and Mr. Paine, named them in the order in which they had been passed—Bayard, Stoneman, Pleasanton, Custer, and Kilpatrick, generals who were severally his commanding officers during the War of the Rebellion. Eight exhausting portages occurred during the day, and an equal number of lakes were crossed after leaving Lake Kilpatrick. The three largest of the latter received from the Captain the names of Gregg, Davies, and Sheridan, distinguished cavalry leaders of the Union army

One of the most expansive bodies of water, seen between Leech Lake and Lake Itasca, had an average width of about five miles, and bore an unpronounceable Indian name, signifying "Blue Snake." To this sheet of water the Captain gave the name of his brother George. Lake George was crossed, and the canoes conveyed to the highest ground in the vicinity. The sun was declining, and, the whole party needing rest, tents were again pitched. Early the following morning, all eager to reach their destination, and fortified by a good night's sleep, the canoes were pushed into a fine sheet of water named by the Captain Lake Paine, after his companion of the Saint Paul *Pioneer Press*. This lake is only a short distance from Lake George, the intervening space being comparatively level, and covered with jack-pines and underbrush. Crossing Lake Paine, another portage of half a mile presented itself, and the River Naiwa was reached, a stream several miles in length. Descending this river a distance of five or six miles, they disembarked and portaged in a westerly direction, reaching another stream, that appeared to be a favorite haunt for wild fowl, which were very numerous, and seemingly unaffected by the approach of man. Paddling four hours up this stream they came to a lake which Captain Glazier believed to be the source of the Eastern Fork of the Mississippi. This water was passed over in twenty minutes, and the name "Elvira" conferred upon it, in memory of a deceased sister of the Captain.

At the southern end of Lake Elvira, the canoes entered its inlet, which flows in a northerly direction, and discharges into the main stream originating in Lake Glazier, not far from the southern end of Lake Bemidji. It was not laid down on the maps, and was named De Soto River by Captain Glazier, in honor of the renowned discoverer of the Mississippi. The day was now drawing to a close, and, nearly exhausted by the portages over the roughest region of Minnesota, it was promptly decided to encamp for the night.

In the morning a heavy fog, rising from a swamp in their front, obscured the trail, and the journey could not be resumed until seven o'clock. Moving forward in Indian file, they rested thirteen times before reaching the shores of Lake Itasca. Between three and four o'clock in the afternoon, their eager eyes beheld the silvery waters of the lake, and in a few minutes the party were floating on its bosom on their way to Schoolcraft Island, near the center of the lake. On this solitary isle, Henry Rowe Schoolcraft encamped sixty years ago, and believed that in the waters that surrounded him he had discovered the long-sought-for Source of the Mississippi. This belief he afterward announced to the world, and for over fifty years the lake was held, on the authority of Schoolcraft, to be the Ultimate Head of the Father of Waters, no one gainsaying it. This, doubtless, was for the reason that very few persons, except Indians, had ever visited it, the region around Lake Itasca being well-nigh inaccessible, and entirely so without a competent guide.

Schoolcraft Island is about three-quarters of an acre in extent, and so densely covered with trees, shrubs, and undergrowth that the Glazier party found some difficulty in clearing a space for their tents. The appearance of Itasca and its environment of forest lands is highly attractive. It is about five miles in length, with an average width of about half a mile. Its greatest length is from southeast to northwest. It has three arms radiating from its center, somewhat like those of a star-fish. One arm points to the southeast, one to the southwest, and the remaining one extends northward to the outlet of the lake.

Chenowagesic, perfectly familiar with the region, informed the Captain that the name of the lake was *Omushkos.* Schoolcraft himself, in the narrative of his expedition, Chapter XXIII, says:

> "I inquired of Ozawindib the Indian name of this lake; he replied, *Omushkos*, which is the Chippewa name of the *Elk*. Having previously got an inkling of some of their mythological and necromantic notions of the origin and mutations of the country, which permitted the use of a female name for it, I denominated it *Itasca*."

Having supped and rested on the island, the exploring party re-embarked on the morning of the twenty-second, at eight o'clock, and began coasting Itasca. Chenowagesic again assured the Captain and his companions that he was thoroughly acquainted with all the streams, lakes, and ponds within a hundred miles, and impressed them with his entire trustworthiness. In coasting the lake they found the outlets of six small streams, two only having well-defined mouths, and four simply filtering into the lake through swampy ground.

Reaching the southern extremity of the southwestern arm of the lake, the canoes were forced, with some difficulty, through a tangled mass of reeds and rushes to the mouth of a stream about seven feet wide, but effectually concealed from view by dense lake vegetation. Encouraged by their guide, the canoes were pointed up this affluent, which was much obstructed by fallen trees and occasional sand-bars. These were, however, removed by the crews, and the boats again urged forward. Elevated land appeared on each side of the stream, that on their right rising to the dignity of a hill. This hill, or ridge, Chenowagesic explained, overhung the Source of the Father of Waters toward which they were speeding, and which separated it from Itasca. This Indian was an exceptionally intelligent man, as well as a faithful guide. The object of their search was soon reached—a large sheet of smooth, transparent water of surpassing beauty Afloat on its surface, the conviction forced itself upon them that the Source of the Mississippi could no longer be a subject of uncertainty The canoes were at once paddled across the lake, a distance of nearly two miles, to a promontory at its southern extremity

This point of land, with its picturesque shore projecting into the lake, gives the latter the shape of a heart, a fitting resemblance for the source of the mighty river Encompassed by high ground, thickly clustered and adorned with trees of diverse kinds, dominated by the stately Norway pine, the waters of this beautiful lake scintillate under the rays of the sun, and sparkle like the luster of a million gems. Its broad surface is singularly free from that opaqueness which mars the beauty of many of the surrounding lakes, including Itasca. It is supplied by springs, some in its bed, but two feeders were found, on careful investigation, under the guidance of Chenowagesic, to originate in sand-hills a few miles to the southward, and flowed into the lake on each side of the promontory; while a third entered on the northwestern shore of the lake. These affluents, small but significant, were named, respectively, Eagle, Excelsior, and Deer creeks. At the extreme point, or cape, of the promontory, a spring was discovered whose water was deliciously cool. The shores of the lake were then investigated.

Returning to the promontory, the party was called into line, and Captain Glazier made a few remarks, expressing his confident belief that they had found the TRUE SOURCE of the Great River, a discovery which had baffled the attempts of previous explorers; and they had therefore added something to the geographical knowledge of the country He dwelt on the error of Schoolcraft in assigning this distinction to Lake Itasca, which was now clearly seen to be merely the first expansion of the river, after leaving its source in the lake they were looking upon. Chenowagesic had told him that the Indian name of this lake was *Pokegama*, which the interpreter explained signified "The Place where the Waters Gather," or, in other words, the Primal Reservoir If such was the case, it was unquestionably the Fountain-head, or True Source, of the Mississippi.

At the conclusion of the Captain's remarks, Mr Paine stepped forward and spoke of the justness of his views, in which the entire party concurred. He then moved that the lake be named GLAZIER, in honor of the man whose determination and perseverance to learn the truth on a subject of so much general interest had successfully accomplished the end he had in view on leaving Saint Paul. The motion of Mr Paine was seconded by the interpreter, Moses Lagard, and adopted by acclamation, Captain Glazier, meanwhile, protesting that he would prefer it should retain its descriptive Indian name of *Pokegama*.

I may here remark that some of Captain Glazier's critics have recently applied the term "Elk" to this sheet of water, a name which, according to Schoolcraft, as we have seen, was the aboriginal designation of Lake Itasca. Lake Glazier is entirely disconnected with Itasca, the two lakes being separated by a high ridge and perfectly independent of each other A perennial stream at the foot of the ridge, up which the party ascended in their canoes, and to which the name of "Infant Mississippi" has been appropriately given, carries the waters of the upper lake to its lower neighbor, on its long route to the Gulf of Mexico. Thus the lake above Itasca is in no sense a part of Itasca, and to call it "Elk" Lake is an anomaly, and an unworthy evasion, a perversion of scientific accuracy, misleading to the student, and, in short, a geographical blunder Itasca has been "Elk Lake" from time immemorial, according to Indian tradition, while Pokegama, since 1881, has been popularly transmuted into "Lake Glazier."

This lake, which proved to be the Primal Reservoir, or Ultimate Head, of the Mississippi, was found by measurement to cover an area of 255 acres, with an average depth of forty-five feet. The results of the First Glazier Expedition were so far satisfactory that, on their announcement to the public through the press, geographers, instructors, and educational publishers were unanimous in their acceptance of the Glazier claim, and a change was forthwith made in all maps of the State of Minnesota.

Some of the opponents of Captain Glazier's published views on the subject have of late maintained that Schoolcraft visited the lake above Itasca in 1832, and Nicollet in 1836. There is not a word in the "Narrative" of the former to indicate that he went south of the island which bears his name. All the evidence points in the opposite direction, and it must be clear to the careful reader that he remained on the island only a few hours. He says he was hurried, having an appointment to meet certain Indians in council at the mouth of Crow Wing River. His map of Lake Itasca does not show the lake to the south of it. Hence it is presumable that he could not have coasted Itasca for its feeders, which, to have been effectually accomplished, would have occupied him an entire day at least. Even if he had done so, the strong probability is that, being hurried, he would not have found the concealed entrance to the stream which led to the lake beyond. Captain Glazier admits that he was largely indebted to his chief guide, and that had it not been for Chenowagesic he would possibly never have discovered the mouth of this important affluent. The time allotted himself by Schoolcraft, as indicated in his "Narrative," would not have allowed him to ascend the southwestern arm of Itasca, much less so to pass up the creek to the important lake beyond it. The conclusion to be drawn from his "Narrative" is, that he was only between two and three hours within the Itascan Basin, and, in his eagerness to depart on his mission to Crow Wing River, he not improbably relied upon his guide, Ozawindib, for whatever knowledge he obtained of Lake Itasca and its surroundings.

If Nicollet saw the Source of the Mississippi, he certainly failed to describe it. He shows on his map only the creek which enters the southern end of Itasca and the ponds through which it passes on to the lake. He doubtless ascended this creek, but the more important stream entering the lake on his left escaped his view, as it would that of ninety-nine persons out of a hundred. If he had ascended this affluent of Itasca, he would at once have discovered that Schoolcraft was in error, that Itasca was *not* the Source of the Mississippi River, and his map would have been differently constructed. The mouth of the inlet that led to the True Source was doubtless hidden then, as now, by a mass of lake vegetation, which so concealed it from view that in 1881 even Chenowagesic had difficulty in finding it. I therefore reasonably conclude that Nicollet, like his predecessor, was deceived in assuming Itasca to be the Source of the Mississippi, the logical inference being that he never saw the beautiful lake to the south of it.

In 1872, Lake Itasca was visited by Julius Chambers. Mr Chambers, during his summer vacation, was not an explorer, but a tourist on pleasure bent, and paddled his canoe on Lake Itasca up to its southern end. Here he discovered the mouth of a creek wide enough to admit his canoe, and, ascending it, came to a pond or expansion of the creek. Believing he had entered an important feeder of the river's source, or rather, as he terms it in a dispatch to the New York *Herald*, the Source itself of "the longest river in the world—a small lake, scarcely a quarter of a mile in diameter, in the midst of a floating bog."

Having myself visited the Headwaters of the Mississippi in the summer of 1891, I became thoroughly convinced, after careful personal investigation, that the Primal Reservoir of the Great River is a body of water lying to the south of Lake Itasca, nearly two miles in diameter, and that there is not the faintest shadow of a bog or morass within at least a mile of it. Its basin is secluded—an elevated ridge dividing it from Itasca—and the surrounding shores are high, and crowned with a dense growth of timber Mr Chambers' description of his boggy pond on Nicollet Creek is proof sufficient to me that he, in common with Schoolcraft and Nicollet, made a serious mistake. The genesis of the "longest river in the world," or, if not the longest, the *finest*, is not in a "floating bog, a quarter of a mile in diameter," but has a much nobler origin. It is to be hoped that Mr. Chambers will pay another visit to Lake Itasca, and correct his error

The Government survey of 1875 doubtless saw the True Source of the river, but did little beyond measuring its area. This was a portion of their duty, as the lake exceeded forty acres in extent. They did not trouble themselves about its relation to Lake Itasca or to the Mississippi, nor did they give much attention to its feeders, for had they done so, they would not have shown on their map an important feeder of Lake Glazier as an affluent of Lake Itasca, thus depriving the former of one of its credentials to the distinction claimed for it, and adding to the importance of the latter Had they possessed the instincts of geographers or explorers, they would have discovered and reported to their chief at Washington that the large lake above and beyond Itasca was the True Head of the Mississippi, and thus forestalled the explorer of 1881, who discovered and announced this important geographical fact to the country.

Hopewell Clarke, a professional surveyor, who was sent out to investigate and report upon Captain Glazier's explorations, confesses that the Government survey of 1875 had made *mistakes*, and excuses their inaccuracies in these words: "Errors will creep into their work; but when we take into consideration the difficulties they had to contend with, it is not to be wondered at." Had the members of this survey of 1875 conducted their investigations with a view to the location of the Source of the Mississippi, and had they traced the affluents of this lake to their springs, they would have been satisfied that it was the Source of the Great River, and not simply a feeder of Lake Itasca, that its size and position entitled it to more consideration than they were inclined to give it.

The result of Captain Glazier's First Expedition was the discovery that Lake Itasca could not—with any regard to geographical accuracy—be considered the Source of the Mississippi, as was taught in all geographies and maps prior to 1881—the period of his visit and discovery; but that the fine body of water above it, the Pokegama of the Indians, was unquestionably the Primal Reservoir and Head of the river; a truth now generally recognized by geographers, encyclopædists, instructors, and map publishers, and controverted by only a few quibblers, who have not themselves visited the region, and hence are essentially unqualified to pronounce judgment in the matter.

Schoolcraft and Nicollet are worthy of the greatest honor for their persevering efforts to reach the Source, and if they failed in the accomplishment of that object, it is no more than many other distinguished explorers have done, in attempts to find the springs of other great rivers. All knowledge is progressive, and geography, in common with history, is open to correction as time rolls on. The beliefs of centuries are sometimes proved to be without foundation, and are cast aside for the results of modern research. The explorations of intrepid pioneers and travelers are yearly adding to our knowledge of the earth, and if the labors of one intelligent and zealous American, with time and means at his command, have resulted in a discovery that those who preceded him in the same line of investigation were in error in their conclusions, shall it be said, in this enlightened day, that he is not justified in declaring his discovery because a few cavilers affect to discredit him?

B.

CRITICS AND CAVILERS.

The controversy concerning the Source of the Mississippi has been confined to an extremely limited circle. Certain critics and cavilers, more or less given to raising objections when a new exposition of an old theory is advanced—especially if the propounder is not of their caste—have controverted the truth of Captain Glazier's account of his discovery, and challenged him to produce proof of his positive assertions. (1) That Lake Itasca possesses no rightful claim to be considered the Source of the Mississippi; and (2) that the True Source of that river is in a comparatively large lake immediately to the south of Itasca, and above it. These are the points in dispute, and the first proposition is, of course, a corollary of the second.

Captain Glazier has repeatedly presented his proofs through the press, and has answered the challenge of his opponents by inviting them to accompany him to the Head-waters of the river and investigate and judge for themselves, volunteering to defray half the expense incurred. This offer they have not accepted, but replied by sending out a person, independently, to represent them, a man who, before setting forth on his mission, paraded in public his determination to support his employers. This offensive display of partisanship in the sacred cause of science passed unreproved by the critics of Captain Glazier, but was not unheeded by his friends. The party referred to proceeded on his mercenary errand, and has since published a report which for subterfuge, evasiveness, and moral obliquity has seldom been equaled. It was, however, indorsed and published with the sanction of his patrons. But the words of the report were no index to the writer's mind. He had looked upon the True Source of the Mississippi if his patrons had not, and could not be otherwise than mentally assured of the truth and scrupulous correctness of the Glazier position. He returned to his employers—*and denied it!* There was little fear of their discovering his duplicity, even if they had wished to do so. The spot is very difficult of access, as I have shown. He plausibly pointed to other lakes, ponds, and streams, and while admitting that none of them had any visible connection with Lake Itasca or the Mississippi, suggested that *probably* the connection was underground! He knew it was the wish of those who had been instrumental in sending him to the Headwaters that he should not return and support the views of Captain Glazier, which views they had previously, in their wisdom, denounced as "fraudulent," and their propounder a "charlatan." They were apparently confirmed in their mistaken belief that Lake Itasca was the Source of the Mississippi. Not so, however, the press and the public. The sentiment was widely expressed that Captain Glazier was not being fairly treated, and the people, prompt to detect and denounce injustice, made their views known, not only in the Northwestern press, but throughout the country I will here subjoin a few examples of these views, of which I have hundreds in my possession.

A correspondent at Worcester, Massachusetts, writes to a Saint Paul daily, in March, 1886:

In 1881 Captain Willard Glazier brought to the notice of the people of this and other countries that beyond Itasca lay the Source of the Great River. Let the men stand up and be counted who, prior to 1881, declared that the lake now named Lake Glazier was the source of the great stream flowing through the nation's heart. Let your correspondent, "Somebody who Knows," furnish the names of these men.
Is Lake Glazier the source of the river? That is the question. Schoolcraft says, "Geographers deem that branch of a river as its true source which originates at the remotest distance from its mouth." Glazier says, "It is the custom of geographers to fix upon the remotest water, and a lake if possible, as the source of a river" In 1881, he claimed the lake in question as the True Source. Let the proposition lately made by him [the offer to defray half the expense of an authorized expedition to decide the question] be accepted in good faith, and his claim stand or fall on its merits. As long ago as 1858, the doubt existed as to Itasca being the True Head. A great claim is made by Captain Glazier; let his claim be met in a spirit of fairness on the part of all concerned; let the verdict be true, free from prejudice, and lasting.

FAIR PLAY.

A writer in the Buffalo *Courier*, in November, 1886, took issue with that journal regarding the discovery of the Mississippi's source:

Editor of the Courier:

In your issue of September 19th there appears a short article dealing "blows without gloves" at Captain Willard Glazier's "pretensions" to having discovered the True Source of the Mississippi in a lake to the south of Itasca. The article appears to have been inspired by a correspondent of *Science*, who objected to Captain Glazier's claim on grounds which I propose to analyze. The correspondent of *Science* begins by asserting that Glazier gave his own name to the lake he discovered, which is an error, originated, probably, by some caviler, jealous that any man should presume to make a discovery who was not officially authorized to do so. One of Captain Glazier's companions, in an article to the Saint Paul *Pioneer Press*, after describing the discovery of the new lake, writes:

"On its one promontory our party landed. After exploring its shores and being marshaled in line, Captain Glazier made a few remarks appropriate to the discovery of the True Source of the Father of Waters, and then the question of a name for the new lake arose. This being left for the Captain's companions to decide, Barrett Channing Paine of Indianapolis, after alluding in warm terms to the time, money, and energy expended by Captain Glazier in the expedition, proposed that it be named LAKE GLAZIER in his honor. The proposition was received with applause and carried by acclamation."

Thus, we see, Captain Glazier did not "give his own name" to the lake. He, on the contrary, we are told, suggested and urged that it should retain its Indian appellation of *Pokegama.*

There is nothing to be found in Schoolcraft's narrative of his expedition to show that he penetrated south of Lake Itasca. He speaks of an inlet to Itasca leading from a smaller lake to the south, but clearly did not visit the smaller lake, and hence did not "discover" it. Nor was it known to exist by Nicollet, who came after him. The latter explorer says that there are five creeks flowing into Itasca. Captain Glazier discovered six, the sixth originating in a lake (not a lakelet) a short distance to the south of Itasca. This lake was not known to Nicollet. It lies nearly due south of the southwestern arm of Itasca. He visited the others, which are mere ponds in comparison, but missed the most important one, probably owing to difficulty of access, its inlet to Lake Itasca being completely hidden by the densest lake vegetation. Such an inlet would probably not have been discovered by the Glazier party but for the information of the Indian guide, whose hunting-ground was in the immediate neighborhood. The "Infant Mississippi" flows from this lake, through which Captain Glazier and his companions forced their way under the guidance of Chenowagesic. The lakelets, or ponds, shown on Nicollet's map have nothing to do with the source of the river; and the map itself, so far as Lake Itasca and its region are concerned, is altogether misleading. Itasca has three arms, or bays, not two, as shown on Nicollet's map.

AN OLD GEOGRAPHER.

George F Cram of Chicago, well known throughout the country as a leading map and atlas publisher, writes, under date December 4, 1886:

"There is no question in my mind but that the Source of the Mississippi is not in Lake Itasca, as we have hitherto been taught, but in a lake immediately to the south of it. The question of the discovery of this lake, which will probably prove to be the True Source, is the subject of a warm contest between Captain Glazier and some school-book publishers who seem to have interests inimical to his. Whatever name may be conferred upon this lake will be determined after these gentlemen have become reconciled, but the question of the source of the Mississippi I think may be considered absolutely settled, and Lake Itasca must lose its reputation for being the Head of that important stream."

A correspondent at Providence, Rhode Island, wrote to the Boston *Herald* under date October, 1886, in response to a criticism by Russell Hinman of Cincinnati. Mr. Hinman was at the time, I believe, connected with an educational publishing house in that city in the capacity of geographer, and, in his letter to the Boston *Herald*, very confidently denied that the claim of Captain Glazier to have located the True Source of the Mississippi had any foundation in fact. It will be understood by the intelligent reader that if the Glazier discovery proved to be correct, it would necessitate an alteration in some of the geographical publications of his firm. Hence, possibly, the denial, which also occurred in a similar instance in New York:

To the Editor of the Boston Herald:

In a recent issue of your paper appears a letter signed "Russell Hinman," to which my attention has only just been drawn. Mr. Hinman writes in the authoritative style of an explorer who has a personal knowledge of the region to which he refers, namely, that around the Headwaters of the Mississippi. If, however, as I suspect, your correspondent is simply a "carpet knight," and gathered his information from sources open to all of us, his tone of authority is, I think, somewhat misplaced. I propose to meet the gentleman's second-hand information with that derived from direct personal knowledge of the subject in debate, and to advance only that which I know to be fact.

For years Lake Itasca has been regarded both by geographers and map makers, as well as by the public generally, as the Source of one of the greatest rivers of the world—the Mississippi.

No injustice is done to the memory of the two early explorers of the

Northwest, Schoolcraft and Nicollet, in the statement that, notwithstanding their many valuable additions to the geographical knowledge of Northern Minnesota, their explorations did not extend to the discovery of the True Source of the Mississippi. Schoolcraft believed it to be Lake Itasca, and Nicollet confirmed him in this error. Glazier, in July, 1881, started for this lake, and learned, upon diligent inquiry at the Government agency at Leech Lake, that the dense forests that surround the Source of the Father of Waters had never been traversed by white men since the visit of Nicollet in 1834, or even by Indians at any time except in winter, when lakes and rivers were frozen up and the whole surface of the country covered with a mantle of snow He also learned through the guides and interpreters who accompanied him that the Indians of these primeval forests did not regard Itasca as the Source of the river; but, while rejecting it, differed among themselves as to what lake really was the Fountain-head.

Captain Glazier determined to thoroughly examine all this region and to locate definitely and forever its True Source. In accordance with this design, he pushed on toward Lake Itasca, intending to make it a starting point for further exploration. Reaching this point, he and his little party camped on Schoolcraft Island, and, after a night's rest, he directed operations toward the lakes and streams of the surrounding country. He closely examined the shores of Lake Itasca for tributary streams, finding but three of any importance. Of these, by far the largest came in at the southern end of the lake, at a point where it is nearly filled with bulrushes and other thick vegetable growth.

Taking two canoes, Glazier ascended this stream, which, though shallow, is rapid, yet so narrow in places that to jump across it would be an easy task. Following its windings, he entered what appeared to be a lakelet filled with rushes. Pushing through this, however, the canoes finally glided out upon the still surface of a beautiful lake, clear as crystal, with pebbly bottom, and shores covered with a thick growth of pine. This lake is formed irregularly in the shape of a heart, having but one marked promontory Captain Glazier measured the length of the lake, and found it to be over a mile and a half, and its width a little less. He found that this lake was supplied by three feeders, which rose in sand hills a few miles from the lake, and, after a thorough examination, became convinced that this beautiful sheet of water was in reality the Source, or Primal Reservoir, of the mighty river. Without much discussion, the members of the party decided unanimously to name it Lake Glazier, in his honor. This is a brief summary of the proceedings of the Glazier expedition, so far as concerns the discovery

Your correspondent states that the existence of such a tributary lake to Lake Itasca has been known for more than half a century I reply that the lake indicated on Schoolcraft's map, published in 1834, and on Nicollet's map, published in 1838, is not the lake referred to by Glazier, or it would have been at once designated as the Source of the Mississippi. If its existence was known, why was it not so designated? The lake is not quite so long as Itasca, but is considerably wider and much deeper, and the stream that unites it with the latter is perennial, and wide enough and deep enough for the passage of canoes. Surely, if this water had been known to previous explorers, they would have pronounced it, as Glazier has done, the Source of the Mississippi. Of the three feeders to the Glazier lake, one enters it from the west, which has its source in a lakelet named "Alice." This feeder is shown on the Land-office map as entering Lake Itasca, which is an error. It enters the Glazier lake at its northern extremity, and of this Captain Glazier fully satisfied himself. Lake Alice lies farther to the south than Lake Glazier, and if the stream issuing from it debouched in Itasca, it would be the veritable source of the river. But it is simply a feeder of the Glazier lake, and hence is entitled to less consideration.

It is claimed for Lake Glazier that it is the True Source of the Great River, and that if it had been visited by the two eminent explorers who preceded Willard Glazier, they would have so recognized and named it. That they failed to do so is conclusive proof that they never saw it.

EXPLORER.

A leading paper of Minneapolis copied the following letter addressed to a Philadelphia daily, in response to two of Captain Glazier's opponents, in which the writer expounds his views upon the Glazier claim, and criticises the critics:

Editor Philadelphia Times:

In an article in *Science*, of a recent date, Henry D. Harrower of New York expresses himself thus: "It is evident that Captain Glazier thinks he was the first white man to visit Elk Lake."

Captain Glazier did visit the lake to which the above misnomer is applied, and every other lake and pond in the vicinity of Lake Itasca; and claims to have been the first to locate a body of water to the south of Itasca, and tributary to the latter, which had not been recognized by any geographical authority as the Source of the Mississippi prior to the summer of 1881—the date of his visit. This lake is the one referred to by Barrett Channing Paine, a member of the expedition, in the extract given by Mr. Harrower in *Science*. Let me here ask, is it not somewhat strange that many of the most prominent geographers and map publishers of the country, who, it is to be presumed, have access to the latest and most reliable authorities, should have accepted the Glazier claim, and changed their maps in accordance therewith, if they had not, after due investigation, been fully satisfied of its genuineness and accuracy? This circumstance alone, in the opinion of many, is almost sufficient to establish Captain Glazier's title, when we take into consideration the fact that exactness is a *sine qua non* in a modern map. . By actual measurement, Lake Glazier was found to be over a mile and a half long and nearly as wide, with an average depth of forty-five feet, which is deeper than any part of Itasca.

There appears to be on the part of Mr Harrower, and a previous correspondent of *Science*, Russell Hinman of Cincinnati, for some occult reason, a disposition to belittle the undertaking of the Glazier party

It was, it is true, simply a private expedition led by an American citizen whose antecedents as a cavalry officer throughout the war for the Union, and since as a popular writer, should, I venture to think, have some weight in the balance where mere credibility is the question at issue. He was not a mere theorist, but an actual explorer, and, as such, his testimony is as worthy of credit as that of any other explorer, especially when confirmed by the intelligent gentlemen who accompanied him. He was not authorized by the Government to proceed to the Headwaters of the Mississippi; and the journey was certainly not made in his own financial interest, as it cost him a considerable sum of money to accomplish it. The expedition appears to have been organized solely in the interest of correct knowledge upon a geographical question of some importance. He traveled over a country which, according to the best authorities he had access to, had never before been trodden by white men, namely, that between Leech Lake and Lake Itasca. In doing so, he discovered a chain of lakes and streams that was not known to exist by any authority he consulted. These he named after distinguished American soldiers and statesmen. Ultimately, he made his way to a lake a short distance south of Itasca, of respectable proportions, which, from all the information he could gather, had never before been known or recognized as the Head of the Great River. If Messrs. Harrower and Hinman had traveled over the same ground, they would be better qualified to pass judgment upon the account given by this intrepid explorer.

Before concluding, I may be permitted to state that according to Schoolcraft the name "Elk Lake" is that by which Lake Itasca was known to the Indians, and is still known to them, and, according to the testimony of Captain Glazier's guides, this name has never been applied by them to any other lake in the vicinity. The lake located by Captain Glazier as the True Source is known as *Pokegama* by the Chippewas, meaning "The Place where the Waters Gather"; and this lake is, without the shadow of a doubt, the Primal Reservoir of the mighty Mississippi.

INVESTIGATOR.

In January, 1887, the Minneapolis *Journal* published the subjoined letter in advocacy of Captain Glazier's claim:

Editor Minneapolis Journal:

The liberal spirit in which you have treated the controversy between Captain Glazier and his critics on the subject of the Source of the Mississippi, leads me to place at your disposal certain facts within my knowledge, in connection with the mooted question.

On what ground do his numerous supporters lay claim that Captain Glazier discovered the True Source of the Great River that divides our continent? At the period of his visit to Lake Itasca and the surrounding region, July, 1881, he made diligent inquiry upon every matter that bore upon the question—whether Lake Itasca was the Source of the Mississippi. He then proceeded to Itasca, via Leech Lake, and found a beautiful lake to the south of it, which, after a careful survey, he discovered to be the undoubted Source of the mighty river, connected, as it was, by a permanent stream with Lake Itasca. As such he located it, and his name was given to it by the companions of his expedition.

Here let me observe, that while William Morrison, in 1804, was probably the first white man who saw Lake Itasca, no one has ever credited him with the discovery of the Source of the Mississippi. In fact, he knew nothing about its relation to that river. He was not an explorer, but a fur trader. Had he known that the Mississippi was an outlet of Itasca, he, and not Schoolcraft, would have been recognized all these years as the discoverer of that lake. On precisely the same ground, others may have seen the lake to the south of Itasca before Captain Glazier, but it is fully admitted that no one who preceded him to that region had assigned it its true character, nor properly placed its feeders. With reference to the latter feature of the subject in dispute, it has hitherto been erroneously supposed that the lakelet to the southwest of Lake Glazier, shown as Lake Alice on Glazier's large map, empties into the southern extremity of Lake Itasca, instead of into the northwestern part of Lake Glazier. This makes all the difference in the world, and proves that the Government surveyors, in running their parallels, failed to trace this stream to its outlet. If it could be established that the creek from Lake Alice debouched in Lake Itasca instead of Lake Glazier, then Captain Glazier and his friends would at once relinquish his claim to have located the Primal Reservoir, or True Source, of the Mississippi. But his knowledge of this feeder is based upon actual investigation, and he knows to a certainty that the lake beyond and above Itasca has at least three feeders instead of two, as shown on the Land-office map. On this ground alone he is entitled to the credit, not only of establishing the fact of the existence of a new, and hitherto unrecognized, Source of the Mississippi, but of proving conclusively that an important feeder is the outlet of a lakelet which has hitherto been misrepresented on the Government maps as falling into Lake Itasca.

GEOGRAPHER.

Apropos of the controversy between Captain Glazier and some members of the Minnesota Historical Society, the Saint Paul *Globe*, the leading Democratic journal of Minnesota, has the following paragraph:

"Captain Glazier makes a fair proposition for the settlement of the controversy between himself and the State Historical Society He proposes a commission of three members, one to be selected by the Minnesota Historical Society, one by himself, and the third by the American Geographical Society, to investigate the matter in dispute by making a tour of exploration to the upper waters of the Mississippi, and settle forever the quarrel about its Source. He further offers to defray one-half of all the expenses of the expedition."

The Chicago *Times*, in the subjoined notice of Captain Glazier's last work, "Down the Great River," gives a succinct but interesting account of the discovery of the True Source, in which the writer evinces a thorough recognition and appreciation of the Captain's labors:

"A most interesting portion of Captain Glazier's 'Down the Great River' is the beginning, where the author gives the details of an expedition made in July, 1881, by himself, with five companions, when he claims, with good grounds, to have fixed the actual Source of the Great River His attention was called, in 1876, to the fact that, though everybody knows the mouth of the stream, there was then much uncertainty about its Source. In 1881, he found time to organize the expedition named, and crossing the country to Itasca embarked in his canoes, and pushed through that lake up a stream flowing into it, and came upon another considerable body of water, fed by three principal streams, originating in springs at the foot of a range of hills some miles farther on. This lake he fixed upon as the True Source, and since his published accounts most of the geographers and map makers have modified their works according to his discoveries. He claims to have been the first to discover and establish the fact that it is the highest link in a chain in which Itasca is another; or, in other words, the True Head of the river. The Indian name of the lake is *Pokegama*, and this Captain Glazier says he would have retained, but was overruled by the other members, who insisted on calling it LAKE GLAZIER."

On February 9, 1887, the State Historical Society, at Saint Paul, is reported to have met and passed certain resolutions, after listening to the reading of a paper by General James H. Baker on the "Source of the Mississippi."

It may be safely assumed that the gallant general knew more of army tactics than he knew personally of the Source of the Great River, and about as much of the latter as was possessed by his otherwise intelligent audience, who were said to have unanimously (?) passed his cut-and-dried resolutions. It is not known that General Baker—at the date of the meeting called to suppress Captain Glazier—had ever been within three hundred miles of the Source of the river, and his inflated resolutions had doubtless, in the absence of personal knowledge of his subject, been based upon information derived from writers whose acquaintance with the True Source was on a level with his own and that of the Minnesota Historical Society generally This learned society innocently believed at the time that no body of water existed beyond Lake Itasca that was tributary to it—ergo, that Itasca was the Source of the Mississippi.

The tone of the resolutions submitted to the meeting is almost beneath criticism; indeed, they bristle with low scurrility They were of a character to convince any moderately informed person, first, that the chairman knew nothing of the Source of the Mississippi, and secondly, that for some unknown reason he was animated by an intense dislike of Captain Glazier, two qualifications that presumably fitted him for the chairmanship of such a meeting. The *dignity, elegance of diction*, and *suavity* of these resolutions were on a par with the treatment Captain Glazier has generally met with from a few members of this Historical Society, who affect to think and act for it as a body

At the meeting referred to, Captain Glazier's younger brother was present, and after the reading of the resolutions respectfully requested to be heard. He naturally objected to the offensive epithets which had been heaped upon his brother, but was peremptorily called to order by Chairman Baker, and not permitted to proceed. A "corporal's guard" of the audience passed the resolutions, while the feeling of the majority was in marked sympathy with young Glazier, who simply attempted to defend his brother from the foul aspersions cast upon him by the self-satisfied clique on the platform. An influential member of the society, from whom one would have expected something more refined than the language of a cow-boy, excitedly called him a *liar!* A disgraceful scene ensued in the hall of this eminently *learned* society, whose motto, evidently, is not *audi alteram partem.*

The first of the resolutions read to the meeting was in these words:

"We hereby express, as the deliberate judgment of this society, that the assertions and assumptions of said Glazier are baseless and false."

By this "society" must be understood some three or four of its officious members who pose as the "society," and their "deliberate judgment" meant simply a determination on their part to suppress Captain Glazier, if possible, for no better reason than that he was not a resident of Minnesota, but of New York. What could a New Yorker know about the Source of the Mississippi? They would have no outsiders come to their State and expose their ignorance to the world by pretending to have discovered that the Source of their magnificent river was not in the sacred Itasca of the renowned

Schoolcraft. Right or wrong, Glazier must be silenced, and restricted from promulgating his heresy *

"*The assertions and assumptions of said Glazier are baseless and false,*" quoth General Baker and his obsequious satellites. This clause of the resolution, couched in the peculiar language of a society whose supposed aim is to educate and refine the people of the State, is, however, a harmless thunderbolt, and may be answered in two words, "*Prove it!*" I venture to affirm from my own personal knowledge that "the assertions and assumptions of said Glazier" were neither "baseless" nor "false," but as well founded and true as that the author of these resolutions was utterly incompetent to pass judgment upon them from his personal ignorance of the question at issue.

Resolution No. II:

"*That he is in no sense a discoverer or explorer.*"

This ungrammatical blow from a literary society of such pretensions is amusing. "A discoverer or *a* explorer" might tumble accidentally from the pen of an unfledged rustic raised on the prairies, but a "learned" society should at least know that a vowel is preceded by the article *an*. We excuse the lapse, however, and generously attribute it to their haste to inflict another telling stroke at their victim.

Captain Glazier's explorations, unlike those of his critics, have extended beyond the limits of Saint Paul, and his discovery of the True Source of the Father of Waters has been recognized by thousands of his intelligent countrymen, including geographers, college faculties, teachers, encyclopædists, and map publishers. It may be confidently affirmed, moreover, that he has "explored" more of the American continent than any fifty members of the Minnesota Historical Society, inclusive of the pretentious gentlemen who denounced him in such unmeasured terms. His work on the "Mississippi" alone affords ample evidence of his exploratory labors and researches in outlying sections of the country.

---

* From conversations I have since had with prominent residents of Saint Paul, I have obtained this knowledge of the "true inwardness" or motive of the opposition, which, as I have already said, was, and continues to be, confined to a very narrow circle of the M. H. S.

Resolution No. III:

"*That the lake which Captain Glazier asserts is the True Source of the Mississippi River is not such in reality, but that the real source of the river is Lake Itasca and its tributaries.*"

Captain Glazier has never claimed that the real Source of the river was not in a "tributary," but denies most emphatically that it is in Lake Itasca. The "tributary" in question is a fine lake above Itasca, separated from the latter by a lofty and extended ridge, and contributes its clear waters through a perennial stream to Lake Itasca and thence to the Mississippi. Lake Itasca has no better title to be considered the Source of the river than Lake Bemidji, except that the former is nearer the True Source than the latter The lake above Itasca, over a mile and a half long, nearly as wide, and forty-five feet deep, which for the past ten years has been known far and wide as LAKE GLAZIER, is claimed as the True Head, the reservoir of its five tributary streams, and hence named *Pokegama* by the Indians, or "The Place where the Waters Gather" This body of water, unknown until 1881 to the Solons of the Historical Society, is claimed by Captain Glazier and his host of supporters as the True Source of the Mississippi, in defiance of the perverse and senseless contention of a few cavilers.

Resolution No. IV:

"*That we feel amazed at the presumption and assurance displayed by Captain Glazier in making his claim; in arrogantly heralding himself to the world as a discoverer; in deceiving historical societies; in publishing maps on which the lake in question is made to appear in a wrong position and four times its proper size, and in persuading publishers to place his name on their maps.*"

Presumption, assurance, arrogance, and deceit are here flippantly cast in the teeth of a man whose only offense consisted in a modest attempt to settle a long-disputed geographical question. He asked no subsidy of the Government or State, but undertook a difficult, nay arduous, journey through a veritable *terra incognita*, entirely at his own cost and in the interest of science. May I respectfully ask these *gentlemen* who make him a target for their vituperative shafts, where is the *presumption* involved in such an act? Many thousands think it was highly commendable in Glazier to put himself to so much inconvenience in order to solve a problem in American geography which would have solved itself in the course of time, when frontiersmen pushed farther forward into the primitive wilderness that surrounds the Head of the river. Was it *presumption* in Stanley to find Livingstone? Was it *presumption* in Nicollet to follow and pass Schoolcraft in his investigations? Is it not rather *presumption* and *assurance* for a few members of this society to thrust themselves before the public and condemn and denounce in such unseemly and opprobrious terms a man who did his best to enlighten them on a topic concerning which they were at the time in dense ignorance? The "presumption and assurance of Captain Glazier" have borne fruit. It is now known that the "great scientist of the Cass expedition" was in error when he coined the word *Itasca* and conferred it upon the sheet of water which he doubtless believed was the Source of the Mississippi. People are no longer in ignorance or doubt as to what is the True Source; that it lies to the south of Itasca, in a lake of no mean pretensions, which in point of beauty and size compares most favorably with its neighbor, and is in every way worthy of the distinction of standing at the extreme head of our greatest river The Minnesota Historical Society may possess its soul in peace; Lake Glazier will survive and be known as such generations after these brilliant critics have been gathered to their fathers, and their society has become more enlightened and consequently less obstructive and unmannerly

The remaining portion of Resolution No. IV is simply exaggerated nonsense, destitute of a grain of truth, and therefore calls only for denial. Captain Glazier made a plain announcement of fact to the public, without any flourish of trumpets. He attempted to deceive no historical society, but invited them to investigate for themselves. And here I will add that no *honest* investigator could arrive at any other conclusion than the one he had reached. The maps he has published are geographically correct—far more so than those of Schoolcraft, Nicollet, or the spurious production of the agent who followed Glazier, and imposed his alleged map of the region upon the public under the ægis of his employers of the Minnesota Historical Society The "lake in question," as

LAKE GARFIELD.
Located by First Glazier Expedition, July 17, 1881.

delineated on the Glazier map, is of correct relative size to Lake Itasca, and is in its right topographical position in reference to the latter lake. Finally, it is almost needless to say that he has no such influence over publishers as that ascribed to him, and if his name has found a place on their maps it has been of their own volition without a word of "persuasion" from him. The folly of such a supposition is worthy of its originators.

Resolution No. V:

"*That the Legislature be requested to pass the Donnelly bill, which fixes the names of the lakes and streams composing the Itasca source of the Mississippi River.*"

Resolution No. VI:

"*That we call upon the various geographical, historical, and other learned societies to co-operate with us in repudiating Glazier's claim.*"

If the Minnesota Legislature would pass a bill removing Lake Glazier from its envied position at the Head of the Mississippi, it would doubtless satisfy the qualms of the Minnesota Historical Society, and forever silence the troublesome Glazier, who has disturbed their learned equanimity to such a degree as to render an appeal to the Legislature necessary. Nothing short of this could have any other effect than to make the quasi-learned society of Saint Paul and their legislators appear supremely ridiculous in the eyes of all intelligent and fair-minded Americans.

The "various geographical, historical, and other learned societies" called upon to co-operate, have, as I am informed, with very few exceptions, shown great hesitation in compromising themselves by obeying the summons; the perverseness exhibited by their Northwestern sister—in her dogged opposition to Captain Glazier, and unreasoning adherence to Lake Itasca—having given rise to a suspicion that, after all, Glazier may be right and the Saint Paul egotists wrong. Anyhow, they could not be expected to "co-operate" in denouncing the gentleman as a "fraud" without first dispatching an exploring party to the Headwaters on their own account, and hence their hesitation to "co-operate." The Saint Paul wiseacres have therefore been left to fight their battle alone; with what result we shall probably learn further on.

The St. Paul *Times*, in 1887, expressed its opinion of the caustic treatment Captain Glazier was receiving from certain members of the Minnesota Historical Society The editor remarks:

"The Minnesota State Historical Society has covered itself all over with glory, and Captain Glazier with ignominy, and the people can now take a rest so far as they are concerned about the rival claims of the discoverers of the Source of the great Father of Waters. General Baker seems to have considered it the society's duty to deal in wholesale denunciation of Captain Glazier's claims, which are apparently as well founded as those of any other discoverer. Schoolcraft was not the first to see Itasca Lake. William Morrison, a pioneer Minnesotian, had a cabin on the island in Itasca Lake twenty-eight years before Schoolcraft visited that region. Yet no one has denied the latter the right to name the lake and island. Why not accord Glazier a similar right under precisely similar circumstances? His claims are supported emphatically by the overwhelming testimony of hundreds of the most distinguished and competent authorities in the Northwest. Glazier did undoubtedly expend much time and treasure in investigating, not only the Source of the Mississippi, but the history of the entire river from its Source to the Gulf. He could have no object, nor could he gain anything by garbling statements when it was as easy for him to publish the truth. As a writer, the sale of whose works depended permanently on the accuracy of their information, he had every incentive to take the greatest pains in getting at the facts. The leading map publishers have indorsed his claims, and do so in a way that leaves no doubt that they placed implicit confidence in him as a careful and trustworthy geographer and historian. Rand, McNally & Co., George T. Cram, A. S. Barnes & Co., and others of the leading publishing houses who have a heavy personal interest in investigating the correctness of everything they publish, tacitly acknowledge Captain Glazier's claims by accepting his views, and reproducing them in their books and maps. The press, pulpit, bar, and Legislature of the State of Minnesota give unqualified assent, through many of their leading members, to the position of Captain Glazier. And the Minnesota State Historical Society assumes toward these gentlemen a very offensive attitude when they stigmatize, by a string of violent and abusive resolutions, his natural and apparently just claims to be considered the first who published his belief that Lake Glazier is the True Source of the Mississippi. The society has acted like a pack of intellectual hobble-de-hoys, and not in the sedate, cautious, and dignified fashion we naturally expect of them. Even if Glazier's claims were as absurd as the society says they are, there is no excuse for turning our Historical Society into an agency for the dissemination of abusive epithets.

From all we can glean, we are decidedly of opinion that the rash conduct of a few members has placed the society in a very ridiculous position, and if they have raised a laugh against themselves they have themselves to blame. The frantic appeals to the world to stand by the Minnesota Historical Society in this matter, as they are embraced in their resolutions, are too absurd for anything. It must mortify any sensible member of the society to read the resolutions published in the *Globe* and *Pioneer Press.* They are decidedly Billingsgatish, and bear on their face a spirit of hostility against Captain Glazier which could scarcely be evoked by a mere love of truth. . On the whole, we prefer to accept Lake Glazier as the name for the body of water which he asserts is the True Source of the Mississippi. "

The Saint Paul *Dispatch,* a leading and widely circulated daily of the capital of Minnesota, has published, since 1881, many editorials upon this subject. I reproduce one that appeared in the issue of March 27, 1887·

"A question has been raised by some members of our Historical Society as to whether Lake Itasca or Lake Glazier is the True Source of the Mississippi. Captain Glazier makes a claim to having located the lake which bears his name as the Primal Reservoir, or True Head, of the river. Upon his announcement to that effect, the world abandoned its previous belief that Itasca was the source, and accepted the Glazier lake as the true fountain of the mighty stream. Later the claim was advanced by certain members of our Historical Society that Glazier was not the discoverer, and was not entitled to any credit. It was said that others had been there prior to his visit and had 'discovered' the lake. But it was not claimed that any one had ever announced it as the Source of the Mississippi, and the best proof of this is found in the assertion of the State Historical Society that it is *not* the Source. It would seem, therefore, that before Captain Glazier is denounced as a 'fraud,' it would be well to settle the question as to who is right about the actual Source—he or the Historical Society. If Itasca is the Source, then Glazier's 'discovery' is unimportant and not worth wasting words about. But if the lake fixed upon by Glazier is the Source, then undoubtedly he is entitled to great credit for discovering a fact of which even our Historical Society seems to be still ignorant. "

A correspondent at Buffalo writes to a Northern New York journal in April, 1887 The Syracuse *Standard* had criticised the Captain's claim to discovery at the Headwaters of the Mississippi in the scurrilous style of the Minnesota Historical Society, and the New York paper copied the *Standard* article, adding its own comments in opposition to Glazier's announced discovery. The Buffalo correspondent replied as follows:

"In the issue of March 23d of your usually well-informed paper, you have given prominent insertion to an article copied from the Syracuse *Standard,* in which the writer commented unfavorably on Captain Willard Glazier's claim. As an old acquaintance of the Captain, I venture to take up the gauntlet in his behalf; and first, I will observe that we have here an illustration of the truth of the proverb, A prophet is not without honor save in his own country ' While honors have been showered on Willard Glazier by the press, geographers, and scientists throughout the land, in his 'own country' he is sneered at as an 'adventurer ' This, however, only indirectly, and probably from inadvertence. He is remembered, not unkindly, by his former classmates of your Wesleyan Seminary, some of whom have recognized him as conferring honor on their *alma mater* by his stirring military career and popular writings, and are his good friends to this day

"The Syracuse *Standard*, from which you copied the scurrilous article, is inconsistent, to say the least. In 1883, it gave its readers a very favorable notice of Captain Glazier's book, 'Battles for the Union,' then just published. It spoke of him as an author 'wielding his pen with surprising facility,' and his descriptions 'abounding with life and interest'; adding, 'the work is full of the momentous incidents of a struggle, the memory of which our brave soldiers love to dwell upon,' etc.

"Glazier was a soldier under Custer and Kilpatrick, and successfully took part in the battles of Cedar Mountain, Manassas, Fredericksburg, Brandy Station, Gettysburg, and other engagements, and was eventually taken prisoner and made the acquaintance of the interior of Libby Prison. He finally made his escape and reached the Federal lines. In his first book, written shortly after the close of the war, we get many glimpses of life in that well-known prison, and numerous pathetic and humorous incidents that fell under his notice. He then wrote 'Three Years in the Federal Cavalry,' in defense of that arm of the service. Then followed 'Battles for the Union' and 'Heroes of Three Wars,' and later a work on the 'Peculiarities of American Cities,' all of which have won glowing eulogies from the press from Maine to California. Lastly, he is about to give to his countrymen a work on 'The Valley of the Mississippi,' having traversed the entire length of the Great River in a canoe for purposes of observation—a distance of over 3,000 miles, and occupying a period of 117 days. Possessed of energy and daring, Glazier, before this, had crossed the continent on horseback from Boston to San Francisco, thus proving himself a thorough American in being able to do anything and everything equally well; 'rushing,' as Shakespeare observes, 'where angels feared to tread.' His 'superficial works' met the demand of the public and have been sold by hundreds of thousands. This fact is usually considered a test of the excellence rather than the superficiality of a book.

"In the article quoted from the inconsistent Syracuse paper, reference is made to an investigation by the Minnesota Historical Society of Captain Glazier's claim to have located the True Source of the Mississippi River. The investigation here referred to was confined to one individual, who wrote an abusive pamphlet on the subject; and the society, composed for the most part of farmers and persons who knew nothing of, or had ever visited, the Headwaters of the Great River, accepted it. The individual in question took exception to Captain Glazier's giving names to sundry lakes and streams he discovered between Leech Lake and Lake Itasca, which had never before been named or probably ever seen by white men. These lakes and streams he named after his cavalry comrades, and the old explorers, De Soto, Marquette, La Salle, Hennepin, and Joliet, and their successors, Beltrami, Schoolcraft, and Nicollet. He also gave the names of Garfield, Sheridan, Bayard, Stoneman, Pleasanton, Gregg, Custer, and Kilpatrick to other bodies of water; and in three cases was guilty of the serious offense of giving the names of his wife and daughter and that of a deceased sister to some small lakes, as an affectionate memento of his visit. This is the worst that can be said of him.

"With regard to the location of the Source of the Great River, Captain Glazier is supported by a host of competent judges, including the Governor of Minnesota and hundreds of representative men of the State; while the fact of the discovery is disputed by only a few persons—scarcely one of whom has ever been within two hundred miles of the Source. The lake located by Captain Glazier as the Primal Reservoir, or True Source, of the Mississippi, is now recognized as such by almost every geographer and map publisher in the country, and by many in Europe."

The opposition to Captain Glazier by the Minnesota Historical Society, located at Saint Paul, partook of an extremely personal, not to say malignant type, about the beginning of the year 1887 It is probably difficult to sympathize with a new truth which dispels the illusion of a lifetime. It should be repeated, however, that this opposition was confined to a very few individuals. These gentlemen were reluctant to surrender the honor that had clung for fifty years to the Itasca of Schoolcraft. They were under the protection of the society, and resolved, by virtue of their position, to suppress the new theory that would displace their idol; and perhaps there is little wonder that prejudice and conservatism were averse to its adoption. The unheard-of proposition that Lake Itasca was *not* the Source of the Mississippi was a heresy that must be met, and its propounder silenced. The subjoined article on the subject of the opposition opportunely appeared in the Saint Paul *Dispatch*, in the month of February, 1887, and doubtless expressed the views of many citizens besides those of the writer·

Editor Saint Paul Dispatch:

The Minnesota Historical Society, it would seem, has been over-hasty in its efforts to influence public opinion against the claim of Captain Glazier. Their report, as read last night, was a document hardly calculated to inspire confidence in thinking people regarding the erudition of what ought to be an institution seeking the truth of history and settling mooted geographical questions. This may have arisen from the peculiar characteristics of the gentleman who was chairman of the committee to whom was delegated the work of preparing the report. However, the society should have ignored it, but, having adopted the same, have laid themselves open to the responsibility of it, if not to the ridicule of sister societies throughout the world. It is not meet nor dignified that a body assuming to be "learned" should lumber up a report of that character—which must be looked to as an authority on this subject in future time—with discourteous language, possibly libelous, and which seemed taken entire from a pamphlet issued from a rival publishing house, and adopted by the committee. It would seem, if the committee had found, in their opinion, no just foundation for Captain Glazier's claims, that our society should have reported in language becoming the society, and with some consideration due that gentleman. They have greatly lowered their standard, and would seem to aspire to be considered a company of gossipy old women. It was also unfortunate that the society refused to listen to Captain Glazier's brother, who had accompanied him to the Headwaters of the Great River, and desired to speak before them. Can it be possible that a society, presumed to be above bias or prejudice, should refuse to hear both sides, preferring to make an *ex parte* report? Is this the position a society claiming public confidence should assume? . A society seeking the truth of history should be content to bear a cross in its mission, or surrender to more patient hands. Captain Glazier was entitled to some consideration from the society as well as the pamphlet of the book publisher referred to. Fair play is dear to every American heart. If he was not entitled to any consideration in the opinion of the savants, as to his alleged discovery at the Head of the Mississippi, he was at least entitled to a patient hearing from the society of our State, but a small portion of the great country for which he fought and suffered a long and weary imprisonment. It would seem a disgrace to our State that the Minnesota Historical Society has assumed the motto, "Strike, and then hear me." Is the Minnesota Historical Society a sort of mutual admiration society, making up reports on quite important questions from pamphlets of rival publishing houses, without hearing both sides; and giving to the world profound conclusions based on *ex parte* information and their own prejudices? Should their one-sided report be a foreclosure of the matter?

A CITIZEN OF ST. PAUL.

The Saint Paul *Dispatch* has believed in and supported the Glazier side of the controversy from its inception; and it will not be considered surprising, therefore, that I find myself more than once quoting from its pungent and ably written articles. In reply to a sheet published in Sauk Centre, Minnesota, whose editor took the side of the Historical Society, and rejected Captain Glazier's claim, the *Dispatch* expressed itself as follows:

"We don't say that Itasca is or is not the Source of the Mississippi. The Historical Society says it is; Glazier says it isn't, and describes another lake which he claims to be the Source. Between the energetic and enterprising Glazier and some of the fossils of the Historical Society we are inclined, however, to believe in Glazier; but before expressing our final opinion as to whether he is right or wrong, we want another exploration made. If the Historical Society and its puny allies, like the Sauk Centre *Tribune*, are so firm in the belief that Itasca is the Source, they should accept Glazier's proposition for an investigation. By not doing so, however, they lay themselves open to the suspicion that they are afraid that Glazier will prove what he says, and thereby leave them open to the charge of being a sublime lot of ignoramuses."

The following article, by one friendly to Captain Glazier, is taken from the Minneapolis *Evening Journal* of December, 1888, and is inserted here to show the animus of some of the Captain's "critics and cavilers," whose perseverance and industry would have been more commendable if exerted in the cause of truth:

Editor Minneapolis Journal:

The vexed question of the True Source of the Father of Waters has again come to the front, and candidates for fame or notoriety are propounding their theories, backed by pretended facts, in the vain effort to dispossess Captain Willard Glazier of the honor conferred upon him by public opinion in 1881; in which year, as you are aware, he published to the world the results of his journey to the Headwaters of the Mississippi. A paragraph relating to the question of the True Source of the Great River has lately appeared in some papers, dated St. Paul, December 1st, drawing attention to what the paragrapher is pleased to denominate, "An instructive and valuable article, with a carefully drawn and accurate map, contributed to the *Pioneer Press*." I would ask you to kindly permit me a few words on this subject, which may be considered of interest to some of your readers. Captain Glazier claims to have located the Fountain-head of the Mississippi, and the geographers, educational publishers, and map makers of the country recognize his claim, while hundreds of the most prominent men of Minnesota, and elsewhere, have borne written testimony to the truth of his published statements. Having been identified with the Glazier expedition to the Headwaters of the Mississippi, I unhesitatingly assert, despite a thousand cavilers like the correspondent of the *Pioneer Press*, that no other water exists that can, with any show of reason or plausibility, be called the Source of the Mississippi, but the body of water which now bears the name of Lake Glazier. The "carefully drawn and accurate map," to which allusion is made in the paragraph referred to, is a meaningless jumble, utterly beyond comprehension, except in that it confirms the Glazier account by placing its delineator's *alleged source* in a relative position to Lake Glazier that, in itself, refutes the theory of the *pond* being the Source of the river. The article in the *Pioneer Press* is evasive, and shows the animus of the writer, whose aim is clearly a desire to propagate an untruth, and by so doing deprive a worthy man of the credit accorded him by his fellow-countrymen. Captain Glazier may not have been the first to visit the lake to the south of, and above, Itasca, but was admittedly the first to locate it definitely, and establish its geographical importance in its relation to the Mississippi, and for this reason is entitled to the same consideration that was accorded to his predecessor, Schoolcraft, who claimed the credit of having "discovered" Lake Itasca, which he probably knew had previously been visited by William Morrison, the fur trader, in 1804. Parties who have visited the region since 1881 are very confused and unsatisfactory in their reports, no two of them agreeing as to the Primal Reservoir; but they make one thing clear, and that is: That the large heart-shaped lake to the south of Itasca—wider and deeper than the latter—is the only body of water worthy of recognition as the Fountain-head of the Great River; all the other ponds and lakelets referred to by them being little more than mud-puddles and bogs, with no outlets, and altogether undeserving of the slightest consideration. The "true source" of the writer to the *Pioneer Press* is one of these frog-ponds, and his so-called "accurate map" is accurate only in this, that it places Lake Glazier where nature placed it, namely, at the Head of the Mississippi.

VERITAS CAPUT.

The Worcester *Spy* published in December, 1888, the following letter from an Eastern correspondent, who appears to have taken an interest in the question of the True Source of the Mississippi.

Editor Worcester Spy:

In an editorial in the *Spy* of last week, something is said of "Lake Glazier," and also of the finding of another lake which, it is claimed, supersedes the claim of Captain Glazier in 1881 in regard to the True Source of the Mississippi. A Mr. Brower, in the St. Paul *Pioneer Press*, it appears, is the champion of this latest source. In his article in the *Press* he claims that an insignificant lake, or pond, *west* of Lake Glazier, is the true source. In this statement, his map, also published, contradicts him, as in the map it is shown that his "true source" is considerably farther north than Lake Glazier, and hence can not be the fountain-head of the Great River. This is not the first time some of these small ponds have been taken to be the source of the river. These ponds were not unknown to Captain Glazier at the time he made his exploration, and put forth his claim. All the lakes, ponds, and feeders in that region were visited, and the result was that the beautiful lake called by the Indians *Pokegama* was selected. In regard to this, Captain Glazier says, "I simply claim to have established the fact that there is a fine lake above and beyond Itasca, wider and deeper than that lake, with woodland shores, with three constantly flowing streams for its feeders, and in every way worthy of the position it occupies as the Primal Reservoir, or the True Source, of the Father of Waters."

No other lake in the region beyond Itasca can compare in any sense with the above-mentioned lake. This fact is known and admitted by the Indians born and reared in that locality, as I have it from them. General Baker's attempt to crush out the claim of Captain Glazier was a failure. Mr. Brower and his later claim can not stand before the facts in regard to the merits of Lake Glazier as the True Source of the Mississippi.

AN EARLY PIONEER OF MINNESOTA.

In January, 1889, an effort was made by a certain educational publishing house in New York to discredit Captain Glazier with the public by denying his just claim to have discovered and located the source of the Mississippi. In reply, the following letter appeared in the *New England Home Journal*, from the pen of a gentleman well known in that section as a wri.er on history and various branches of science, who is also a member of several learned societies in this country and Europe:

Editor Home Journal:

A feeble attempt has lately been made to prove that the claim of Captain Willard Glazier to have discovered the true source of the Mississippi, rests upon no other foundation than that of "literary piracy and fraud." If this were true, concerned with him in this attempt to foist upon the public this fraudulent claim, we find a long list of hitherto reputable names of men who fill high positions in the civil and educational world. Prominent among the number in Minnesota are the Governor, two ex-Governors, five Mayors, six editors, and six superintendents of schools. In the country at large, eighteen educational publishers, fourteen map publishers, together with the indorsement of four colleges and several leading institutions of learning. His claim also receives the sanction of several educators and map publishers in other countries. The above are only a few of the indorsements received by the Captain, yet we are told that his claim is all moonshine; that they who have sanctioned all this, know not what they are talking about!

C.

A leading Saint Paul daily, of March 4, 1889, treats in an editorial of a certain phase of the opposition to Captain Glazier. Persons residing in Saint Paul, hearing of the proceedings of the Historical Society, or rather of a few of its officious members, denounced the latter as most unfair to the Captain, and unbecoming the society Knowing nothing of the locality of the Headwaters from personal inspection, their attempts to impose their views upon the public could be characterized as nothing less than rash and presumptuous, if not worse:

" . . The State Historical Society and its estimable secretary appear to have reached a stage of excitement, in the consideration of

Captain Glazier's claims, which far exceeds that of any other individual or interest concerned. Two years ago the society passed resolutions denouncing Captain Glazier as an 'adventurer,' and of course denying to him the credit of discovering the True Source of the Mississippi, and thereafter went to the Legislature, virtually asking that its resolutions be spread out on the statute books of the State in the form of a legal enactment. They selected, strangely enough, as the instrument of the undertaking, Ignatius Donnelly, who, as a discoverer, historian, and literary oracle, would, we fear, run serious risk of faring quite as badly as Glazier at the hands of that erudite establishment, should the occasion demand an expression of its opinion regarding him. They failed, however, in the undertaking, and now, two years later, propose to repeat their efforts.

"We do not assume the championship of Captain Glazier. That is not at all necessary We do not pretend to say whether the lake which now appears on the State map as the True Source of the Mississippi River should or should not be called Lake Glazier. But we would like to know how the State Historical Society, or any other body, expects to determine the True Source of the Mississippi, or the true discoverer of that Source, by the passage of resolutions or the enactment of legislation. The students of this question, either now or hereafter, can not be expected to care a rap what the State Legislature thought, or what the Historical Society made its members believe it thought, on the subject. This kind of legislation is about on a par with certain mediæval practices which involved the barbarous sacrifice of human life in order to establish the correctness of their opinions as to the hereafter."

In a review of Captain Glazier's notable work on the "Mississippi," in which the author describes in detail his journey to the Headwaters, and discovery of the Source of the Great River, the *Popular Science Monthly* for April, 1889, refers to his claim in the following words:

"In this book, Captain Glazier relates the story in full, of his journey in 1881, by the aid of an Indian guide, 'across country,' from Brainerd, Minnesota, to Lake Glazier, south of Lake Itasca, and his determination of it as the real Source of the Mississippi River. The journey was made first to Leech Lake, which is on one of the main affluents of the Upper Missi sippi—and is the seat of an Indian agency—and thence up a chain of lakes and portages, through a territory of which very little, if anything, was definitely known, to Itasca Lake; around Itasca Lake to a stream flowing into it; up that stream to 'Lake Glazier,' and around that lake until the author and explorer was satisfied that nothing important was likely to be found above it. . . . As determined by the author, Lake Glazier is 1,585 feet above the level of the ocean, and is 3,184 miles from the Gulf of Mexico. . . . Captain Glazier's claims to be the discoverer of the True Source of the Mississippi have been disputed by some persons who have affirmed that the lake which has been named after him was not unknown to Schoolcraft, and that it has been visited by hunters. The Captain replies to these objectors by affirming that no matter how many persons may have known of the existence of that body of water, he was the first to explore it, to gauge its dimensions, and to determine that it is the Ultimate Source of the Mississippi; and he cites a large number of declarations of geographers, and of men versed in the history, geography, and traditions of Minnesota, which support his claims in this shape. He represents Glazier Lake, though its superficial area is less, as being wider and deeper, and containing more water than Itasca Lake. The story of the explorer's journey is very pleasantly narrated. "

The Philadelphia *Evening Telegraph*, a journal read largely by scholars and scientists, gives its sanction to the Glazier discovery of the True Source of the Mississippi in the following extract from an editorial:

" It appears quite clear that Lake Itasca never possessed any title to the honor conferred upon it by Schoolcraft in 1832 of giving birth to our magnificent river. One reason alone is given to account for our ignorance of its True Source, namely, it was outside the usual track of the fur traders, and in a region scarcely ever visited by Indians or white men. Schoolcraft had pronounced Itasca to be the source, and no one up to the date of Captain Glazier's explorations felt sufficiently interested in the matter to investigate or dispute its claim.

"It was long suspected that the Mississippi had its Fountain-head higher up than Lake Itasca, and in July, 1881, an expedition led by Captain Willard Glazier discovered a lake to the south of Itasca—hitherto unrecognized in our geographies—a mile and a half in diameter, and falling into the latter by a permanent stream—the Infant Mississippi. Beyond this there appears to be no water connected with the river, and hence Lake Glazier is now the recognized source of the Mississippi. . "

If any fair-minded and unprejudiced critic of the Glazier claim reads the foregoing extracts, let it be understood that these shafts of the exponents of public opinion are not aimed at him, but at those only who have assumed the prerogative of censorship, for the reason that by some accident they find themselves in the position of leadership in a society claiming to be "learned."

The discovery of the True Source of the Mississippi was made over ten years ago, and published to the world, in a plainly written narrative, by the discoverer, a man entitled to be believed, and to be treated with some consideration. The discovery is now virtually recognized and accepted by every geographer and scientist in the country who has given attention to the subject; but continues to be denied by a few pseudo-critics, associated with the Minnesota Historical Society at Saint Paul, who persistently stultify themselves, and endeavor to mislead the public by solemnly asserting that Lake Itasca is the Source, in defiance of all evidence to the contrary; and this for no better reason than because Schoolcraft, sixty years ago, so believed and asserted!

It must not be forgotten by the reader, in estimating the value of this opposition, that these same cavilers have never personally risked a visit to the source of the river, and hence their egregious assumption of authority in determining an important question in geography has, to say the least, placed them in a very equivocal light before the country; for evidence of which I have simply to refer the reader to some of the preceding extracts.

C.

CORRESPONDENCE RELATING TO FIRST EXPEDITION.

The intelligent reader of this Appendix, it is hoped, will feel in some degree interested in what I respectfully submit for his consideration, in explanation and justification of the facts involved in this discussion. From a large mass of correspondence now lying before me, I have selected a few letters bearing upon these facts, which go to show how wide-spread is the popular belief that the position taken by Captain Glazier is unassailable. It is founded upon the personal observation and most painstaking investigation of a man of no ordinary intelligence, who has staked his reputation as a well-known author on the positive assertion that Lake Itasca possesses *no claim whatever* to be considered the Source of our greatest river, a truth so palpable and patent to the sense of sight as to be beyond the sphere of doubt to any rational mind.

The correspondence here reproduced will show that, in the belief of the writers, Glazier located the True Source of the Mississippi River in a beautiful sheet of water *beyond* Itasca, and emptying into the latter through a permanent outlet; further, that despite the unreasoning opposition of a few critics, the press and the public have already yielded him the credit of setting at rest a long-discussed geographical question.

Barrett Channing Paine of Indianapolis, formerly a reporter on the staff of the Saint Paul *Pioneer Press*, addressed the following letter to that journal, under date August fourteenth, 1881. Mr. Paine accompanied Captain Glazier to the Source of the Mississippi on his First Expedition, and descended with him, in his canoe, throughout the entire length of the river to the Gulf. While at the Headwaters, and during the descent of the river, Mr Paine addressed long accounts of the journey and discovery to the *Pioneer Press*, as well as to many of the leading papers of cities on the banks of the Mississippi. In the whole of this correspondence, he expressed his firm personal belief in the truth of Captain Glazier's contention that the Source of the Mississippi is not in Lake Itasca, but in the fine lake immediately beyond it.

After giving a detailed account of the journey from the shore of Itasca Lake, he proceeds:

"*Editor Saint Paul Pioneer Press:*

"At last our longing eyes rested upon the waters of Itasca. Soon after, we were floating on its placid bosom, and after a pull of about two miles reached Schoolcraft Island. This island is about three acres in extent, and so covered with underbrush that we could with difficulty clear a place for a camp. The island has but few trees of any size, the most prominent of which is the pine, and on one of these we blazed our names and the date of our arrival. Lake Itasca is not at all the sort of lake I had expected to see, being a rather large and fine body of water, with an extreme length of about five miles and an average breadth of nearly a mile. It has three arms of nearly equal size, and the island on which we camped is situated near the point where they come together The lake was fixed upon as the Source of the Mississippi by Schoolcraft in 1832, and until now its title has been undisputed. Inquiries instituted by Captain Glazier, however, developed the fact that though few among the Indians and trappers who had visited that section believed Itasca to be the Source, there was some controversy as to whether another lake situated *beyond* Itasca, and pouring its waters into it, had not the strongest claim to that distinction. We were fortunate in having among our guides an Indian, named Chenowagesic, who had hunted and trapped for years on all the surrounding lakes, and had even for a number of years had his wigwam on Schoolcraft Island, and planted corn on that historic spot. He stated that a lake beyond Itasca had always been considered by him, and other Indians thoroughly familiar with the locality, as the True Source of the Father of Waters.

"Acting on this information, we started for the upper, or southern, end of the lake early next morning, finding, when we reached it, that it terminated in bulrushes and what seemed to be a swamp. Our guide, however, took us through the rushes, and we found that a small but swift stream entered here, up which, with difficulty, we pushed our canoes. This stream flows from one of the prettiest lakes we had seen on our trip. The shores are high and covered with verdure, and the lake, which is nearly round—its regularity being broken by but one point—has a greatest diameter of nearly two miles. Into this lake flow three principal streams, which rise in sand hills at distances ranging from one to two miles from the lake.

"Having previously estimated the volume of water flowing into Itasca by all the streams contributing to it, and found the one from this lake much in excess of that of others, we held a little meeting on the promontory, and unanimously voted to call the new-found Source Lake Glazier, in honor of the leader of our party.

"In regard to this lake being the True Source or Primal Reservoir of the Mississippi I have but little doubt, though I am not quite positive as to the rules followed in determining the source of a river. It seems customary to select a lake as the source, when practicable, and for that reason this honor was given to Itasca, though Schoolcraft must have surmised that other streams of more or less magnitude flowed into Itasca. In regard to this other lake to the south, he must have been in entire ignorance, owing perhaps to the rushes and dense lake growths at the mouth of the creek which led to it. "

I produce another of Mr Paine's descriptive letters, printed in the Saint Louis *Globe-Democrat*, August, 1881. Mr. Paine, a man of rare intelligence, it will be seen, was thoroughly convinced in his own mind, from personal investigation, that the lake to the south of Itasca was the *Source* which had been so long sought in vain.

"*Editor Saint Louis Globe-Democrat:*

"Lake Itasca for many years has been regarded both by geographical societies and map makers, as well as by the public generally, as the Source of the grandest of rivers—the mighty Mississippi. But geographical knowledge, like all other knowledge, is of little consequence if it is not progressive, and in its history we have seen the firmly rooted beliefs of centuries torn up and tossed aside by the explorations and reasoning of intrepid travelers, who, respecting truth and facts more than mere theory, have accepted nothing without proof, merely because others have so accepted it. This is the ground occupied by Captain Willard Glazier in his explorations in search of the Source of the Mississippi.

"Starting for the Headwaters of this great river in July last, he learned that the dense forests which surround the Source of the Father of Waters were rarely penetrated by white men, or even by Indians, at any time except in winter, when lakes and rivers were frozen up, and the whole surface of the country covered with snow.

"He also heard, through the interpreter and Indian guides who accompanied him, that the aboriginal inhabitants of these primeval forests did not regard Itasca as the Source; but spoke of another lake, broad and beautiful, which lay beyond Itasca, and poured its clear water into the accepted Source through a small stream. Captain Glazier determined to thoroughly examine all this region, and settle definitely and forever the problem of the True Source of the Mississippi.

"Acting in accordance with this resolution, he pushed on toward Itasca, intending to make it a starting-point for further exploration. Reaching this objective point after innumerable hardships, we camped on Schoolcraft Island, and after a night's rest he directed operations toward the lakes and streams of the surrounding country We closely examined the shores of Lake Itasca for tributary streams, finding but three of any importance. Of these the one by far the largest came in at the extreme head of the lake, at a point where it is nearly filled with bulrushes.

"Taking two canoes, Captain Glazier ascended this stream, which, though shallow, is rapid. Following its windings, we entered what appeared to be a lake filled with reeds and rushes. Pushing through this barrier, however, the canoes soon glided out upon the still surface of a beautiful lake, clear as crystal, with pebbly bottom, and its shores covered with a thick growth of pine. This lake is formed in the shape of a heart, having but one marked promontory Its greatest length is about two miles and its width about a mile and a half.

"We found that this fine lake was fed by at least three rivulets, which rose in sand hills a few miles from the lake; and thoroughly convinced that this body of water was the True Source of the Mississippi, our leader proclaimed it as such. Without waiting for much discussion, the party decided unanimously to call it Lake Glazier, in his honor. Expressing his thanks for this mark of their appreciation, Captain Glazier said that though he firmly believed the lake to be the Source of the river, he should relax none of his vigilance on the trip through the unknown part of the great stream, but would carefully examine all water flowing into the Mississippi, in order to be positive as to its origin."

The succeeding letter is one of many that appeared in 1881, the period of the First Glazier Expedition to the Headwaters of the Great River. Every leading paper from Saint Paul to New Orleans contained correspondence relating to the discovery of the "True Source," and it would require a volume to reproduce all or even one-half of these communications to the press by parties interested in the question:

SAINT LOUIS, MISSOURI,
September 19, 1881.

Editor Saint Louis Post-Dispatch:

Lake Itasca has been considered to be the source of the Mississippi for so many years that any man who disputes its title to that honor is looked upon as a radical, and one bent upon upsetting all one's preconceived geographical ideas. Still it seems to be a fact that Lake Itasca is not the Source, and has no greater claim to being called so than Lake Cass or Lake Bemidji or Lake Pepin. This was discovered by Captain Willard Glazier, who headed an expedition last July, and started for the Headwaters of the Mississippi. Reaching Lake Itasca after a journey of great difficulty, he camped on Schoolcraft Island, and thoroughly examined the lakes and streams which contribute their waters to the Great River. The various theories and stories heard from his Indian guides were considered as clews, and faithfully followed up until their truth or falsity was ascertained. Success at length crowned his labors, for a beautiful lake was found beyond Itasca, and in the direct line of the course of the river, which proved to be the farthest water—the extreme Head of our grand Mississippi. This lake is said to be about two miles in diameter, with clear water and beautiful surroundings, fed by several springs, and one of the prettiest of its size in Minnesota. The stream which flows from it into Itasca is very rapid, but narrow.

HISTORICUS.

The following extract is from a letter received by the present writer, in May, 1884, from Paul Beaulieu, interpreter to the White Earth Indian Agency, Minnesota. Beaulieu is a very intelligent French-Canadian. He has lived all his life within seventy miles of the Head of the Mississippi. His letter was in answer to an inquiry as to the views of the people of that section concerning Captain Glazier's discovery He writes:

WHITE EARTH INDIAN AGENCY, MINNESOTA.

I would respectfully state that according to the ideas of the people of this section for scores of years past, in alluding to Lake Itasca, which is known only as Elk Lake, or *Omushkos*, by the Indians, it was never considered by them as the Head or Source of the Father of Running Waters, or May-see-see-bee. I have received the map you sent me showing the route of exploration of Captain Glazier, 1881, and am well acquainted with his chief guide, Chenowagesic, who has made the section of country explored by Captain Glazier his home for many years, and who has at length proved the truth of his often-repeated assertion, when maps were shown him, that a lake beyond Itasca would in time change an important feature of those maps, and that Lake Itasca can not maintain its claim to being the Fountain-head of Ke-chêê-see-be, or the Great River. The map, as outlined by Captain Glazier's guide, Chenowagesic, is correct, and it is plain to us, who know the lay of this whole country (I mean by the word *us* the Chippewa tribe in particular), that *Lake Glazier* is located at the right place, and is the highest lake on the great Mississippi, and therefore the Source of that river.

Respectfully yours,

PAUL BEAULIEU.

A correspondent writes to the Boston *Times*, August 29, 1886, as follows:

Editor Boston Times:

A glance at the map of the United States will show that the great river of North America—the Mississippi—has its Source in Northern Minnesota, flowing at first in a northerly direction, then suddenly darting off at right angles to the eastward, and then again continuing its course in a southerly direction until it finally mingles its flood with the Gulf of Mexico—a distance from its source of 3,184 miles. It is of the origin of this great river I purpose to speak here. Can a river have two sources? Now it is a debated point at the present day whether Lake Itasca or Lake Glazier is the Fountain-head of the Father of Waters. The former lake, as everybody knows, was discovered by Schoolcraft in 1832, the latter by Glazier in 1881. Lake Glazier lies in latitude about 47°, and as the river flows at first to the northward, it is necessarily beyond the source assigned to it by Schoolcraft. Hence it follows, that Lake Glazier, if the premises are correct, is the Primal Reservoir of the Mississippi, always granting that the alleged discovery is sufficiently authenticated. As evidence in his favor, Captain Glazier states that in July, 1881, he fitted out an Expedition, composed of himself and three or four others, accompanied by an interpreter and Indian guides, and with the necessary canoes and supplies started from Saint Paul for Northern Minnesota, with the intention of reaching Lake Itasca, and setting at rest the vexed question of its claim to be the Source of the Mississippi. According to the accounts published at the time in almost every newspaper, from the extreme north to the extreme south of the Great River, and copied into many of the leading papers of the Eastern and Middle States, he not only reached Itasca, but soon discovered that the famed lake of Schoolcraft was not the Source; that, in fact, another lake, nearly as large as Itasca, existed farther up—that is, farther south; that this latter was a beautiful sheet of water, nestling among the pines, known to the Indians as *Pokegama;* and, moreover, that it discharged itself by a respectable stream—the Infant Mississippi—into Itasca. One of Captain Glazier's Indian guides, rejoicing in the euphemistic name of Chenowagesic, had previously told him of the existence of this lake, and its connection with Itasca, and, therefore, with the Mississippi, and piloted him and his party into it. This Indian, who is said to have been middle-aged, very intelligent, and very faithful and reliable, told him, further, that no white man had ever been seen there; his own hunting-ground was in the immediate vicinity; and the Captain and his associates could readily believe that the locality had probably never before been visited by civilized men, for the very good reason that it is well-nigh inaccessible. After surveying the new lake and its feeders, the former of which he found nearly circular, and nearly two miles in diameter, and his companions having formally christened it after their leader, the Captain and his party descended the stream connecting it with Itasca in their canoes, and passing through the latter lake, started on the long voyage, they had originally contemplated as part of their plans, down the Great River to the Gulf of Mexico. After one hundred and thirty-eight days of paddling, and many hairbreadth escapes, they made the Gulf. But the news of the discovery of the new Source of the Mississippi had reached New Orleans before them, as it had reached Saint Louis before their arrival at that city on their way down. The news was considered of sufficient importance by the New Orleans Academy of Sciences to warrant their calling a special meeting of the members, and inviting Captain Glazier to lay before them the details of his discovery. Fully satisfied as to the validity of his claim, highly complimentary resolutions were passed, recognizing the discovery. On his return journey to Saint Louis, Captain Glazier was officially invited to lay before the members of the Missouri Historical Society some account of his explorations in Northern Minnesota, and again the fact was duly indorsed, by resolution, that Lake Glazier is the True Source of the Mississippi. Since that date—January, 1882—other scientific bodies have, after due investigation, given their recognition to the genuineness of the discovery. The maps of some of the leading map publishers have been corrected, and Lake Itasca no longer figures on them as the source of the Great River, Lake Glazier having taken its place. The school geographies of several publishers likewise give Lake Glazier as the Source.

All this evidence seems conclusive of the authenticity and credibility of the claim of Captain Willard Glazier, albeit we are reluctant to give up the good old poetic name of Itasca. The world moves, however, and we must move with it. Glazier's name, like those of De Soto, Marquette, La Salle, Hennepin, and others, will, we venture to think, be indissolubly associated, for all time, with our grand old river.

Good-by, Itasca! Thy beautiful name loses none of its sweetness, though shorn of its glory MAY-SEE-SEE-BEE.

The following is copy of a letter sent to General J H. Baker of the Minnesota Historical Society, Saint Paul. *No reply was vouchsafed, or the slightest notice taken of it.* Glazier, although for many years a member in good standing of the G. A. R., evidently made a mistake in approaching so important a personage—albeit a comrade—with an offer to submit facts of which he was personally cognizant. The letter, *unacknowledged*, I here insert:

SYRACUSE, NEW YORK,
January 17, 1887

General J H. BAKER, Saint Paul, Minnesota.

DEAR SIR AND COMRADE: I have just learned through my brother, now in your city, that you are a member of the Minnesota Historical Society and take considerable interest in the controversy concerning the True Source of the Mississippi. It occurs to me that you might possibly like to be put in possession of a few facts relative to the mooted question. If I am right in this supposition, I shall be pleased to place at your disposal such matter as I have at my command, and in the meantime, remain,

Yours in F C. and L.,
WILLARD GLAZIER.

I subjoin a letter to Governor A. R. McGill of Minnesota. The intention of this Appendix is to give as nearly as possible a concise and truthful account of the controversy that followed upon the announcement of the discovery of the True Source of the Mississippi. A letter to the Governor was thought advisable at a time when the Historical Society's paid agents were publishing coarse and calumnious articles against Captain Glazier in a fruitless attempt to discredit him before the public. It is needless to add that in this case a courteous reply was received by the writer

CAMDEN, NEW JERSEY,
February 18, 1887

To Governor A. R. McGILL, Saint Paul, Minnesota.

DEAR SIR: Permit me to address you on the subject of Captain Willard Glazier's claim to have located the True Source of the Mississippi River. It is the general belief that the opposition to this claim originated with a firm of school-book and map publishers in New York City, whose single motive was to advertise themselves and their wares, and this firm appears to have secured an advocate in a very active member of your State Historical Society, named Baker. This man has not scrupled in his attempts to discredit, and, if possible, dishonor my friend by an energetic and interested opposition to his claim to have been the *first* white man to locate the True Source of the Mississippi.

And right here I will say, that from a long and most intimate acquaintance with Captain Willard Glazier, I know him to be eminently precise, cautious, exact, and conscientious in everything he says and does, and would be the last man in the world to advance a theory that he knew to be groundless, or in the slightest degree open to question.

His title to respectful consideration is founded, in a measure, on his honorable military record during the war of the Rebellion, and the authorship of several popular works—mostly relating to military affairs. He is scrupulously truthful, and his moral character, in every respect, beyond impeachment.

In July, 1881, I assisted him in organizing his expedition to the Headwaters of the Mississippi; and although I did not accompany him beyond Saint Paul, am thoroughly posted on every step of his progress to Lake Itasca and the lake above it, which stands at the head of the Great River and is its True Source.

Mr. Baker, who appears to be running the Minnesota Historical Society, has greatly belittled himself in the estimation of every one outside the society by the malevolent course he is adopting. Captain Glazier has offered to pay one-half the expenses of a commission of competent engineers and surveyors to proceed to the lake he has located as the True Source, and to abide by their decision on the subject. Can anything be fairer or more liberal than this, or afford stronger proof of his honest faith in his discovery, and therefore of his title to be accredited with it? I have the honor to be, very respectfully,

Your obedient servant,
PEARCE GILES.

About the commencement of the year 1887, while at Syracuse, New York, Captain Glazier was advised by friends in Saint Paul that scurrilous and libelous articles were appearing in the local press concerning him, having reference to his claim to have located the Source of the Mississippi. Newspapers reached him containing letters from his critics of the Historical Society, and the writers, not satisfied with denying his claim, attempted to injure him in public opinion by denouncing him as "a fraud" and "an adventurer." He thereupon started for Saint Paul, and on his arrival in that city hastily wrote the subjoined letter. In this, no word unbecoming a gentleman appeared. He confined himself to placing the grounds of his claim before the reader, and made very little reference to the defamatory language of his traducers.

With reference to the proposition to the Historical Society, in the last paragraph of his letter, it is significant that no notice was taken of it, and if one may judge from the newspaper comment of the time, the learned society was afraid, if they accepted his liberal offer, that the "adventurer" might establish his claim and so place them in an undignified predicament before the public.

MERCHANTS' HOTEL,
SAINT PAUL, MINNESOTA,
February 12, 1887

EDITOR SAINT PAUL DISPATCH: I have come to Minnesota in 1887 to claim the credit which was very generally accorded me by press and people in 1881. I do not ask for anything which is not in justice mine, and if I am unable to win my case without descending to *personalities and mud throwing*, I prefer to lose it. I was taught in the schools of the East that Lake Itasca was the source of the Mississippi River, and when I reached this State in 1881, ascertained that its title was still unquestioned by white men. To quote from my recent letter to the *Pioneer Press:* "Those who have been my most persistent critics in this controversy opened the battle with the assertion that Lake Itasca was the undoubted Source of the Mississippi, and that, at the time of my expedition, there was nothing of an exploratory character in Northern Minnesota." How well they have been able to justify their position will be developed as we advance.

For many years prior to 1881, I had been of the opinion that Lake Itasca occupied an erroneous position in our geography In fact, I had become satisfied, through conversations with straggling Chippewas in the Northwest, that the red man's ideal river did not rise in the lake described by his white brother, but that there were other lakes and streams beyond that lake, and some day the truth of their statements would be verified.

Thoroughly convinced that there was yet a field for exploration in Northern Minnesota, I resolved, in 1876, to attempt a settlement of the vexed question concerning the Source of the Mississippi, at an early day. Finding the opportunity I sought, in 1881, I came to Saint Paul in June of that year, accompanied by Pearce Giles of Camden, New Jersey. Here I was joined by my brother George of Chicago, and Barrett Channing Paine of the *Pioneer Press.*

Having completed arrangements, I left Saint Paul on the morning of July fourth, with Brainerd as our immediate objective. Short halts were made at Minneapolis, Monticello, Saint Cloud, and Little Falls, on our way up the river. Brainerd was reached July seventh. This town is situated near the boundary of the Chippewa Indian Reservation, and is the nearest place of consequence to Lake Itasca. Here I again halted to further inform myself concerning the topography of the country; to decide upon the most feasible route to our destination, and to provide such extra supplies of rations, clothing, and general outfit as might be considered essential to the success of our undertaking. After consulting my maps, I concluded that while Schoolcraft and Nicollet had found Itasca by going up the river through Lakes Winnebegoshish, Cass, and Bemidji, the most direct course would be by way of Leech Lake and Kabekanka River.

A careful study of the route to Leech Lake, with a few valuable suggestions from Warren Leland, one of the oldest residents of Brainerd, led us to seek conveyance to the former place over what is known in Northern Minnesota as the Government Road.

While at the Leech Lake Indian Agency, we obtained valuable information concerning the peculiar characteristics of the Indians on the Chippewa Reservation. At this place, it was our good fortune to meet the Post Missionary, Rev Edwin Benedict; Major A. C. Ruffee, the Indian Agent; Paul Beaulieu, the veteran Government Interpreter; Flatmouth, head chief of the Chippewas; White Cloud, chief of the Mississippis, and several others, well known at the Agency Through conversations with these parties, I learned that pioneers of that region were of the opinion that the lake located by Schoolcraft was the Source of the Mississippi; but the Indians invariably claimed that the Great River had its Origin in a beautiful lake above, and beyond, Itasca. Paul Beaulieu, who is perhaps the best authority in Minnesota on the subject, having lived for more than sixty years within its borders, said, in substance, that Chenowagesic, the most intelligent Chippewa of his acquaintance, had made the Itasca region his home for many years, and that he had always asserted, when maps were shown him, that a lake above Itasca would in time change a feature of those maps, and confirm his statement that "Lake Itasca could not longer maintain its claim to being the fountain-head of Ke-chee-see-bee, or Great River, which is named May-see-see-be by the Chippewas."

Three days were spent at Leech Lake, during which time we secured an interpreter, Indian guides, and birch-bark canoes. Everything being in order, we launched our canoes on the morning of July seventeenth, wishing, as previously explained, to approach Itasca by a different route from that employed by Schoolcraft and Nicollet, who went up the Mississippi from Lake Winnebegoshish. I crossed Leech Lake, and ascended the Kabekanka River, thence in a direct westerly course, through twenty-one lakes, alternated by as many portages, reaching Itasca between two and three o'clock on the afternoon of the twenty-first.

The work of coasting Itasca for its feeders was begun at an early

LAKE SHERIDAN.

hour on the morning of the twenty-second. We found the outlets of six small streams, two having well-defined mouths, and four filtering into the lake through bogs. The upper end of the southwestern arm of Itasca is heavily margined with reeds and rushes, and it was not without considerable difficulty that we forced our way through this barrier into the larger of the two open streams which enter at this point. This stream, at its mouth, is seven feet wide and three feet deep. Slow and tortuous progress of between two and three hundred yards, brought us to a blockade of logs and shallow water. Determined to float in my canoe upon the surface of the lake toward which we were paddling, I directed the guides to remove the obstructions, and continued to urge the canoes rapidly forward, although opposed by a strong and constantly increasing current. On pulling and pushing our way through a network of rushes, similar to that encountered on leaving Itasca, the cheering sight of a transparent body of water burst upon our view.

This lake, the Chippewa name of which is *Pokegama*, is about a mile and a half in its greatest diameter, and would be nearly an oval in form but for a single promontory at its southern extremity, which extends its shores into the lake so as to give it in outline the appearance of a heart. Its principal feeders are three creeks, two of which enter on the right and left of the headland, and have their origin in springs at the foot of sand hills from two to three miles distant. The third stream is but little more than a mile in length, and is the outlet of a small lake situated to the southwestward.

Assuming that the statements of my party are clearly indisputable concerning the lake which I claim as the Source, it must be admitted:

I. That Lake Itasca can not longer be maintained as the Fountain-head, for the reason that it is the custom, agreeably to the definition of geographers, to fix upon the *remotest* water, and a lake if possible, as the source of a river.

II. That Schoolcraft could not have seen the lake located by me, else he would have pronounced it the Source, placed it upon his map, and described it as such.

III. Nicollet, who followed Schoolcraft, could not have been aware of its existence, as he gives it no place upon his map, or description in the narrative of his expedition.

IV The Government survey is in error in showing that the outlet of the lakelet to the southwest of my lake debouches in Lake Itasca.

Whatever the verdict, and regardless of the name applied to it, the lake to the south of Itasca was certainly not known to the white inhabitants of Northern Minnesota prior to 1881. Lake Itasca was still recognized as the Origin of the river, was placed upon the maps, and taught as such in all the schools of the country

I simply claim to have established the fact that there is a beautiful lake above and beyond Itasca, wider and deeper than that lake, with woodland shores, with three constantly flowing streams for its feeders, and in every way worthy of the position it occupies as the Primal Reservoir—the True Source of the Father of Waters.

In conclusion. it was with no intent to deprive Schoolcraft, Nicollet, or any other explorer who preceded me of their well-earned laurels, that I announced the True Source of the Mississippi. Having entered the lake to the south of Itasca and definitely located its feeders, I became satisfied that it was the Primal Reservoir of the Great River, and so announced it to the geographical world. This is the head and front of my offending.

The Minnesota Historical Society has now re-affirmed that Lake Itasca is the Fountain-head. If this is true, then "Lake Glazier" is of little more importance than any other of the ten thousand lakes of Minnesota. If I am right and the Historical Society is wrong, then I submit, in the name of justice, am I not at least entitled to considerate treatment?

So confident am I of the rightfulness of my claim, that I make this proposition to the Minnesota Historical Society, that this question may be settled for all time: That the gentleman who introduced bill "No. 207," withdraw the same and substitute one of the following tenor: That the Legislature commission three persons, one to be selected by the Governor, one by the American Geographical Society, and one by myself, who shall be empowered to employ competent surveyors to visit the Headwaters of the Mississippi, and report their decision on this matter to the next session of the Legislature of this State, for the passage of a bill formulated on their investigations and findings.

If this is done I will, as I have before offered to do, deposit in some National bank of Saint Paul sufficient funds to cover one-half the expense of the expedition, provided the Minnesota Historical Society, or any person or persons, will furnish the other half. Can I offer a fairer proposition? If not accepted, my case is prejudged. If accepted, let the State of Minnesota and the geographical world abide the issue, as I am willing to do.

WILLARD GLAZIER.

Rev John C. Crane of West Millbury, Massachusetts, a writer and recognized authority in the East upon matters pertaining to general history, science, and geography, expressed his views on the claim of Captain Glazier in the following letter to the Saint Paul *Dispatch:*

WEST MILLBURY,
December 10, 1888.

Editor Saint Paul Dispatch:

My attention has been called to the communication of J. V Brower, published in a Saint Paul paper recently All the letters in opposition to the claim of Captain Glazier show so much spite and venom against the Captain that I can not refrain from lending him a hand, although I think him well able to take care of himself. In the map published with the Brower article in the *Pioneer Press*, he tries to prove that the lake south of Itasca, which is found to be wider and deeper than the lake of Schoolcraft, is not the True Source of the Mississippi. I make the statement that what he says is the Source is nothing but an insignificant lakelet or pond compared with the Glazier lake. A glance at the map of that region will convince any one in possession of an unprejudiced mind, which is the largest lake in that region beyond Itasca with requisite feeders and all the requirements of the Source of a river. A puddle among the sand hills, dribbling its tribute along, can not dispute the right of Lake Glazier. Mr. Brower claims that a pond to the west of the Glazier lake is the Source. But in this his own map contradicts him, as on that map his Source and the stream entering the west arm of Itasca would be much farther to the north than Lake Glazier, and therefore can not be the Source. I have no hesitation in saying that Captain Glazier was cognizant of all that Mr. Brower claims. I know the region well, and don't believe that an Indian can be found in that locality but will say that he believes Lake Glazier to be the Primal Reservoir, and therefore the Head of the Father of Waters. With one fell swoop of Brower's pen, one lake of Nicollet disappears; the Government surveyors of that region have clanked their chains and stuck their pins in the wrong place. It was reserved for a party of hunters, "out for a day's shooting," to discover in a frog-pond the fountain-head of the mightiest river in our land. Schoolcraft says that "the True Source of a river is a point at the remotest distance from its mouth," but connected with this statement are other points to be considered. The proportions of the lakes claimed as the Source, and the depth of water, are also to be taken into account. Shall we ignore *Pokegama*, or Lake Glazier, two miles long, a mile and a half wide, and forty-five feet deep, for an insignificant pond? Thirty years ago the writer was a resident of Minnesota, and even then the idea was advanced that Itasca was not the Source of the Great River. For a long time after Captain Glazier announced the lake named after him by his companions as the True Source, no one disputed the truthfulness of his claim. Few men have had so many ovations from individuals and societies as he. Jealous and interested parties since that time have sought to stamp out his claim and the author of it. If these gentlemen are sincere in their desire to settle this much-discussed question as to the True Source of the river, why do they not accept Captain Glazier's proposition? He has offered to pay one-half the cost of an expedition, fully equipped, that shall settle the question on its merits, if his opponents will pay the other half. The fact is they dare not do it. Time has only strengthened Captain Glazier in the belief that his lake is the True Source of the Mississippi. In that belief the writer coincides.

One word and I have done. Mr. Brower, in his article in the *Pioneer Press*, alludes to the "so-called Captain Willard Glazier." If holding a captain's commission, bearing the broad seal of the great Empire State, in one of the companies of a daring cavalry regiment, and tasting the horrors of nearly all the rebel prisons in the late war does not entitle a man to be called "Captain," then I should like to be informed what qualifications are necessary. J. C. CRANE.

Bearing upon the subject of the True Source of the Great River, the following from a "Student" of the question, resident in the East, will be found apt and well reasoned:

ROCHESTER, February 20, 1887.

Editor Saint Paul Dispatch:

Your paper of the 18th inst. has just come under my notice. You say that the State Historical Society proposes to sit down on Captain Willard Glazier's claim to have located the True Source of the Mississippi. From information that has reached me, I am of the opinion that not many intelligent citizens of Minnesota will be found to "sit down" with them. One thing is certain: that Itasca is not the Source. No one in his senses will now affirm that it is; and if the lake to the south of it, and falling into it, is not the Source, where is it to be found? The lakelet to the southwest—marked "Alice" on the Glazier map—which empties into Lake Glazier, is simply a feeder of the newly located Source, and, according to the Glazier survey, is erroneously marked on the Land-office map as falling into Lake Itasca. This little fact makes all the difference in the world.

Captain Glazier's opponents will find it uphill work to convince sensible men that the True Source of the Mississippi is not in the lake in which he has placed it. If this lake had been seen before he visited it in 1881, he was certainly the first man, as it appears to me, to announce it to the world as the True Source, and should, in common fairness, have the credit that attaches to a first discovery.

STUDENT.

An open letter from Captain Willard Glazier to the Minnesota Historical Society, published widely in Minnesota and the States bordering upon the Mississippi.

PHILADELPHIA, March 20, 1889.

To the President and Members of the Minnesota Historical Society.

GENTLEMEN: I have just noticed in the Saint Paul papers that the question of the Source of the Great River is again occupying your attention, although I had long since concluded that the several expeditions which have followed mine of 1881 had sufficiently enlightened your honorable body upon the mooted topic to enable you to make satisfactory deductions as to the veracity and validity of my published statements.

It is now nearly eight years since I published the fact that Lake Itasca was not the Source of the Mississippi, but that another lake to the south of it was the Fountain-head of the river. During the interval that has elapsed since 1881, I have been criticised by a few persons, some of whom claim to have visited the region, and by others who have never been within hundreds of miles of it. At this late date, however, nearly eight years after my announcement, and notwithstanding the silly antagonism of a few opponents, I am as firmly convinced as I was on the twenty-second day of July, 1881, that the heart-shaped lake to the south of Itasca, and falling into the latter, is the True Source of the Mississippi, and that Lake Itasca, therefore, has no title whatever to this distinction. I have been before the world for many years, and am well known to thousands of my fellow-countrymen, not one of whom, I venture to say, would accuse me of ever stating what I did not believe to be true. Yet these would-be critics and detractors have not scrupled to charge me with falsifying, and almost every other crime short of murder in the first degree, because I have had the temerity to assert, and re-assert, the truth upon a subject about which I am thoroughly cognizant, and of which I have no more doubt than I have of the existence of the Mississippi itself, or of my own identity

What possible excuse there can be for visiting that region at a time when the locality is covered with ice and snow, is to me and many others incomprehensible. Permit me to express the honest conviction that personal consideration for two or three persons in the great State of Minnesota appears to have had more influence in the deliberations of your society, than a desire to establish a geographical truth. Those who have been recently commissioned to report on the topography of the country at the Headwaters of the Mississippi, are apparently visiting that section with the aim, and probably the determination, of disproving me, the quibbling of their letters to the press showing most clearly that they are gone in search of anything but geographical facts. If it really was the opinion of your learned body that another expedition was necessary to remove all doubt upon the subject, why dispatch an individual on this mission who is well known to you to be personally inimical to me. Why not have appointed some one to represent my side of the question, or at least some one known to be unprejudiced and disinterested? Can it be possible that you have forgotten my offer made two years ago, when this question was under discussion before the Legislature? Believing, then, that it was your wish to see fair play, and that you desired to go on record as advocates of the truth, I respectfully submitted: "'That the Legislature commission three persons, one to be selected by the Governor, one by the American Geographical Society, and one by myself, who were to be empowered to employ competent surveyors, visit the region, and report their decision to the next Legislature of your State, with a view to the passage of a bill on the subject. If this is done," I added, "I will deposit in some National bank of Saint Paul sufficient funds to cover one-half the expense of the expedition, provided the Minnesota Historical Society, or any person or persons, will guarantee the other half. If not accepted, my case is prejudged. If accepted, let the State of Minnesota and the geographical world abide the issue, as I am willing to do." This proposition was submitted February 12, 1887, and I felt much gratified at the time that my proffer to your society was received with general approval by the press throughout the country, and that your local papers were especially pleased, and pronounced it just and fair. But notwithstanding this, and my willingness to meet you half-way in any movement tending to a just and impartial decision upon the merits of the question, the impression at Saint Paul seemed to be, that, having been drawn into an error, you would employ no one to represent you who was not committed or pledged to your side of the controversy Is this a fair and proper course to pursue? Would it not inspire greater confidence in your candor and impartiality to have the investigation made by entirely disinterested persons, on whose report full reliance could be placed? I feel sure that a majority of the members of your society have a sufficient sense of honor to realize that it is very *unfair* to employ two persons to investigate and report upon a subject which has engaged the attention of half a dozen others, one of the former having, as is well known, prejudged the case, and avowed himself a bitter opponent to me—although I have never, to my knowledge, seen the man or held any communication with him. I am confident you will candidly admit that nothing can be more inequitable than to commission a man to confirm himself and disprove his adversary, without giving the latter even a hearing. The apparent anxiety of certain members of your society would seem to indicate that there is considerable uncertainty in your camp as to the late reports of J. V Brower and others upon whom you have relied for a correct statement of facts, and I shall not be surprised, if in the end you arrive at the conclusion that their veracious reports are very contradictory, and therefore altogether untrustworthy If Mr. Brower's first statement of his views, published in the *Pioneer Press*, was an honest presentation of the case, what ground can there be now for sending him out a second time to make another report, in which, of course, he will not fail to verify himself.

If my memory serves me, it was the argument of your society, in 1887, that Lake Itasca was the source of the Mississippi, and that nothing beyond this lake was worthy of consideration. Now that I have, in the opinion of thousands, established to the contrary, you do not, I believe, assume that Itasca is the Primal Reservoir; but, in order to throw discredit upon my announcement of 1881, you dispatch a delegation of one or two individuals to that quarter, for the well-understood purpose of giving prominence to two or three ponds and rivulets which have a doubtful existence during the summer months. This conduct, gentlemen, is unworthy of an institution claiming the title of "Historical Society," and I have faith to believe that the great majority of the intelligent and fair-minded citizens of Minnesota, in and out of your society, will be disposed to place the credit of locating the True Source of the Mississippi where it properly belongs.

Permit me to inquire again, what excuse you have for your latest expedition? Have you not already accepted the statements of those who followed me? Why not accept their maps as conclusive, instead of sending them back to re-investigate their first investigation. Has not this flimsy farce been carried far enough? Have you sent J. V Brower back to the scene of his late operations for the reason that *his maps confirm my statements?* If so, I fear eternity itself will find you only at the threshold of your researches.

I conclude by re-asserting that the lake to the south of Itasca, and connected therewith by a perennial stream, is the Primal Reservoir or True Source of the Mississippi; that it was not so considered prior to the visit of my expedition, in 1881, and that my party was the first to locate its feeders correctly, and discover its true relation to the Great River. I have the honor to be,

Very respectfully yours,

WILLARD GLAZIER.

The Minneapolis *Spectator* is the leading literary journal of that city, and contains, among other valuable matter, comments on current topics. The following contribution is from a lady who appears to have given some attention to the subject:

315 Market Street,
Camden, New Jersey, March 10, 1889.

Editor Minneapolis Spectator:

From time to time, in taking up a newspaper, I have noticed various comments and opinions concerning the location of the True Source of the Mississippi, and on Captain Glazier's claim to the discovery which removes old Itasca from the prominent position she has held so long, to give place to a more potent, although smaller, rival. Apropos of this subject, I have read with great interest a recent letter in the Saint Paul *Dispatch*, setting forth very convincingly, to my mind, the validity of Captain Glazier's claims, and making his position unassailable, except by those in whom a certain animus is not wanting, as in the case of Mr Fletcher Williams, Secretary of the Historical Society, Saint Paul, whose weak and spasmodic attacks call forth my indignation.

The only concern I have in the matter springs from a love of fair play, which is an instinct, I suppose, common to most of us; and the interest of the rising generation, the "young idea," which may be erroneously led to "shoot" in the wrong direction, when in three-fourths of the schools the pupils are taught that Itasca must give place to Glazier, and in the other fourth, not that there is no Lake Glazier, but that it is such an infant as yet that they want Itasca to hold the reins a few years longer, even if the school children do run the risk of not giving a correct answer to the question, "What is the Source of the Mississippi?" Mr. Fletcher Williams would evidently like to ignore Captain Glazier's claims if he could do so.

Mr. Williams! as the secretary of the State Historical Society, you ought to be above using scurrilous language. Let Mr. Williams study up his subject and not attack a man whose claims, to quote one of our geographies, "are emphatically supported by the overwhelming testimony of hundreds of the most competent and distinguished authorities in the Northwest," on the strength of the disbelief of himself and three or four of his friends, who in all probability have never seen the Source of the Mississippi. If it is so easy, as Mr. Williams claims, to prove Captain Glazier in error, why not do so? If it is not worth while to do so, why does Mr. Williams enter into the question at all? Is it from a weakness for casting opprobrious names at an adversary who is known to thousands to be worthy only of respect?

I take a further interest in the question from having been one of a party who discussed the subject in the Jamestown public schools some few years ago. We read everything we could find pertaining to it, from Schoolcraft to Glazier, and unanimously agreed upon giving Captain Glazier the credit of the discovery, in the absence of well supported denials of his claim. It is abundantly clear that the lake claimed by Captain Glazier was entirely unrecognized by the geographical world, including Messrs. Schoolcraft and Nicollet, up to the year 1881, the date of the Glazier expedition. If Mr. Williams has determined to take Lake Glazier from us, what will he substitute as the true source, for all geographers and historical societies agree now that Itasca has had its day, and can never more gain recognition as the head of our greatest river.

Let our discoverer have his laurels and wear them now, not waiting, as many of our great explorers have done, for their achievements to be blazoned forth only after death has claimed them. The knowledge that their efforts have been recognized and appreciated in this life is far more to them than any posthumous honors can be. That Captain Glazier's claims will be universally recognized sooner or later is an axiom that can not be gainsaid.

Yours for the right and fair play,

MRS. F K. HUNT.

A New Yorker pays his respects to J V Brower, and criticises his report in the *Pioneer Press:*

NEW YORK, May 30, 1889.

Editor Winona Republican, Minnesota:

I have just noticed in one of your Saint Paul contemporaries, an article with the singular heading, "Lakes like Links Secretly Connect the Plateau Reservoir with the Mississippi's Apparent Source."

The article with this incomprehensible heading is accompanied by an imperfect and very inaccurate map of the Headwaters of the Missi.sippi. The writer—J V. Brower, I presume—as usual, affects an authoritative tone, and if his readers allow themselves to be duped by his inflated and positive style of treating the subject, they will find themselves egregiously in error in the matter of the correct location of the Source of the Mississippi.

As was observed by a writer in a late issue of the Saint Paul *Dispatch*, this person was altogether unfitted to undertake the task assigned him by certain members of your Historical Society, inasmuch as he had predetermined, at any cost, to deprive Glazier of his well-earned laurels. The report now before me is all fustian. This Lake No. 3 is little more than a puddle, having no permanent connection with the Mississippi, a fact he would soon discover if he went out there in July or August; whereas the stream uniting his "Elk" Lake and Lake Itasca is perennial.

The dimensions he gives of No. 3 on his map are out of all proportion to its real size; compared with the Glazier Source it is simply an insignificant pond, and no part of it extends farther south than the lake he persists in calling 'Elk Lake'—which the geographer designates "Lake Glazier." This latter body of water covers an area of 255 acres, whereas Lake No. 3—named on the Glazier map "Wolf Pond" —is less than 30 acres in extent. Again: The comparative distances Brower gives between the two lakes (Glazier and No. 3) and Lake Itasca, viz., 8,315 feet and 1,100 feet, are altogether misleading; but this is a matter of little importance, as the southern extremity of Lake Glazier extends in reality considerably farther south than No. 3 (Wolf Pond).

Lake Glazier is the only respectable body of water to the south of Itasca that presents a shadow of claim to be considered the Head of the Great River, and with all deference to the Fletcher Williams' clique, it will be held to be the True Source of the Father of Waters until the next cataclysm deprives us of the Mississippi, and the flourishing city of Saint Paul on its banks.

GOTHAM.

D.

VOICE OF THE PRESS.

The opposition to the Glazier claim of a few recalcitrant members of the Minnesota Historical Society, who still persisted in their adherence to the Itasca of Schoolcraft, had the effect of inciting inquiry into the merits and authenticity of the important discovery that Lake Itasca possessed no title whatever to the distinction so long conferred upon it, of standing at the Head of our matchless river. The attention of the Press throughout this country, Canada, and Europe has, since 1881, been frequently occupied with the question herein discussed, and geographers and others have contributed to it their views on the subject, in which the general belief prevails that Itasca is not the Source of the river, and that the fine lake to the south, unknown to Schoolcraft or Nicollet, or to the public, until located by the First Glazier Expedition, is the Primal Reservoir or Fountain-head of the Mississippi. In confirmation of this, I invite attention to the opinions of the Press of many cities.

Saint Paul Dispatch.

" We are glad to be able to sustain anew the legitimate claims of this brave and adventurous man. We believe that, had he lived in the times when heroism of the grandest type was an essential to the conduct of Mississippi exploration, he would not have been found wanting in the qualities which, in those days, did so much to aid one's faith in the innate grandeur of human character. Captain Glazier set out to test the correctness of the generally accepted theories of scholars as to the place of the rise of the Mississippi River; he made the test, and found that those theories were not correct. He has given to the world the record of his discovery, and, if we are not wholly at fault, he has done much to perpetuate his own name thereby."

Northwestern Presbyterian, Minneapolis.

"All who live in the valley of America's greatest river will be especially interested in knowing something of its Source, its course, and the cities that line its banks. Since De Soto first discovered the Father of Waters, in 1541, many eminent explorers have been associated with its history. Marquette, Joliet, La Salle, Hennepin, La Hontan, Charlevoix, Carver, Pike, Cass, and Beltrami preceded Schoolcraft. The last named discovered a lake which he supposed to be the Source, but the Indians and the missionaries said there was a lake beyond. A learned few believed them. It remained for some explorer to make further investigation, and publish the truth more widely to the world. This was done by Captain Glazier, in 1881, who visited the lake, explored its shores, and found it to be wider and deeper than Itasca."

Saint Paul Times.

" Captain Glazier's claims are supported emphatically by the overwhelming testimony of thousands of the most distinguished and competent authorities in the Northwest. Glazier undoubtedly expended much time and treasure in investigating not only the Source of the Mississippi, but the geography and history of the entire river, from its Source to the Gulf. The leading map publishers have indorsed his claims, and do so in a way that leaves no doubt that they place implicit confidence in him as a careful and trustworthy geographer and historian. Rand, McNally & Co. and George F. Cram of Chicago; Matthews, Northrup & Co. of Buffalo; A. S. Barnes & Co. of New York; University Publishing Company of New York; W & A. K. Johnston of Edinburgh, Scotland; MacMillan & Co., London and New York; W M. Bradley & Brother, Philadelphia, and many others of the leading publishing houses, who have a heavy personal interest in investigating the accuracy of everything they publish, acknowledge Captain Glazier's claims by accepting his views, and reproducing them in their books and maps. The press, bar, pulpit, and Legislature of the State of Minnesota give assent, through many of their leading members, to the position of Captain Glazier "

Chicago Times.

"The most interesting portion of Captain Glazier's 'Down the Great River' is the beginning, where the author gives the details of an expedition made, in 1881, by himself with five companions, when he claims, with good grounds, to have fixed the actual True Source of the Great River His attention was called, in 1876, to the fact that, though everybody knows the mouth of the stream, there was then much uncertainty about the Source. In 1881, he found time to organize the expedition named, and crossing the country to Itasca, embarked and pushed through that lake up a stream flowing into it, and came upon another considerable body of water fed by three streams originating in springs at the foot of a curved range of hills some miles farther on. This lake he fixed upon as the True Source, and since his published accounts many geographers and map workers have modified their works according to his discoveries. He claims to have been the first to discover and establish the fact that it is the highest link in a chain in which Itasca is another; or, in other words, the True Source of the river. The Indian name of the lake is ***Pokegama***, and this, the author says, he would have retained, but was overruled by the other five, who insisted on calling it LAKE GLAZIER. For the particulars of the interesting story the reader must be referred to the volume itself. Captain Glazier is an old traveler and a practiced writer. The manner of his journey down the Mississippi enabled him to see well all there was to see, and he enables his readers to see also."

Chicago Herald.

"For half a century or more it has been understood that Lake Itasca was the Source of the Mississippi River, but Captain Willard Glazier has exploded this theory by a canoe voyage undertaken in 1881. The results of his investigations were given to geographers at the time and accepted as satisfactory and complete. Maps were at once changed by the map publishers, and LAKE GLAZIER, a tributary of Lake Itasca, was set down as the True Source of the 'Father of Waters.' The story of Captain Glazier's adventures is told by him in a book entitled 'Down the Great River,' which is entertaining as well as being of importance as a contribution to the geography and history of this country Together with two companions and several guides, Glazier first discovered that the lake now bearing his name was the True Source of the Great River, and then journeyed by canoe from that point to the mouth of the Mississippi, a distance of 3,184 miles."

Chicago Inter Ocean.

"Readers of 'Soldiers of the Saddle,' 'Capture, Prison-Pen, and Escape,' and other writings of Captain Glazier, will require no urging to read the entertaining volume 'Down the Great River.' It is an account of the discovery of the True Source of the Mississippi River, with pictorial and descriptive views of cities, towns, and scenery gathered from a canoe voyage from its Headwaters to the Gulf. For fifty years American youth have been taught that 'the Mississippi rises in Lake Itasca,' until Captain Glazier, in this memorable journey of one hundred and seventeen days in his canoe demonstrated the error, and mapped the facts so accurately as to settle the question for all time. Leading geographers and educational publishers have already made changes in their maps, and given due credit to Captain Glazier and his new lake. To say the Mississippi rises in Lake Glazier is only doing simple justice to the intrepid explorer, and hero of many battles."

Chicago Evening Journal.

"However the knowledge may affect the world at large that the Source of the mighty Mississippi is other than generations of geography students have been taught that it was, there is little doubt left that we have all been in the wrong about it, and that this most peerless river was born, not in Itasca's sparkling springs, but in another wider and deeper body of water that lies still farther south and bears the name of its discoverer—LAKE GLAZIER. . . ."

Detroit Commercial Advertiser.

". . . Captain Glazier undoubtedly accomplished a great work.

The source of the Mississippi had ever been an unsettled question, unsatisfactory attempts at discovery having been made and various ill-founded claims put forward; but the subject for the last half century has been constantly agitated. It remained for Captain Glazier to finish the work begun by De Soto in 1541, and positively locate the True Fountain-head. That the lake from which the Great River starts, known by the Indians as Lake Pokegama, should be re-named LAKE GLAZIER, seems an appropriate honor for the resolute explorer. "

New York Students' Journal.

" Captain Willard Glazier discovered the True Source of the Mississippi River. This discovery is one of the most important contributions to the geography of this country during the past half century It seems marvelous that, up to the year 1881, the geography of one of the States of the Union was so poorly known that it had hitherto been supposed that Lake Itasca was the Source of the great Father of Waters."

Brooklyn Eagle.

"Captain Glazier's very clear map of the Great River shows the True Source to be south of Lake Itasca—accepted by Schoolcraft in 1832 as the Headwaters, in disregard of the stream entering its southwestern arm. To Captain Glazier belongs the identification of the Fountain-head of the Mississippi."

Popular Science Monthly.

"In 'Down the Great River,' Captain Glazier relates the story in full of his journey in 1881, by the aid of an Indian guide, 'across country,' from Brainerd, Minnesota, to 'LAKE GLAZIER,' south of Itasca Lake, and his determination of it as the real source of the Mississippi River. . . LAKE GLAZIER is in latitude about 47° N., is 1,585 feet above the level of the sea, and is 3,184 miles from the Gulf of Mexico. Its area is less than that of Lake Itasca, but it is deeper and contains more water than the latter The story of the explorer's journey is very pleasantly narrated."

Philadelphia Dispatch.

" In 1832, Henry Rowe Schoolcraft reached Lake Itasca, but failed to search for its feeders, and thus missed the discovery of the True Source of the Mississippi. Jean Nicolas Nicollet reached the same point four years later, and was satisfied that his journey was successfully concluded. Nothing further was done for forty-five years, during which time it was believed that Lake Itasca was the Source; but Captain Glazier pushed his explorations farther, and, by following a feeder of Lake Itasca, was rewarded by discovering, to the south of Itasca, a beautiful body of water a mile and a half wide. This was the True Source. His labors were promptly recognized by various learned societies and by scientists and geographers, and to-day the lake, which bears the name of the discoverer, is acknowledged to be the Primal Reservoir of the Great River."

Grand Rapids Telegram-Herald.

" . Captain Glazier, in his search for the True Source of the Mississippi, has corrected a geographical error of half a century, and located the fountain-head in a lake above and beyond Lake Itasca. He discovered this lake on the twenty-second day of July, 1881, Chenowagesic, a Chippewa brave, being his guide. The lake, out of which flows the infant Mississippi, is about two miles in its greatest diameter. Its Indian name is *Pokegama*, but Glazier's companions insisted on naming it after their leader . "

Albany Argus.

"Readers of newspapers are doubtless familiar with the controversy as to the True Source of the Mississippi. Captain Willard Glazier, known as the writer of a number of popular works, made an expedition, in 1881, in search of the starting point of the Great River. Reaching Brainerd, on the Mississippi, he crossed the country to Leech Lake. Here, on July 17th, he launched his canoes and paddled through the Portage River and a chain of lakes lying to the west of Leech Lake. With a few detours he came to Lake Itasca, which had heretofore been popularly accepted as the source of the river. Coasting around this for tributaries, he found a creek due south which connected with a beautiful lake about two miles in diameter. As this seemed to meet the geographical requirements, being the most distant portion of tributary water from the mouth, it was pronounced to be the Source, and the Indian name, *Pokegama*, changed to Lake Glazier by the companions of the explorer."

Boston Traveler.

"In 1881 Captain Willard Glazier determined to test his theory, and that of several other geographers, that Lake Itasca was not the real source of the Mississippi, and undertook an expedition fraught with innumerable difficulties, but successful in establishing the correctness of his belief. For beyond Lake Itasca, and connected with it by a stream, he found another lake nearly as large as Itasca, and which proved to be the True Source of the Great River."

Boston Commonwealth.

"Captain Willard Glazier, whose writings are so widely and favorably known, achieved probably the most lasting reputation in 1881, when he made his expedition to the Source of the Mississippi. The results of that expedition he has put in a book. Starting from Saint Paul on the 4th of July, 1881, equipped with canoes and accompanied by Indian guides, he set forth with the object of ascertaining if Lake Itasca were really the source of the 'Father of Waters,' as had been so long supposed. He reached Lake Itasca, and after a careful examination of this lake, discovered that it was not the head of the river, but that there was a lake still higher up, to which he pushed on with his canoes through a narrow inlet. This lake has since been known by the name of its discoverer, 'LAKE GLAZIER,' and has been accepted by geographical authorities as in reality the True Source of the great American River."

Philadelphia Evening Telegraph.

"It appears quite clear that Lake Itasca never possessed any title to the honor conferred upon it by Schoolcraft, in 1832, of giving birth to our magnificent river. One reason alone is given to account for our ignorance of its True Source, namely, it was outside the usual track of the fur traders, and in a region scarcely ever visited by Indians or white men. Schoolcraft had pronounced Itasca to be the Source, and no one up to the date of Captain Glazier's explorations felt sufficiently interested in the matter to investigate or dispute its claim.

"It was long suspected that the Mississippi had its Fountain-head higher up than Lake Itasca, and in July, 1881, an Expedition led by Captain Willard Glazier discovered a lake to the south of Itasca, a mile and a half in diameter, and falling into the latter by a permanent stream. Beyond this there is no water connected with the river, and hence LAKE GLAZIER is now recognized as the True Source of the Mississippi."

Chicago Geographical News.

" The real facts in the case are that all the investigations made since Captain Glazier's discovery tend to show very conclusively that the True Source of the river is in the lake lying a short distance south of Itasca; and that Glazier was the first who discovered and proclaimed the Source to be in that lake. This being the case, it seems but just that the honor of the discovery should be no longer withheld from him. At all events, our school geographies should teach the truth as to where the Source really is."

The Buffalo Times.

" The source of the Great River has been sought for at different times by travelers of nearly every nationality. In 1805, the United States Government sent Lieutenant Pike to explore the region in which the Mississippi was supposed to have its origin; and in 1820, Governor Cass of Michigan undertook a similar task; but they were unsuccessful in their attempts to trace the river to its origin, for its True Source remained still unknown. In 1832, Henry Rowe Schoolcraft explored Lake Itasca, which he regarded as the Head of the great stream. It had long been suspected, however, that the Mississippi had its Fountain-head higher up than Lake Itasca; and in July, 1881, an Expedition, led by Captain Willard Glazier, discovered a lake to the south of Itasca, nearly two miles in diameter and forty-five feet deep, falling into Itasca by a permanent stream. Lake Glazier is now generally recognized as the source of our great midland stream."

Cleveland Leader.

"Captain Glazier has added to his long and varied experiences the discovery of the True Source of the Mississippi. He found it in a hitherto unrecognized lake to the south of Itasca He started with his brother and one or two other white men, and having arrived at Leech Lake, obtained birch-bark canoes, and one or two Indians, and set out in search of the Source. Having reached Lake Itasca, the lake which has heretofore been regarded as the Source, he resolved upon a thorough exploration of the adjacent regions. The outlets of six small streams were found in Itasca. Trusting to an Indian guide, they entered the largest one, and followed it along some distance. After paddling for some time, another lake was found, and christened by the party 'Lake Glazier—the Source of the Father of Waters.' This lake is nearly two miles in diameter and forty-five feet deep. "

Indianapolis Journal.

". . In 1881, Captain Glazier, having doubts of the accuracy of previous explorations at the Headwaters of the Mississippi, set out to verify them, or to discover, himself, the True Source of the Great River. This he did, after an interesting and remarkable overland journey through the wilds of Northern Minnesota. He discovered and demonstrated that the True Source of the Mississippi is not Lake Itasca, as had been long claimed, but a lake to the south of that and emptying into it, which he located, and it has since been named Lake Glazier in honor of the discoverer. "

National Republican, Washington, D. C.

" The birthplace of the Father of Waters is not Lake Itasca, as generally received, but LAKE GLAZIER, in its vicinity, which, by a small stream, flows into Itasca. LAKE GLAZIER, so named from its discoverer, Captain Willard Glazier, has three feeders, Eagle, Excelsior, and Deer creeks. This latest geographical claim is supported by ample testimony from highest and wide-spread authorities."

Ohio State Journal.

"It seems strange that for nearly fifty years, up to 1881, no new thing had been discovered concerning the great Mississippi, whose Source in the vast wilderness of the Northwest was supposed to be in Lake Itasca. In that year, however, Captain Willard Glazier, an adventurous spirit, determined to finally solve the mystery of the Source of the 'Father of Waters,' and also to navigate its entire length from Source to Sea. Accordingly, he traced with infinite hardship the narrowing stream above Itasca until its True Source was finally reached in what is now known as LAKE GLAZIER."

Philadelphia Public Ledger.

"By the discoveries of Captain Willard Glazier, made in 1881, Lake Itasca is dislodged from its former eminence as the Source of the Mississippi, the real Headwaters of that mighty stream being traced to LAKE GLAZIER, a distance of 3,184 miles from the Gulf of Mexico."

The Wheeling Intelligencer.

"Until this journey was made, the Source of the Mississippi was universally placed in Lake Itasca, whereas Glazier and his party demonstrated that a higher basin, now put down in all the new maps and geographies as LAKE GLAZIER, is really the Primary Reservoir of the Mississippi. It seems almost incredible, but is nevertheless true, that for over forty years previous to 1881, when Captain Glazier made his discovery, it was accepted as settled that Lake Itasca was the remotest body of water from the mouth of the Mississippi. The falsity of this theory, however, has been established, and an important discovery given to the geographical world. No discovery rivaling this in interest and importance has been made on the American continent for half a century "

New York Christian Nation.

"Strange as it may seem, the True Source of the Mississippi was not known until 1881, but was erroneously supposed to take its rise in Lake Itasca, until that well-known traveler and popular writer, Captain Willard Glazier, took it into his head that the first end of the long river was not really known. And as Columbus resolved to discover a new world, so Captain Glazier determined to find the real Source of the Mississippi. He set forth in the month of May, 1881, from New York to the 'far West,' to put his long-cherished theory to the test, and with what result the world was made acquainted at the time by the public press. Many men have worked and schemed for years to gain fame, but Captain Glazier, in the heroic discharge of a self-imposed duty, in 117 days made his name immortal."

Philadelphia Inquirer.

"Several years ago Captain Glazier, while meditating upon the exploits of De Soto, Marquette, Father Hennepin, and La Salle, the heroic old explorers, who led the way to the Great River of North America, regretted that although its mouth was discovered by the Chevalier La Salle nearly two hundred years ago, there was still much uncertainty as to its True Source. . The discovery and final location of the source of the Mississippi has now received general recognition in this country and Europe, and there certainly seems to be no doubt of the validity of Captain Glazier's claim. His account of the discovery is very entertaining reading."

Burlington Hawkeye.

"In the summer of 1881, Captain Willard Glazier, well known as a popular writer, made a remarkable canoe voyage from the Source of the Mississippi down its entire length to the Gulf of Mexico. Prior to starting on this unprecedented voyage, he organized and led an expedition to the Headwaters of the river in Northern Minnesota, with a view of setting at rest the vexed question as to the True Source of the mighty river. Captain Glazier and his party left Saint Paul, duly equipped with canoes and commissariat, July fourth, 1881, and arrived at Lake Itasca July twenty first. Thence, by the aid of his Indian guides, he penetrated to another lake beyond Itasca, and connected therewith by a stream which is a continuation of the Mississippi, and at that point is simply a narrow creek. The lake thus entered by Captain Glazier is the True Source of the Father of Waters. LAKE GLAZIER now appears on the maps as the source of the Great River "

Camden Post.

" Starting for the Headwaters of the Mississippi in July, 1881, Captain Glazier tells us in the narrative of his journey that he learned that the dense forests which surround the Source of the Father of Waters were rarely penetrated by white men, or even by Indians except in the pursuit of game in the winter. He also learned through his Indian guides and interpreter that the inhabitants of these primeval forests did not regard Itasca as the Source of May-see-see-bee, but that another lake, broad, deep, and beautiful, which lay above Itasca, and poured its clear waters into that lake, was the true head of the river. The Captain determined to thoroughly examine all this region, and to settle forever the question of the veritable Source of the Mississippi. In accordance with this design, he at length, after many difficulties, found himself on Schoolcraft Island in the center of Lake Itasca, and after a night's rest directed operations toward the lakes and streams of the surrounding country He examined the shores of Itasca for tributary streams, finding but two of any importance. Of these, the largest came in at the extreme head of the lake, the mouth of which was filled with bulrushes. Taking two canoes, he and his party ascended this stream. Following the windings, and pushing through the obstructions, the canoes suddenly glided out upon the still surface of a comparatively large lake, clear as crystal, with pebbly bottom, and shores covered with a thick growth of pine. The greatest length of this lake is about two miles and its width a mile and a half. Captain Glazier, feeling thoroughly convinced that this fine body of water was the True Source of the Mississippi, proclaimed it as such, and his companions decided unanimously to name it Lake Glazier in honor of their leader. One of the party was an attaché of the Saint Paul *Pioneer Press*, and this gentleman dispatched an account of the discovery to his paper. Since that period, the newly discovered Source has engaged the attention of the press throughout the country, which, with one or two exceptions, has unqualifiedly accepted Captain Glazier's account, and given him the credit due; and the maps of Minnesota now show LAKE GLAZIER instead of Lake Itasca as the Source of the Great River. . "

Pittsburg Press.

". The mystery which surrounded the regions of Lake Itasca, the accepted Source for nearly fifty years, and the paucity of information concerning the lake, were sufficient incentives to lead Captain Glazier, in 1881, to organize an Expedition to carry the exploration farther than had been done by any previous explorer. It resulted in a complete success, as he not only succeeded in reaching Lake Itasca, but, following the lead of an Indian guide, he made the discovery that there was still another lake above Itasca, and connected therewith by a permanently flowing stream—the Infant Mississippi. This lake was the real Source of the river, and was named 'Glazier' in honor of the man who had planned and led the expedition. It has been so placed on maps issued by educational houses, not only in this country, but also in Canada and Europe. . "

New York Observer

" To Captain Glazier is undoubtedly due the honor of tracing the Father of Waters, the great American river, up to its True Source in the network of lakes that occupies the northern portion of the State of Minnesota, a task attended with more difficulties and embarrassments than it might appear to involve to the careless observer. "

Minneapolis Star News.

" On the 22d day of July, 1881, the traveler and author, Captain Willard Glazier, discovered a silvery lake nestled among the pines of Northern Minnesota, and situate to the south of Itasca. He also discovered that a swift current flowed continuously from his new-found wonder to what was supposed to be the Source of the Father of Waters. Further investigation revealed the fact that the lake he had discovered was the True Source of the Mississippi. The lake is known to the Indians as *Pokegama*—'the Place where the Waters Gather.'

" Captain Glazier was induced to explore the Headwaters of the Mississippi by Indian tradition, which denied Schoolcraft's theory of Itasca. In the early part of Glazier's expedition he met Paul Beaulieu, the veteran interpreter at the Leech Lake Government Agency, who told him that Schoolcraft was in error. Fortified with this idea, he set out to discover the True Source of the Father of Waters. . To Captain Glazier is due all the glory and honor of discovering to modern geographers the True Head of our Great River."

Philadelphia Times.

"If one has labored under the impression that at this late date in our history every nook and corner of the United States has been discovered and mapped by enterprising explorers, it now seems conclusive that one has been mistaken. Captain Willard Glazier has discovered the True Source of the Mississippi, which is not, as we have been led to believe from our boyhood, in Lake Itasca, but in another lake to the south of it. Unlike Mr. Donnelly in his attempt to dethrone Shakespeare, he succeeds in proving his theory to the satisfaction of the most competent judges, to wit, the geographers and educational publishers of the country. These accept the new Source by placing it on their maps and calling it after the discoverer, 'Lake Glazier.' "

Boston Beacon.

"On July 22, 1881, Captain Willard Glazier discovered what is now known to be the True Source of the Mississippi, in a lake beyond Itasca, about six miles in circumference, which, by the expedition accompanying him, was given his name, and so, after half a century, the origin of the Father of Waters is at length settled beyond a doubt. . . ."

Portland Express.

"Captain Glazier and the members of his Expedition went in search of the True Source of the Mississippi. The expedition exploded the long-held theory that Lake Itasca was the Source of the Father of Waters, and its True Source was discovered and accurately located. As a result of the discoveries made by Captain Glazier, all the atlases, geographies, and encyclopædias marked the change of the Mississippi's Source, and although the discoveries were not credited for a time, their accuracy has since been established with the above results."

Troy Budget.

"Probably nothing has done more to establish Captain Glazier's reputation than his explorations at the Headwaters of the Mississippi. Different travelers, of world-wide fame, had fixed upon different lakes as the Source of this 'Father of Waters,' and geographers and map makers had for years regarded the matter as settled, and recorded Lake Itasca, on the authority of Schoolcraft, as the sought-for Source. Led by the whisperings of Indian traditions, that told of other lakes, still farther on, Captain Glazier determined to test the accuracy of these shadowy reports. His persistence was amply rewarded. He has turned a new leaf in the geography of that region, which neither the jealousy of rival interests nor the torsion of adverse criticism has been able to turn backward. The water which he discovered, and which his companions very appropriately called Lake Glazier, has become historic. It has been adopted by the best geographers and by the best map makers as a final settlement of the question of the actual Source of the Mississippi River"

The foregoing will probably be sufficient evidence to the reader that the "Voice of the Press" was distinctly heard in support of the discovery of 1881, and in justification of the man who possessed the moral courage to question a popular, but groundless, theory, and the pluck to overthrow it, in the face of contumely, insult, and mean detraction of interested and prejudiced pseudo-scientists. Barely one-third of the press articles in my possession, all in support of the Glazier claim, are given, but *quantum sufficit.*

E.

CORRESPONDENCE RELATING TO SECOND EXPEDITION.

The Second Glazier Expedition to the Headwaters of the Mississippi was undertaken in August and September, 1891, and some of the correspondence that preceded it is here given. The object of this second visit is plainly indicated in the following letter addressed by Captain Glazier to the Secretary of the Wisconsin Historical Society, Madison. Letters of similar tenor were also sent to several gentlemen, including scientists, secretaries of geographical societies, heads of colleges, and others who, it was thought, from their position in the literary and scientific world, would naturally be interested in the solution of an important geographical question which had attracted so much attention. To all of these letters courteous responses were received, the result being that some accepted the invitation, while more were unable to spare the necessary time from their business and professional occupations. All, however, wrote encouragingly, and expressed their approval of the proposed plan of another and final effort to establish the truth as to the real Source of the Great River

447 Jackson Street,
Milwaukee, Wisconsin,
June 24, 1891.

The Secretary, State Historical Society, Madison, Wisconsin.

Dear Sir: Having concluded to re-visit the Headwaters of the Mississippi, accompanied by a few gentlemen interested in the topography of that region, I take the liberty of informing you of my purpose. I may explain that my object in making this second journey is not to seek confirmation of my published statements on the subject of the True Source of our Great River, for upon this question I am so thoroughly satisfied of my correctness that no amount of cavil or opposition can affect my conclusions in the slightest degree—but, mainly, for the satisfaction of the gentlemen—geographers, scientists, editors, and others—who will join me as members of the expedition and see for themselves the beautiful lake above Itasca, which I claimed, after careful survey, to be the Source of the Mississippi; and which I assert, on the testimony of all American geographers, was never so considered prior to the visit of my exploring party of 1881, when its true relation to the river was revealed and established. These gentlemen will probably testify over their signatures as to the results of their investigations, the effect of which may possibly be, to remove the doubts of some who still affect to believe Lake Itasca to be the Source—an error which I have combatted for the last ten years.

It has occurred to me, dear sir, that you are presumably interested in the elucidation of an important geographical problem which has attracted so much of public attention, and may possibly like to become a member of our party of investigators, and thus be enabled to form your own conclusions from observations made on the spot. Should you favor me by accepting my invitation, a cordial welcome will await you, and I shall do my best to make the journey as agreeable and pleasant as possible. Having already been over the ground, I shall have no difficulty in piloting my companions by the nearest and best route to our destination.

I am at present organizing an expedition for the journey, and shall be very pleased to hear from you on the subject of my proposal. I am,

Very respectfully,

WILLARD GLAZIER.

Rev John C. Crane had been for some years in doubt as to the real Source of the Mississippi, and expressed a strong desire to become a member of the Expedition. Mr. Crane is well known in the East as a magazine writer on historical questions.

WEST MILLBURY,
May 24, 1891.

CAPTAIN WILLARD GLAZIER, Milwaukee, Wisconsin.

MY DEAR SIR: It has been my great desire for the past few years to visit the Headwaters of the Mississippi. Time after time I have taken up your maps and others bearing on the region, to see if I was right in my premises and conclusions. I have said to myself: Are you not prejudiced in the matter? Is not the source somewhere else? In vain! I could not convince myself that I am wrong in accepting your lake to the south of Itasca. By what process of reasoning men can come to any other conclusion, I can not understand. I appreciate your desire to know and publish the truth on this important geographical question, and will go with you if possible.

Very truly yours,

J C. CRANE.

Rev. George A. Peltz, D. D., LL. D., pastor of the Temple Baptist Church, Philadelphia, believes Lake Glazier is the Source of the Mississippi, and regretted his inability to accompany the party.

THE TEMPLE, BROAD AND BERKS STREETS,
PHILADELPHIA, June 9, 1891.

DEAR CAPTAIN GLAZIER: Your kind letter of the 3d inst. was a surprise, and I thought I must say "yes," and journey with you through the Northern Wilderness. But I have been obliged to change my conclusions as I have thought the matter over. I fear, as I grow older, I am getting too heavy for explorations, so I am sure I would not help your party much. I thank you for your remembrance of me, but must decline the honor, which I do with much regret. I wish you all success. May you silence your adversaries so effectually that they will never trouble you again. Yours very sincerely,

GEORGE A. PELTZ.

General Edward W Whitaker of Washington, D. C., late chief of staff to Generals Custer, Kilpatrick, and Sheridan, regretted his inability to accompany the Glazier party on account of official engagements.

WASHINGTON, June 14, 1891.

CAPTAIN W GLAZIER, Milwaukee, Wisconsin.

MY DEAR CAPTAIN: Your letter of June 11th at hand. Thanks for your invitation. I note the dates you mention for commencing your march north, and see clearly that my engagements for the reunion of 1st Connecticut Cavalry and the G. A. R., at Detroit, will deprive me of the great pleasure of being with you and your company of "pioneers." I truly regret this, and trust you will be able to rout the enemy without the aid of, Yours very sincerely,

E. W WHITAKER.

George Thompson, editor of the Saint Paul *Dispatch*, would have much liked to join the Glazier Expedition to the Headwaters, but was unable to absent himself on account of business pressure.

OFFICE OF THE *Dispatch*,
SAINT PAUL, MINNESOTA,
June 15, 1891.

CAPTAIN W GLAZIER, Milwaukee, Wisconsin.

DEAR SIR: Your letter of June 10th I found on my desk on my return from a short vacation. The invitation to accompany you on your trip to the Headwaters, much as I should like to go for many reasons, I am very sorry to say I cannot accept, as my duties are so numerous that they will not permit of my absence for any length of time. With regard to a representative of the *Dispatch* going with the party, I hope to be able to send one. I understand that a delegation, appointed by the Governor to locate a park near the Source of the river, will start shortly, and, on that account, as well as a strong desire to acquire a certain knowledge, I should like to accompany your party, or the other, or send a representative with both. Very truly yours,

GEORGE THOMPSON.

George F. Cram of Chicago, Book, Map, and Atlas Publisher, would have been pleased to see the Source of the Mississippi.

415–417 DEARBORN STREET,
CHICAGO, ILLINOIS,
June 22, 1891.

CAPTAIN WILLARD GLAZIER, Milwaukee, Wisconsin.

DEAR SIR: I am pleased to acknowledge receipt of your favor of the 20th inst., and thank you for the invitation you extend to me. I do not know, at present, if it will be possible for me to leave my business and be present with you on your trip, although I would exceedingly like to do so, both for the satisfaction of seeing the Source of the Mississippi, and also for the very pleasant summer outing which it will undoubtedly be. . . You have my best wishes.

Yours very truly,
GEORGE F CRAM.

Hon. D. Sinclair, editor Winona *Republican*, had business engagements which rendered it impossible to join the expedition.

Republican OFFICE,
WINONA, June 23, 1891.

CAPTAIN WILLARD GLAZIER, Milwaukee, Wisconsin.

MY DEAR SIR: . . I have deferred answering your invitation, hoping that I might be able to so arrange my affairs as to accompany you on your expedition to the Source of the Mississippi. This, however, I find it impossible to do, on account of business engagements outside of my regular newspaper work. I regret this very much, as it would have afforded me the greatest pleasure; all the more so, inasmuch as I have strongly sympathized with your views in the gallant contest you have made with our Minnesota savants of the Historical Society Thanking you very cordially for your invitation, I am,

Very truly yours,
D. SINCLAIR.

Dr A. Munsell, editor Dubuque *Trade Journal*, accepted the invitation to accompany Captain Glazier and his party

Trade Journal OFFICE,
DUBUQUE, June 29, 1891.

CAPTAIN GLAZIER, Milwaukee, Wisconsin.

DEAR SIR: I am pleased with the plan of your journey to the Headwaters of the Mississippi, and, in answer to your invitation, shall find pleasure in accompanying the expedition in August. I am already impressed with the idea, from all I have heard and read of your former expedition, pro and con, that Itasca is not the Source, and shall be only too glad to look over the field myself, and form my conclusions from ocular evidence. I will be prepared to join you in a tramp through the wilderness whenever you are ready to start. I have, as you are aware, given considerable attention to the subject that interests you so much.

Yours very truly,

A. MUNSELL.

W. H. Gamble, a prominent geographer of Philadelphia, while recognizing the importance of a second expedition, was unable to accept the invitation, for reasons which he assigns.

618 CHESTNUT STREET,
PHILADELPHIA, June 30, 1891.

CAPTAIN WILLARD GLAZIER, Milwaukee, Wisconsin.

. . I appreciate your kindness in tendering me an invitation to visit with you the Headwaters of the Mississippi, but am afraid it will be impossible for me to accept, as I shall be at that time unusually deep in my United States geological work, our contract expiring this fall; but I assure you there is nothing would please me more than to make one of your interesting party of explorers. The knowledge gained by a tramp over the field would be of vast service to me, and I think to others, for my plan would be to follow up the drainage and locate its proper Reservoir, which, I have no doubt, from all I have learned, would be in the Glazier Lake, in accordance with the topography as I now understand it. I have just completed, for the Pennsylvania Railroad Company, a large drawing of the United States, representing their system and connecting lines. I have placed Lake Glazier as the Source of the Mississippi. This drawing will be circulated throughout Europe as well as America—North and South.

W H. GAMBLE.

George H. Benedict of Chicago, Map and Wood Engraving, could not avail himself of the invitation.

175-177 SOUTH CLARK STREET,
CHICAGO, July 6, 1891.

CAPTAIN WILLARD GLAZIER, Milwaukee, Wisconsin.

DEAR SIR: Your polite invitation to accompany your Expedition to the Source of the Mississippi is received, and I regret very much that it will be quite impossible for me to leave my business for the length of time it would require to make the trip and investigation you contemplate. With many thanks for your invitation, and wishing you success, I am,

Yours truly,

GEORGE H. BENEDICT.

Professor A. N. Husted of the State Normal College, Albany, New York, appreciated the invitation, but was unable to accept it, for domestic reasons.

31

STATE NORMAL COLLEGE,
ALBANY, July 8, 1891.

MY DEAR CAPTAIN GLAZIER: I greatly appreciate your invitation to make one of your party to proceed to the Source of the Mississippi. Under other circumstances I should be most happy to avail myself of it, but am compelled to decline on account of the severe illness of Mrs. Husted, which has detained us here since our "Commencement." I am, however, very sensible of your courtesy in thinking of me as a possible addition to your corps of explorers. Believe me that to see the Source of the great Mississippi, and enjoy the society of your select party, for a time, would be a very great pleasure to me. Wishing you a successful trip and more well-earned honors, I remain,

Sincerely yours,
A. N. HUSTED.

H. H. Rassweiler, Geographer, Chicago, would have been very glad to form one of the party, but business engagements precluded his doing so.

515 WABASH AVENUE,
CHICAGO, July 9, 1891.

CAPTAIN GLAZIER, Milwaukee, Wisconsin.

DEAR SIR: Your favor of the 4th inst. is received, and I thank you for your invitation to accompany you on your contemplated trip to the Headwaters of the Great River. Nothing that I can think of in the line of recreation, adventure, and interesting research would give me more pleasure than just such a trip as you propose undertaking. But I regret to say that I can not go. Business appointments already made forbid me the pleasure. Thanking you again for your very kind invitation, I am,

Very truly yours,
H. H. RASSWEILER.

Charles H. Ames of the firm of D. C. Heath & Co., Educational Publishers, Boston, Massachusetts, said he could not think of a vacation for some months to come, as it was the busiest season of the year in the educational publishing business.

BOSTON, July 13, 1891.

CAPTAIN W GLAZIER, Milwaukee, Wisconsin.

DEAR SIR: Your attractive invitation to join an exploring party at the Headwaters of the Mississippi in August is received. Nothing would please me more, and especially to make the journey in company with such gentlemen as I am sure you will bring together on the occasion. An acceptance of your invitation is, however, for me, utterly out of the question. It is the busiest season of the year in educational publishing, and I can not think of a vacation for some months to come.

Please accept my thanks and best wishes for the fullest success of your expedition, and believe me, Very truly yours,

CHARLES H. AMES.

Charles Lubrecht, New York, Map and Chart Manufacturer, was unable to leave his business, but sent good wishes, and believed the Second Expedition would result in establishing Captain Glazier's claim.

195 PEARL STREET,
NEW YORK, July 13, 1891.

CAPTAIN WILLARD GLAZIER, Milwaukee, Wisconsin.

DEAR SIR: I thank you for your invitation to accompany your party, and assure you nothing would afford me more pleasure than roughing it with you for such an object. But my business will not permit my absence for so long a time as you state. I can only send you my best wishes, and feel convinced that this Second Expedition to the Source of the Father of Waters will fully and forever establish in all doubting minds—if there are any left—your rightful claim as its discoverer. I am,

Very truly yours,

CHARLES LUBRECHT.

Dr. Charles E. Harrison, Davenport, Iowa, Secretary and ex-President Academy of Natural Sciences, accepted invitation to accompany the Expedition.

DAVENPORT, July 15, 1891.

CAPTAIN WILLARD GLAZIER, Milwaukee, Wisconsin.

MY DEAR SIR: Your letter is at hand. I thank you for your invitation to a member of our Academy to join your Expedition to the Itascan Basin, and will endeavor to find one, who would not only be acceptable as our representative, but would do honor to you and your party Unfortunately, most of our members are men of business and pressed for time, but I hope to be able to find some one who will avail himself of your invitation. I have spoken to Professor Barriss on the subject, but fear it will be impossible for him to go, as he is getting well along in years and his feeble health would not permit him to undergo the necessary fatigue. Our President—Mr. Thompson—Professor Barriss, and other officers and members, unite in urging me to represent them, but I hesitate to do so from the fact that I make no claims as a scientist, only a lover of nature and nature's works. Have devoted some attention to archæology, having done considerable investigation of the mounds in this vicinity I have served the Academy for many years in all the official capacities. May I ask the length of time to be occupied by the trip? I am,

Very truly yours,

CHARLES E. HARRISON.

NOTE.—In a subsequent letter, Dr. Harrison concluded to accept the invitation to represent the Academy, and accompanied the Glazier party, leaving Minneapolis August seventeenth.

D. S. Knowlton, editor Boston *Times*, accepted invitation to join the investigating party

THE *Times* OFFICE,
BOSTON, MASSACHUSETTS,
July 20, 1891.

DEAR CAPTAIN GLAZIER: Your favor of June 26th was duly received, and after giving the matter full consideration, I accept your invitation to join you on a tour of observation at the Headwaters of the Mississippi. I will arrange the vacations of those in the office and adjust my own affairs so as to allow of my absence for a month or so. I very much wish to make one of the party, and things point that way now. Should there be any change in the date of departure from Minneapolis, will you kindly advise me? You can readily appreciate that I am ordinarily pretty busy, and have many interests which it is difficult to neglect, or be away from for a month. But I am counting most earnestly upon being one of your party, and thank you for the invitation. We New Englanders want to know all about the "Great Northwest," and especially the exact location of the mighty Mississippi's cradle.

Very truly yours,
D. S. KNOWLTON.

James O. Griffin, Registrar Cornell University, in the absence of President Adams in Europe, endeavored to comply with Captain Glazier's request.

OFFICE REGISTRAR
CORNELL UNIVERSITY, ITHACA,
July 24, 1891.

CAPTAIN WILLARD GLAZIER, Milwaukee, Wisconsin.

MY DEAR SIR: In reply to your letter of invitation addressed to President Adams, I beg to say that he is now absent in Europe, and will not return until September; but I will place your letter in the hands of Professor H. S. Williams, of the department of Geology and Paleontology, and request him to recommend to you, if possible, a gentleman to represent us in your party I am,

Very truly yours,
JAMES O. GRIFFIN.

Professor H. D. Densmore, Beloit College, had arranged to join the Glazier Expedition, but found at the last moment that he could not absent himself from the College at the time appointed for the departure from Minneapolis, and recommended a substitute.

BELOIT COLLEGE,
August 11, 1891.

CAPTAIN GLAZIER, Minneapolis, Minnesota.

MY DEAR SIR: I find, at the last moment, that I can not accompany you. Your trip would take me into the beginning of my term work, which it does not seem advisable for me to encroach upon. I am *very sorry* indeed not to form one of your party. I can do no better than commend to you as a substitute Mr. Albert Whitney, son of Professor H. M. Whitney He is a graduate, and a genius in woodcraft. You would find him a valuable acquisition as an explorer.

Again expressing my regrets, I am,

Very sincerely yours,

H. D. Densmore.

The replies to letters of invitation could be largely multiplied, but the few I have inserted above will suffice to show the spirit in which the invitation was received, and the interest manifested in the proposed Expedition.

F.

AFTER THE RETURN.

Having presented to the reader a few of the letters received by Captain Glazier before the departure of the Expedition on its errand of investigation, it will possibly be deemed pertinent to the purpose of this Appendix to submit others written by various members of the party *after their return.* These show the very decided opinions formed on the subject that engrossed attention at the Headwaters—the exact location of the Source of the Mississippi. They will further expose the mendacity of certain parties who maliciously invented and attempted to spread the falsehood that the investigating party were "divided in their conclusions as to the True Source of the River."

The New York *Herald* printed the following communication from D. S. Knowlton, editor of the Boston *Times*.

WADENA, MINNESOTA,
September 4, 1891.

To the Editor of the New York Herald:

On Saturday morning, August 22d, the Glazier Expedition left Park Rapids, Hubbard County, Minnesota, by wagon train, to visit the Headwaters of the Mississippi River. Their object was to carefully investigate the streams and lakes tributary to Lake Itasca, take measurements and photographs, and report to the public impartially upon the facts as found. The value to the world of these investigations lies in the fact that there is, particularly in Saint Paul, some controversy as to what should be considered the Ultimate Source of the Father of Waters.

In 1832, Schoolcraft located Itasca as this Source. In 1881, Captain Willard Glazier, the author and traveler, claimed to have discovered, and to have been the first to announce, the true relation of the Mississippi to the lake south of the southwest arm of Lake Itasca. As it was a lake of large dimensions, he proclaimed it the True Source.

It was quite generally considered to be so for a number of years. Then a controversy arose, and lately the Minnesota Historical Society, who denominate the Glazier Lake as Elk Lake—the early name of Itasca—have explored another stream entering Itasca a little farther to the west, called Nicollet Creek, and have located the Source of the Great River up that valley.

The members of this Second Expedition were: Captain Willard

Glazier of Albany, New York; Pearce Giles of Camden, New Jersey; John C. Crane of Worcester, Massachusetts, historian, author, and genealogist; Charles E. Harrison of Davenport, Iowa, who has held nearly all of the executive offices of the Davenport Academy of Sciences; A. Munsell of Dubuque, Iowa, editor and publisher of the Dubuque *Trade Journal*, and well known in the business circles of that city; F. J. Trost of Van Loo & Trost, the Toledo photographers, who took many photographs of the lakes' tributaries and surrounding hills; W S. Shure of York, Pennsylvania, artist; D. S. Knowlton, editor of the Boston *Times;* Albert W. Whitney of Beloit College, Beloit, Wisconsin, botanist to the expedition; E. M. Horton, surveyor and civil engineer; Oliver S. Keay of Park Rapids, assistant surveyor and guide, and Louis Delezene of Park Rapids, cook. We were also accompanied a part of the time by Hon. C. D. Cutting and Frank Cutting of Howard County, Iowa; and A. R. Cobb, postmaster at Park Rapids, and editor of the Hubbard County *Enterprise.*

Miss Alice Glazier, Captain Glazier's daughter, was the only lady to accompany the expedition. She has decided ability as a water-colorist and sketcher.

Saturday evening overtook us twenty-two miles from Park Rapids. Schoolcraft Island, in Lake Itasca, was reached by nightfall the next day.

Early Monday morning, August 24th, we paddled down the southwest arm of Itasca, and pitched a permanent camp on a ridge, some thirty feet high, overlooking and separating Lake Itasca on the north and the Glazier lake on the south. The latter is a beautiful body of water, at least 255 acres in area. It flows into Itasca by a stream 1,100 feet in length, which has been named the *Infant Mississippi.*

The feeders of Lake Glazier are as follows: Skirting the lake along its eastern shore, one hears, fifty feet away, the water pouring in a cascade from an iron spring, some fifty feet from the edge of the lake, and at least fifteen feet above it. Next comes Deer Creek, which is 6,864 feet long; Horton Creek is 1,188 feet long, flowing from a lake 396 feet wide; Excelsior Creek is 8,778 feet in length, its source being two and two-third miles from Itasca. Eagle Creek is 4,356 feet long, and flows from Lake Alice, a picturesque sheet of water nine and a half acres in extent.

These tributaries enter the lake in natural bays, which are separated from each other by wooded ridges jutting into the lake.

It having been claimed by some that the Mississippi has its Source up Nicollet Creek to the west, the party made an equally careful investigation of the running water tributary at that point. Nicollet Creek was chained from its mouth through Nicollet's First Lake—not over three acres in extent—and Nicollet's Second Lake—not over twelve acres in extent—to its starting-point, above the second lake. The most remote running water issues from a series of springs 7,307 feet from Itasca, a little over one and two-fifths miles. These springs are at the foot of a high ridge or divide, which was examined carefully. I can not see how they can be considered otherwise than the source of the creek. No connecting running water was found flowing from Nicollet's Third Lake over the divide or from the region beyond.

By comparing the figures given, it is seen that the distance of the most remote running water from Itasca flowing through Glazier Lake—the source of Excelsior Creek—is 6,799 feet more than the most remote running water entering Itasca through the Nicollet Creek—an excess of nearly one mile and a third in favor of the Glazier Basin. . .

Our long tramps being practically completed early Saturday afternoon, August 29th, the entire company crossed the Glazier lake in canoes to the highest promontory on its southern shore. Captain Glazier there delivered quite an address beneath the same trees under which he halted in 1881. He said that he then became satisfied that this beautiful lake was the True Source of the Mississippi, for the reason that it is above and beyond Itasca; that it flows into that lake through a perennial stream, and that it has five permanent feeders leading to the swamps and sand hills from one and a half to two and a half miles southward.

Camp was broken Monday, August 31st, and we arrived at Park Rapids Tuesday evening. The members of the party drew up and signed a statement covering their observations, without Captain Glazier's knowledge. I will give the concluding paragraph:

"Investigation and observation lead us to the conclusion that the basin drained by the feeders to Lake Glazier, and emptying into Lake Itasca at the southeast corner of its southwest arm, is considerably larger than that drained by the stream emptying into the south side of the southwest arm—Nicollet Creek; and that running water can be traced at a much greater distance from the outlet of Glazier Lake into Lake Itasca than from the other outlet referred to."

D. S. Knowlton.

Letter to the Minneapolis *Tribune* from Albert W. Whitney, botanist to the expedition:

Park Rapids, Minnesota,
September 3, 1891.

The Second Glazier Expedition to the Headwaters of the Mississippi returned to this place last evening. The party left Minneapolis on Monday, August seventeenth. Most of the week following was spent on the route, in the cities of Saint Cloud, Brainerd, Wadena, and Park Rapids, and in getting ready to start into the woods. At Brainerd the party received a pleasant call from Miss Lotta Grandelmeyer, a great-granddaughter of William Morrison, who was the first white man to see Lake Itasca. At Park Rapids the party was increased by the addition to its ranks of Hon. C. D. Cutting and son, of Iowa; H. R. Cobb, postmaster and editor of the Hubbard County *Enterprise;* E. M. Horton, civil engineer and surveyor; O. S. Keay, assistant surveyor and guide, and Louis Delezene, cook.

Saturday morning the journey from Park Rapids was begun, and the heavy-laden wagons rolled over the prairie for a few miles and then plunged northward into the somber forest. The road is about as bad as could well be imagined; up and down the steep inclines of the Kettle Moraine, and over great glacial bowlders, to say nothing of washouts and stumps and mud-holes. Lake Itasca was reached on the second day, and as the sun threw his setting rays across its sedgy waters, tents were pitched on the island where fifty-nine years ago Schoolcraft landed, and which now bears his name. Lake Itasca is a body of water consisting of the anomaly of three arms without a body, radiating from a point which almost coincides with Schoolcraft Island. The water is not very clear, but quite deep. The shores are fringed with a few rods of sedges and wild rice, where one may occasionally catch sight of a deer ready to dart back into the forest which encircles the lake; now the banks are steep and covered with birch and poplar, and occasional pieces of fine pine; now they are low and thickly grown with tamarack.

Monday was spent in moving camp to the ridge of high land separating Lakes Itasca and Glazier. There lay spread out before our gaze the two lakes; elsewhere a limitless expanse of pine and birch, save in the opening about us, where grew in gay profusion quantities of golden-rod, asters, and painted-cup, while off toward the water was revealed the beautiful face of the fringed gentian. By the way, I never saw this flower in such wonderful beauty and quantity as along the road on the way back; it was a glorious vision of blue.

I think every member of the party, without exception, was surprised at the extent and beauty of the Glazier lake as it first dawned upon our view. In size and character, I should say, it very much resembles Lake Harriet, near Minneapolis. Its shape is roughly oval. Its greatest length is about one and one-fourth miles; its width, from one-half to three-fourths of a mile. Its area is 255 acres; its depth, about 45 feet. Many of its characteristics are those of Itasca; the difference between them lies in the greater height of the hills which surround the Glazier lake and in its much clearer and purer waters.

Lake Glazier is connected with Itasca by a creek. This creek has a brisk current, and we found carried enough water to afford to our large boats passage between the lakes. Lake Glazier is fed by at least four tributaries; they all flow northward. The largest is Excelsior Creek. This originates in seepage springs in a tamarack swamp; these springs were found by measurement to be 8,778 feet from the Glazier lake.

Eagle Creek rises likewise in a tamarack swamp 6,798 feet from Lake Glazier; 1,518 feet from its source it passes through Lake Alice, a beautiful little sheet of water, 924 feet in length, and of an area of about 9⅝ acres. Deer Creek from its source to Lake Glazier is 6,864 feet. Horton Creek is a small stream 1,188 feet in length. It has its source in a lily pond of about 2½ acres. Besides these streams there are on the east shore of the lake several iron springs, one of which pours its waters in a cascade down the face of fifty feet of a hill.

Lake Glazier is just as worthy of the name of lake as is Itasca, and in interesting features and picturesqueness far surpasses it Its waters are full of fish. Casual trolling between the long tramps and exploring campaigns which formed the daily programme always resulted in the capture of plenty of pickerel, pike, rock-bass, and crupples. One morning, besides numerous smaller fry, two fish were caught which together weighed twenty-five pounds. Ducks are not very numerous, but of course the season is yet rather early. While speaking of game, let me not forget to chronicle our two bear adventures. Mr. Bear in both cases was wise enough to appear before our "amateur" hunters, and both were relieved, I venture to say, with mere salutes.

The only other important feeder of Lake Itasca is Nicollet Creek, which enters Itasca about a quarter of a mile west of the outlet of the creek from Lake Glazier. This was carefully explored and measured from mouth to source. It drains a tamarack swamp and has several small feeders. Its total length is 7,307 feet. Near its head it passes through two small bodies of water, which have been called "Nicollet's First and Second Lakes." The former of these, and nearest to Itasca, is a lily pond of about three acres. The second is a small lake of about twelve acres in extent, but of no especial beauty or interest. A few feet beyond this, and one is confronted by a high ridge of land. While gazing up at the splendid pines which crown its summit, one of our party discovered the source of Nicollet Creek by stepping in, up to the knees, in a spring which bubbles up at its base. Whatever importance Nicollet Creek may have as a feeder of Lake Itasca, it is certain that this must accrue to it in virtue of its career below the ridge and this spring.

Itasca is supplied by two principal sources. One of these drains a tamarack swamp, has nothing worthy to be called a *lake* in its course, and has a source 7,307 feet from Itasca. The other is a narrower stream, but flows from a fine lake, the source of whose principal feeder is 14,106 feet from Itasca.

These are the facts in regard to Lakes Itasca and Glazier, and their feeders, which our party have to present. Our time has been principally spent in their careful acquisition, and it was no easy matter, in this country of tamarack swamps, floating bogs, underbrush, and mosquitos, to obtain them.

As to pronouncing judgment in the matter of the Source of the Mississippi, I, at least, and I think I may safely say each member of the party, feels that it is not his province. We hope that we have more or less perfectly presented the facts in regard to the question. Let the people, by the help of able geographers, use these facts in coming to a conclusion as to the True Source of the Great River.

ALBERT W WHITNEY.

Dr A. Munsell gives his account of the investigations at the Headwaters of the Mississippi, in which he participated as a member of the Second Glazier Expedition:

Everybody knows that in 1832 Henry Rowe Schoolcraft, a distinguished American explorer and ethnologist, sought the Source of the Mississippi River. He reached a lake having three sprawling arms and a central island. From this lake, at the extremity of its northern arm, through an outlet thirty feet wide, the water found an outward flow. After camping a few hours on the island, he concluded that here was the Ultimate Source and Primal Reservoir of the Great River. He inquired of his Indian guide the name of the lake, and was told *Omushkos*—a word that means "Elk." He then departed, and for fifty years this body of water, which he re-named "Itasca," continued the accepted Source of the river, the island, meanwhile, being honored with his name.

In 1881, Captain Willard Glazier of Albany, New York, soldier, traveler, and author, by reason of information derived from Indians, became impressed with the conviction that uncertainty yet rested on the origin of the river, and that its True Source was probably beyond Itasca. Entertaining this view, he organized a party and proceeded to a further exploration of the Headwater region. Reaching Itasca on the twenty-first of July, 1881, he entered the lake and paddled for Schoolcraft Island, where tents were pitched that night. Meanwhile, Chenowagesic, his chief guide, had informed the Captain that some years previously he had lived in that region, making it his hunting-ground within the distance of one hundred miles. He also declared that the beginning of the river was beyond Lake Itasca. On the morning of the twenty-second of July the search was vigorously commenced. In coasting the lake, two streams were found having distinct inlets, and four that indistinctly percolated through bogs. Chenowagesic insisted that one of the two streams near the extremity of the southwestern arm led to a lake beyond Itasca. The right stream was at length discovered, and the canoes pushed through. A lively flow of water soon revealed itself, and, with enthusiasm, a difficult passage through it was made, when suddenly a most beautiful lake appeared. This body of water was immediately paddled across to a promontory on its southern shore, which, projecting into the lake, considerably indents its marginal outline. The general shape was deemed to be oval, and its greatest diameter nearly two miles. On coasting the lake, three tributary streams were found and traced to their origins, two of them to springs issuing from sand hills and one proceeding from a small lake. The streams were at once named by the Captain, *Eagle*, *Excelsior*, and *Deer* creeks, and the lakelet at the head of Eagle Creek was called Lake *Alice*. As nothing but mere feeders flowed into the newly discovered body of water, Captain Glazier deemed it to be the Ultimate Source of the Mississippi; that Itasca received its waters, and, as an expansion of the river only, sent them onward in their course toward the sea. A few remarks from the Captain reminded them of the importance of their work, and the effect it would have in making a new revelation concerning the real Source of America's greatest river. At the instance of Mr. Paine, a member of the expedition, and by a unanimous vote, with the exception of the Captain's, the body of water was formally named Lake Glazier. Six volleys were fired over the water—a volley for each member of the party.

The announcement of the new Source was soon made known to the world, and Captain Glazier, already noted as an author and traveler, became still more so by the publication of another book, entitled "Down the Great River." Geographers, scientists, and map publishers, as well as the settlers of Northern Minnesota, immediately accepted the truth of a new Source to the Mississippi.

But the Minnesota Historical Society, which vaunts itself as "a co-ordinate branch of the State Government," several years after the announcement of the location of the True Source of the river, bestirred itself to controvert and deny the genuineness of the discovery, and denounced the discoverer as an "adventurer" and a false guide. By lobbying the Legislature, the Society procured the passage of a law prohibiting the use in the public schools of the State of any map or geography showing Lake Glazier as the Source of the Mississippi. Captain Glazier, however, stoutly adhered to his position, would retract nothing from his published statements, and the controversy waxed warm. An agent of the Society was dispatched to the Headwaters, with instructions to report on the real Source of the river, and disprove the Glazier theory. This agent complicated matters on his return by reporting four new sources to the river. One of these was ascertained by hypothetically tunneling a ridge, following ooze through a bog, and ultimately draining from a distant lake by tapping its bottom. Another, in very despair, gave the source a heavenly origin, the agent reporting that "All our rivers have their sources in the clouds," a truism scarcely coming within the definition of "physical geography." The map publishers intensified the controversy, it is conjectured, with a view of delaying any necessary changes in their maps. They also arranged to have the recent International Congress at Berne, Switzerland, conservatively pass on the Source question of the Mississippi, and name *Itasca* as still the origin of the river. All this, and other reasons, gave rise to the

SECOND GLAZIER EXPEDITION.

For the purpose of ascertaining accurately the actual Source of the Mississippi, several geographers, scientists, editors, and others, volunteered to accompany Captain Glazier, in August, 1891, to the Headwaters of the river. All preparations being completed, the party left Park Rapids, a frontier town nearest to the Headwaters, on the morning of the 22d in three wagons. The way was rough and through a wilderness. Twenty miles out, we camped for the night. Next day, the 23d, reached Lake Itasca in the afternoon, and camped for the night. A permanent camp was established the 24th on the high ridge separating Lake Glazier from Lake Itasca. Camp Trost, on Lake Glazier, was named in honor of Fred J. Trost of Toledo, Ohio, a skilled photographer and experienced sportsman. He has taken one hundred views in the headwaters region of scenes in camp and woods, and places of prominence and interest. The tents on Camp Trost were occupied seven days, or rather nights, for during the day all hands were constantly out and hard at work in their respective spheres. Exploring squads went in every direction, all over the so-called Itasca Basin, and noted every rivulet, spring, bog, pond, and lake. The two surveyors chained the length of all the streams and triangulated for distances across water. Whitney, the botanist, industriously inquired into the flora, not neglecting the fauna, of the region, and also determined the flowing volume of water at important points connected with the inlets of feeders to Lakes Itasca and Glazier, and the inlets and outlets of the main Mississippi stream in this, the locality of its infancy. Dr. Harrison gathered mineralogical and small zoological specimens while aiding in the common work of exploration. The journalists observed, took notes, and were more or less active, in company with the surveyors, in taking measurements of affluents and locating springs. Briefly, and by way of summary, the work done by this Expedition may be given: First, Pine Creek, named by Captain Glazier in 1881, and since variously called "Nicollet River" and by other names, was thoroughly investigated. Its upward trace commences at the extreme end of the southwestern arm of Itasca. The trace was followed into, and out of, a lily-covered pond of about three acres; thence into, and out of, a larger, or twelve-acre collection of water, from which it proceeds to its origin in a boggy spring at the base of a high ridge that divides the valley of this creek from the basin of Lake Glazier and its numerous feeders. The entire length of the creek was chained and found to be 7,307 feet, or about a mile and two-fifths. Over the ridge and beyond, in the general depression on the hither side of the *Hauteurs de Terre*, or heights of land, that divides the Mississippi water-shed from that of the Red River of the North, numerous isolated bogs, ponds, lakelets, and lakes were seen and noted.

Examination next began at the mouth of the Infant Mississippi—a perennial stream that unites Lakes Glazier and Itasca. Upward, its course begins near the end of the southwestern arm of Itasca, on the east side, and leads into Lake Glazier. LAKE GLAZIER is a beautiful body of water, having a surface of 255 acres and a depth of 45 feet. Next to Itasca it is the largest single collection of water in the headwaters region. In general shape it is oval, with longer and shorter diameters of nearly two miles and one mile. Its waters are deeper than those of Itasca, purer, and more abound with fish. The growth of vegetation and forest about it is of the same general character as that which borders Itasca, but is more dense and green. The outline is gently irregular and pleasingly sinuous. A bold rocky promontory, fifty feet high, rises from the lake on the south side, while a high ridge elevates the bank on the east. Though perhaps a hundred pure springs pour through their rivulets into Lake Glazier, its main feeders are:

EAGLE Creek, leading out at the northwest, proceeding directly west, and then south to its origin in Lake Alice; which, further, has a rill feeder 1,518 feet long. The entire distance of the commencement of the minor feeder to Lake Alice, from the mouth of the Infant Mississippi in Lake Itasca, is 9,878 feet.

EXCELSIOR Creek, directly south, has a length of 8,788 feet, and its origin, a spring, is 14,106 feet distant from the mouth of the Infant Mississippi.

DEER Creek and HORTON Creek are both on the south, the former rising in a spring and the latter in Whitney Pond. Deer Creek is 6,864 feet long, and its source is 13,904 feet from Itasca. Horton Creek is 1,188 feet long, and its source, Whitney Pond, 396 feet. The area of Whitney Pond is two acres, and the distance to its extreme southern end from Itasca is 8,492 feet.

SHURE Spring is situated on the hillside of the east bank of Lake Glazier, at a horizontal distance of probably 80 feet, and vertical elevation of 40 feet above the lake level. Its stream would fill a three-inch pipe, and leaps in a lively rush down the hill. It has been named after Mr. Shure's wife, Florence Cascade. The spring and cascade are objects of pleasing interest, and the water strongly chalybeate.

Other features of Lake Glazier may be alluded to. The promontory causes a pronounced bay on each side of it. The beach on the southeastern side is composed of fine white sand, which reminds one of the seaside. Near the southwestern shore is an eagle's nest in the top of a Norway pine. It appears to be about five or six feet in outside circumference. Captain Glazier saw it there in 1881, and Chenowagesic told him it had been there for forty years previously How many eaglets have been, and will be, nurtured in that maternal home may be left for the imagination to conjecture.

A most pleasing effect is experienced by the beholder on seeing this lake the first time, and particularly from any of the high lands surrounding it. He is surprised at viewing so large a sheet of water, and his attention is riveted many moments on its unusual beauty.

On August twenty-ninth, the investigating labors of the Expedition closed, and in the afternoon the party assembled on the promontory There Captain Glazier addressed us. He reviewed the history of the Mississippi's Source, and complimented his hearers on the care taken and the diligence shown in the examination of the region. He said their work was important, and would be regarded with interest by every inhabitant of Minnesota, the Mississippi Valley, this country, and the geographical world generally. In the final decision of what is the True Source, geographers would value and consider the work we had done. Mr. Crane, on behalf of his companions, responded briefly and appropriately

The Flag which had floated over every camp, and had accompanied Captain Glazier to the same region in 1881, was hoisted to a tree-top to remain as a memento of the Second Glazier Expedition. Twenty-five volleys were fired as a salute—six for the party of 1881 and nineteen for the party of 1891. All then entered the canoes and enjoyed a leisurely stroll of observation at an hour when the air was balmy, the breeze gentle, and the declining sun cast a glow of cheerful light over beautiful Lake Glazier.

Sunday, August 30th, was spent quietly in camp, writing up journals and preparing for the morrow's retreat toward civilization. Mr. Crane closed the day with divine service in front of the camp. In an admirable discourse he proclaimed the gospel call to his hearers. When the sermon and prayer ceased, a spontaneous choir sang "Nearer My God to Thee," followed by the doxology and benediction. Thus closed our Sabbath day

The entire region had been traversed, and every rill, rivulet, stream, bog, and collection of water carefully examined. In addition to the topographic and hydrographic facts mentioned in this letter, the following general statements may be made:

Itasca is simply not the Source of the Mississippi; a perennial stream connects it with another lake nearly as large, and above and beyond it.

The largest feeder to Lake Itasca is 7,307 feet long from mouth to source, while the largest feeder to Lake Glazier is 8,778 feet from mouth to source, and at the same time its mouth is 8,907 feet from Itasca, making its total length of water surface connection with Itasca 16,214 feet. In view of all these facts, it is evident that Lake Glazier, a body 255 acres in surface, draining the basin in which it lies, and being the most remote Reservoir receiving and supplying water to the great stream, should be held to be the True Source of the Mississippi River.

A. MUNSELL.

From Winfield Scott Shure, correspondent of the *Age*, York, Pennsylvania

LAKE GLAZIER, MINNESOTA,
August 31, 1891.

EDITOR THE *Age:* This morning found myself and tent-mate up before the day, coasting Lake Itasca in search of water-fowl. We returned before breakfast with a goodly number, but before doing so paddled our canoe down the Mississippi a few rods from the point where the river leaves Itasca, and after viewing the winding infant stream, and vainly wishing we could paddle on and on until we reached the Gulf of Mexico, retraced our course.

As the dawn grew into early day, and the sun rose in all his splendor, a gentle breeze came from the south and fanned the mirror-like surface of the lake into ripples, and ere long the white-caps ran high. We therefore deemed it unadvisable to go forward with our freight, or those of our party least fitted for battling with a storm; but our leader, who desired to again gaze on the beautiful lake to the south of Itasca, called for two volunteers to man a boat and take him and his daughter and the guide across the lake. Mr. Trost and I responded, and after coasting it for more than an hour, paddled into the mouth of the Infant Mississippi—the stream flowing from Lake Glazier into Lake Itasca. Following the stream until we encountered a fallen tree across it, we were compelled to disembark.

In our haste to see the Real Source of the Father of Waters, we hastened to a point from which the guide told us the lake could be seen. Mounting the crest of the ridge, I took a sweeping glance at the lake before us, then turned my attention to our leader and his daughter Picture in your mind Captain Glazier's delight as he realized that he had again, after ten years, reached this spot, and had been able to bring with him men from all parts of the country; men who would honestly investigate, and who were competent to judge, and render an impartial decision on the question at issue between him and his critics. Picture his satisfaction at this moment when, after men had said, "There is no such lake in existence;" "nothing but a mud-hole which dries up entirely in the summer;" "has no connection with Itasca," and many other things of like character, he was able to show to honest men a beautiful, well-defined lake, running off in the distance nearly two miles from where we stood, covering an area of 255 acres, and connected with Itasca by a permanent stream, up which we had just run our boat bearing five persons.

All freight and passengers had been landed on the ridge, a camp-site selected, tents pitched, and many of the odd turns necessary to camp comfort had been attended to, and when finally the "Stars and Stripes" had been hoisted over our encampment, and the shades of evening began to deepen into night, we were settled in our permanent quarters—Camp Trost.

On the evening of the above date, as we all sat around the camp-fire, our leader addressed us briefly, referring to the purposes of this, his Second Expedition, and the pending questions for settlement. He said his desire was that each one would so thoroughly explore the country surrounding the Mississippi's Source, that they would all be prepared and qualified to render an intelligent and a decided verdict. He also expressed his willingness to place the result entirely in our hands.

At "roll-call" the morning of August twenty-fifth, all expressed a desire to see Pine or Nicollet Creek, to which a pretended investigator has lately tried to give prominence, and to that point we first directed our steps. The surveyors chained the creek, measured its width and the volume of water. About a mile from the point where it enters Itasca, we came to a pond about three acres in area, and covered with lily-pads. Passing this pond, a short distance farther on we came to a second lakelet. These two ponds, or lakelets, are the so-called Nicollet's "First and Second Lakes." "Nicollet's Third Lake" is divided from the former two by a ridge about fifty feet high. I am firmly of the belief that if geographers can find nothing of more importance beyond Itasca than Nicollet Creek, Schoolcraft's lake would still claim its old distinction. Going farther south a distance of six miles, we came to Lakes Whipple, The Triplets, Morrison, and Hernando De Soto, in turn, the last named pronounced by the "investigator" above referred to the Source of the Mississippi. Notwithstanding all traces of running water tributary to Itasca had stopped at "Nicollet's Second Lake," we were all curious to see "Lake Hernando De Soto." Imagine our disgust when, after a tramp of six miles, through a forest almost impassable, which took us five hours, we saw the lake—the place where a lake had been—a lake with three arms, two of which had dried up; a lake having neither inlet nor outlet. We felt we had been duped by misrepresentation into this toilsome, fruitless journey We next turned our attention to Lake Glazier and its feeders.

One by one the questions giving motive to our toilsome undertaking are answering themselves. There is a lake beyond Itasca, well defined, and surrounded by high hills; a lake with five permanent feeders, two of which have their origin in ponds as large as "Nicollet's Second Lake." Lake Glazier, the one referred to, has an average sounding of forty-five feet, and a surface of 255 acres. It is connected with Itasca by a stream twenty feet in width. All this is the result of careful surveys. After a thorough investigation, and in view of all the facts, together with full cognizance of the geographical definition of the source of a river, I, with every member of the party, am prepared to say that Lake Glazier is the Source of the Mississippi; that Captain Glazier was right in 1881, as has been verified in 1891. He was the first to coast this lake and explore its feeders, and the first to establish its true relation to the Mississippi. He was the first to map it and its affluents, and to make its existence known to geographers and the world. Schoolcraft was not the first white man to see Itasca, yet he was the first to connect it with the Mississippi, and to him is accorded the merit of the discovery of the supposed source. In like manner should be accorded to Captain Glazier the credit of discovering the True Source of the river.

Saturday, August twenty-ninth, our investigations at the Headwaters were completed, and in the afternoon we all assembled on the picturesque promontory at the southern end of Lake Glazier. Here the Captain addressed us, and reviewed his labors in 1881, and ours in 1891. He appealed to us in the strongest terms to be just, candid, and unbiased in rendering our verdict to the public as to what we honestly believed to be the extreme head or True Source of the river.

The report of the surveyors was then read, and the members of the party, without a single exception, expressed their fullest concurrence with it.

Sunday we rested, and in the afternoon religious service was conducted by Rev H. Crane, in front of the camp and facing Lake Glazier

August thirty-first. We break camp this morning and start on our journey back to civilization and our homes, and if we are worn and sunburnt, we are all most happy to be able to report unconditional success of our trip in every particular. The lake to the south of Itasca, named in 1881 Lake Glazier, is beyond question the Source of the Mississippi.

W S. Shure.

G.

EDITORIAL COMMENT.

The Second Glazier Expedition to the Headwaters of the Mississippi evoked much favorable comment from the press. Credit was awarded the Explorer for his praiseworthy effort to settle the long-disputed question of the True Source of the Great River and the successful issue of his enterprise. Captain Glazier's Report in full, on the return of the Expedition, was addressed to many of the Geographical and Historical Societies, and published in most of the leading journals of the country

Minnesota enjoys the distinction of having within her borders the cradle of the mighty river, and is entitled to be heard first. We therefore quote from the columns of her leading journals, beginning with the *Dispatch* of Saint Paul, in which the following editorial introduced the Glazier Report on the Results of the Expedition of 1891:

"Elsewhere in to-day's issue of the *Dispatch* is given the Report of Captain Willard Glazier to the President of the American Geographical Society upon the Source of the Mississippi River. It is a long document, but should not be briefly glanced at on that account. Captain Glazier has the pleasing faculty of arranging facts and figures in a most effective and entertaining manner, and of expressing himself clearly and forcibly. There is not a dry or prosy sentence in the whole of this Report. It presents in very interesting form all the information which has been gathered relative to an important geographical question upon which there has been some little difference of opinion.

"The main points of the dispute about the Source of the Mississippi are quite generally known, and the corroborative light which is now thrown on the claim made by Captain Glazier, after his first visit in 1881 will be received and read with a great deal of satisfaction by the many who have felt all along that he was in the right. Even should the facts now published not be accepted by the opponents of the Captain—and so bitter and unreasoning is their hostility to him that it is probable they will decline to accept even this Report—the public in general will have benefited much by his explorations.

"The Report opens with a succinct review of the situation prior to and after his Exploration of 1881. Lake Itasca had long borne the credit of being the head of the Great River, but Captain Glazier was led to the belief that an error had been made, and that the True Source lay beyond Itasca. On the twenty-second of July, 1881, he located a basin of water south of Itasca as the Primal Reservoir, and made public his discovery This lake has been since known as Lake Glazier. Its Indian name was *Pokegama*—the 'place where the waters gather.' His announcement of the finding of a Reservoir beyond Itasca was greeted with a storm of criticism and unbelief by unfriendly and jealous parties, and he has had to stand the abuse of those who had no ground for argument. 'The antagonism,' he says, 'thus developed by an honest attempt to establish a geographical truth, together with the fact that, even at this late day, some of our leading educators still believe in the error of Lake Itasca, led me to decide upon another visit to the Itasca Basin, having for its object the most thorough investigation and a final settlement of the vexed question which had occupied the attention of geographers for over ten years.'

"He then proceeds to describe his preparations for the Second Expedition, and introduces us to the members of his party, all gentlemen of education and good standing, whose indorsement or refutation might be accepted without question. They set out on August seventeenth, 1891, and lost no time in making their way to the scene of action.

"Having reviewed the explorations of those who preceded his earlier visit, and briefly referred to recent investigations, he presents in detail, from his daily field-notes, the observations of his Second Expedition. One noticeable feature of these field-notes is the very evident desire manifested by Captain Glazier to be accurate in all his measurements and thorough in his investigations. Honesty of purpose is everywhere apparent. The daily work is minutely, but not tediously, described, and the Report embraces a vast quantity of valuable information. Subjoined to it are the individual indorsements of all the members of the party.

"Whatever may be the final outcome of the investigation, it can not be successfully disputed that Captain Willard Glazier has done more than any other explorer to demonstrate the absolute correctness of the location of the Head of the Mississippi. More than ten years ago he fitted out an Expedition at great expense, and after careful research and scientific investigation presented the results of his explorations, tending to overthrow the established or accepted claim that Lake Itasca was the Fountain-head of the Great River His exhaustive treatise was at once made a theme of universal discussion, and for a considerable period it was the one important question written and talked about by the leading geographical students of the country Like all modern innovations, however, Captain Glazier's claims were subjected to severe and searching criticism, and by some to ridicule and virulent opposition.

"'Who was this daring discoverer who ventured to take issue with the history and traditions of the early decades?'

"The fact that the published reports of Captain Glazier raised such a cyclonic outburst was in itself sufficient to prove that his claims were worthy of consideration, and notwithstanding the pronounced opposition of a few whose opinions were considered valuable, the new theory was accepted by most of the leading geographers.

"Thus the contention has been going on ever since the First Expedition of 1881. Last summer Captain Glazier again organized an expedition and spent some time at the Headwaters, with the result that every member of his expedition confirmed his claim in regard to the True Source of the River."

The Winona *Republican* in February, 1892, published Captain Glazier's report in full, preceded by the following editorial.

"The Report of Captain Willard Glazier's Second Expedition to the Headwaters of the Mississippi, herewith published, is a paper of sufficient popular interest to insure for it a general and an attentive perusal. The circumstances attending this second visit of Captain Glazier to the Source of the Great River are more or less familiar to the readers of the *Republican*, but in the Report now made public they are so succinctly yet clearly reviewed as to give the narrative a new and personal interest that attached to no preceding reference to the subject under notice. For half a century Lake Itasca had been regarded as the source of the Mississippi, but Captain Glazier was led to the belief that an error had been made, and that the True Source lay beyond. In July, 1881, he personally visited the Headwaters, and after a close and careful exploration located a lake south of Itasca as the Primal Reservoir. This lake, known to the aboriginal inhabitants of that region as *Pokegama*, has since been placed on many maps, and is generally designated Lake Glazier. The claim of Captain Glazier to having made this discovery was vigorously contested by certain interested parties, and the discoverer subjected to the severest personal criticism. Undismayed by the assaults made upon him, Captain Glazier determined to fortify his position by a second and still more thorough investigation. On this occasion he was accompanied by a party of gentlemen of education and high standing in the several communities where they reside, whose indorsement or disproof of his views might be regarded as conclusive in relation to all the physical facts coming under observation. The result is now before the public and the testimony should be weighed according to its merit. It is particularly to be noted in perusing Captain Glazier's Report that his observations were carried on with much care and apparent accuracy. The measurements were made by an expert, and all the investigations were participated in, and are unqualifiedly indorsed by the individual members of the party. Honesty of purpose is manifest throughout.

"Amid all the contention and doubt, thus far one thing is certain: No such careful and thorough exploration of the Headwaters of the Mississippi has been made by any other investigator as that recently completed by Captain Glazier. If, in the interest of historic truth and geographical accuracy, his claim is to be frowned down, the evidence upon which it is done ought not to be less trustworthy or convincing than that presented in his behalf. We strongly recommend a careful perusal of his Report, which is addressed to the Hon. Charles P Daly, LL. D., President of the American Geographical Society "

From the Washington *Star*

"The question of what lake or stream is the True Source of the Father of Waters is one that has agitated geographers for several years. The inclination is to accept the results of Captain Willard Glazier's explorations—that of 1881, confirmed and extended by that of 1891—as conclusive. The history of the discovery of the Source of the Mississippi, while not so thrilling as the history of the discovery of the source of the Nile, is more interesting and important to Americans.

"Before Schoolcraft's report of 1832, the existence of the Source in Lake Itasca, or its vicinity, was not known. Although several surveys were made subsequently, it was not until the Glazier Expedition of July, 1881, that the Source was finally located south of Itasca in a comparatively large lake called after the discoverer. If geographers were not inclined to trace the sources of rivers, where possible, to lakes, rather than to flowing streams, Excelsior Creek, the longest feeder of Lake Glazier, would be considered justly as the Fountain-head of the Great River of North America."

From the Davenport *Democrat.*

"Dr. Charles E. Harrison is at home again after his wanderings about the Headwaters of the Mississippi as a member of the Glazier party, representing the Davenport Academy of Sciences. He had fully as interesting and instructive a trip as he expected, and is glad he went.

"The party was composed of between fifteen and twenty persons, among them Miss Alice Glazier, the only daughter of the head of the Expedition. The start was made from Minneapolis, August seventeenth. The train was left at Park Rapids, and wagons were taken to Lake Itasca, which was reached August twenty-third. The wagon journey was fraught with much interest, but not with much comfort. The party walked by preference. They do not have paved streets up there, but some of the roughest country to be found in the Mississippi Valley; no settlers, no roads, no civilization; but wilderness, hard work, deer, and bears. A member of the party shot a bear *en route*.

"Camps were pitched after the first day on a height of land separating Lake Itasca from Lake Glazier. Thence the party explored the region. The two surveyors went ahead and the members of the party followed. Dr Harrison saw enough to convince him that Captain Glazier has a valid claim to the honor of being the man to make the first announcement that Lake Itasca is not the Source of the Mississippi, but that the other lake to the south of it is. Lake Itasca had been visited by white men at the very opening of the nineteenth century, but it remained for Schoolcraft, in 1832, to make the announcement that it was the source. Captain Glazier was the man to make formal announcement of the fact that the lake to the south, and not Itasca, is the True Source

Dr Harrison is well satisfied that Lake Itasca has little relation to the Mississippi beyond that possessed by Lake Pepin; the river simply flows through it. The members of the party, after looking over all the ground in the most careful manner, came to the conclusion that the claim of the Captain is well founded, and that the majority of the geographers have done the right thing in following his lead as they have done. Dr. Harrison says he went there with the intention to be critical and find fault, if there were any evidences of crooked work on the part of Captain Glazier, but admits that all was fair and square, and there is nothing to indicate that Captain Glazier is not fully entitled to the credit he claims."

From the Minneapolis *Times:*

"Lake Glazier is the Source of the Mississippi River.

"That is the unanimous verdict of the gentlemen who have just returned from an Expedition to the Headwaters of the Great River. They have made a report of their explorations in which facts are given which establish to their satisfaction the fallacy of all other theories. That Lake Itasca is only the *approximate* source of the Mississippi has long been known. The real source has been the subject of a long dispute among geographers. Itasca is fed by running water, and the Ultimate Source of the Mississippi could only be ascertained by tracing the 'sources' of Itasca. In 1881, Captain Willard Glazier explored the waters about Lake Itasca, and came to the conclusion that the lake now known as Lake Glazier was the actual source of the big river. Then some one else traced Nicollet Creek up to the three Nicollet ponds, and made the contention that the real source of the Mississippi was the last of these ponds, misnamed lakes. The same party afterward changed his mind and pronounced 'Lake Hernando De Soto' to be the Source. Captain Glazier has never weakened on his theory that the Glazier Lake is the real Source, and the party above referred to has stubbornly argued in favor of the 'De Soto Lake.' The controversy has awakened great interest throughout the country. A short time ago a party was organized to explore the Headwaters of the river and ascertain the facts relating thereto. Captain Glazier headed the expedition, but none of the gentlemen who accompanied him were prejudiced or influenced in any way. It was a large party, composed of geographers, scientists, editors, surveyors, and men of good standing, all of whom, we are informed, were strangers to Captain Glazier.

"The trip through the wilderness from Park Rapids to the Headwaters was by no means a pleasant one. It was slow and tedious work to get the horses and wagons through the wild forest, and the trail was so rough that the travelers found it necessary to walk the greater part of the distance. After a two days' tramp the expedition reached the east arm of Lake Itasca about noon on Saturday, August twenty-second. After a short rest they launched their canoes and conveyed themselves and their chattels to Schoolcraft Island, on which they pitched their tents Saturday evening. The party remained on the island over Sunday. They were a very tired lot of people, and a Sunday's rest was never so much appreciated by them before.

"The party removed their tents from Schoolcraft Island to the shore of Lake Glazier Monday morning, and encamped on the high ridge separating that lake from Lake Itasca. Then began the work of exploring the waters. They made a careful examination of Lake Itasca, and found that it had no affluents of any consequence except Nicollet Creek and the stream that connected Itasca with Lake Glazier. Nicollet Creek was traced to the Nicollet ponds, as far as there was running water. The distance was carefully measured, and it proved to be 7,309½ feet from Lake Itasca to the farthest of the Nicollet lakelets. Then considerable time was spent in examining Lake Glazier and its feeders.

"It was ascertained that Excelsior Creek was the longest one flowing into Lake Glazier, it measuring 8,778 feet. The distance from the mouth of Excelsior Creek to the creek connecting Glazier and Itasca lakes was found to be 4,229 feet. The length of the connecting creek measured 1,100 feet. This made a total distance of 14,107 feet from Lake Itasca to the source of Excelsior Creek. Therefore, if the source of the Mississippi is the farthest point from whence there is running water, it stands out clearly that the source of Excelsior Creek is the source of the Mississippi. And as Excelsior Creek is merely a feeder to Lake Glazier, that lake should figure as the Real Source of the Great River. These were the conclusions of all the members of the expedition, without exception.

"The expedition did not overlook the 'De Soto Lake.' A long tramp from the south shore of Lake Glazier over a swampy ridge brought the party to this so-called lake. They made a thorough examination of it, and failed to find that it had either inlet or outlet. In fact, the party became thoroughly convinced that the 'De Soto' was nothing more than a dead lake or pond. How any of its boggy water could possibly reach the Mississippi is a question they were unable to solve."

From the Philadelphia *Telegraph:*

"The Second Glazier Expedition to the Headwaters of the Mississippi River returned to Park Rapids, Minnesota, last evening. The party claims that the Glazier Lake is the Real Source of the Great River of North America. It was found to cover an area of 255 acres, and is connected with Lake Itasca by a creek about 1,100 feet long. The lake is fed by four tributaries, besides which streams there are, on the east shore, several iron springs. The only other important feeder of Lake Itasca is Nicollet Creek, which enters Itasca about a quarter of a mile west of the outlet of the creek from Glazier Lake. Itasca is supplied by two principal affluents. One of these, Nicollet Creek, drains a tamarack swamp, has nothing worthy of the name of a lake in its course, and has a source 7,307 feet from Itasca. The other is a narrower stream, but flows from a fine lake, the source of whose remote feeder is 14,106 feet from Itasca."

From the Dubuque *Trade Journal:*

"It is a singular fact that neither governments nor religious associations have ever achieved anything remarkable in aid of discovery in either the realm of abstract or concrete science. History shows that individual energy and talent have always led in innovations and the establishment of principles that make for truth and the enlightenment and welfare of mankind. On the part of the Government, when not willing to be a bar to progress, and designedly obstructive, its efforts are usually placed in the hands of mediocre persons because they happen to be partisans seeking the emoluments of position and influence. Religious associations, being sectarian and dogmatic, are apprehensive, and fear the least interference with their doctrines, mysteries, and faith. Within their domain anything conceived to be like 'vain babblings and oppositions of science falsely so-called,' is not tolerated, and short work is made of it by persecution. The reason of all this is not inscrutable, for neither science nor philosophy is within their purview The proper functions of government are the conservation of the State and the protection of life, liberty, and property of the individual, as far as may be consistent with the enjoyment of the same rights by others. The function of the religionist is to conserve the faith and practice its duties.

"It is the individual initiative, self-denying, and laborious action that solves difficult problems, makes successful discoveries, and accomplishes anything that ultimately results in increasing knowledge. That their efforts should ever be interfered with, cramped, or impaired by hirelings of official and corporate regulation, is indeed to be regretted by every one who sincerely desires the benefit of truth and the welfare of his race.

"An instance of the kind alluded to is now presented in Minnesota. A controversy is raging there concerning the True Source of the Mississippi River, between Captain Willard Glazier and the Minnesota Historical Society The latter claims to be a 'co-ordinate branch of the State Government,' and its partisan officials leisurely enjoy place and profit. Long ago the Society heard that Itasca was a lake in their State, which Schoolcraft visited in 1832, and supposed it to be the Source of the Mississippi River This, the paid employes of the Historical Society accepted without disturbance to its somnolent movements, and rested in contented ignorance of the True Source, as well as of everything else in that region. The chronic hypnotism of the Society continued until 1881, when Captain Willard Glazier, a New Yorker, having doubts about Itasca being verily the source, explored the Headwaters of the river, and exploded the error. This being a geographical matter, and the fact of the newly discovered Source a geographical truth, one is puzzled to know what a purely historical society had to do with it. Nevertheless, the Society aroused itself from its Rip Van Winkle slumbers, and boldly proclaimed a denial, and stoutly insisted that Itasca was the ultimate origin. Since then, at the expense of the tax-payers, some examination about and beyond Itasca has been made under the management of one J. V. Brower. It was clearly seen that Itasca must go out into the cold. But jealousy of the foreigner would not permit the acceptance of his discovery, and another Source of the river must be devised. So, entirely ignoring the beautiful Lake Glazier, 255 acres in area, the Minnesota Falstaff first glanced at 'the clouds, the source of all our rivers,' then traced a feeder of Itasca a short distance through two ponds to a spring at the foot of a hill. Hypothetically, the hill was tunneled, and onward the hero went. Isolated bogs, ponds, and lakelets were found, all within a compass of five or six miles square, and situated in a general depression of ground. Archæological science now seized Brower, and to his imagination a glacier once roughly scooped out this region in which pools, rills, Lake Glazier, Lake Itasca—all—are now situated. The huge chunk of ice on melting formed a prehistoric lake, which has since subsided to the present aspect of the locality of the Headwaters of America's most noted river. This he proudly named 'Lake Upham,' divided it into 'Greater, Midway, and Lesser Ultimate Reservoir Bowls,' and presented his farrago to the Minnesota Historical Society, as 'Itasca Basin, the Source of the Mississippi.' Finally, the learned theorizer suggested to his employers that a 'legislative enactment prohibit unauthorized, erroneous, and deceptive changes in the State map, so assiduously persisted in from mercenary (!) motives.'

"Now, gentle reader, when you have perused the foregoing, just remember that while the Minnesota Historical Society was in happy ignorance of any topography beyond Lake Itasca, Captain Willard Glazier entered those northern wilds and found a beautiful body of water beyond Itasca, and connected with it by a perennial stream. He correctly mapped its feeders, stated its relation to Itasca, and pronounced that body of water the True Source of the Mississippi. This is what the Society, by its instrument, Brower, seeks to supplant by substituting the dried bed of an extinct, hypothetic, prehistoric lake, from whose now three arid and jack-pine covered 'ultimate reservoir bowls' water is supposed to ooze into Lakes Glazier and Itasca. Than this can vagary farther go?"

From the Chicago *Inter Ocean.*

"The controversy as to the Source of the Mississippi River has placed before the public a vast amount of new information of an interesting character. In 1881, Captain Willard Glazier made an Expedition to the Headwaters of the Mississippi, and announced that he had discovered that Lake Itasca could not be regarded as the True Source of the Great River. He found a fine lake to the south of Lake Itasca, since called Lake Glazier—and which he claimed was the True Source of the Mississippi, 3,184 miles from the Gulf of Mexico, with an elevation above the ocean of 1,582 feet. Captain Glazier started from Brainerd, Minnesota, on the twelfth of July, 1881, intending to go to Lake Itasca, or the Headwaters of the Mississippi, and make a canoe voyage to the Gulf. In the course of this expedition he discovered the new lake to the south of Itasca. He started from there in a canoe, and made the long journey down the Mississippi, reaching the Gulf of Mexico November fifteenth. On his return he published the narrative of this expedition, and claimed the discovery of the True Source of the Mississippi.

"August seventeenth last, Captain Glazier and several gentlemen, interested in the question of the Source of the Great River, left Minneapolis to make a second survey. They made a careful investigation of Lake Glazier, and in their Report pronounce it a beautiful sheet of water over a mile and a half in length and nearly as wide, in extent 255 acres, its depth forty-five feet. Lake Glazier is connected with

Itasca by a permanent stream 1,100 feet long. This has a brisk current, and carried enough water to afford passage to the boats between the two lakes. The Glazier Lake is fed by four tributaries, the largest of which is Excelsior Creek, one mile and five-eighths long. A careful report is also made of Nicollet Creek. The first of the Nicollet 'Lakes' is described as a pond of about three acres; the second, a lakelet about twelve acres in extent; the third, beyond a high ridge, is about ten acres in extent. The party of explorers unanimously decide in favor of Lake Glazier as the True Source of the Mississippi."

From the Albany *Knickerbocker*:

"Ever since Captain Glazier announced that the True Source of the Father of Waters was not the Itasca Lake, in contravention of the geographers, he has been made the target of much scientific and non-scientific abuse. This has frequently been the lot of discoverers and explorers, from Columbus to Mungo Park—even down to our own Stanley

"We learn from the Saint Paul *Dispatch* that the Glazier Expedition was in camp on the northern shore of Lake Glazier, Minnesota, August twenty-fifth. A member of the exploring party writes to our contemporary an interesting account of the expedition which is being made by wagon from Park Rapids, the nearest civilized point to the Head of the River. The party was organized to investigate the grounds upon which Captain Glazier bases his claim to have located the True Source of the Mississippi, and is composed of several scientists and geographers. The correspondent of the *Dispatch*, whose impartiality may be reasonably supposed to be above question, has this to say on the merits of the controversy:

"'I may here remark that I have but little faith in Mr. Brower's numerous and fantastical sources. I have carefully watched the nature and progress of his controversy with Captain Glazier, and can scarcely attribute his errors to misinformation, but rather to an unworthy desire to disprove by any means, fair or foul, Glazier's claim to have definitely located the True Source of the river in 1881. I believe Mr. Brower has, at different times, announced several lakes and ponds as sources of the Mississippi. The conclusion is forced upon me that he is most probably no nearer the truth in his last venture—some particulars of which are given in his report to his Excellency the Governor—than he was in his first. Captain Glazier, on the other hand, in 1881, announced to the world that the Source of our majestic river was unquestionably in a lake of comparatively large dimensions lying to the south of Itasca Lake, and persistently adheres to his announcement, with the full force of conviction, at the present day Nothing can move him from his position; not even the wooden 'monument' erected by his ambitious adversary on the crest of the ridge which separates Itasca from the True Source, by which it is conspicuously evident that Mr. Brower hopes to perpetuate his own name as the chronicler of a proved error innocently made by the ethnologist Schoolcraft. I have very little doubt that Captain Glazier's position on this question will eventually be confirmed by the unanimous concurrence of geographers and competent judges.'"

BIRD'S-EYE VIEW OF LAKE GLAZIER.

H

INDORSEMENT.

In this last section of the Appendix, I respectfully present for the reader's consideration the indorsements and views, *First*, of persons long resident in Minnesota, to whom the question of the Source of the Great River may be supposed to be one of more than ordinary interest, and who, from their proximity to its Headwaters, are, doubtless, in some respects better qualified to pronounce upon the weight of evidence adduced in support of the Glazier claim. *Secondly*, the Indorsements of geographers, educational publishers, and others who have given attention to the subject and arrived at decided conclusions; and *Thirdly*, the unanimous testimony of the Committee of Investigation of the SECOND GLAZIER EXPEDITION, who thoroughly examined and surveyed every lake, pond, and stream, and every foot of ground at the Head of the river, with the single object of locating its True Source.

I.

RESIDENTS OF MINNESOTA.

From Hon. A. R. McGill, Ex-Governor:

"Captain Glazier's claim to be the discoverer of the True Source of the Mississippi seems reasonable, to say the least. I have been a resident of Minnesota twenty-six years, and never until Captain Glazier's expedition heard the claim of Itasca being the Source of the Great River seriously questioned."

From Hon. Horace Austin, Ex-Governor:

"I think that it would be a very proper thing to do under the circumstances that Captain Glazier's services should be recognized by the passage of a bill by the Legislature giving his name to the lake which is the Real Source of the Mississippi."

From Hon. W. H. Gale, Ex-Lieutenant-Governor, Winona:

"I have been a resident of Minnesota for more than twenty-eight years, and I believe it was the generally accepted opinion of the people

of this State that Lake Itasca was the Source of the Mississippi River, until after the expedition of Captain Willard Glazier, and his publication to the world that another lake south of Lake Itasca was the True Source, to which lake has been given the name of LAKE GLAZIER. This is now generally recognized as the True Source and Head of the Mississippi, and Captain Glazier as the man who first made known that fact to the world."

From F. W. Seeley, Adjutant-General:

"I desire to say, in justice to Captain Glazier, that, having been a resident of Minnesota for twenty-five years, and quite familiar with the geography of the State, it is my belief that he was the first to discover the True Source of the Mississippi River and publish it to the world."

From Moses E. Clapp, Attorney-General:

"From such information as I have on the subject, I am convinced that the actual Source of the Mississippi had not been recognized prior to the published accounts of the explorations of Captain Willard Glazier."

From H. W Childs, Assistant Attorney-General:

"There is, in my opinion, no reason or ground for disputing Captain Glazier's claim to have located the body of water now undoubtedly regarded as the Source of the Mississippi River, and appropriately named LAKE GLAZIER."

From Gus. H. Beaulieu, Deputy U. S. Marshal, District of Minnesota:

"Having been born and raised in the State of Minnesota, and a resident of White Earth Indian Reservation, and being familiar with the Indian traditions, I certify that Itasca Lake had never been considered the Source of the Mississippi by the best-informed Chippewa Indians. Although I had never seen any published maps to the contrary, prior to the expedition of Captain Glazier in 1881, from the best information I have among the Indians, I now regard LAKE GLAZIER as the True Source of the Mississippi River. I regard his chief guide, Chenowagesic, as the best authority among the Indians regarding the section of country about the Headwaters of the Mississippi, and consider him thoroughly reliable."

From W S. Tingle, St. Paul Globe:

"After a study of the literature of the subject, I am convinced that the lake to which the name of GLAZIER was given by the Glazier exploring expedition is undoubtedly the True Source of the Mississippi, and that Captain Glazier was the first to call general public attention to the fact."

From Major Will E. Haskell, Editor Minneapolis Tribune:

"There can be no longer any doubt, when the question is carefully considered, that the credit of discovering the True Source of the Mississippi belongs to Captain Willard Glazier. Captain Glazier's discovery has now become an accepted geographical fact, and future generations of school-boys will speak knowingly of LAKE GLAZIER, as we did in our youth of Itasca."

From Rev. W T. Chase, Pastor First Baptist Church, Minneapolis:

"There seems no room for reasonable doubt that the actual Source of the Mississippi had never been recognized until Captain Glazier made its discovery in 1881."

From Rev. J. L. Pitner, Pastor M. E. Church, Minneapolis:

"I am convinced that the Real Source of the Mississippi was not known prior to 1881. I am quite sure the claims of LAKE GLAZIER are not ill-founded, and in its deep, cool bosom the Great River takes its rise."

From J. S. McLain, Evening Journal, Minneapolis:

"I have no reason to question the claim that the body of water which bears the name of LAKE GLAZIER is the Source of the Mississippi."

From Ex-Mayor Pillsbury, Minneapolis:

"I am satisfied that Captain Willard Glazier was the first person that discovered, and made public the discovery, of the True Source of the Mississippi."

From Hon. Samuel E. Adams, Monticello, Member of the Minnesota Historical Society:

"I have no doubt of the correctness of Captain Glazier's statement and that he discovered the new Source bearing his name."

From John H. Elliott, Secretary Y. M. C. A., Minneapolis:

"I have no hesitation in saying that I believe LAKE GLAZIER to be the Real Source of the Mississippi."

From Hon. J. G. Lawrence, Ex-Senator, Wabasha:

"I certainly believe Captain Glazier is entitled to the credit of discovering the True Source of the Mississippi."

From Judge John P. Rea, Ex-Commander-in-Chief G. A. R., Minneapolis:

"I am satisfied that LAKE GLAZIER is the True Source of the Mississippi."

From Judge L. A. Evans, Ex-Mayor, St. Cloud:

"I believe LAKE GLAZIER is the True Source of the Mississippi."

From Albert Shaw, Tribune, Minneapolis:

"Unquestionably, Captain Glazier may claim the credit of having called public attention to the lake beyond Itasca. He was the first who attached geographical importance to it. That the lake will always be called LAKE GLAZIER, I have no doubt; nor do I doubt the propriety of the name."

From G. M. Wing, Secretary Northwest Indian Commission, Minneapolis:

"The lake which Captain Glazier has located is, no doubt, more properly the True Source of the Great River than Lake Itasca. Captain Glazier was the first to discover that fact, and that should entitle him to the honor of naming it."

From Rev. Andrew D. Stowe, Rector Trinity Church, Anoka:

"This is to certify that from the testimony of Indians and half-breeds living at White Earth Agency, Minnesota, during my residence there of two years, I am persuaded that LAKE GLAZIER, instead of Itasca, is the Real Source of the Mississippi."

From D. Sinclair, Winona:

"In the autumn of 1862 I spent several weeks in that portion of Northern Minnesota extending from Crow Wing to Leech Lake, and the country about Red Lake, in company with Paul Beaulieu, the well-known Indian guide and interpreter During a conversation as to the Source of the Mississippi, Beaulieu informed me that Lake Itasca was not the Real Source of that river, but that a smaller lake, located a short distance south of Itasca, was entitled to that distinction. After investigating the matter recently, I have no doubt of the genuineness of Captain Glazier's claim to be the person who first publicly established the fact that the lake which now bears his name is the True Source of the Mississippi River."

From William A. Spencer, Clerk United States District Court, Saint Paul:

"I have resided in Minnesota upward of thirty years, and until recently have always thought that Lake Itasca was the Source of the Mississippi; but after an examination of the claim of Captain Glazier to be the discoverer of the True Source, I am satisfied his claim is well founded."

From O. C. Chase, Chairman County Commissioners, Otter-Tail County:

"From information received, I am fully satisfied that Captain Glazier was the first person to publicly announce the True Source of the Mississippi."

From John J. Ankeny, Postmaster, Minneapolis:

"From the best information I can obtain, I am persuaded that the Source of the Mississippi had not been recognized prior to the published accounts of exploration by Captain Willard Glazier in 1881. I think, therefore, he is entitled to the credit of the discovery."

From P. P. Swenson, Sheriff, Hennepin County:

"After a residence of thirty-two years in the State of Minnesota, until recently I have always supposed that Lake Itasca was the Source of the Mississippi River. I am now well informed of its True Source being LAKE GLAZIER, having personally traversed that section of the State."

From John F. Peterson, Register of Deeds, Minneapolis:

"I have resided in Minnesota for the past eighteen years, and fully believe that LAKE GLAZIER is the True Source of the Mississippi."

From C. P. De Laithe, Superintendent of Schools, Aitkin County:

"I recognize LAKE GLAZIER as the Source of the Mississippi River. Have resided in Aitkin for several years."

From J. H. Hallett, Brainerd:

"I recognize the lake discovered by Captain Glazier as the Real Source of the Mississippi. Have been an Indian trader for the past fifteen years."

From Hon. N. Richardson, Little Falls, Judge of Probate of Morrison County:

"I have resided on the banks of the Mississippi for thirty-one years. Met Captain Glazier at Little Falls with his exploring party, that visited the headwaters of this river in the summer of 1881. From information derived from sources that I consider reliable, I regard LAKE GLAZIER as the True Source of the Great River. Have been a member of the Minnesota Legislature for three terms."

From O. L. Clyde, First Lieutenant National Guard, Little Falls:

"I have been a resident of Northern Minnesota for twenty years, and always supposed that Lake Itasca was the source of the Mississippi. I never heard anything to the contrary until the year 1881, when Captain Glazier explored the Upper Mississippi, and made his report of the same. I now recognize LAKE GLAZIER as the True Source of the Great River."

From Moses La Fond, Little Falls:

"LAKE GLAZIER is now considered the True Source of the Mississippi. I am one of the old pioneers of this State, having resided in the northern section for over thirty-two years, and was a member of the Legislature in 1874."

From R. Cronk, of the Government Survey, Sauk Rapids:

"This is to certify that I was compass-man on the survey of township 143 north, range 36 west of 5th principal meridian, which embraces Itasca Lake (the Indian name of which I understood to be *Omushkos*, or Elk Lake), and hereby affirm that LAKE GLAZIER is the only well-defined body of water emptying into Lake Itasca, and in my opinion is the True Source of the Mississippi."

From Hon. T. G. Healey, Ex-State Senator, Monticello:

"Have resided in Monticello since 1856. I regard LAKE GLAZIER as the True Source of the Mississippi River, and it is now so regarded by the people living in this section of Minnesota."

From Freeman E. Kreck, Postmaster, Aitkin:

"I have been a resident of Aitkin County since 1881; have been county auditor for past two years, and for a time proprietor and editor of the Aitkin *Age*. Since Captain Glazier's explorations I do not hesitate to say that I believe LAKE GLAZIER to be the True Primal Reservoir of the Mississippi, and I think I voice the sentiment of the majority of the residents of this section."

From A. Y Merrill, County Attorney, Aitkin:

"I believe that the lake claimed to have been located by Captain Glazier is the Real Source of the Mississippi River"

From J. W. Wakefield, Aitkin:

"Resident of Minnesota for thirty years. Personally acquainted with Chenowagesic. Indian trader more than fifteen years Thoroughly familiar with the Chippewa language. I recognize LAKE GLAZIER as the True Source of the Mississippi River"

From Lyman P. White, Ex-Mayor, Brainerd:

"I have been a resident of Brainerd since 1870. Built the first house in Brainerd. Have had charge of the town site for the Lake Superior and Puget Sound Company for sixteen years. I met Captain Glazier on his Mississippi trip, and fully indorse his claim to have discovered the True Source of the Mississippi.

From W. W Hartley, Brainerd:

"Have been a resident of Brainerd for the past fifteen years. Editor and publisher of the *Tribune* from 1875 to 1881, and postmaster from 1879 to 1886. Met Captain Glazier and his party here in 1881, both en route to the source of the Mississippi River and on their return voyage by canoe to its mouth. Have no recollection of ever having heard any other than Lake Itasca claimed to be the Source of the Mississippi prior to the Captain's expedition. LAKE GLAZIER has since been accepted and is believed to be its Source."

From J. H. Koop, Postmaster, Brainerd:

"Have been a resident of this State for sixteen years. Met Captain Glazier at the time he made his expedition of discovery to the Source of the Mississippi, and I recognize the lake bearing his name as its True Source."

From N. H. Ingersoll, Editor Brainerd Dispatch:

"I fully indorse the statement that Captain Glazier was the first to proclaim to the world the True Source of the Mississippi."

From Rev. Fletcher J. Hawley, D. D., Rector of St. Paul's Episcopal Church, Brainerd:

"I have been a resident of Brainerd since 1880, and have not heard any one question the truth of Captain Glazier's claim to have discovered the True Source of the Mississippi to be in LAKE GLAZIER."

From W. W. De Kay, Red Wing:

"From such information as I have upon the subject, I regard the lake located by Captain Glazier, to the south of Itasca, as the True Source of the Mississippi. I have resided in Minnesota for thirty-three years."

From William Moore, Superintendent of Schools, Lake City:

"Knowing the facts in regard to Captain Glazier's discovery of the True Source of the Mississippi, as brought out by public discussion, I am convinced that he is justly entitled to be considered the discoverer of the Source of the Mississippi River."

From George C. Stout, Mayor, Lake City:

"I have no doubt that Captain Glazier is fully entitled to the honor of first discovery of the True Source of the Mississippi River."

From D. O. Irwin, Postmaster, Lake City:

"I am convinced that the actual Source of the Mississippi had not been recognized before the published account of explorations by Captain Glazier; and I regard LAKE GLAZIER as the True Source of the Great River."

From H. L. Smith, Editor and Proprietor of the Graphic, Lake City:

"I am fully convinced that LAKE GLAZIER is the Real Source of the Father of Waters. Have resided in Minnesota seventeen years."

From F. J. Collins, Mayor of Wabasha:

"I have no doubt that Captain Glazier is fully entitled to the credit of having discovered the True Source of the Mississippi River. I have resided in Minnesota thirty-one years."

From Hon. James G. Lawrence, Ex-State Senator, Wabasha:

"I believe Captain Glazier is certainly entitled to the credit of discovering the True Source of the Mississippi, in a lake above Lake Itasca, now named after him, LAKE GLAZIER."

From D. L. Dawley, Principal of Schools, Wabasha:

"I believe Captain Glazier to be the real discoverer of the True Source of the Mississippi River."

From William Tubbs, Postmaster and Ex-County Auditor, Monticello:

"Have resided in Minnesota twenty-nine years. LAKE GLAZIER is regarded by the people generally of this section as the True Source of the Mississippi."

From W. J. Brown, Principal of the High School, Monticello:

"I consider LAKE GLAZIER to be the True Source of the Mississippi, and know of no other. I teach the same in the public schools of this place, as also do my assistants."

From Commander A. H. Fitch, Anoka, J. S. Cady Post, G. A. R., Department Minnesota:

"I am fully convinced that the body of water known as LAKE GLAZIER since 1881 is the True Source of the Mississippi, and not Lake Itasca."

From J. M. Tucker, M. D., Hastings:

"I believe Captain Glazier's claim to being the discoverer of the Real Source of the Mississippi is *just*, and have never heard it questioned. It must stand as one of the facts of history."

From Daniel O'Brien, Police Justice, Hastings:

"I am satisfied that the lake to the south of Itasca, located by Glazier in 1881, is the True Source of the Mississippi, and that Captain Glazier is entitled to whatever credit there is in the discovery."

From J. R. Lambert, Ex-Mayor, Hastings:

"It has been a generally accepted fact that Lake Itasca was the Source of the Mississippi River, and like many others who have preceded me in giving testimonials in favor of Captain Willard Glazier's claim as the discoverer of a body of water now known quite generally as LAKE GLAZIER, and so represented in many of our standard geographical works, I cheerfully admit that Captain Glazier is entitl.d to credit as the discoverer."

From S. Westerson, Chairman Board of County Commissioners, Hastings:

"It seems to be clearly proven that there is a lake—now called LAKE GLAZIER—which is the True Source of the Mississippi, discovered by Captain Willard Glazier in the year 1881, and that said Captain Glazier was the first man to make it public. The honor, therefore, in my estimation, is due to him."

From B. B. Herbert, Editor The Republican, Red Wing:

"After a careful examination of the claim made for and against the reputed discovery of the Head of the Mississippi by Captain Willard Glazier, I am convinced that he was the first to question the received statement that Lake Itasca was its Source, and first to connect the lake which some respectable geographers have called by his name with the Mississippi as its Source. Having lived in Minnesota, on the banks of the Mississippi, for nearly thirty years, had any other person claimed to have discovered any other Source than Lake Itasca, I should have been informed thereof."

From S. B. Sheardown, M. D., Winona:

"I believe that Captain Glazier is entitled to the credit of discovering the Real Source of the Mississippi River. I have been a resident of Minnesota over thirty-one years."

From Judge A. F. Storey, St. Vincent:

"I have no hesitancy in saying that there can be no question but that LAKE GLAZIER is the True and Primal Source of the Mississippi River."

From James A. Thompson, Postmaster, Leech Lake:

"I am of opinion that LAKE GLAZIER is the Source of the Mississippi. I have talked on this subject with some of the Indians who accompanied Captain Glazier on his exploring expedition in 1881, and they all say it is the last lake; that they went all the way in their canoes, and could go no farther. It is the general belief here that LAKE GLAZIER is the True Source."

From Paul Beaulieu, United States Interpreter, White Earth Indian Agency:

"I would respectfully state that according to the ideas of the people of this section of country, for scores of years past, in alluding to Lake Itasca, *which is known only as Elk Lake by the original inhabitants of this part of the country*, was never by them considered as the Head or Source of the Father of Running Waters, or May-see-see-bee, as it is by them named. I received a map showing the route of exploration of Captain Willard Glazier, 1881, and being well acquainted with his chief guide, Chenowagesic, who has made the section of country explored by Captain Glazier his home for many years in the past, and who has proved the truth of his often-repeated assertion, when maps were shown him, that a smaller lake above Lake Itasca would in time change a feature of those maps, and proclaim to the world that Lake Itasca can not any longer maintain its claim as being the Fountain-head of Ke-chee-see-be, or Great River, which is called May-see-see-bee by the Chippewas. The map as delineated by Captain Glazier's guide, Chenowagesic, and published by the Glazier party, is correct; and it is plain to us who know the lay of this whole country (I mean by *us* the Chippewa tribe in particular, also the recent explorers for pine) that LAKE GLAZIER is located at the right place, and is the last lake on the longest stream of the several rivers at the head of the Great Mississippi."

From J. O. Simmons, Little Falls:

"Have been a resident of Little Falls for the past twenty-nine years; county attorney and justice of the peace for several years. Would state that I am personally acquainted with the half-breed Indian interpreter, Paul Beaulieu. Have known him since June, 1857, and know him to be a person of intelligence, great experience, and personal knowledge of the northern portion of Minnesota, which up to very recently has been a vast wilderness occupied only by the Chippewas. Have often conversed with him relative to the country north of us, and speaking of the Mississippi, have heard him say that Lake Itasca was not the Fountain-head; that there was a stream emptying its waters into Itasca from a lake a short distance above the latter, and which, in his opinion, was the True Source. Since Captain Glazier's exploration, I accept the lake bearing his name as the True Source of the Mississippi."

II.

GEOGRAPHERS, EDUCATIONAL PUBLISHERS, AND OTHERS.

ROYAL GEOGRAPHICAL SOCIETY,
LONDON, January 12, 1885.

CAPTAIN WILLARD GLAZIER, New York, U. S. A.

DEAR SIR: I am happy to be able to send you a copy of the January number of the proceedings of our Society . Your discovery is considered a distinct addition to our knowledge of the geography of the Mississippi basin, and well worthy of publication by the Society.

Your obedient servant,
H. W BATES,
Assistant Secretary and Editor.

George W. Melville, the famed Arctic Explorer, writes:

PHILADELPHIA, PENNSYLVANIA,
February 5, 1885.

CAPTAIN WILLARD GLAZIER:

DEAR SIR: Your very interesting paper and map of the discovery of the Source of the Mississippi came to hand this morning. Having but a single number of your paper, I can form but an inadequate idea of your labor and patience, except by a look at your map, which is a very good one, and shows an immense amount of labor; in fact, I am astonished at the amount of work done in so short a space of time as is shown on your track chart.

I am gratified at being made the recipient of your favor; and with sentiments of the highest esteem and regard for a worthy brother in the world of science, I am, dear sir,

Very respectfully,
GEORGE W MELVILLE,
Chief Engineer, U. S. Navy.

Geographers and educational publishers of America and Europe have not only made the necessary changes in their maps of Minnesota, but have expressed their recognition and acceptance of the Glazier discovery in letters addressed to friends of the Captain. Among these may be mentioned: Rand, McNally & Co., George F Cram, George H. Benedict & Co., of Chicago; Matthews, Northrup & Co., Buffalo; A. S. Barnes & Co., Prof. James Monteith, Gaylord Watson, and Appleton's Encyclopedia, New York; W & A. K. Johnston, Edinburgh, Scotland, Macmillan & Co., London and New York; Warne & Co., London, England; Chambers' Encyclopedia, Edinburgh, Scotland, A. Hartleben, Wien, Austria, F A. Brockhaus, Leipsic, Germany; W. M. Bradley & Bro., Cowperthwait & Co., E. H. Butler & Co., T. Elwood Zell, and W. H. Gamble, Philadelphia; John Lovell & Son, Montreal, Canada, and others of less prominence.

From Maury's Manual of Geography:

"PAGE 56. Minnesota is crossed by the ridge or 'Height of Land' which separates the Valley of the Mississippi from the northern slope of the Great Central Plain. On this elevation, 1,600 feet above the sea, both the Mississippi and the Red River of the North take their rise, the one flowing south and the other north. The crest of the 'Height of Land' is crowned with lakes of clear water LAKE GLAZIER, one of these, is the Source of the Mississippi. "

From Professor J. W Redway of Philadelphia, an eminent geographer and scientist:

PHILADELPHIA, September 9, 1887

CAPTAIN WILLARD GLAZIER.

DEAR SIR: . You will have the satisfaction of knowing that by your exertions and enterprise an error of more than fifty years' standing has been made apparent. The world owes you a debt for determining an important question in geography

Sincerely yours,

J W REDWAY.

From Messrs. Harper & Bros., New York:

EDUCATIONAL DEPARTMENT.

" . Recent exploration and survey establish the fact that LAKE GLAZIER has the best claim to the distinction of standing at the head of the Father of Waters. School geographies, generally, are being corrected to show it."

From W & A. K. Johnston, Edinburgh, Scotland, Geographers and Engravers to the Queen:

"You have the satisfaction of having done a great work in settling the vexed question of the Source of your mighty river. For this, all interested in geography are indebted to you."

From Rand, McNally & Co., Map Makers and Publishers, Chicago:

"As to the Source of the Mississippi, we gave it considerable attention in preparing our new map of Minnesota, and finally fixed it as LAKE GLAZIER. This, we consider, has the best claim."

From George F Cram, Map and Atlas Publisher, Chicago:

"I mail you to-day a copy of the corrected map of Minnesota, showing LAKE GLAZIER as the Source of the Mississippi."

From Messrs. Cowperthwait & Co., Philadelphia:

"We have added LAKE GLAZIER to our school maps as the Source of the Mississippi."

From Matthews, Northrup & Co., Art Printers, Buffalo, New York:

"We regard Lake Glazier as the True Source of the Mississippi, and are so showing it on all maps, etc., issued by us."

From Fred Warne & Co., Publishers, London, England:

"Pray accept our very cordial thanks. The alteration in the Source of your great river has been noted, and we shall gladly avail ourselves of the information to make the correction in our atlases."

From Herr F. A. Brockhaus, Leipsic, Germany:

"Captain Willard Glazier.

"Dear Sir: I beg to present my sincere congratulations on your important discovery of the True Source of the Mississippi River, and thank you for the map illustrating your expedition."

From A. S. Barnes & Co.'s "Complete Geography," New York:

"The Source of the Mississippi is Lake Glazier, a small lake from which water flows into Lake Itasca, which until recently was thought to be its Source."

From the University Publishing Company, New York:

"We think Lake Glazier is important enough to outrank Itasca as the Source of the Mississippi."

From W M. Bradley & Bros., Philadelphia:

"Lake Glazier appears on our large Atlas of the World, and on Mitchell's Atlas, as the True Source of the Mississippi."

From John Lovell & Son, Educational Publishers, Montreal:

"The testimonials from leading citizens of Minnesota, and others, tell convincingly in Captain Glazier's favor."

From George H. Benedict & Co., Map Engravers, Chicago:

"Lake Glazier is now acknowledged to be the True Source of the Mississippi, and will soon appear as such on all maps."

From Gaylord Watson, Map and Chart Publisher, New York:

"I shall show Lake Glazier as the Source of the Mississippi on my maps."

From P. O'Shea, Catholic Publisher, New York:

"I have come to the conclusion that Lake Glazier is the True Source of the Mississippi, and intend to give it as the Source in the new editions of my geographies."

From Geo. H. Adams & Co., Geographical and Art Publishers, New York:

"We recognize LAKE GLAZIER as the Source of the Mississippi River. We believe Captain Glazier's claim to be the discoverer of the True Source is now very generally admitted by all map publishers of this country."

From Map and School Supply Company, Toronto:

"We consider LAKE GLAZIER the Source of the Mississippi River, and are having it appear on all our latest maps as such."

From John S. Kendall, President National School Furnishing Company, Chicago:

"CAPTAIN WILLARD GLAZIER.

"DEAR SIR: I am glad to see the entire narrative of your voyage "Down the Great River" in book form. There is no doubt about your expedition having added largely to our rather limited stock of information regarding the country around the Headwaters of the Mississippi. I deem it a graceful and fitting compliment to give your name to the lake south of Itasca."

From Colonel George Soulé, President of Soulé College, New Orleans:

"I recognize the correctness of Captain Glazier's claim, and shall teach that the Source of the Mississippi is LAKE GLAZIER."

From R. L. Abernethy, A. M., D. D., President of Rutherford College, North Carolina:

"I am satisfied that LAKE GLAZIER is the True Source of the Mississippi, and that Captain Glazier is entitled to the honor of the discovery."

From G. H. Laughlin, A. M., Ph. D., President of Hiram College, Ohio:

"Captain Glazier has rendered an invaluable service to the science of geography. I am glad that the school geographies are being corrected so as to indicate LAKE GLAZIER as the Source of the Father of Waters."

From Marcus Ward & Co., Map and Atlas Publishers, London, England:

"We are having the necessary alterations made in all our maps, and future editions will give LAKE GLAZIER as the Source of the Mississippi."

From M. Dripps, Map and Atlas Publisher, New York:

"I will avail myself of Captain Glazier's discovery by showing on my future maps of the United States its True Source in LAKE GLAZIER."

From T. L. Flood, Editor, The Chautauquan, Meadville, Pennsylvania:

"Judging from the vast amount of evidence, I have no hesitation in saying that I believe LAKE GLAZIER to be the Source of the Mississippi."

From William Collins, Sons & Company, Publishers, Glasgow, London, and Edinburgh:

"We shall give effect to the discovery of the True Source of the Mississippi in the next issue of our maps."

From H. L. Turner, President, Western Publishing House, Chicago and New York:

"We shall at once modify our representation of the Mississippi's Source on our maps of the country, for the reason that we fully accept Captain Glazier's report and claim."

From J. R. Spaulding & Company, Map Publishers, Boston:

"We think Captain Glazier's claim as to the Source of the Mississippi is correct, and LAKE GLAZIER will appear as the True Source hereafter in our publications."

From John B. Alden, Publisher of "Alden's Manifold Cyclopœdia" and "Home Atlas of the World," New York:

"LAKE GLAZIER is considered the Head of the Mississippi River, and is being taught as such in our public schools."

From Professor John Jasper, Superintendent of Schools, New York City:

"Our teachers are beginning to accept LAKE GLAZIER as the Source of the Mississippi."

From J. L. Smith, Map Publisher, Philadelphia:

"Having given considerable attention to the merits of the claim presented by Captain Willard Glazier to have definitely located the Source of the Mississippi, I am of the opinion that the lake to the south of Itasca should be recognized as the Primal Reservoir or True Fountain-head of that river, and that Captain Glazier is entitled to the credit of having been the first to discover this fact and call public attention to it."

From E. H. Butler & Company, Educational Publishers, Philadelphia:

"We would state that in our own new series of geographies just published we make Elk Lake, south of Lake Itasca, the Source of the Mississippi. We also recognize the fact that this lake is called LAKE GLAZIER, and we presume that the latter title will eventually be established."

From T. Elwood Zell, Publisher of Zell's Enclyclopædia, Philadelphia:

"Captain Glazier has discovered the True Source of the Mississippi in a lake now bearing his name. It would seem that his claim is undoubted."

From Professor James Monteith, Author of Barnes' Complete Geography, etc., New York:

"The lake known as LAKE GLAZIER is, in my opinion, the Source of the Mississippi, and not Itasca Lake. Captain Willard Glazier deserves great credit for demonstrating this lake to be the True Source. It is sometimes called Elk Lake, but I prefer to call it LAKE GLAZIER."

From the Moses King Corporation, Map Publishers, Boston:

"There is a large amount of testimony in favor of LAKE GLAZIER. Rand, McNally & Co., the map-makers of Chicago; Matthews, Northrup & Co., of Buffalo, with whom we are connected, and others, incorporate LAKE GLAZIER into their maps as the Source of the Mississippi; and we incline to the belief that the balance of opinion is in favor of this lake as the True Source."

From Herr A. Hartleben, a leading Publisher of Germany:

"I congratulate Captain Glazier on his important discovery of the Source of the Mississippi River, and shall have great pleasure in bringing the subject to the notice of our Geographical Society."

From "Alden's Manifold Cyclopœdia," New York:

"Glazier Lake (Indian name Pokegama), a small body of water in Northern Minnesota, the Source of the Mississippi River, which flows from it as a stream a few feet wide and connects it with Lake Itasca, which lies to the northward. LAKE GLAZIER is in latitude about 47° N.; is 180 miles in a direct line northwest from Minneapolis, and not far from a mile and a half in greatest diameter. It is estimated to be 1,582 feet above sea-level, and 3,184 miles from the river's mouth in the Gulf of Mexico. Itasca was long deemed the Source, until the discovery of the lake beyond by Captain Willard Glazier (born in Fowler, St. Lawrence County, N. Y., August 22, 1841; great-grandson of a Massachusetts Revolutionary soldier, and himself a soldier in the war against secession). Having heard from the Indians of lakes beyond Itasca, he explored the region, and in his canoe entered LAKE GLAZIER, July 22, 1881. Thence he traversed the entire length of the Mississippi in canoes, from its Source to the Gulf of Mexico."

From W Dundas Walker, Editor, Chambers' Encyclopædia, Edinburgh, Scotland:

"I will be glad to take advantage of the information so kindly placed at my disposal, and congratulate Captain Glazier on his important discovery."

From Professor D. L. Webster, Editor, Webster's Encyclopædia, Chicago:

"The Glazier Expedition resulted in the location of the True Source of the Mississippi. That 'Truth is mighty and will prevail,' was never better evidenced than in the event which has placed the Fountain-head of the Great River in the lake beyond Itasca."

The following extract from the "International Encyclopædia" places LAKE GLAZIER first in the chain of lakes which constitute the Headwaters of the Mississippi:

"Mississippi River. The sources of this great river are LAKES GLAZIER, Itasca, Traverse, or Bemidji, lying among hills of drift and bowlders in the midst of pine forests and marshes."

From American Supplement to the Encyclopædia Britannica:

"The Mississippi has its source in LAKE GLAZIER, south of Lake Itasca, Minnesota, 47° 34′ N. lat., 95° 2′ W Long. The greatest width of this lake is a mile and a half, and it is deeper than Itasca, with which it is connected by a shallow stream about six feet wide."

From Appleton's Annual Encyclopædia, 1885:

"Lake Itasca, which has been distinguished as the head of the Mississippi for fifty years, must, it seems, yield that distinction to a smaller lake, about a mile and a half in length by a mile in width lying farther south, discovered by Captain Willard Glazier in 1881, and named for him LAKE GLAZIER."

From Armstrong's Encyclopædia, Published by F. J. Schulte, Chicago:

"The necessary changes in regard to the Source of the Mississippi will be made in the next edition of my Encyclopædia."

Several of the Passenger Agents of our great railways whose lines run through Northern Minnesota have signified their intention to give LAKE GLAZIER its proper place on their railway maps and illustrated time-tables. The following are a few of the number:

From E. A. Ford, General Passenger Agent, Pennsylvania Lines West of Pittsburg:

"I have instructed our advertising clerk to call the attention of our engravers to the fact that the Source of the Mississippi River should hereafter be shown as LAKE GLAZIER, instead of Lake Itasca."

From J. S. Tebbets, General Passenger Agent, Union Pacific Railway:

"I thank you for the information in regard to our railway map, and have sent instructions to our engravers to make the necessary corrections in the next issue, showing LAKE GLAZIER as the Source of the Mississippi."

From J. R. Wood, General Passenger Agent, The Pennsylvania Railroad Company:

"We will make the correction in the next issue of the maps issued by this company which will cover the points mentioned by you, namely, LAKE GLAZIER, the True Source of the Mississippi. Please accept our thanks."

From J. E. Hannegan, General Passenger Agent, Burlington, Cedar Rapids, and Northern Railway:

"I shall arrange to have our map plates corrected so as to show the True Source of the Mississippi River, and am glad you have called my attention to this matter."

III.

REPORT OF THE COMMITTEE APPOINTED TO SUPERINTEND SURVEY AND INVESTIGATIONS AT THE HEADWATERS OF THE MISSISSIPPI—1891.

CENTRAL HOUSE,
PARK RAPIDS, MINNESOTA,
September 2, 1891.

TO WHOM IT MAY CONCERN: The undersigned were among the members of a party who have just returned from a visit to the region around Lake Itasca in company with Captain Willard Glazier for the purpose of investigating it, and ascertaining the facts concerning the Headwaters of the Mississippi River.

The party, while invited by Captain Glazier, were under no obligations to him, directly or indirectly; and their purpose was to see for themselves, and to report impartially to the public, upon the facts ascertained by personal observation.

The following statement has been formulated by us as a committee, and is hereby presented, without Captain Glazier's knowledge:

I. Two streams were found entering the southwest arm of Lake Itasca—one to the southwest, known as Nicollet Creek; the other to the southeast, flowing from the Glazier Lake.

II. Nicollet Creek was traversed from its mouth up through Nicollet's First and Second Lakes. The creek was still farther traced until its source was found in a number of springs, to the southeast of which is a ridge varying in height from twenty-five to forty feet. The distance from Lake Itasca to these springs was chained and found to be 7,307 feet; this being the remotest distance, in that direction, of running water. The ridge was ascended and crossed to Nicollet's Third Lake, so called, and the region beyond traversed for several mil s.

III. The stream flowing from the Glazier Lake to Lake Itasca was chained, also the Glazier Lake; and its tributaries were followed up and chained. There are five tributaries to this lake, which is 1,100 feet from Lake Itasca, as follows: On the east side, fifty feet from the bank a spring flows in a cascade to the lake. DEER CREEK is 6,864 feet long. EXCELSIOR CREEK is 8,788 feet long, making the distance from its source, through the Glazier Lake to Lake Itasca, 14,106 feet. HORTON CREEK is 1,188 feet long, flowing from a lake two acres in area. EAGLE CREEK is 4,356 feet long, flowing from Lake Alice, 924 feet long, and Lake Alice has a tributary 1,518 feet long.

IV The distance of the most remote running water from Lake Itasca flowing through the Glazier Lake to Itasca—the source of Excelsior Creek—is 6,799 feet more than the distance from Lake Itasca of the most remote running water flowing into Itasca through Nicollet Creek.

V The Glazier Lake has an area of 255 acres. It is a clearly defined body of water, many times larger and more imposing than any or all of the bodies of water emptying into Lake Itasca through Nicollet Creek; and observation and investigation lead us to the conclusion that the basin drained by the feeders to the Glazier Lake, and emptying into Itasca at the southeast corner of the southwest arm, is larger than that drained by the stream emptying into the south side of the southwest arm—Nicollet Creek; and that running water can be traced at a much greater distance from the outlet of the Glazier Lake into Itasca than from the other outlet referred to.

(Signed) JOHN C. CRANE,
DANIEL S. KNOWLTON,
C. E. HARRISON,
FRED J. TROST,
A. MUNSELL,
W S. SHURE,
A. W WHITNEY,

Committee of Investigation of the Glazier Expedition, 1891.

Before closing this Appendix, I may be permitted to say that, in nothing I have advanced, have I, knowingly, overstepped the bounds of truth. As the reader will probably gather, I feel very strongly that an injustice has been done by certain parties to a citizen who deserved nothing but commendation at their hands for his meritorious and disinterested labor in a field neglected by others, and, I may add, especially by those who have been foremost in attacking him. The conduct of these parties would have been less open to censure, if they had refrained from the use of language unbecoming gentlemen, and supposed men of learning, and confined themselves to controverting the position of Captain Glazier by producing *reliable* counter-evidence to prove that he was in error in his conclusions. This, however, being impossible, recourse was had to abuse of a malignant character, for which there was no excuse.

As will be seen, Captain Glazier has numerous friends and supporters throughout the country—men of intelligence and standing—and I am thoroughly persuaded that among people generally, competent to entertain an opinion upon the subject in controversy, an overwhelming number will be found to uphold his views.

I conclude by reiterating that I am thoroughly convinced from my own observations made on the spot in the month of August, 1891, and confirmed by the competent and disinterested testimony of every member of the expedition, that Lake Glazier, lying immediately to the south of Lake Itasca, is the PRIMAL RESERVOIR, or Ultimate Source, of the Mississippi River.

PEARCE GILES.

CAMDEN, NEW JERSEY,
January 24, 1893.

www.ingramcontent.com/pod-product-compliance
Lightning Source LLC
LaVergne TN
LVHW010523100826
845148LV00001B/78